AF531083

KENTUCKY
ACROSS THE LAND

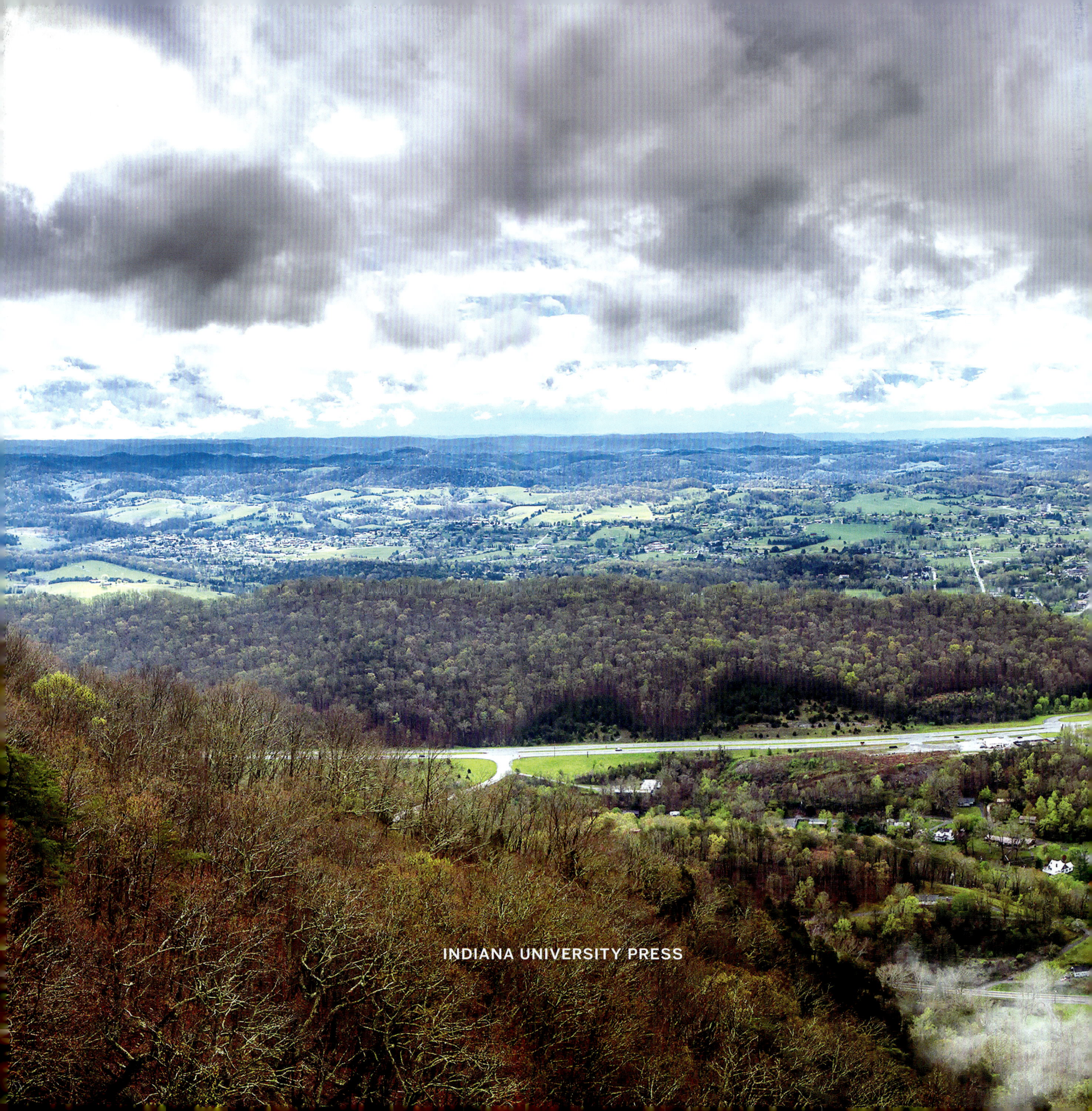
INDIANA UNIVERSITY PRESS

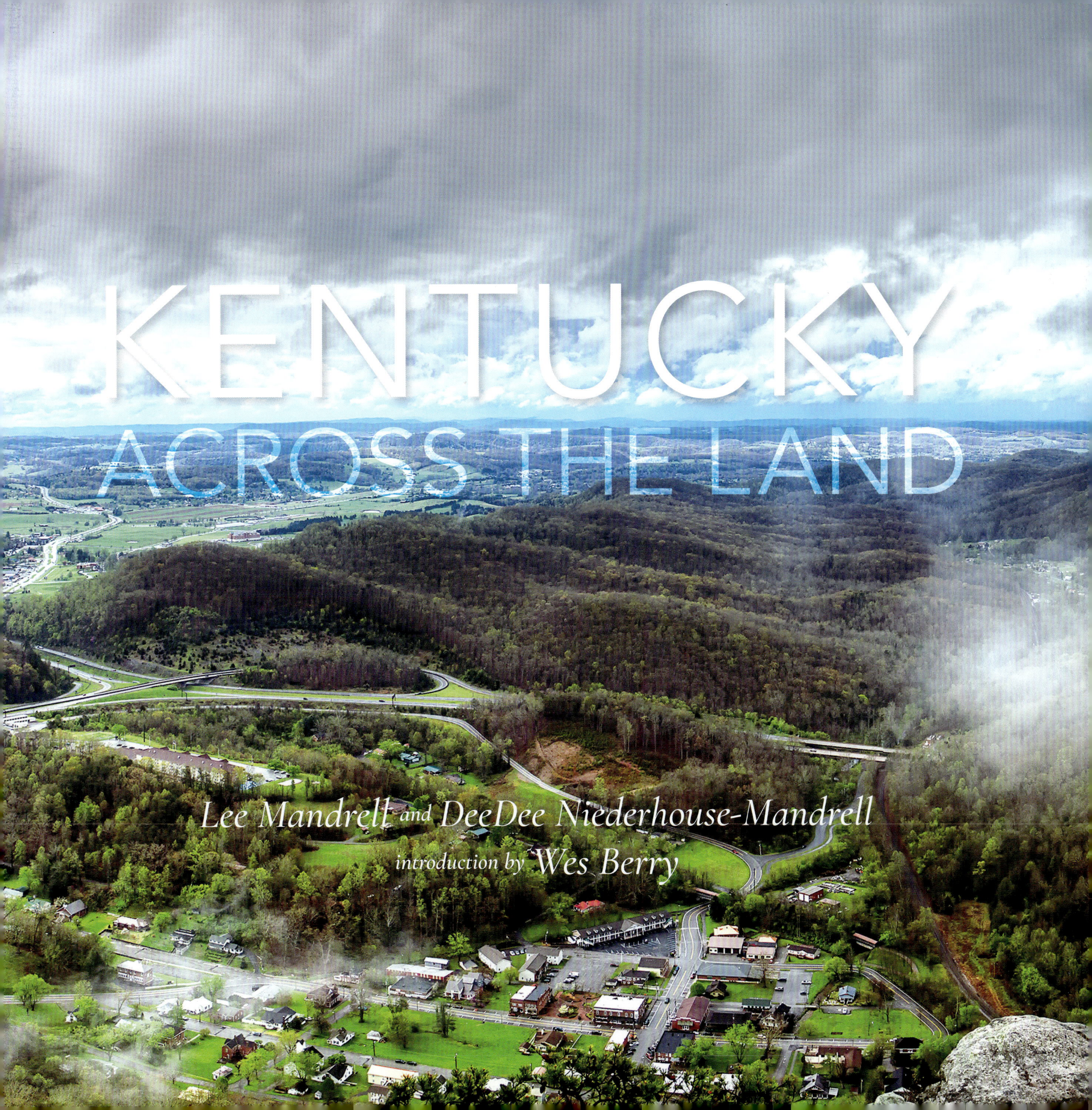

KENTUCKY
ACROSS THE LAND

Lee Mandrell and *DeeDee Niederhouse-Mandrell*

introduction by *Wes Berry*

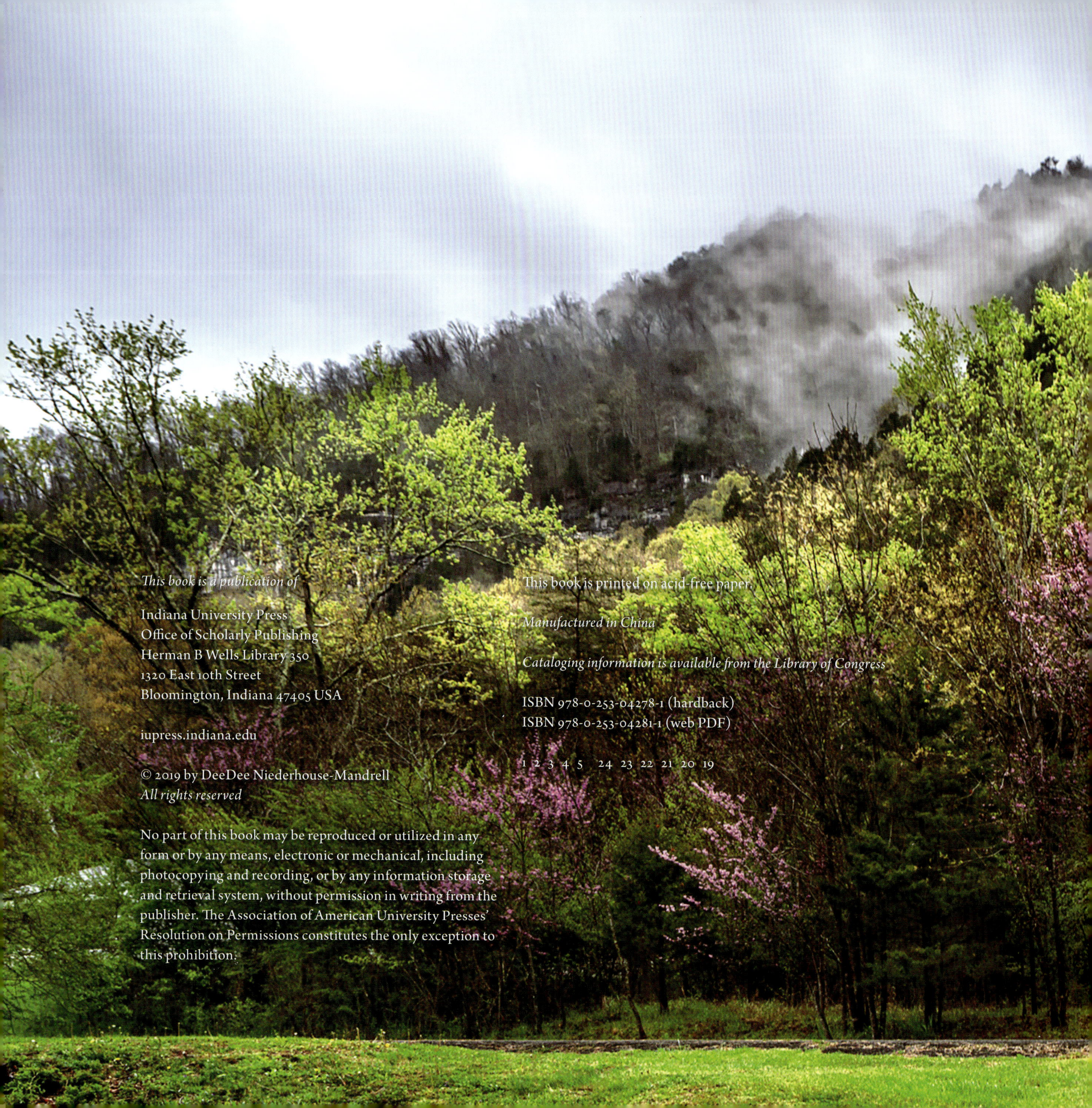

This book is a publication of

Indiana University Press
Office of Scholarly Publishing
Herman B Wells Library 350
1320 East 10th Street
Bloomington, Indiana 47405 USA

iupress.indiana.edu

This book is printed on acid-free paper.

Manufactured in China

Cataloging information is available from the Library of Congress

ISBN 978-0-253-04278-1 (hardback)
ISBN 978-0-253-04281-1 (web PDF)

1 2 3 4 5 24 23 22 21 20 19

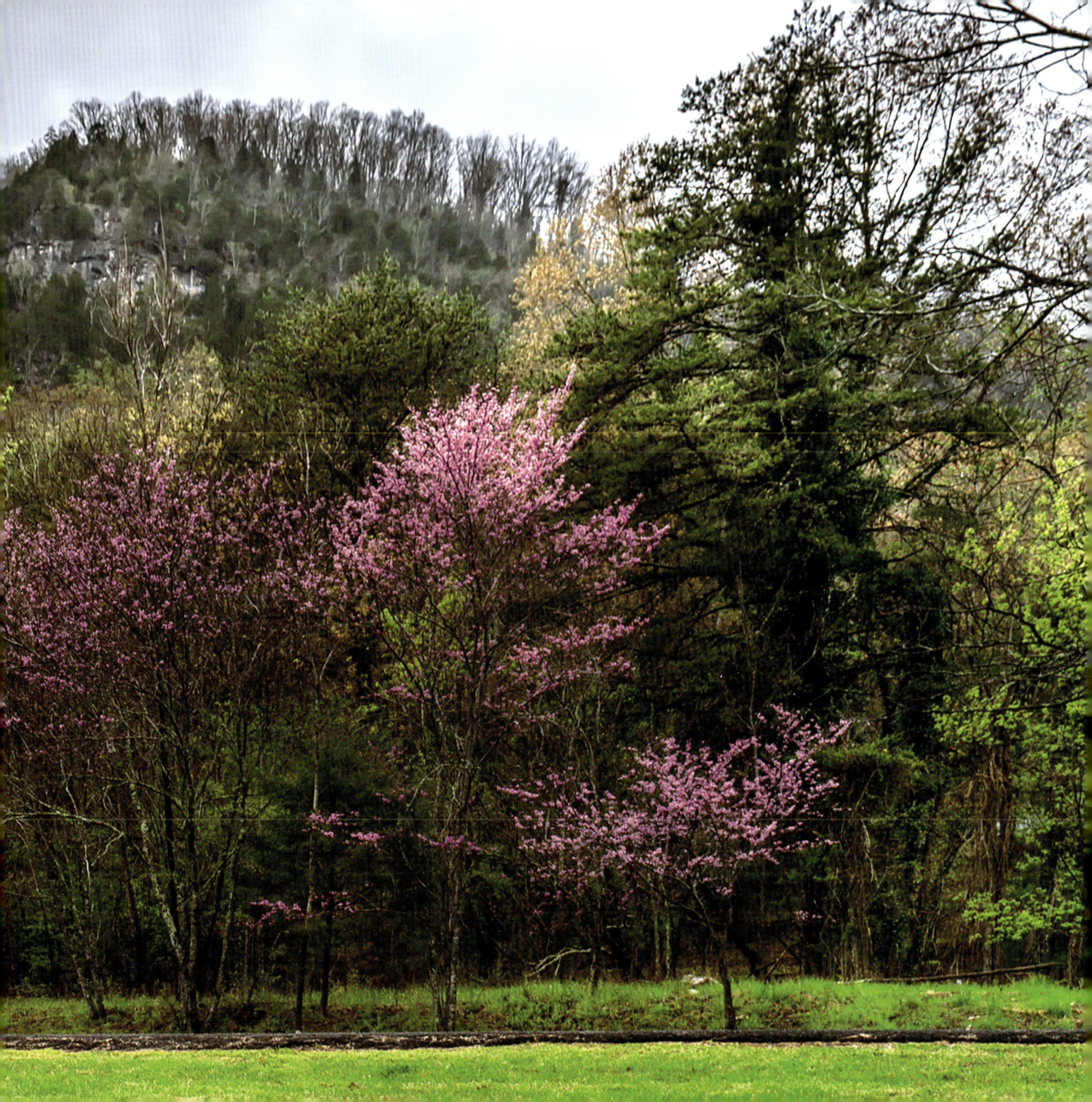

CONTENTS

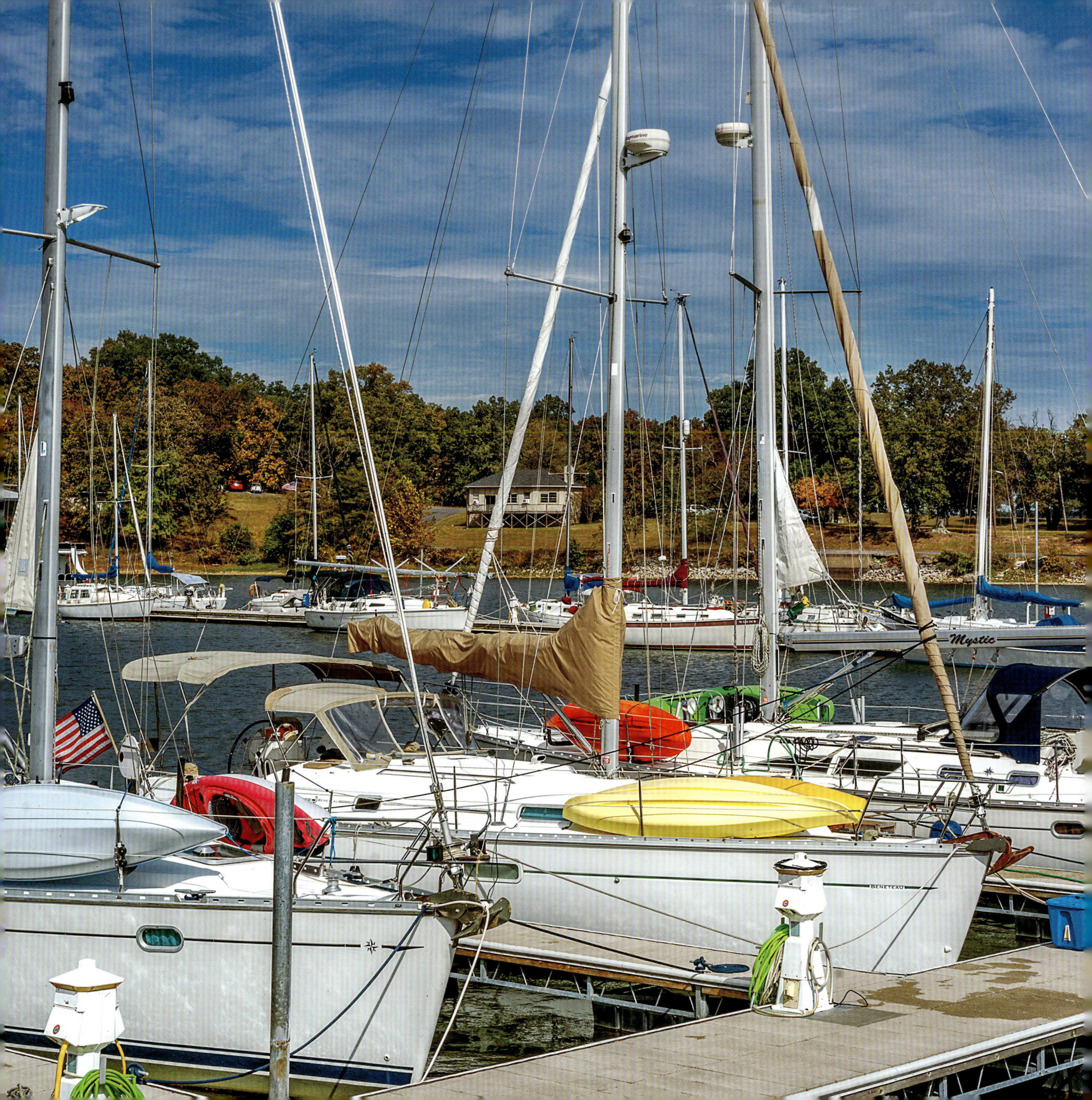
Mystic

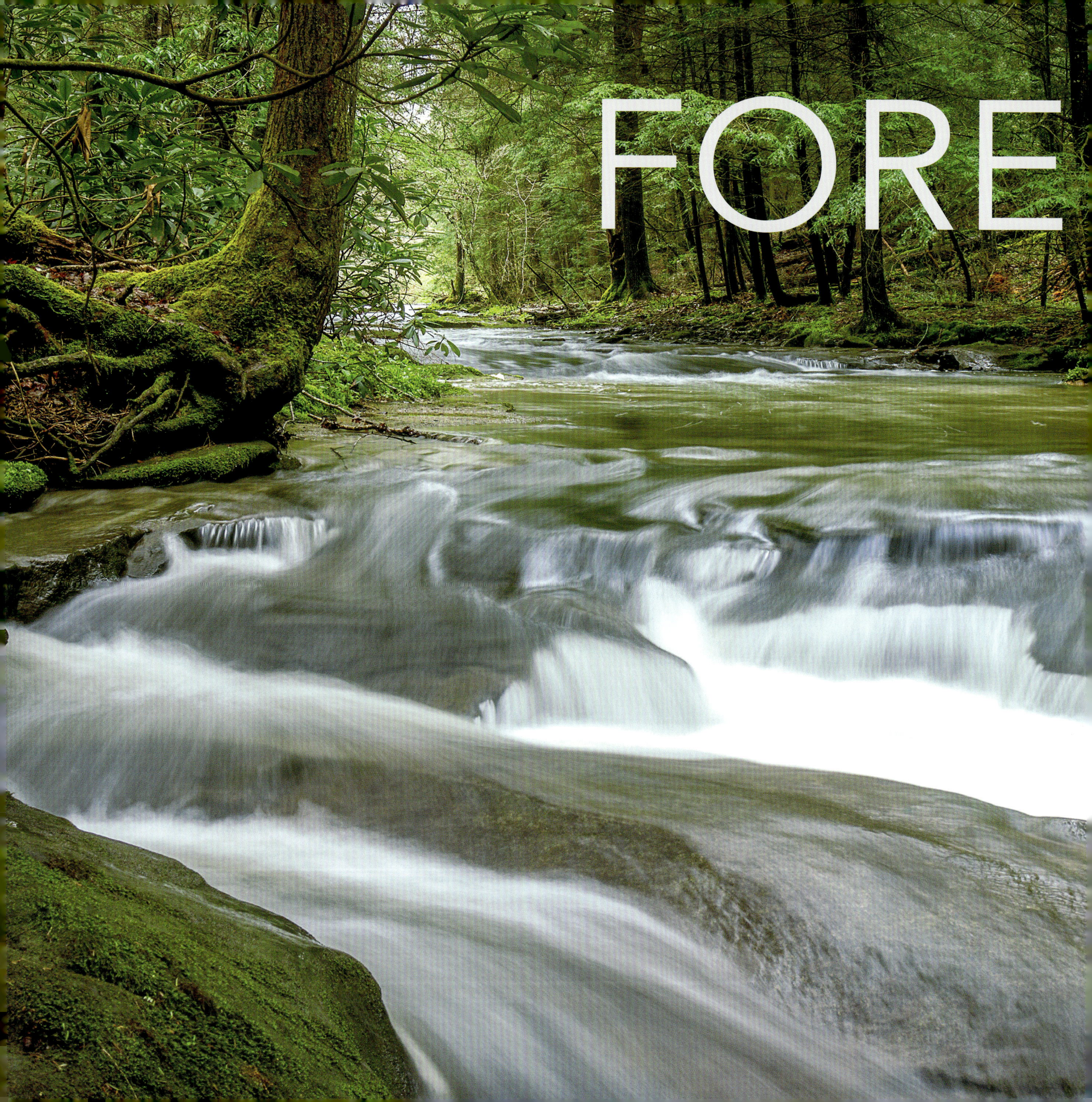

FORE

Cross the Ohio River at Louisville and head south a bit, and pretty soon you see that the glaciers that scoured much of the Midwest stopped shy of this green, rolling, undulating land called Kentucky. Actually, heading south from those glacial leftovers named the Great Lakes, the flattened midwestern cornfields turn to hills and trees south of Indianapolis, and then across the Ohio River, itself formed by glaciation, the highway cuts get more dramatic—rock faces rise up from Interstate 65 as the 18-wheelers chug up the knobs near Clermont, the first of many long ascents and declines as you move towards Elizabethtown. Head east from E-town, and the Bluegrass Parkway toward Lexington passes through long sloping hills and forested farmlands. Southeast of Lexington the hills give way to the piedmont of the Appalachian Mountains. Take a right at Elizabethtown, and the predictable hills eventually flatten out in the western part of the state—but there are still scattered smaller humps on the landscape leading up to the big bluffs overlooking the Mississippi River at Columbus. It's rare to see a big piece of flatness in Kentucky.

We have diverse forests, especially in the eastern mountains where northern species like Virginia pine converge with tropical species like bigleaf magnolia. Many oak and hickory varieties appear statewide and also walnut, beech, and yellow poplar. In the western region, there are sweetgum and cypress.

When I lived in the upper Midwest awhile and dreamed of Kentucky, images of my native Barren County flooded my head: the green hills of pasturelands dotted with cattle, the tobacco fields bordered by stands of hardwoods, and streams leading into creeks that lead into rivers that are frequently dammed. My home river, called Barren River (which Thomas Jefferson names in his *Notes of the State of Virginia* published back in the 1780s), was impounded in 1964 to make Barren River Lake. My maternal granddaddy, a dozer driver, helped build the earthen dam that stopped up that river.

The whole state is rich in water. I spent my youth seeking crawdads and salamanders in the streams around our rural home; wading Peters and Skaggs Creeks fishing for bass and stocked rainbow trout; canoeing Skaggs from Ritter's Mill right below where Nobob Creek runs into it and paddling miles to the still waters of Barren River reservoir; camping out on Barren River with the same granddaddy who built the dam and hunting frogs all night by johnboat, the air loud with the jug-of-rum croaking of big bullfrogs. This state, according to David and Lalie Dick's *Rivers of Kentucky,* "has more miles of navigable waterways—more than 1,500 miles—than any state of the United States except Alaska," which includes "more than 13,000 miles of streams, more than 50 man-made reservoirs, and 1,500 miles of water surface." We got surface streams and underground streams and occasionally streams of whiskey when a bourbon warehouse collapses.

Daniel Boone reputedly said, "Heaven must be a Kentucky kind of place," and no wonder, since Boone was viewing a land of abundant forests and waters and wildlife. It's still beautiful, even after all the river damming and mountain removing and stream filling and highway building. Kentucky remains a largely rural state, with only four cities exceeding fifty thousand people. It's an agrarian landscape with some temples of sublimity, like the water-sculpted natural arches of the Red River Gorge and the thundering white veil of Cumberland Falls and the world's longest cave system, Mammoth Cave of the Green River valley.

Hike the trails. The prehistoric bison and mammoths are gone, but off I-65 at Cave City a giant *Tyrannosaurus rex* statue beckons travelers to Dinosaur World. The gray and red wolves have been eradicated, but wild turkey and deer sightings are common in the woods and along the country roads. Our burley tobacco culture is mostly a thing of the past, with far fewer people growing the human-sized green plant these days, but relics of the crop remain in the weathered tobacco-hanging barns scattered across the land from the Mississippi River in the west to the mountains in the east. These days, in autumn, west of Hopkinsville, aromas of dark-fired tobacco perfume the air as farmers cure the green plants hung in tiered barns over smoldering slabs of hickory and sawdust, turning the leaves from green to dark brown over several days of smoking. Whenever I pass by these tobacco barns after the harvest and whiff those low-burning fires I get hungry for barbecue, which is also wonderfully plentiful in the dark-fired tobacco region. Many Kentuckians, for better and worse, like their wood-smoked meats and tobacco. West Kentucky barbecue joints serve up smoke-bathed sliced mutton, pulled pork, pork ribs, and beef brisket—you know, familiar barbecue fare—but also add to their barbecue pits (because of regional demand for smoke-flavored things) chubby rolls of bologna and deli-style turkey breasts. West Kentuckians even smoke city hams that have already been smoked and cured in ham factories.

What's this have to do with landscapes? Drive around the western Kentucky backroads and highways in the summer months and you'll sniff the landscape. Those barns and barbecue pits and preferences for hickory wood for flavor are all part of the cultural package. Travelers can also see a lot of one-room country churches, tall PVC pipe crosses in symbolic groupings of three, and billboards of the Ten Commandments (and other billboards announcing HELL IS REAL) along Kentucky's roadways. The Revival of 1800 began in western Kentucky and led into the evangelical Second Great Awakening. If you eat meat, you can fill up on mutton and more at various picnics hosted by Catholic churches nearly every weekend from spring to fall.

The past bleeds into the present in the form of church houses, crosses, and billboards; tobacco barns; and polystyrene and fiberglass dinosaurs. You can see the real past, sort of, in northern Kentucky at Big Bone Lick State Historic Site, a natural history park dedicated to Ice Age mammals like giant ground sloths and mammoths that visited the salt licks back in the day. The park also keeps a small bison herd—a throwback to the land's prehistoric bison. In western Kentucky, the Land Between the Rivers, called LBL (Land Between the Lakes National Recreation Area), has a bison and elk prairie as well. Or visit the preserved log homes of the kind President Lincoln lived in or the living history of our sweet-smelling bourbon rickhouses filled with beautiful white-oak barrels.

This is starting to sound like a state tourism ad. I swear they ain't paying me to write this. But seriously, folks, this heaven of a place holds beauty around many corners—over many hills and up the hollers and deep in the earth—as revealed by the photos that follow. Drive around this state and pay attention to the long-formed natural history, all that water sculpting that created the sublime arches, caves, and waterfalls. Soak up the cultural history of the tobacco barns and church houses. Feel the humid green engulf you while driving through a forest in summer. Roll down the windows, slow down, and listen to the red- and yellow-hued leaves crunching under tires in the fall. Park the car. If you can, walk through the woods and fields of our still-state-funded historic and recreational parks and natural areas. If you can, get a boat, canoe, or kayak and take a float on some miles of our abundant waters. I bet you'll see great blue herons, as close as we're likely to get to real dinosaurs, if you spend enough time on the right waterways and observe.

There's plenty of obviously pretty in this state, like the manicured horse farms—the old stone and blackboard fences and well-kept horses made healthy by the soils that birthed the grasses the region is named after—along with the quaint bourbon distilleries. And if you're looking for it, there's the kitsch of vibrantly painted manufactured dinosaurs; a 68,000-pound, 120-foot-tall baseball bat; a biblically scaled Noah's Ark; and a concrete obelisk two-thirds the size of the Washington Monument rising up out of the cornfields at Fairview to commemorate the lost president of the lost Confederacy.

The photos that follow feature mostly the obviously pretty. Enjoy the abundance—the natural and cultural richness—of this land called Kentucky.

Dr. Wes Berry
"THE HUNGRY PROFESSOR"

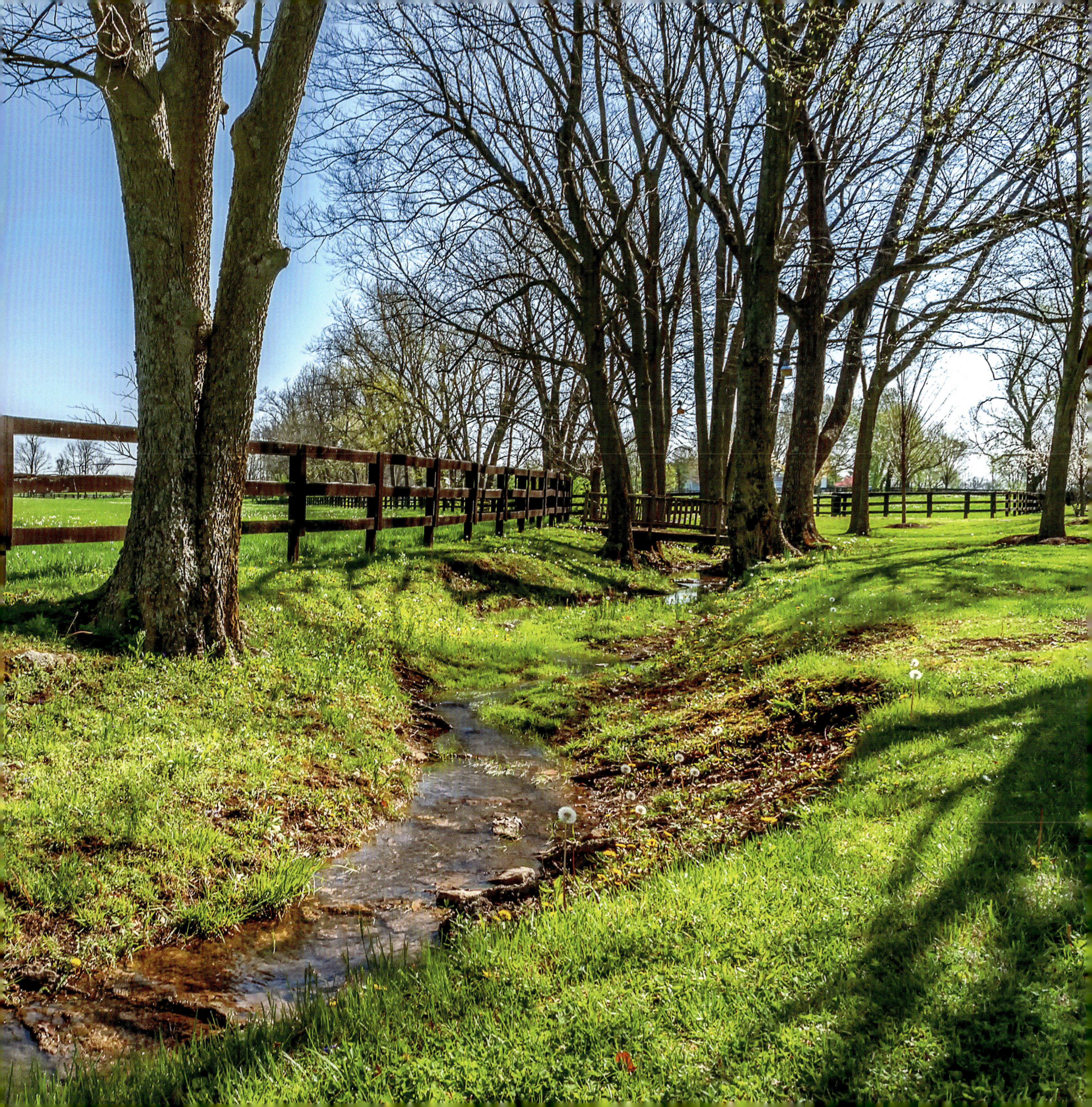

Larry Bennett, I want to say thank you for your friendship and all of your help and advice over the years. I am a better person for knowing you and I have always appreciated you. I will never forget you or your teachings and lessons and will carry those with me the rest of my life. You are one of a kind for sure. I hope you enjoy this book in your retirement and in your new home.

Uncle Joe and Aunt Illa, thank you for all you do. Uncle Joe, you crack me up, and Aunt Illa, you make me smile. It's a great combination.

Lee

We would like to thank all of the employees of the city, state, and national park systems across the country. We would also like to include those of you who work in nature preserves, conservancies, and natural resources. Without each of you and your dedication none of us could really enjoy what is publicly available everywhere in this country, and we never take any of it for granted. We appreciate all of your efforts and hard work in making the outdoors a better place for everyone. We do enjoy the time we get to chat with some of you while we are out. We always come away a little more educated than when we arrive and are always up for learning new things. Thank you.

Gary Dunham, we can't thank you enough for all of your help and input. Thank you . . . again.

To the team at IU Press: We both really appreciate all of your hard work and input and willingness to guide us in the right direction to make sure our books are the best that they can be. We both rely on each person's expertise and skill, be it wordsmithing, writing, design, marketing advice, acquisitions, or other areas. All of you are class acts to work with and our books are all the better for what each of you has contributed. We are very well aware of it, and we are in your debt and try to be as easy to work with as we possibly can. Thank you for being available on a moment's notice. Thank you to each of you.

Lee and DeeDee

ACKNOWLE

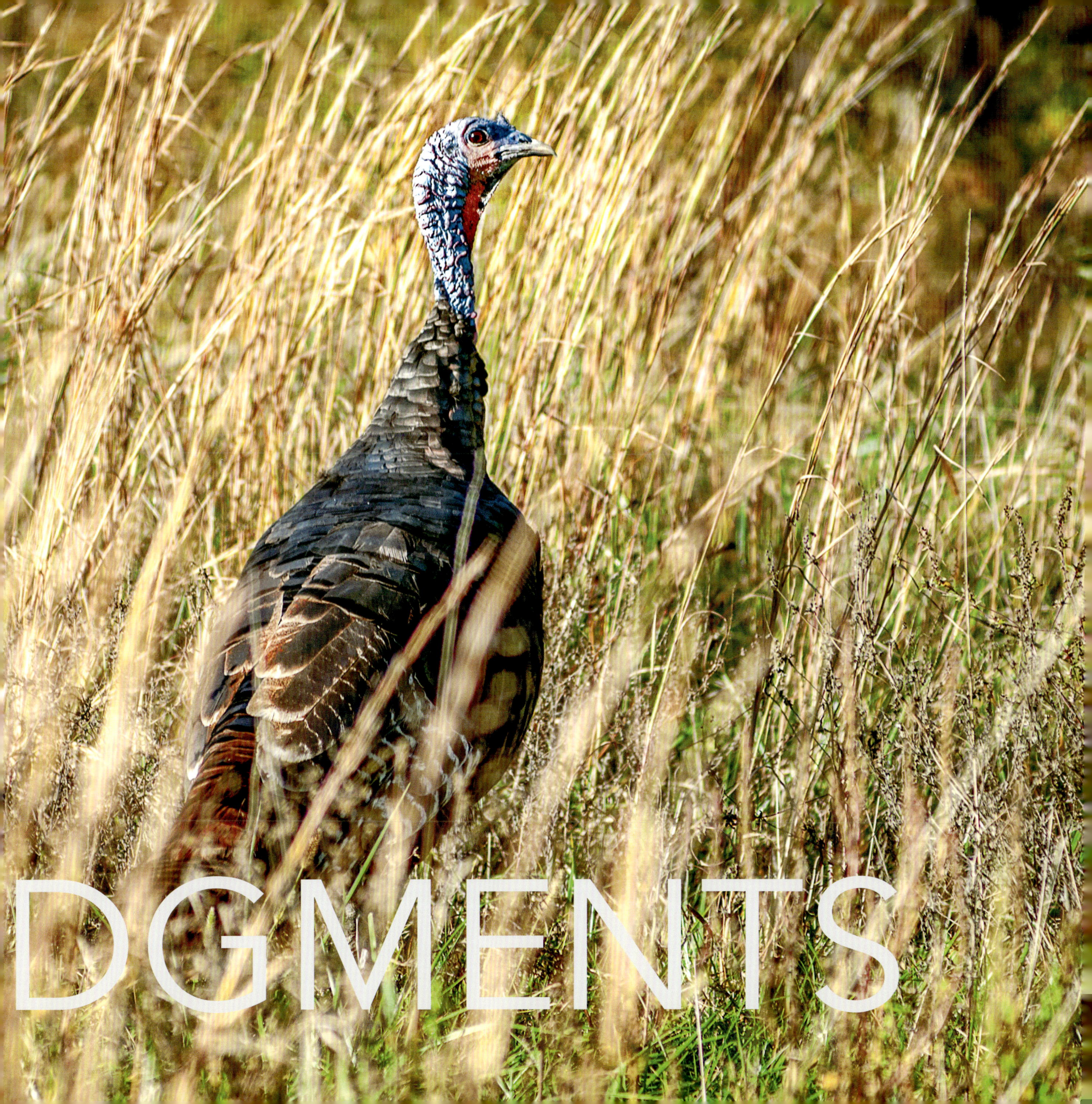
DGMENTS

KENTUCKY
ACROSS THE LAND

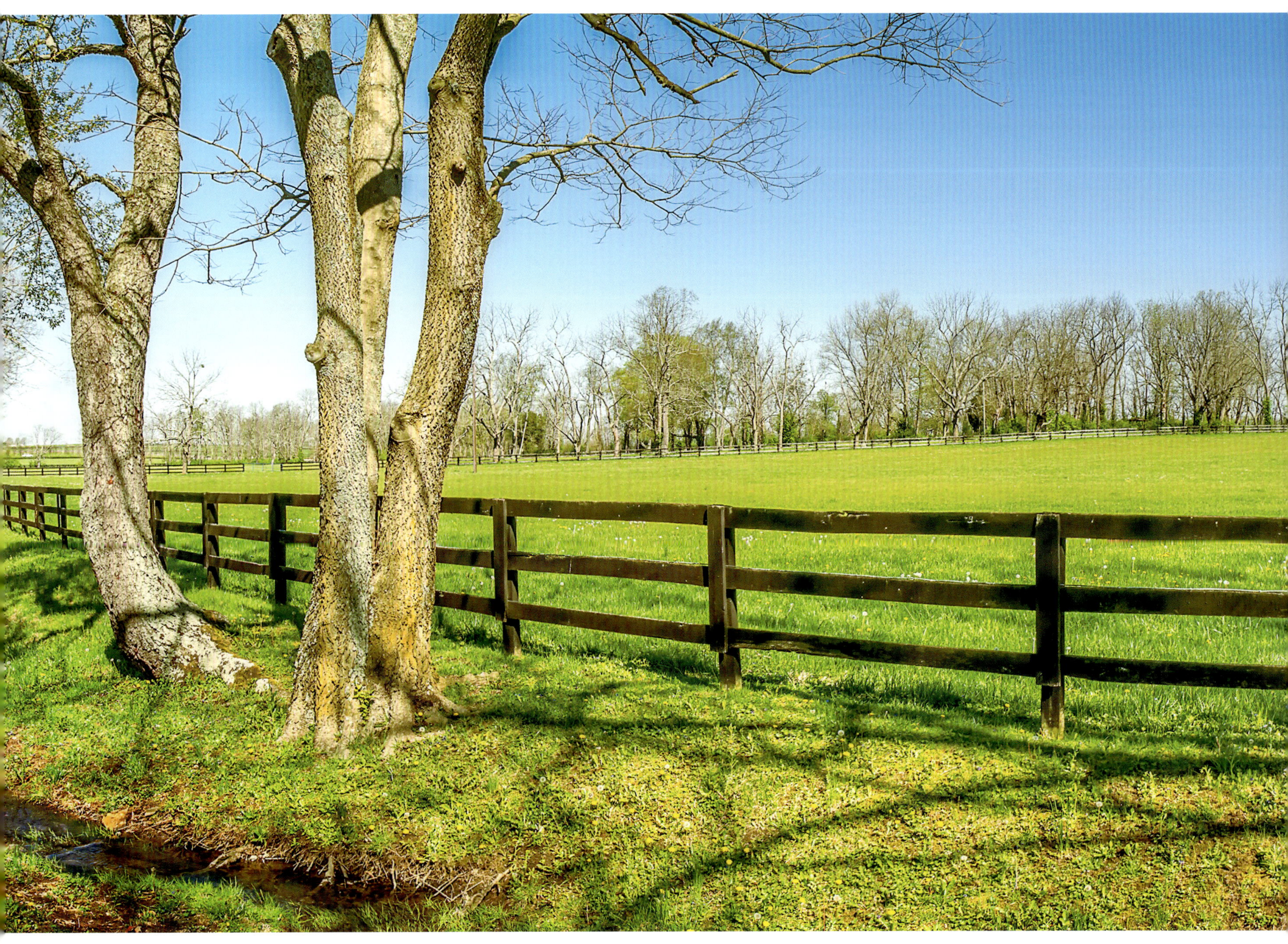

GALLERY

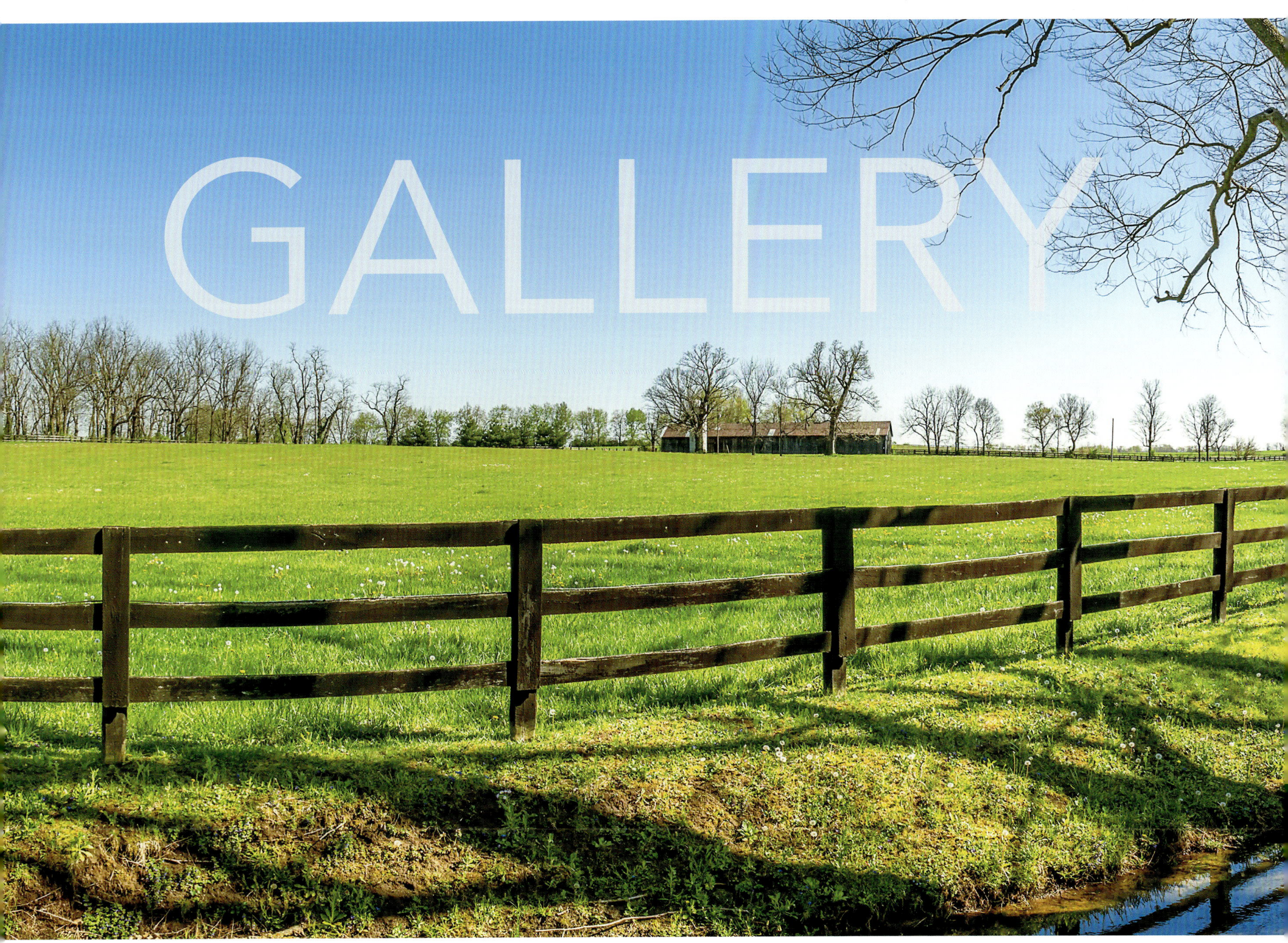

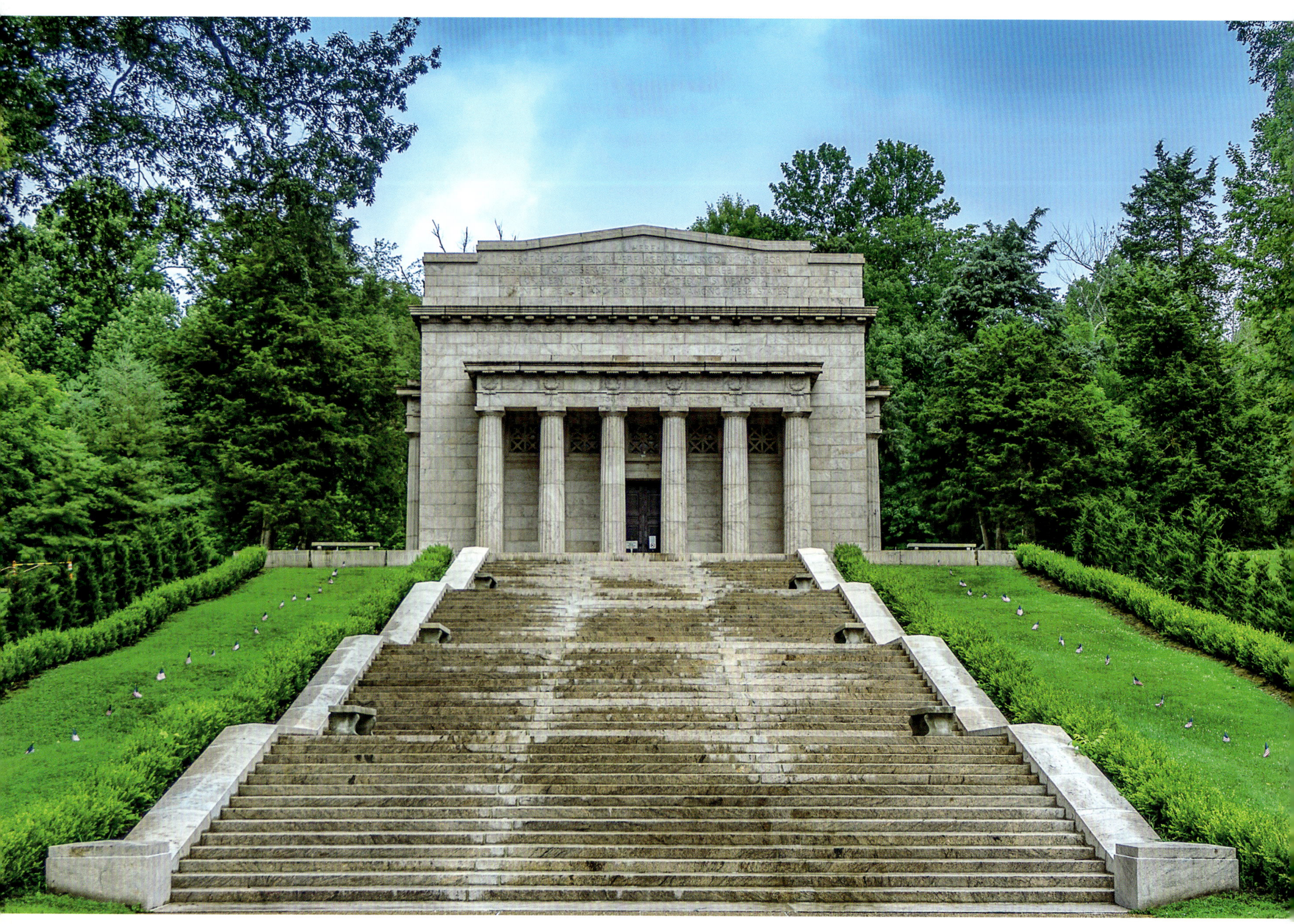

A symbolic birth cabin believed to mark the site of the birthplace of Abraham Lincoln is enshrined in the neoclassical Memorial Building at Abraham Lincoln Birthplace National Historical Park.

Big South Fork River as it passes by the historical site of the Blue Heron Mining Community in Big South Fork National River and Recreation Area.

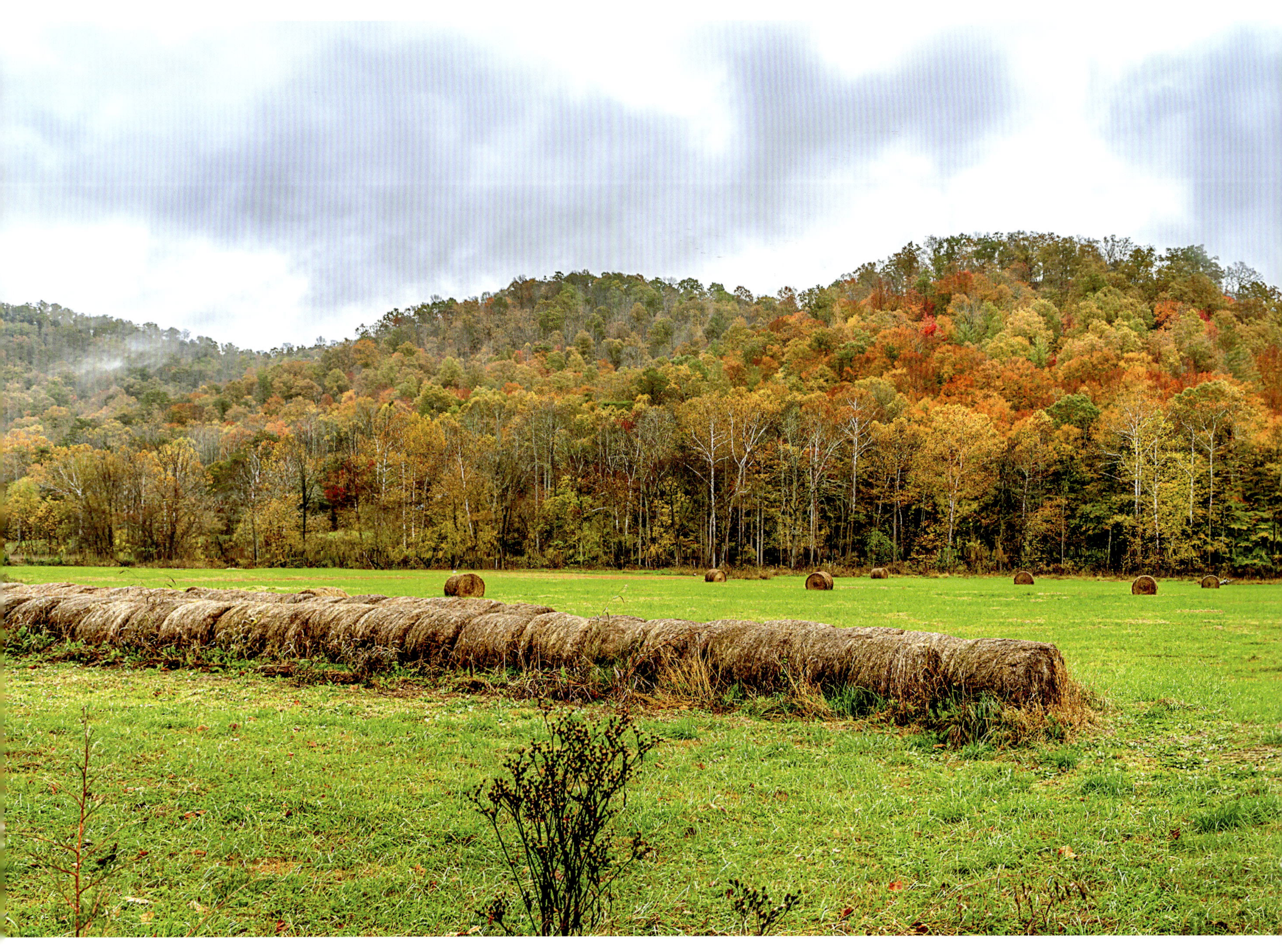

Fall color on the Kentucky hills warms the soul.

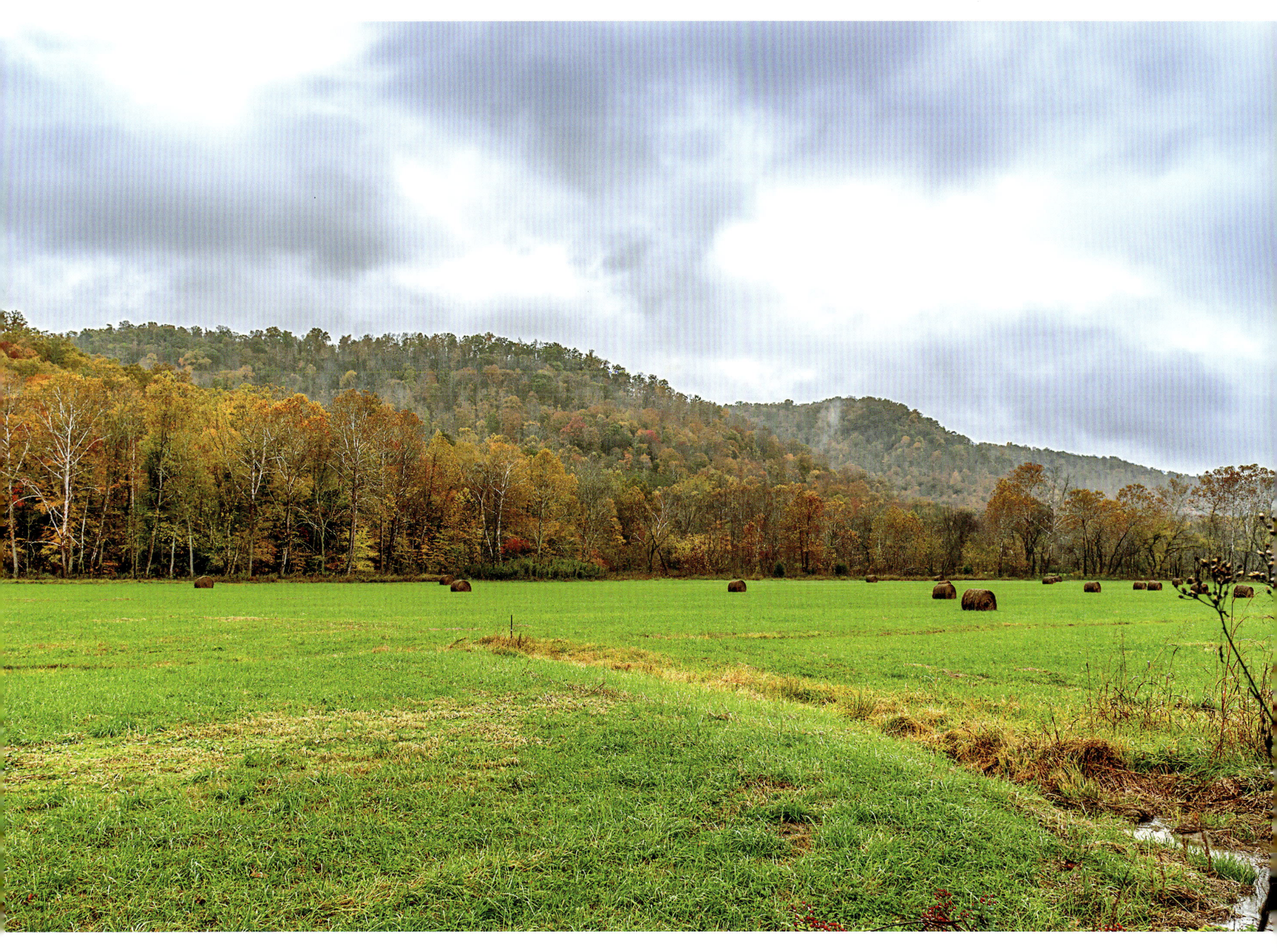

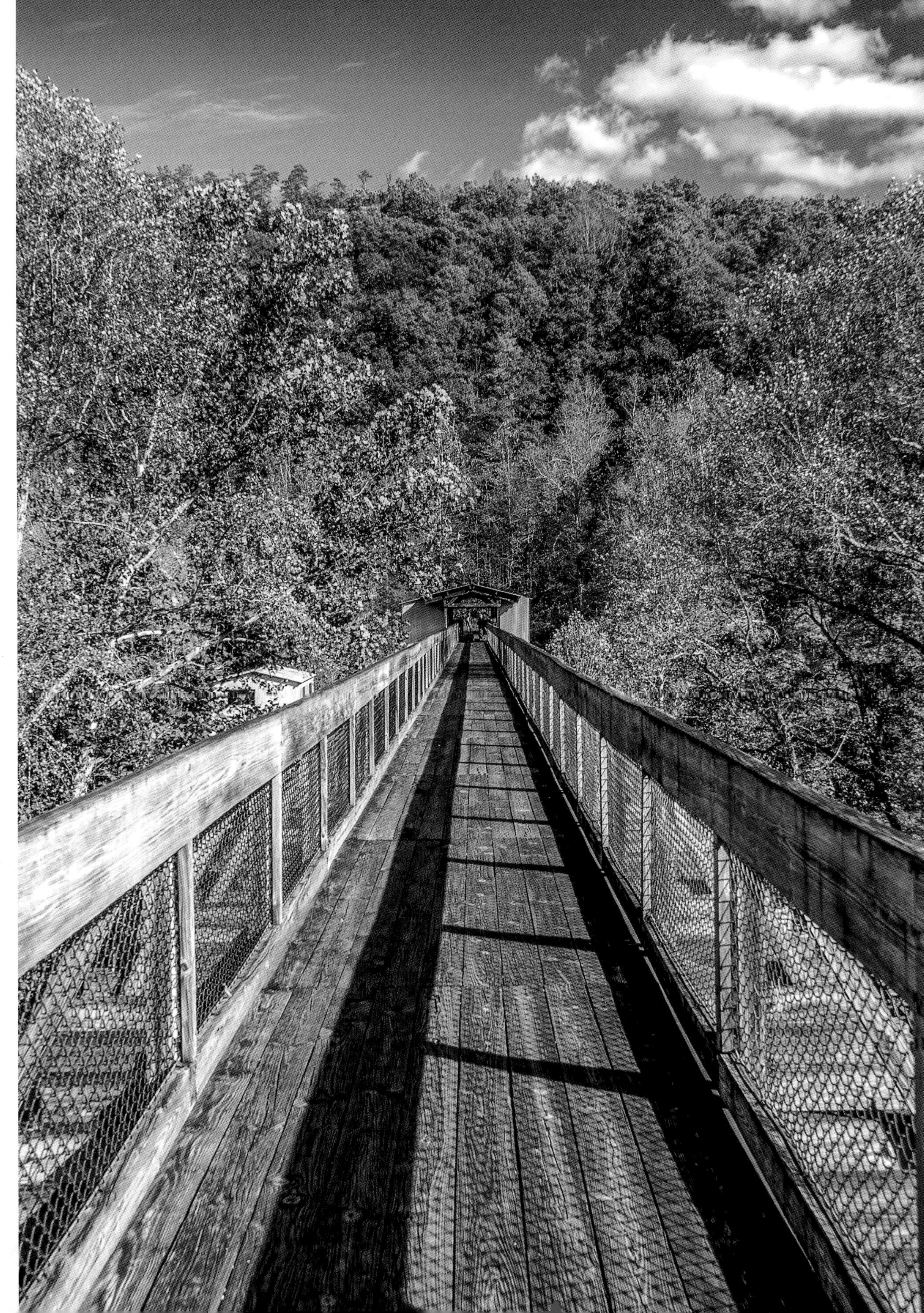

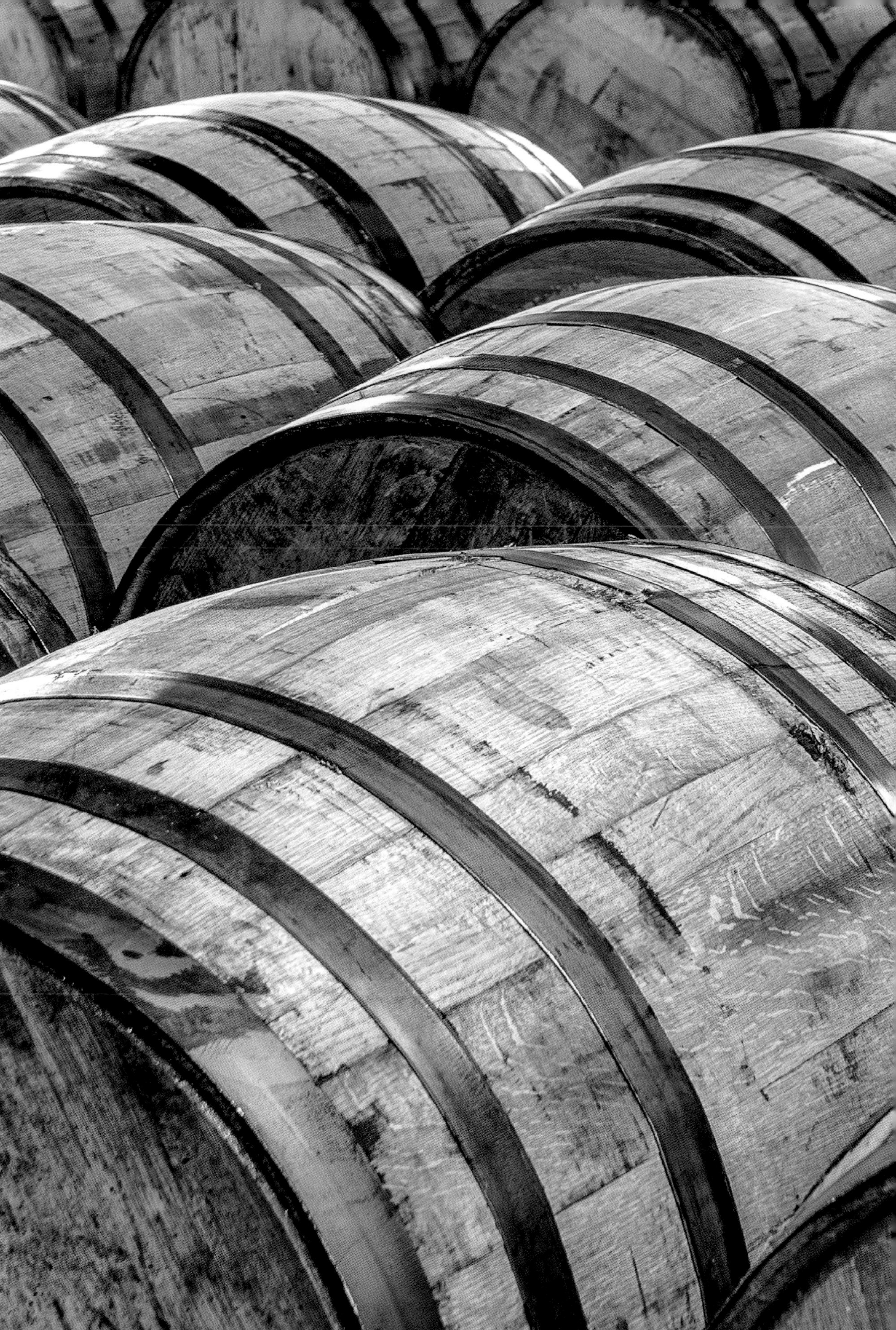

New barrels await inspection before they are filled with Buffalo Trace bourbon.

FACING
Tipple Bridge crosses the Big South Fork River at the historical site of the Blue Heron Mining Community.

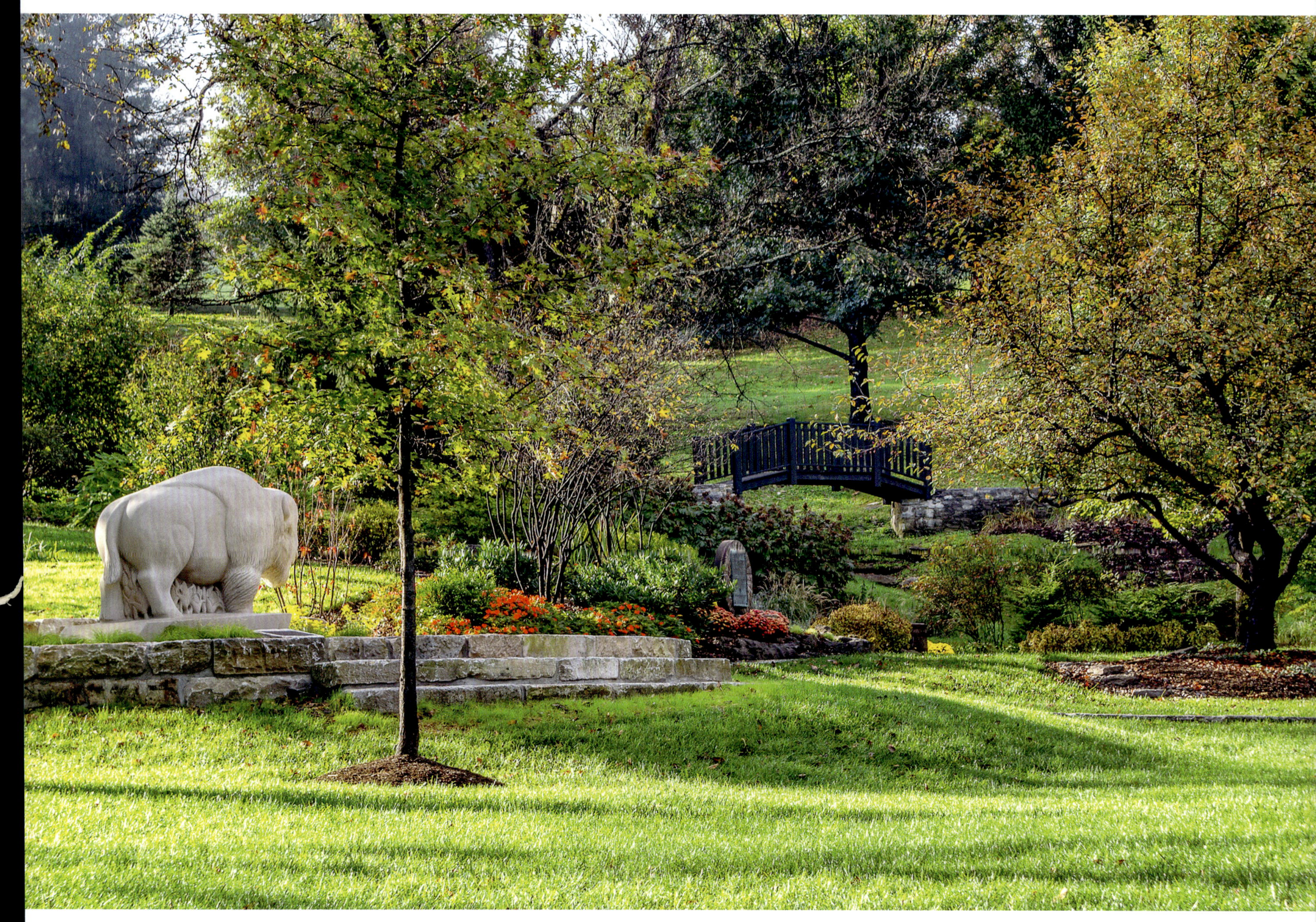

The gardens at Buffalo Trace Distillery offer a picturesque setting for visitors.

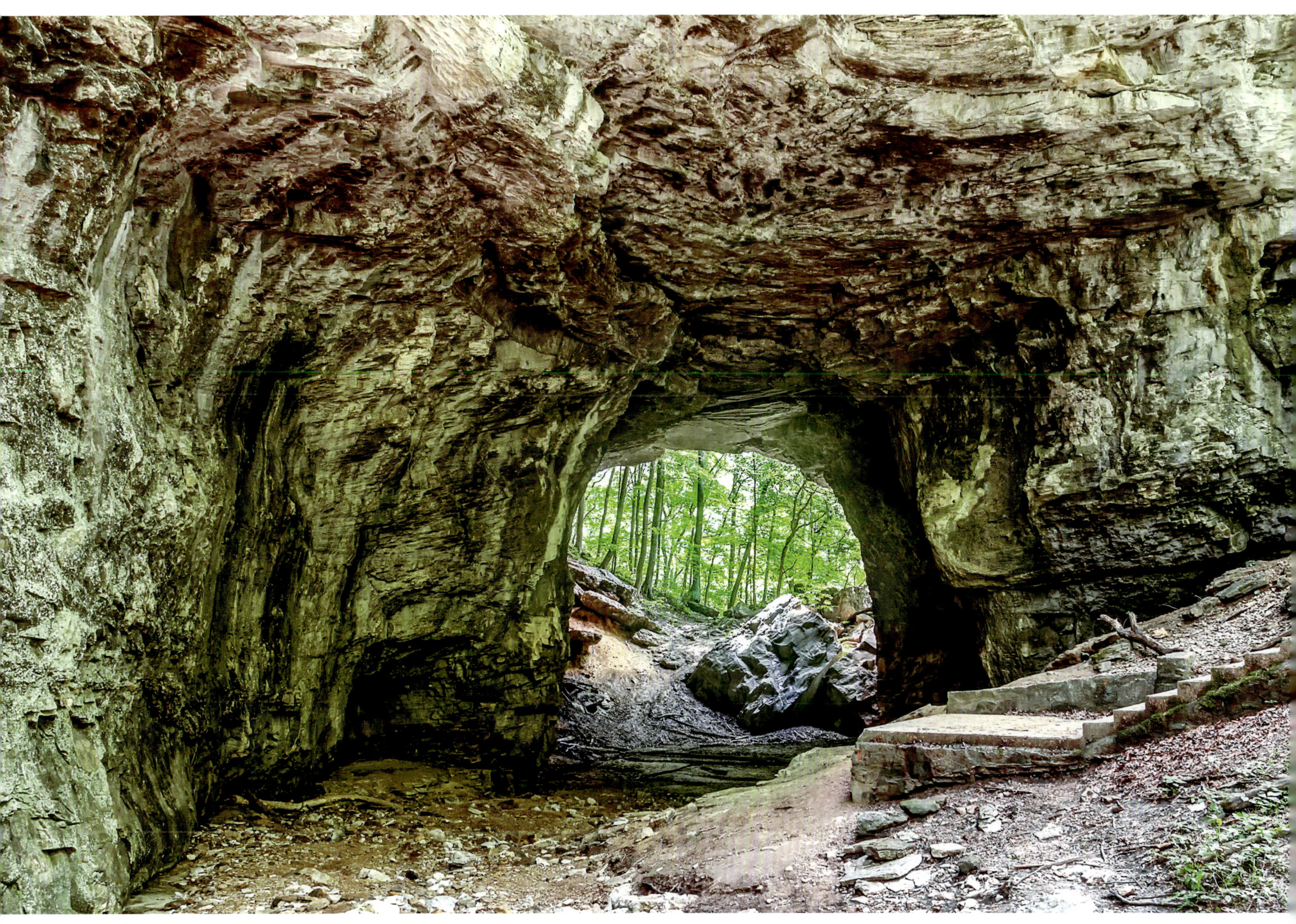

Exploring Smoky Bridge along the Three Bridges Trail at Carter Caves State Resort Park.

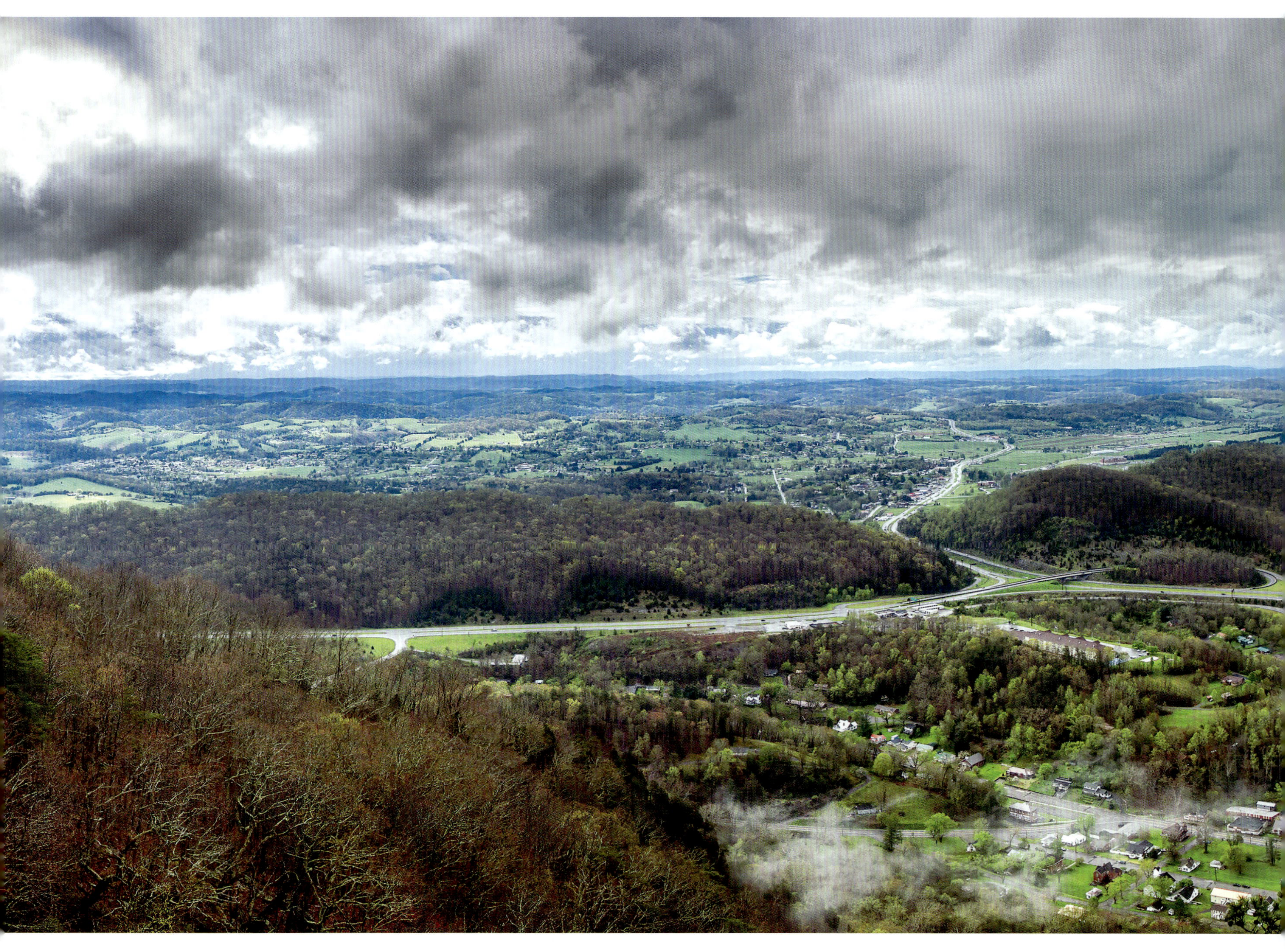

As far as you can see from the heights of Cumberland Gap National Historical Park.

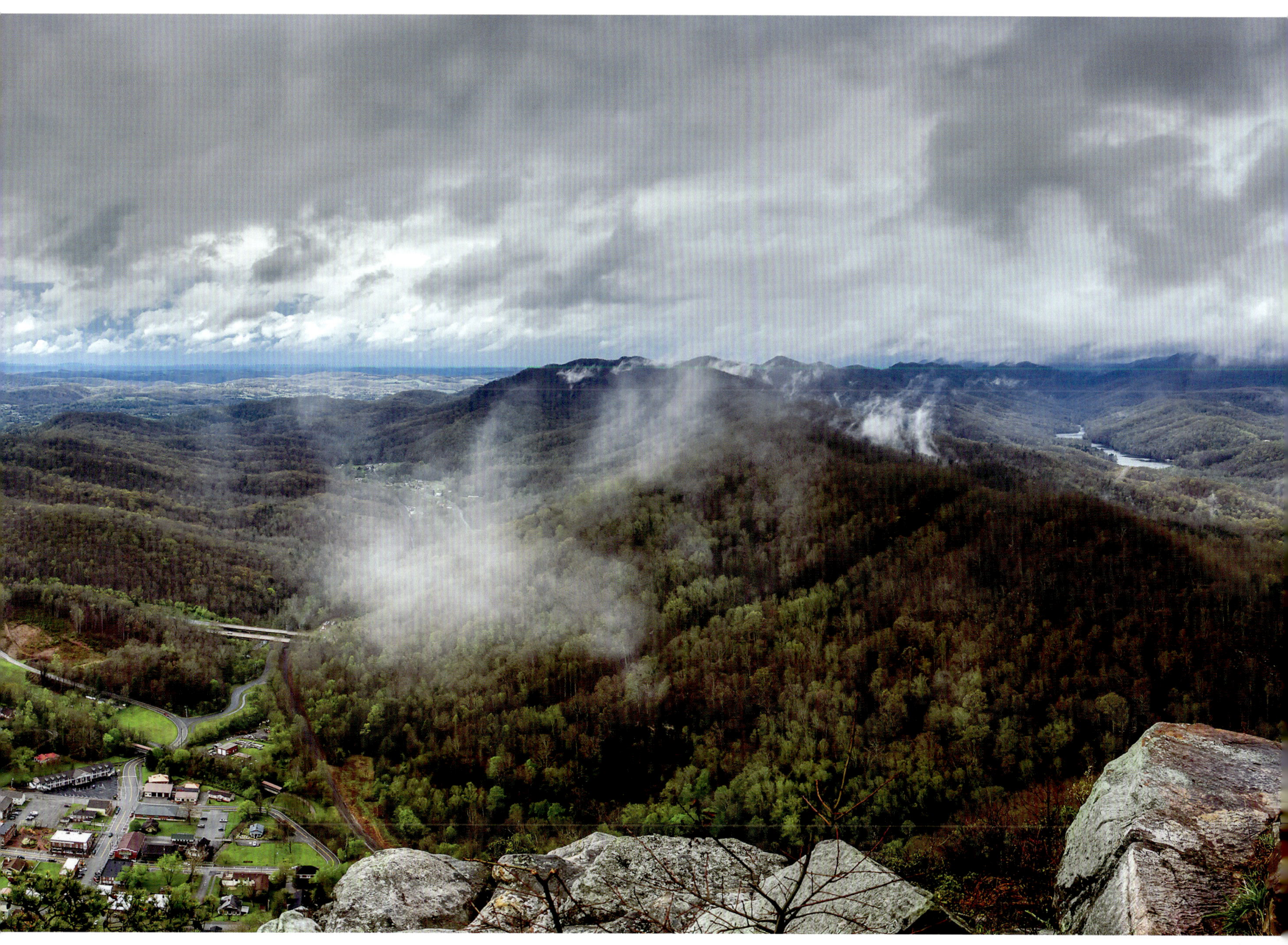

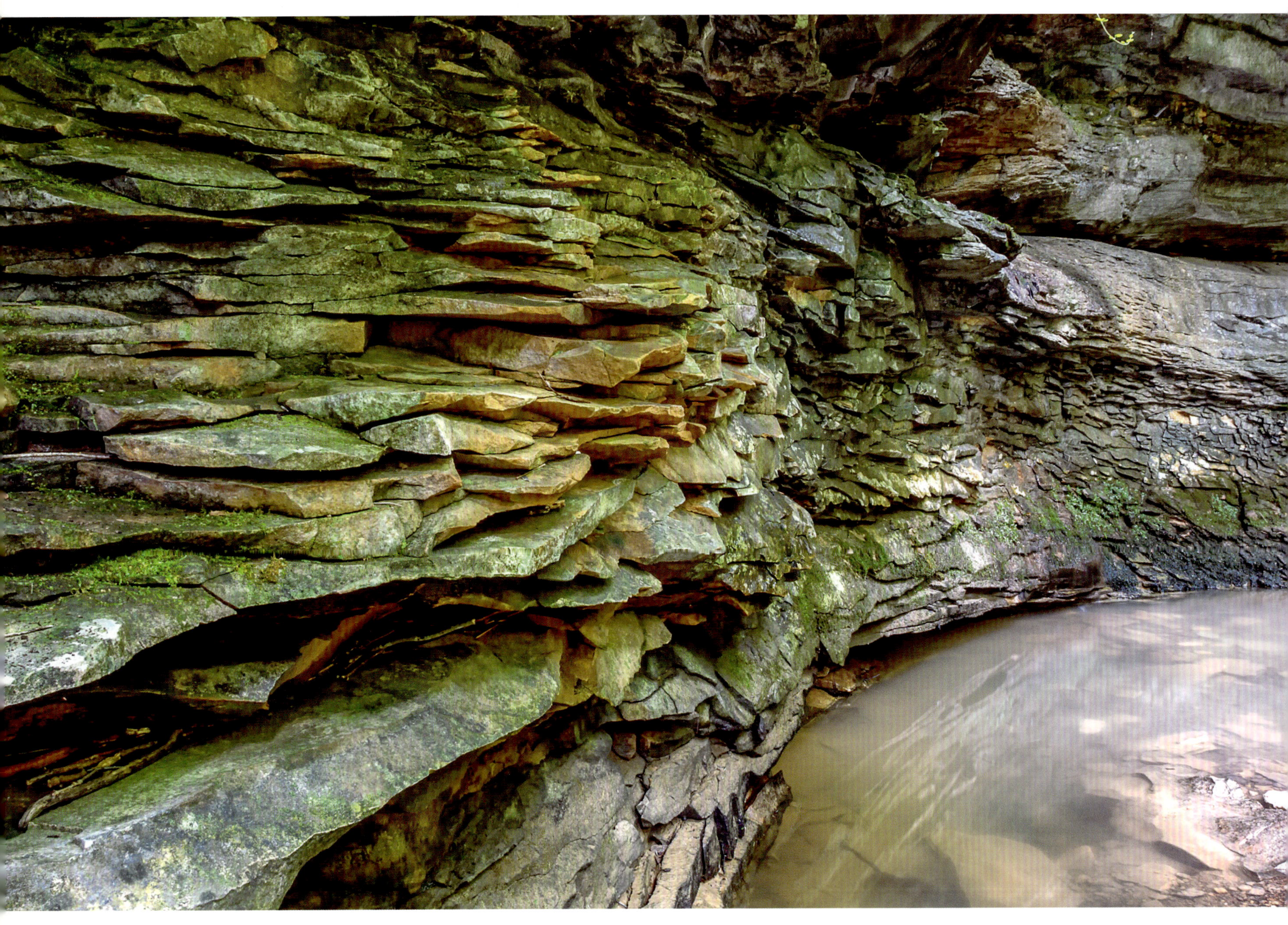

Layers of stone showing years of erosion and environmental change in Horn Hollow Cave at Carter Caves State Resort Park.

Signs of fall at Cove Spring Park in Frankfort, Kentucky.

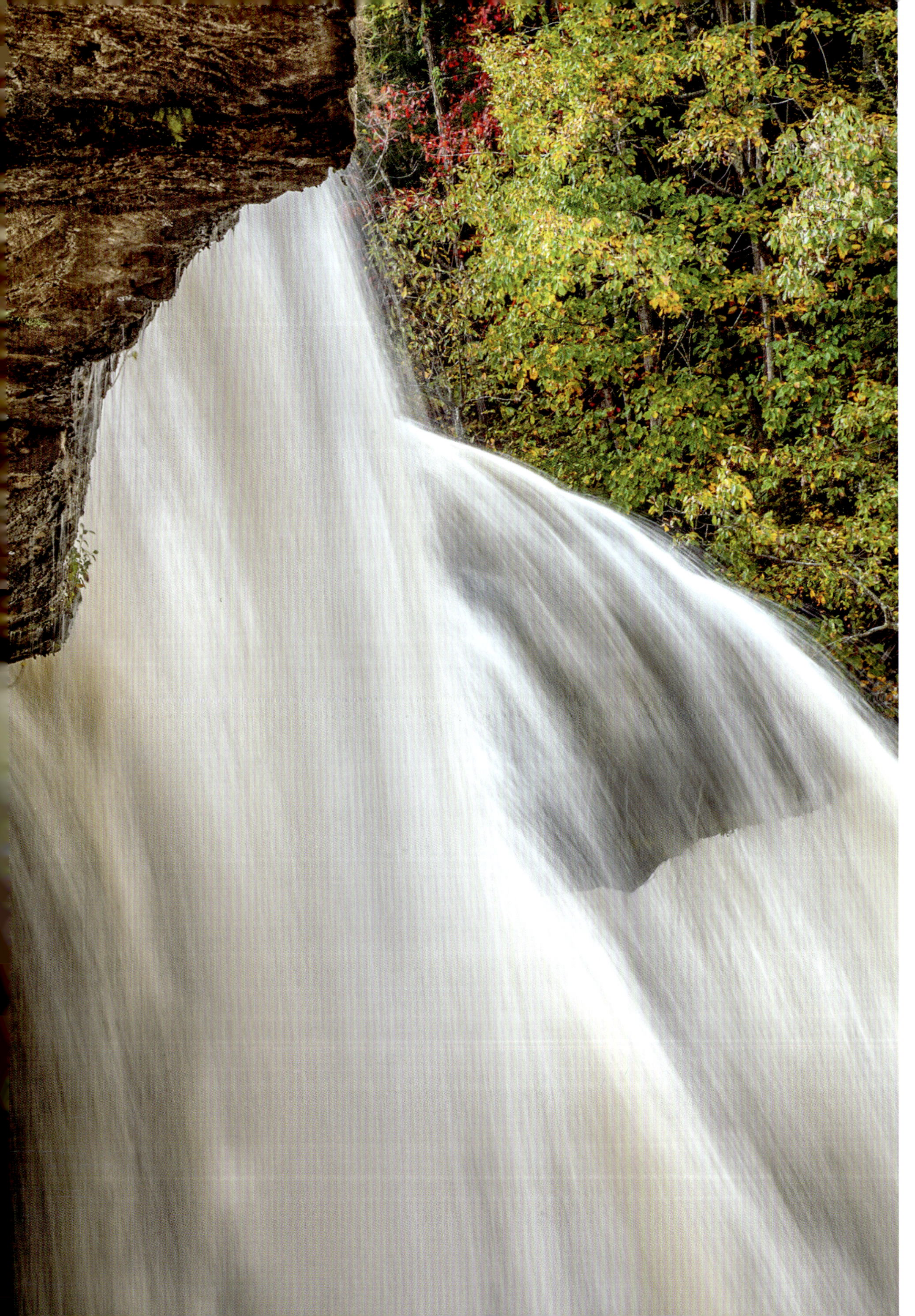

A view through
Cumberland Falls
at Cumberland Falls
State Resort Park.

Sunshine on the whiskey barrels at Buffalo Trace Distillery.

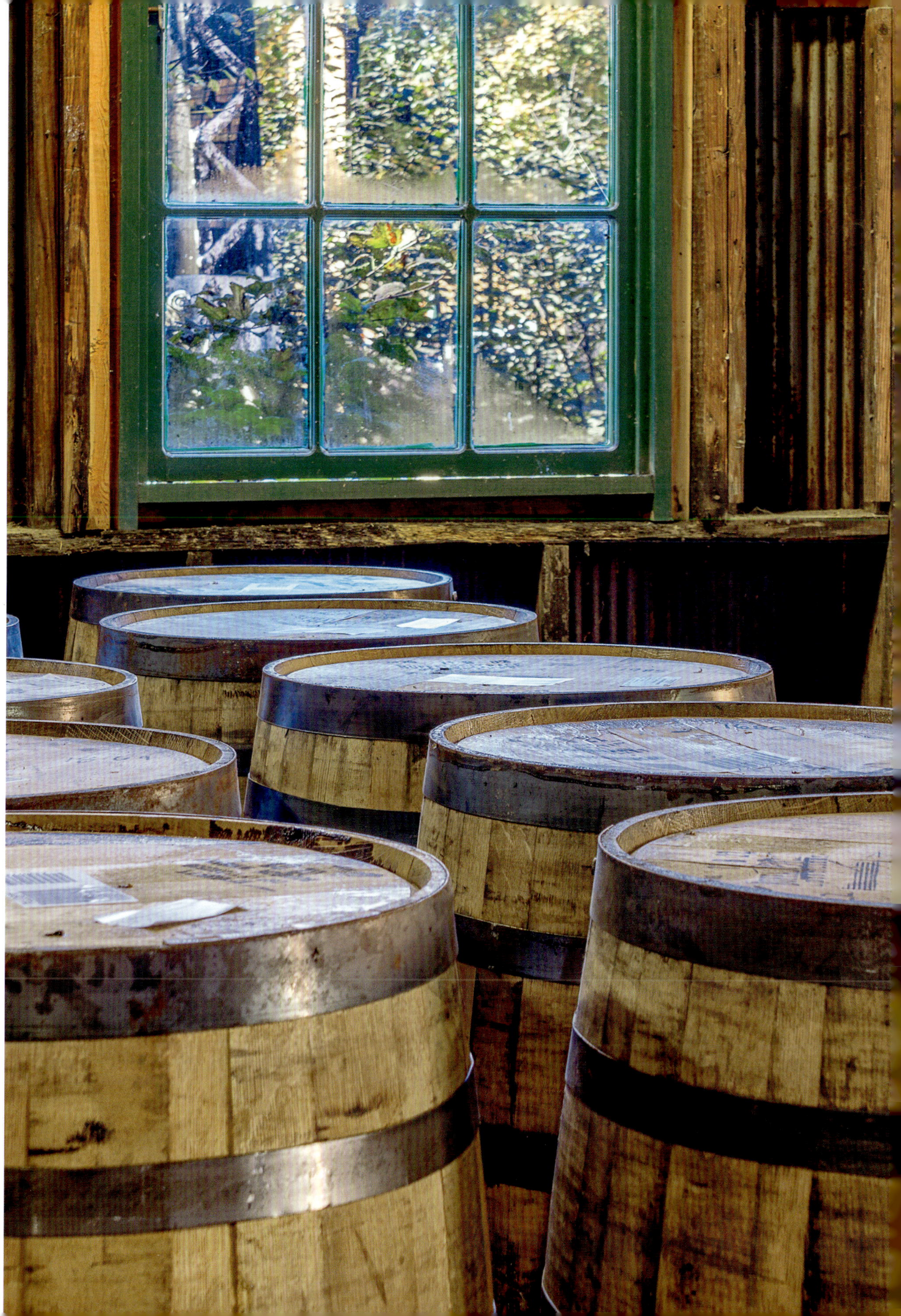

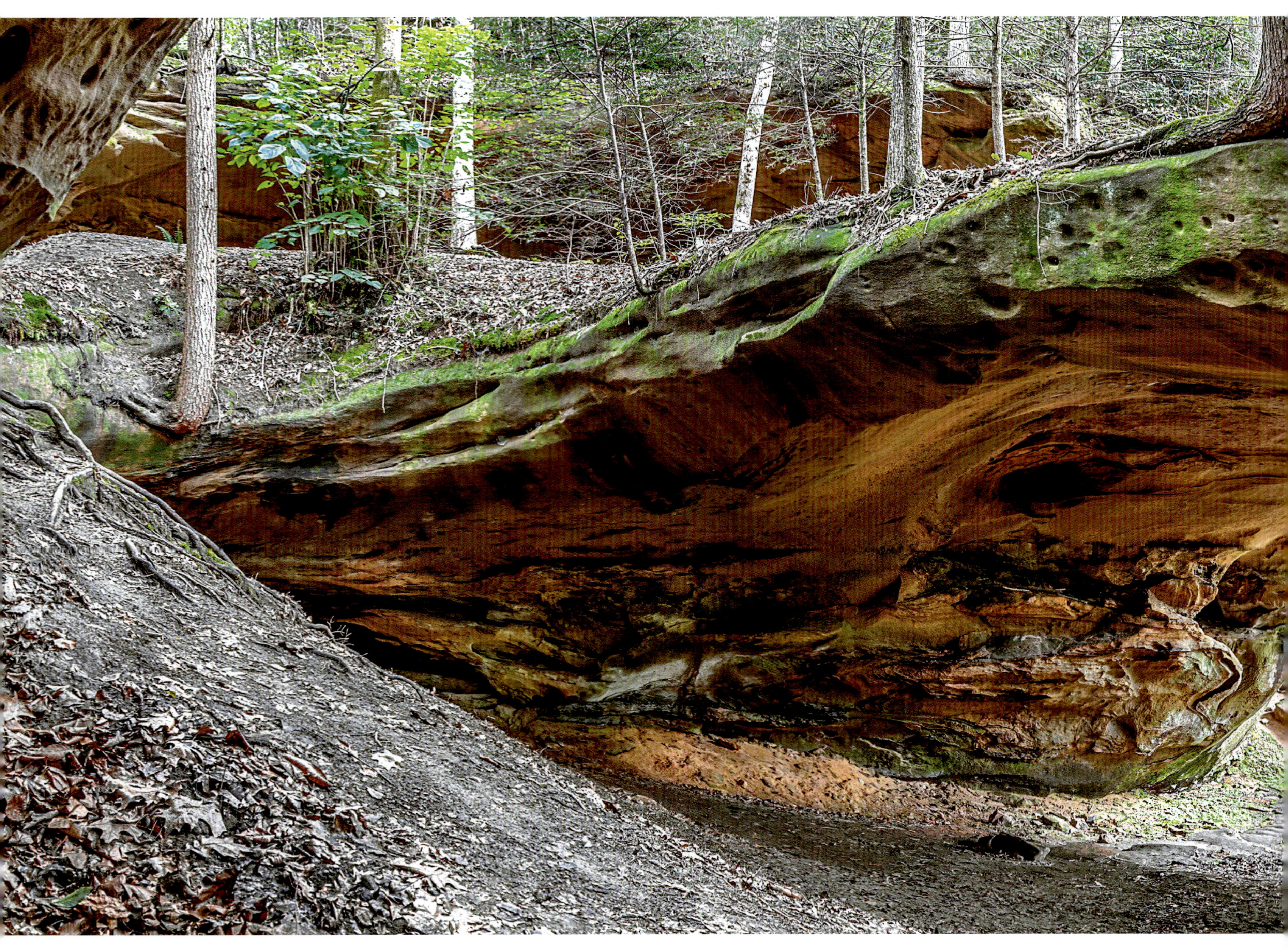

A shaft of light reveals hidden textures and features at Yahoo Arch.

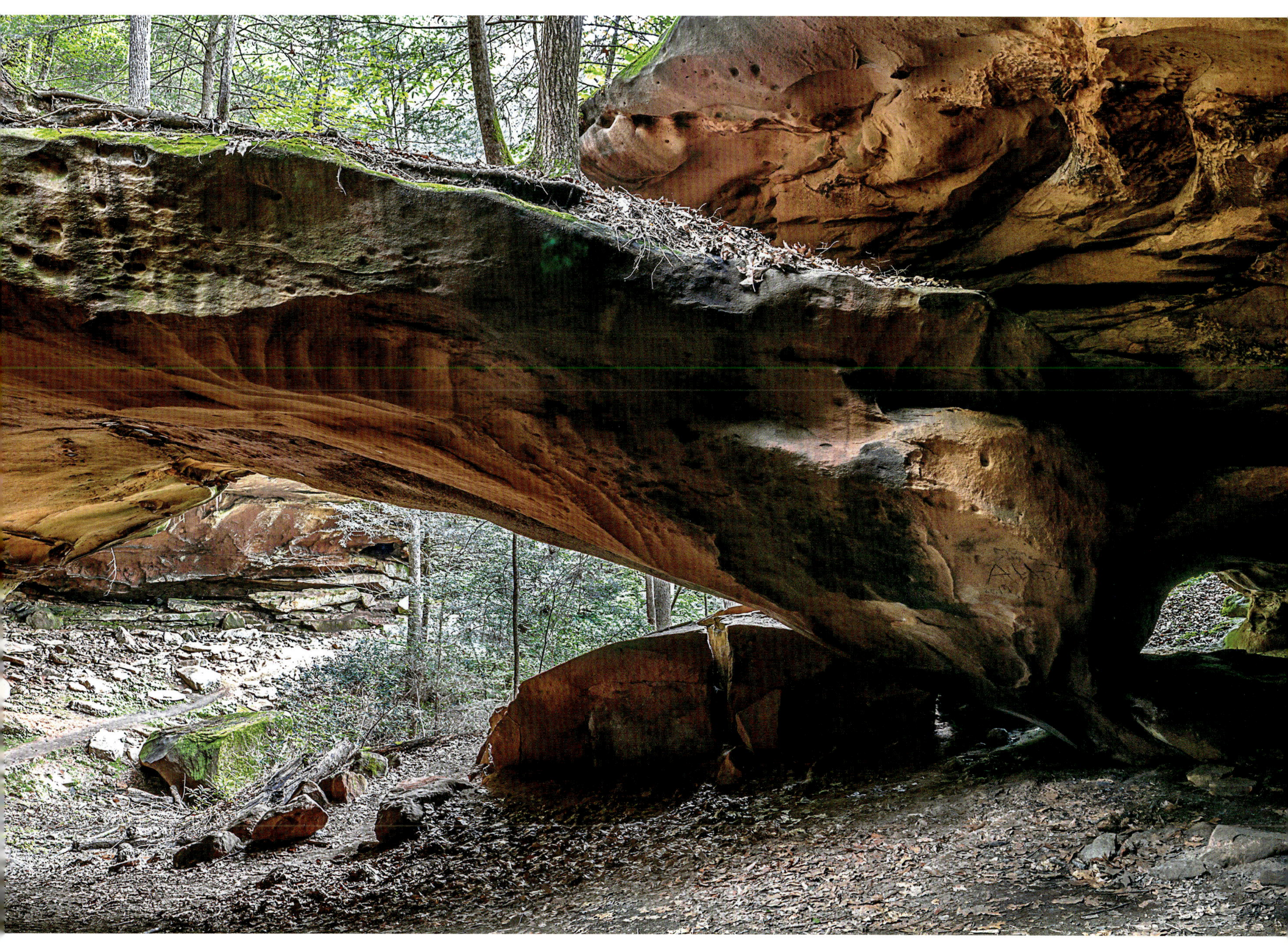

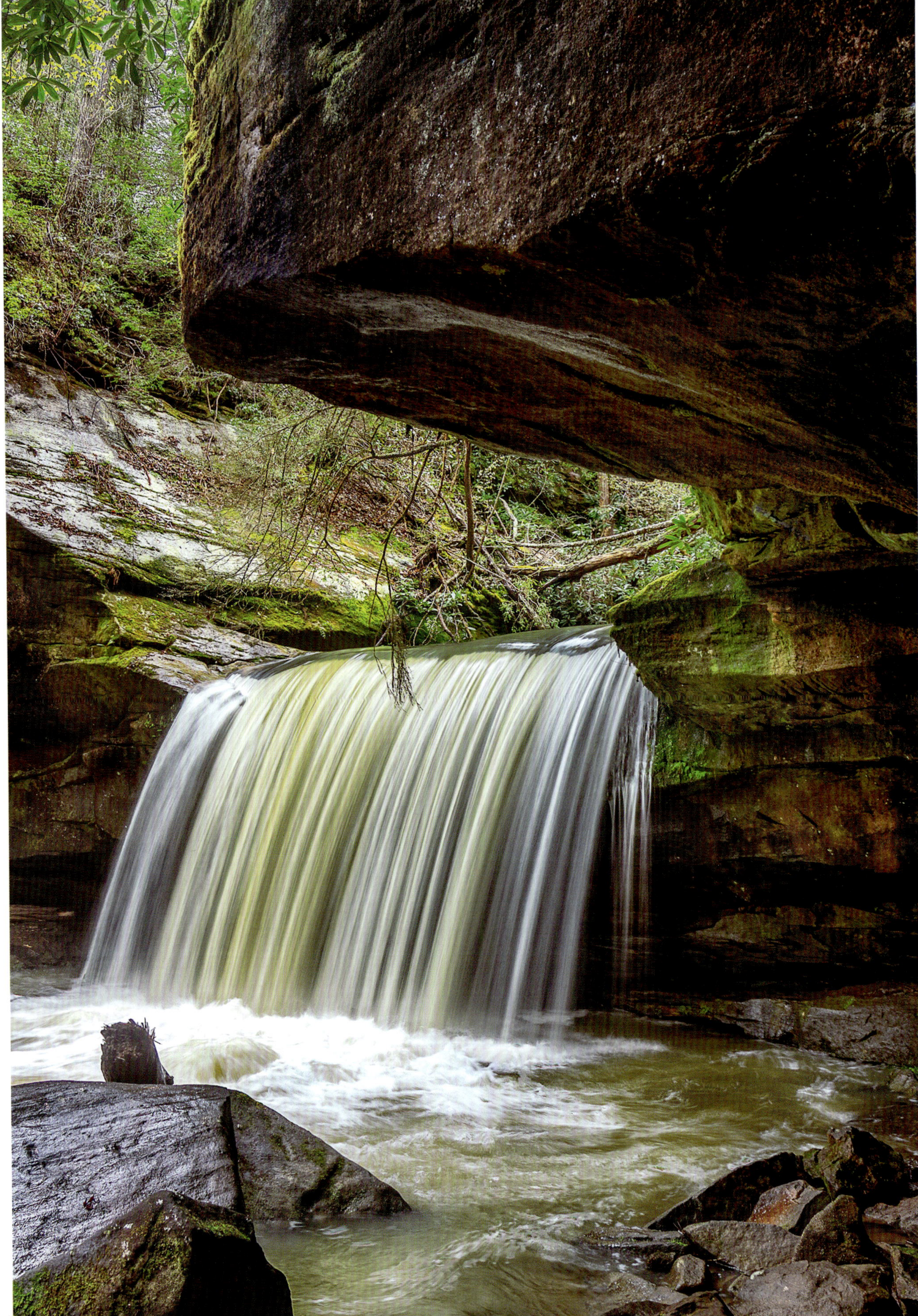

After a heavy rain, water finds its own path to the Cumberland River, creating an ephemeral waterfall.

FACING
Although the name is not pleasant, Dog Slaughter Falls is one of the most beautiful sights in the Cumberland Falls State Resort Park.

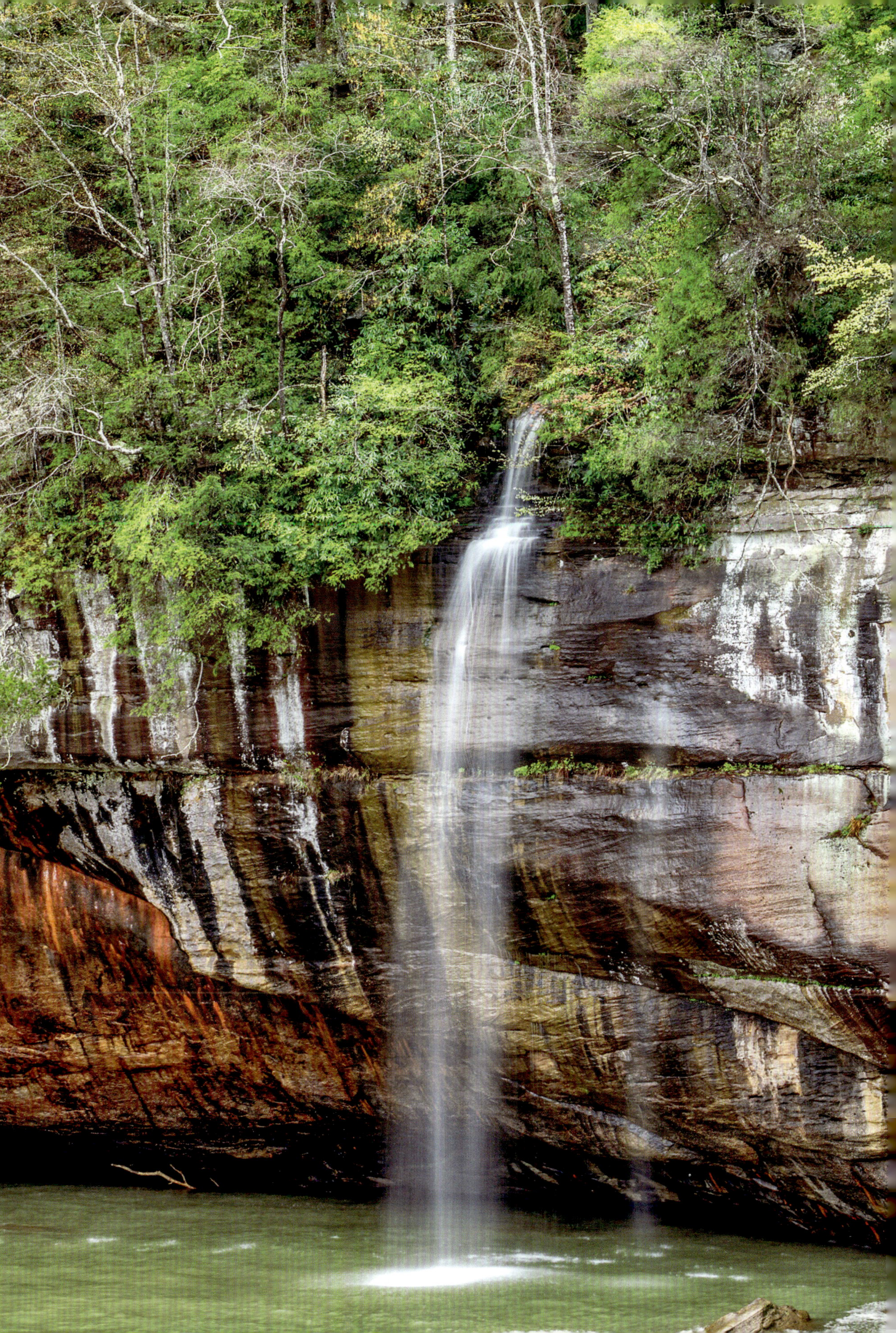

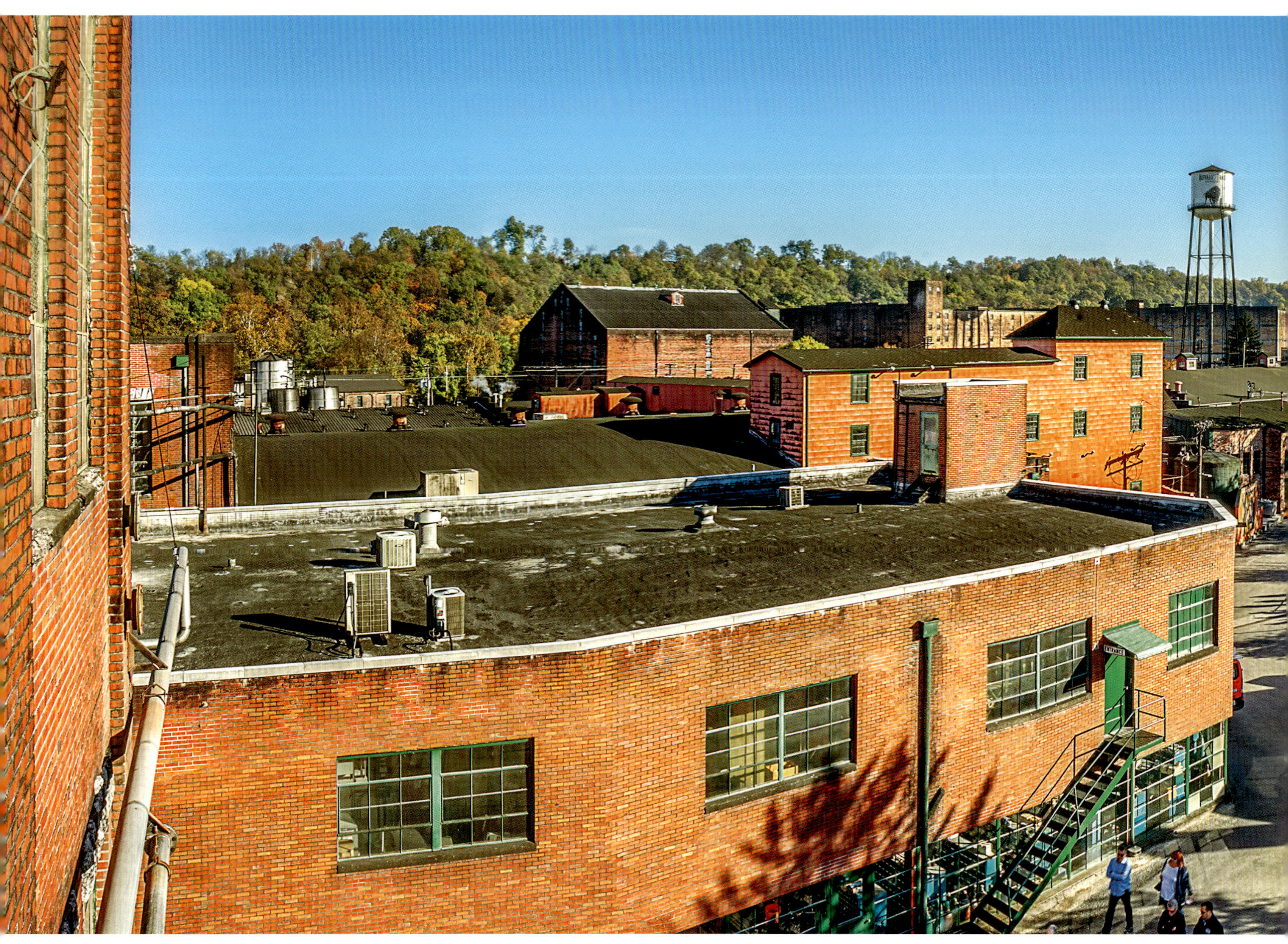

Rich colors at Buffalo Trace Distillery on a bright summer day.

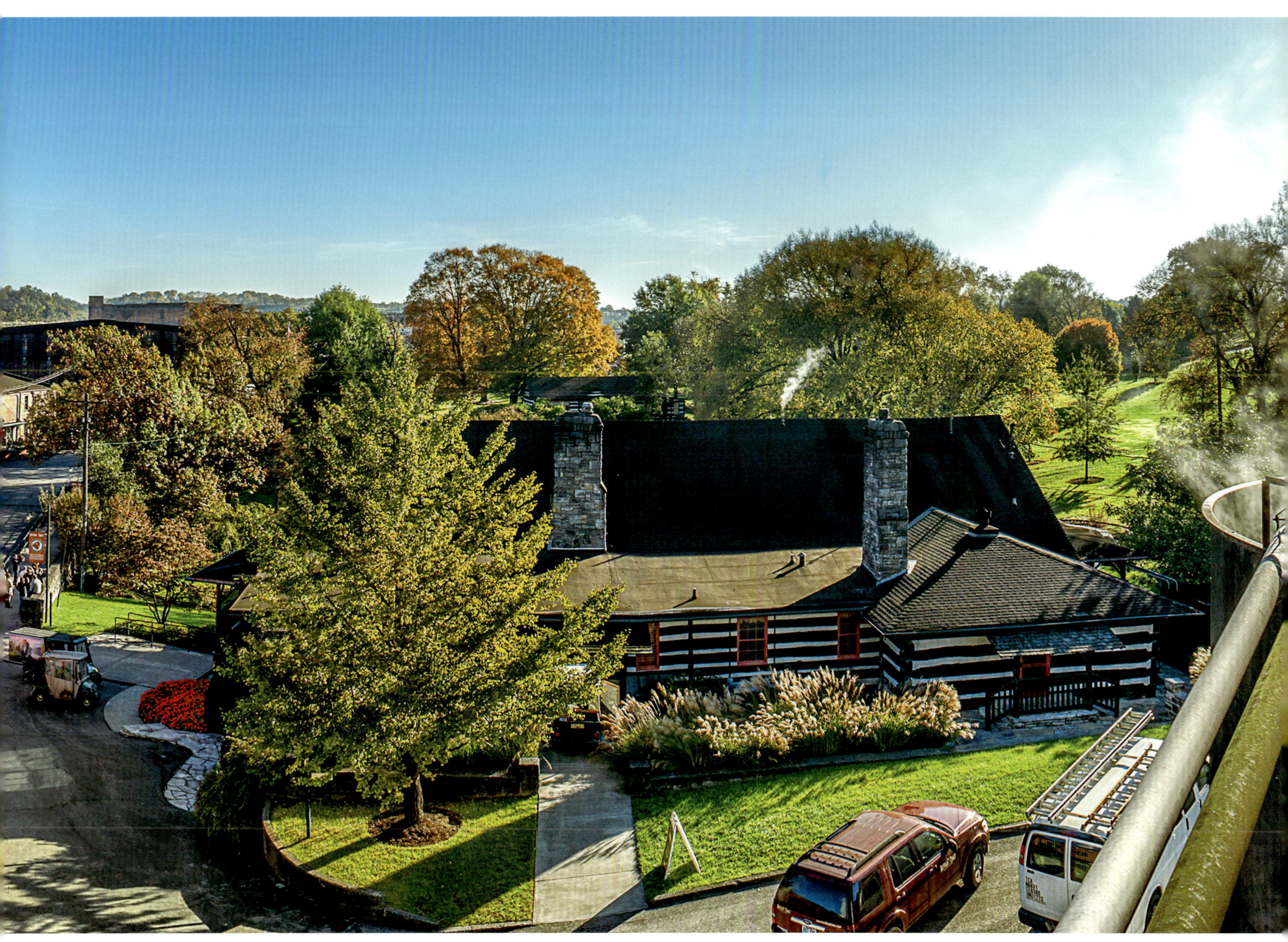

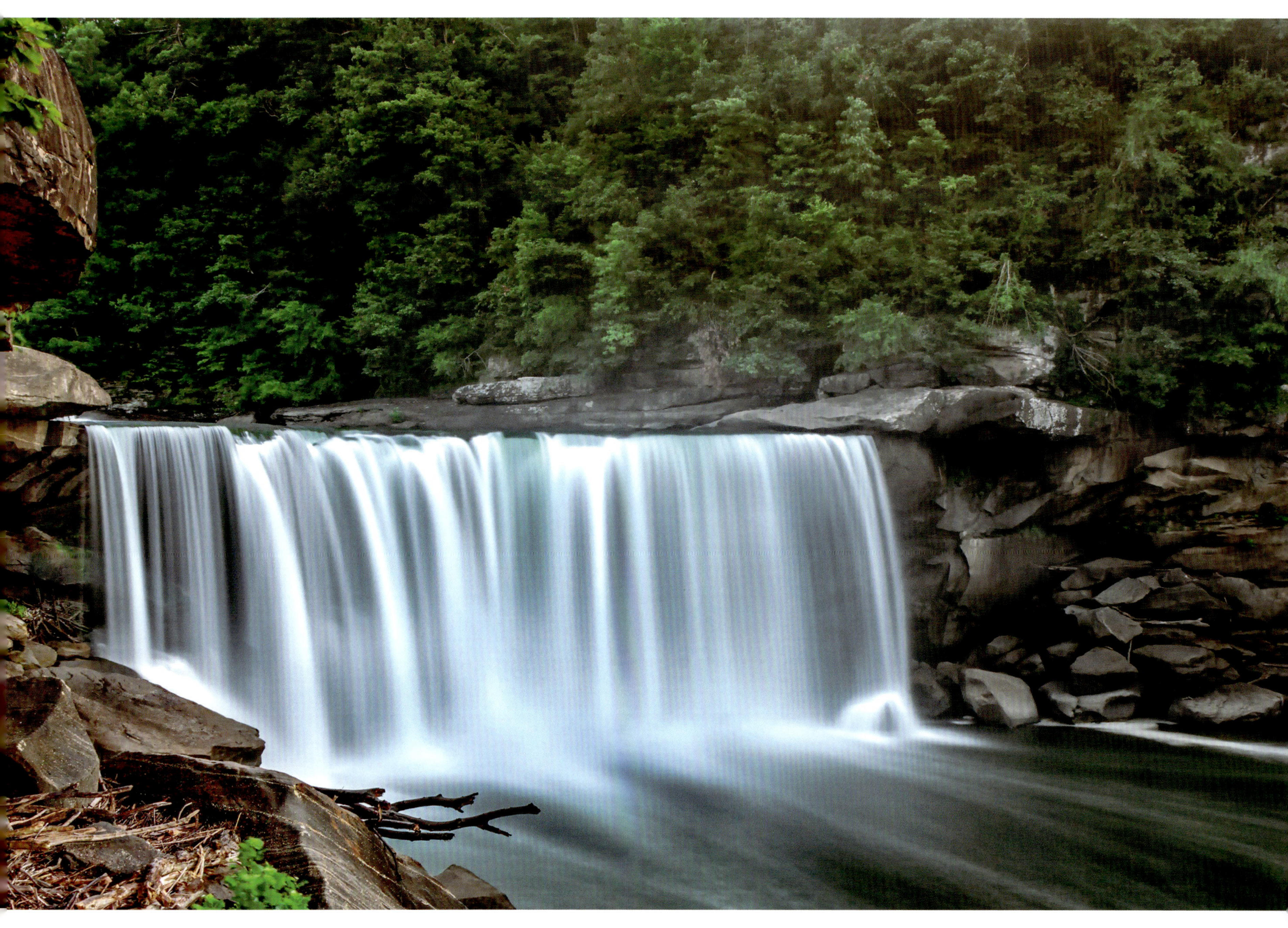

A sixty-eight-foot drop through the mist in the Cumberland River at Cumberland Falls State Resort Park.

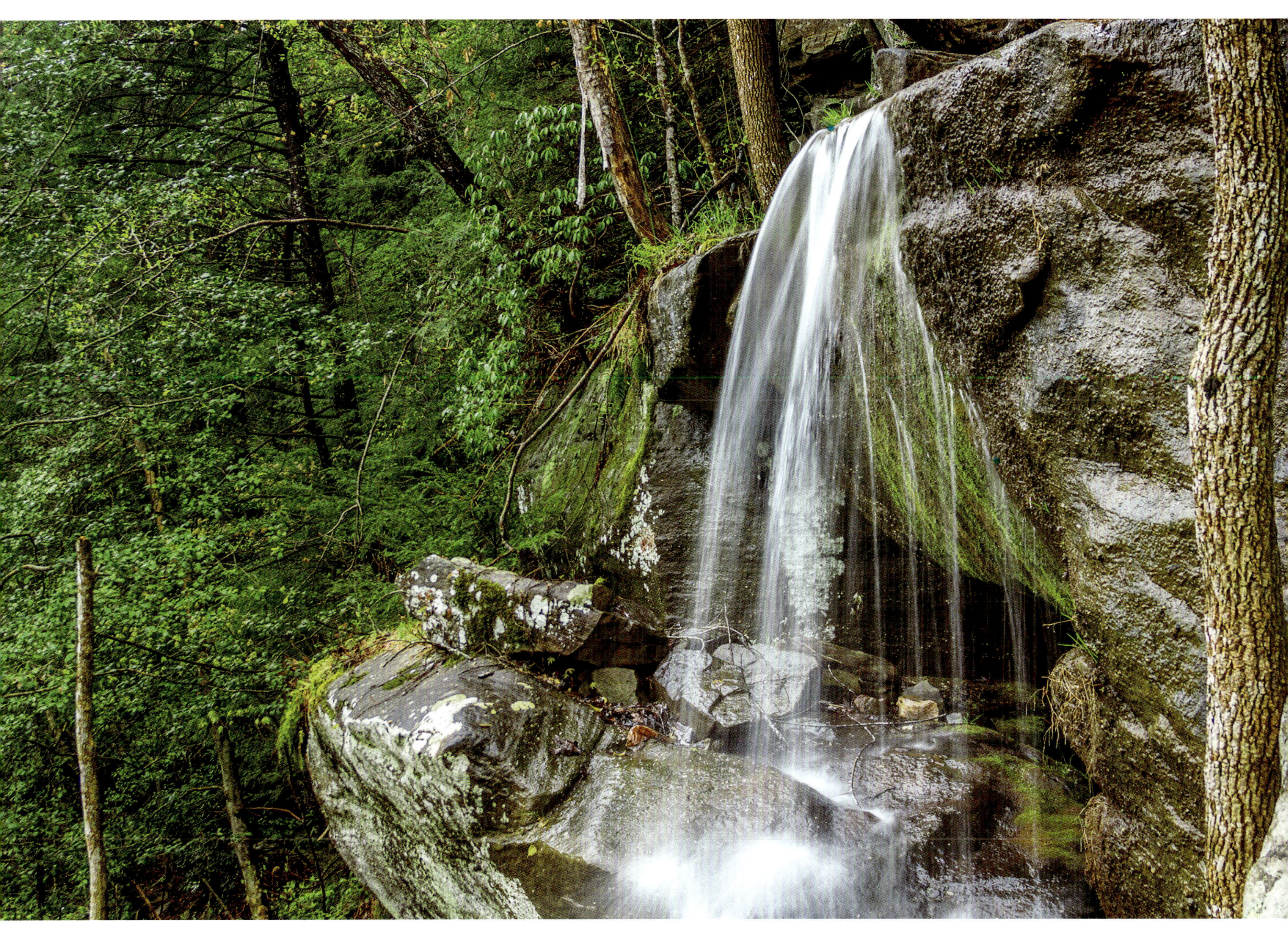

A small stream becomes a racing waterfall after several days of rain. Cumberland Falls State Resort Park.

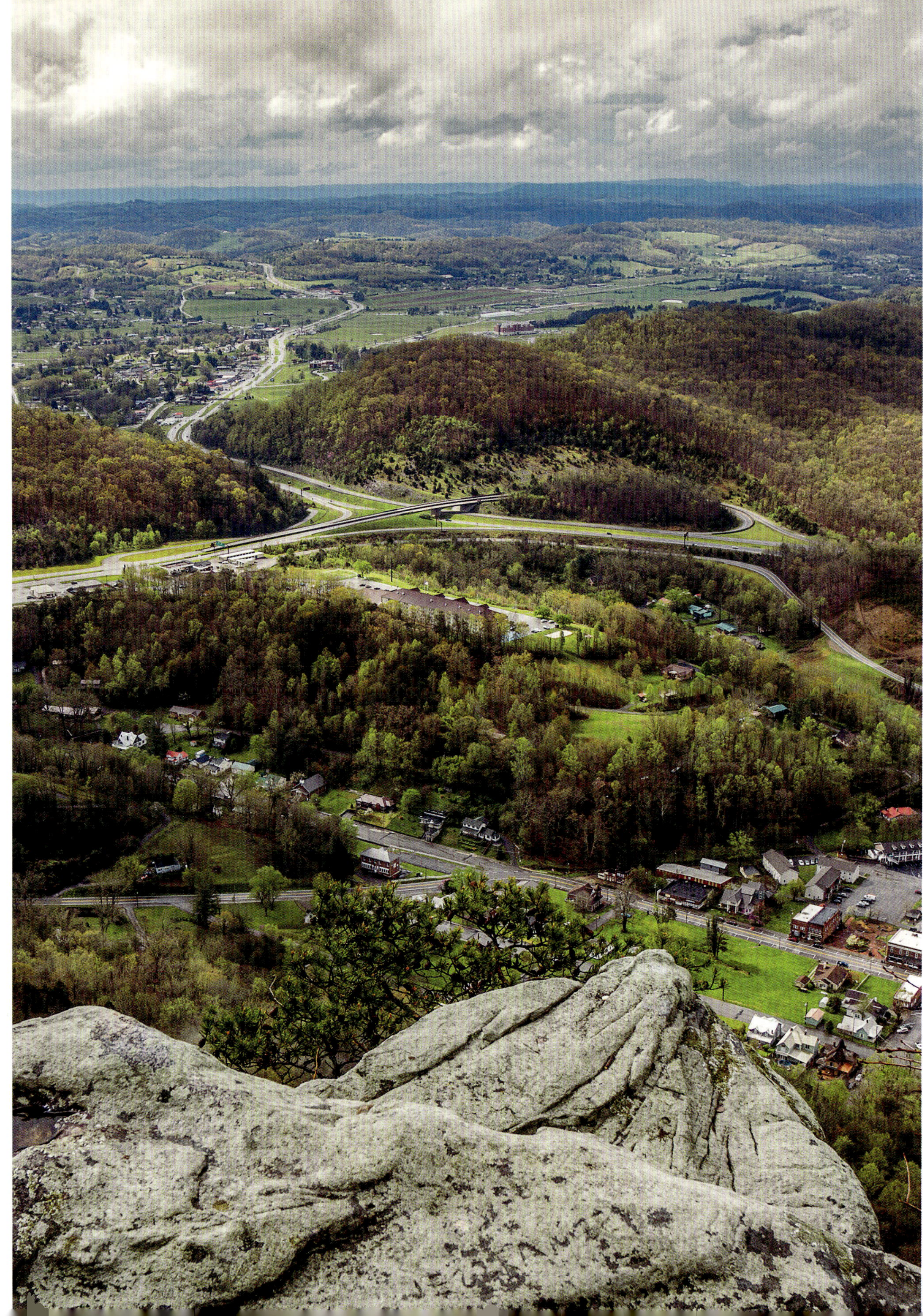

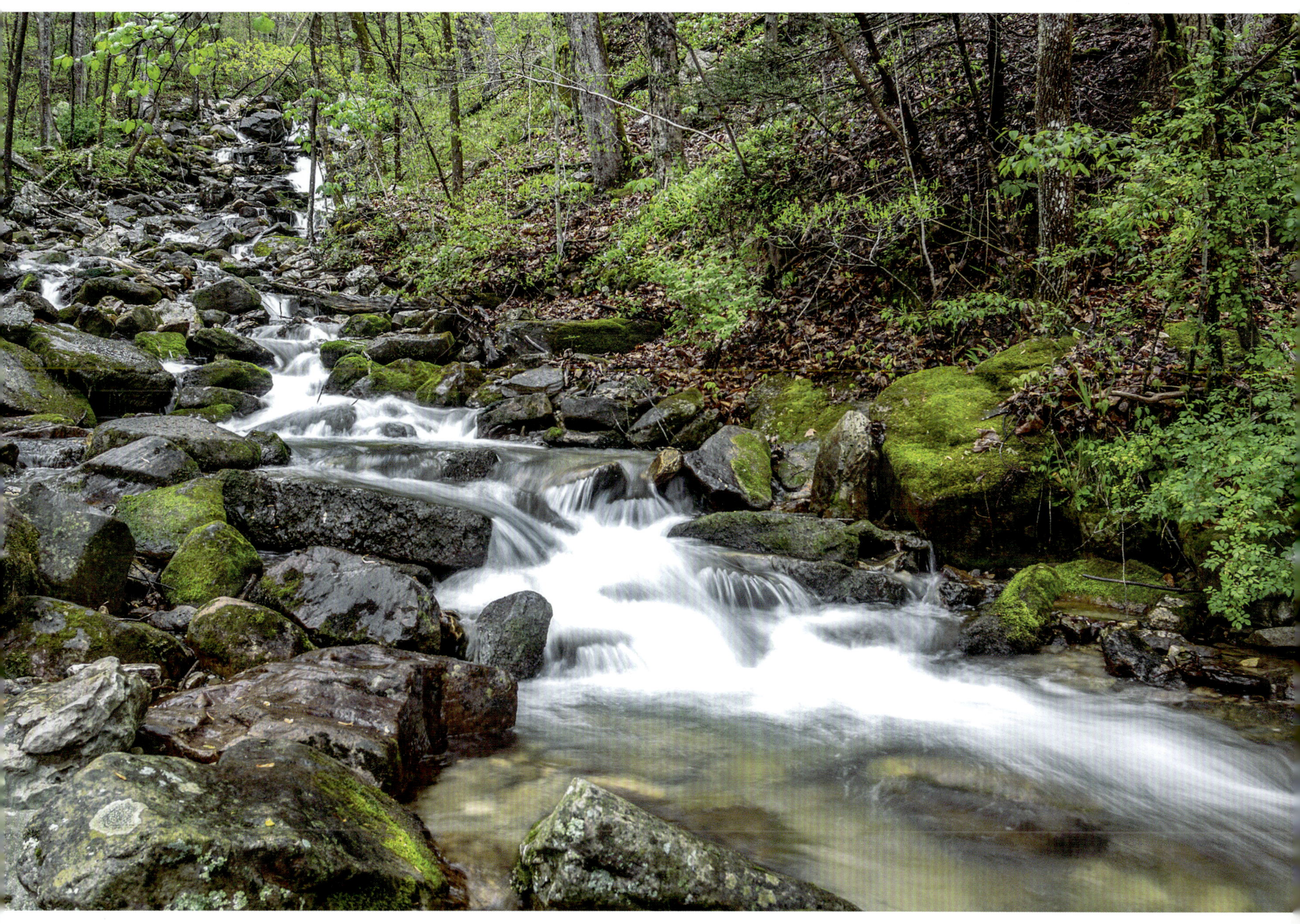

A mountain stream with small cascades makes an inviting place to sit and relax for a moment.

FACING A view from 2,440 feet above it all at Cumberland Gap National Historical Park.

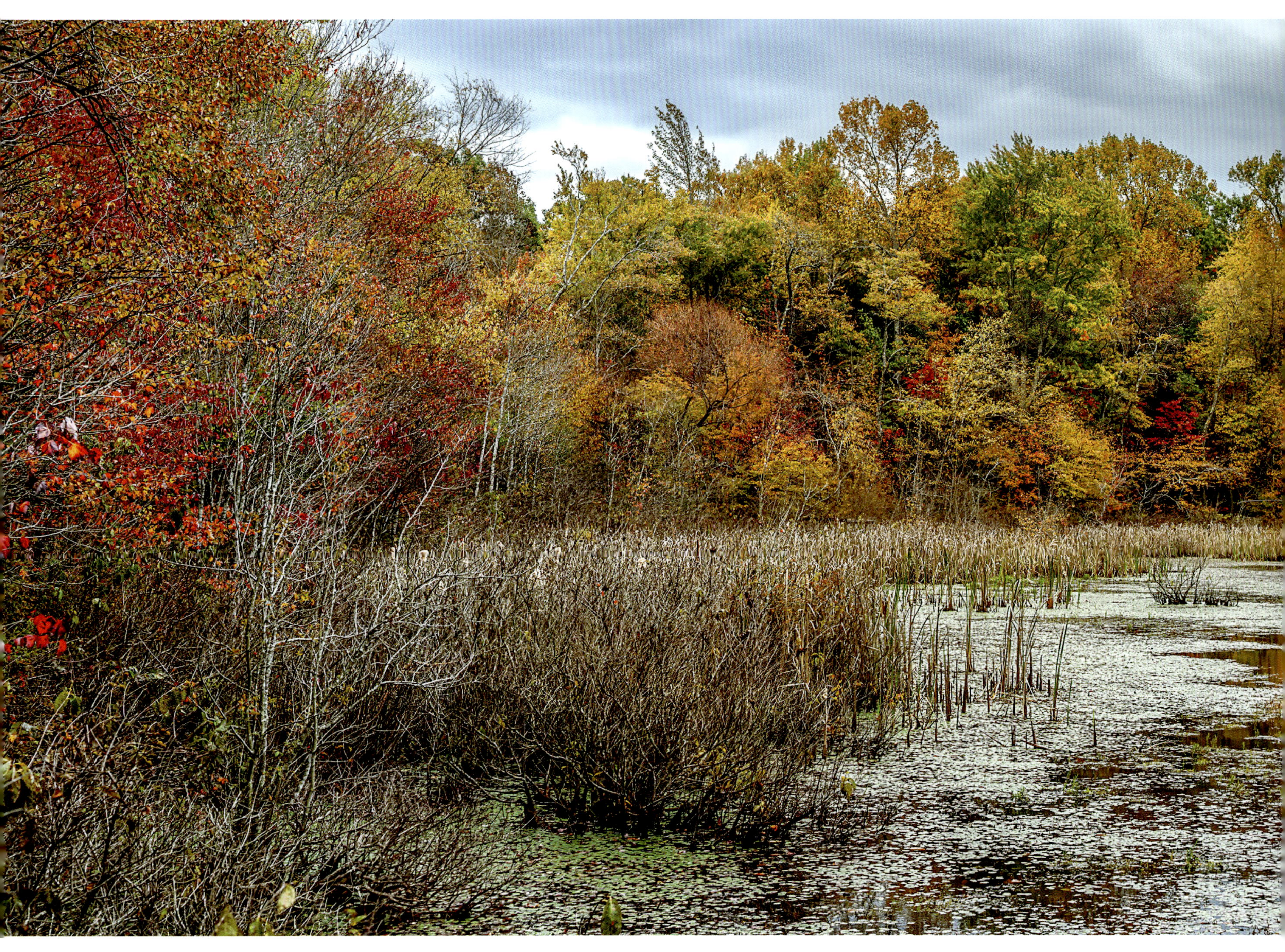

Sloan's Crossing Pond in Mammoth Cave National Park offers quiet beauty on an autumn day.

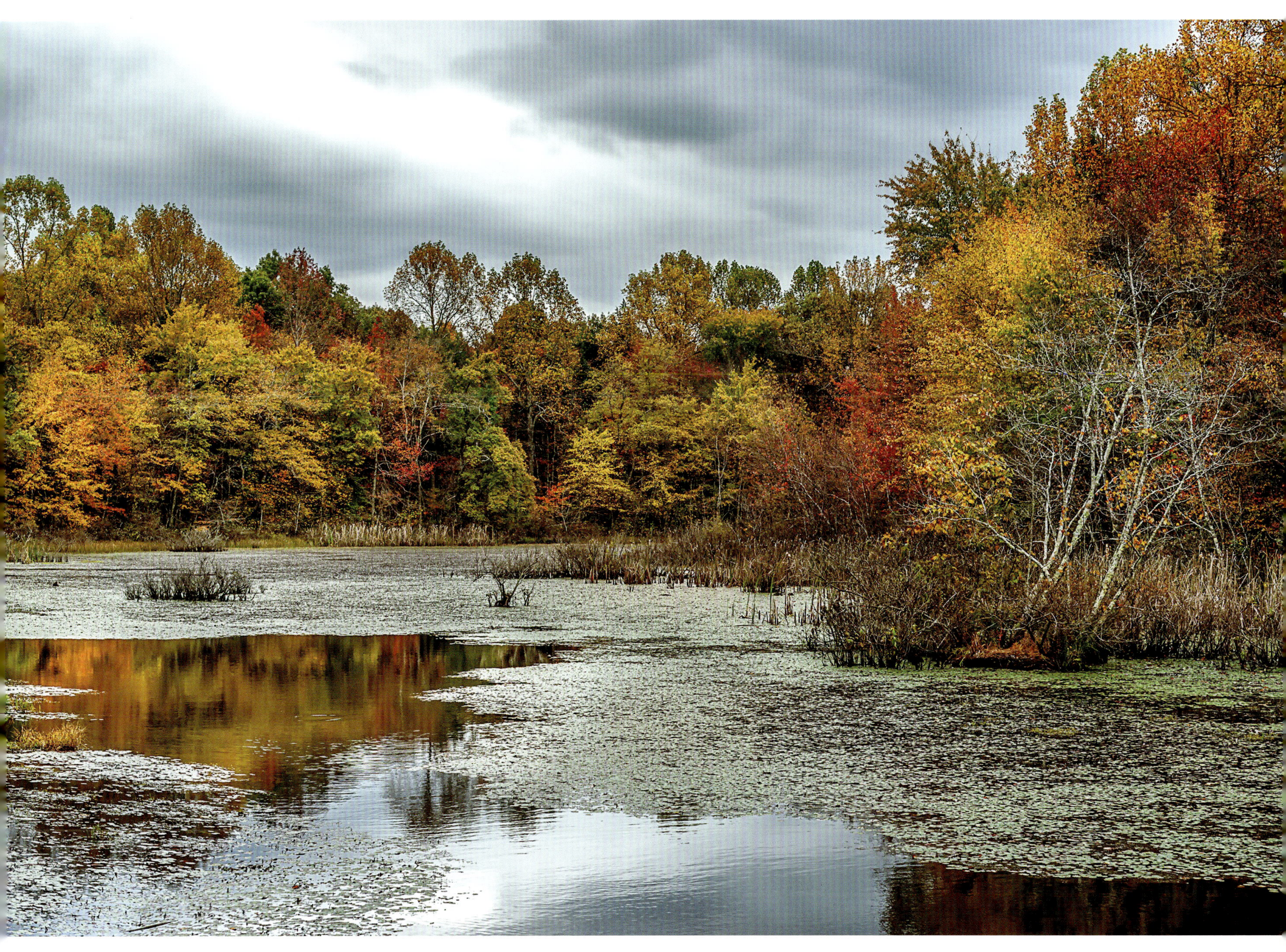

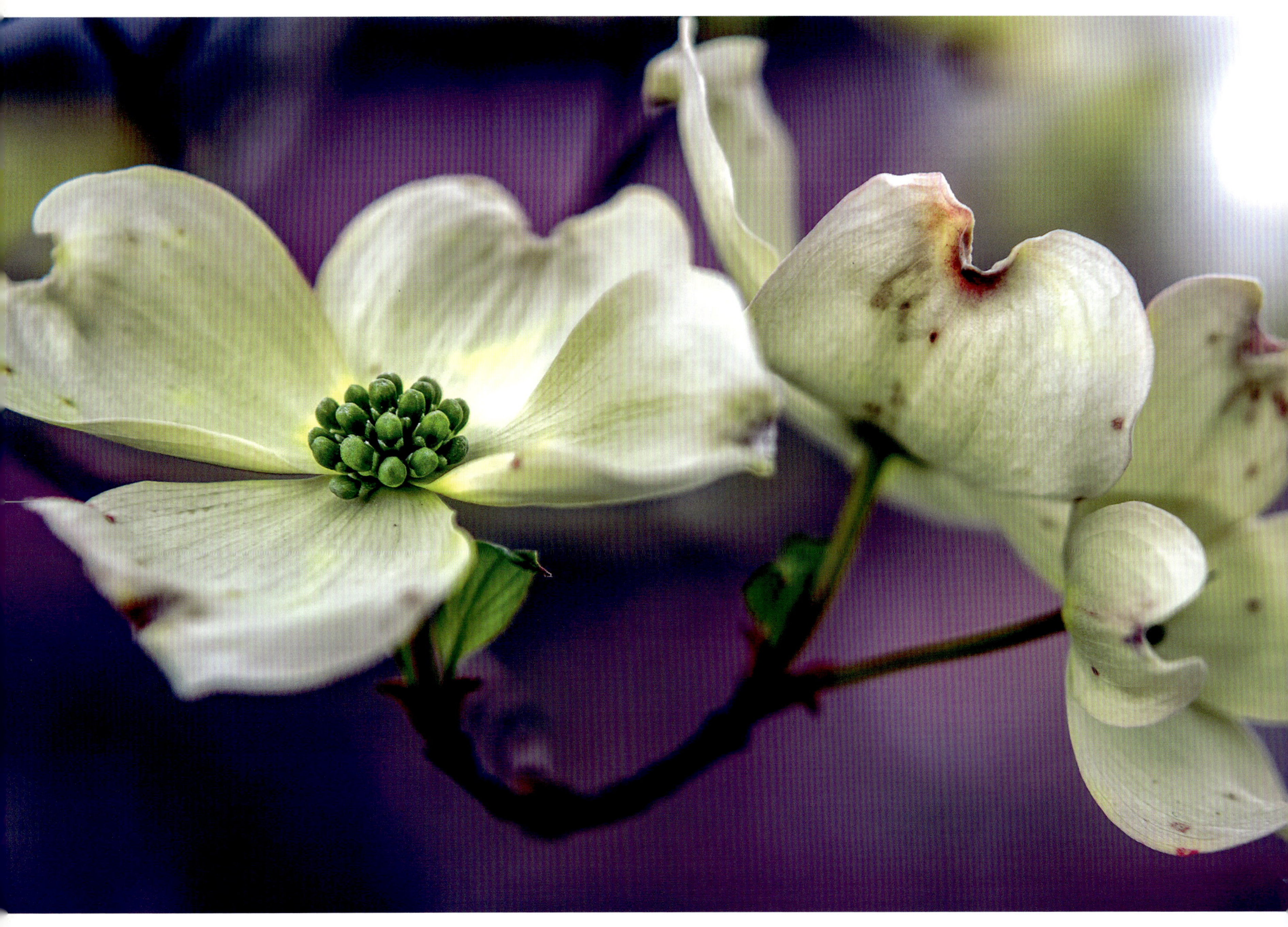

Dogwoods are abundant in the Kentucky Landscape.

Eagle Creek spills into the Cumberland River at Eagle Falls.

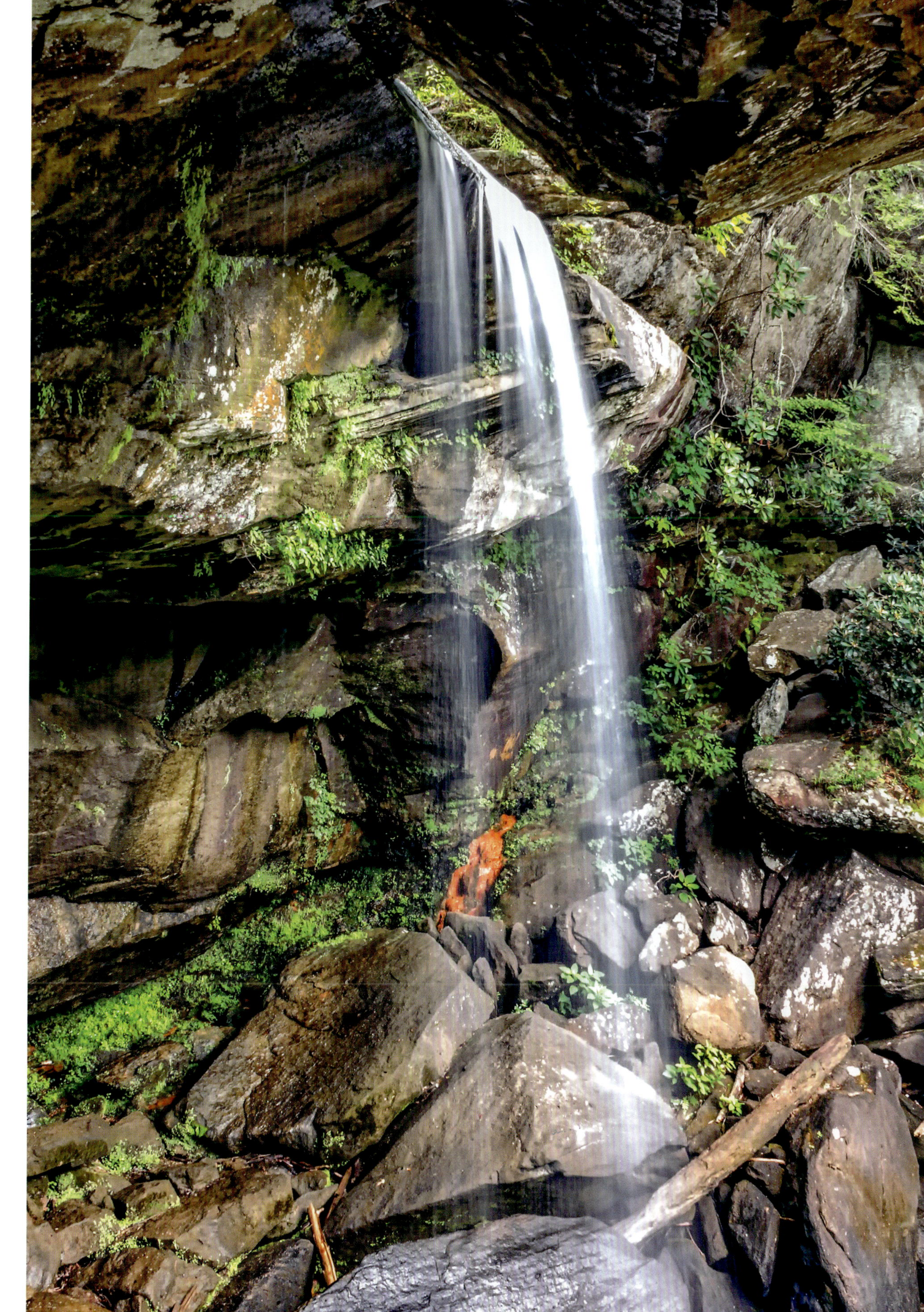

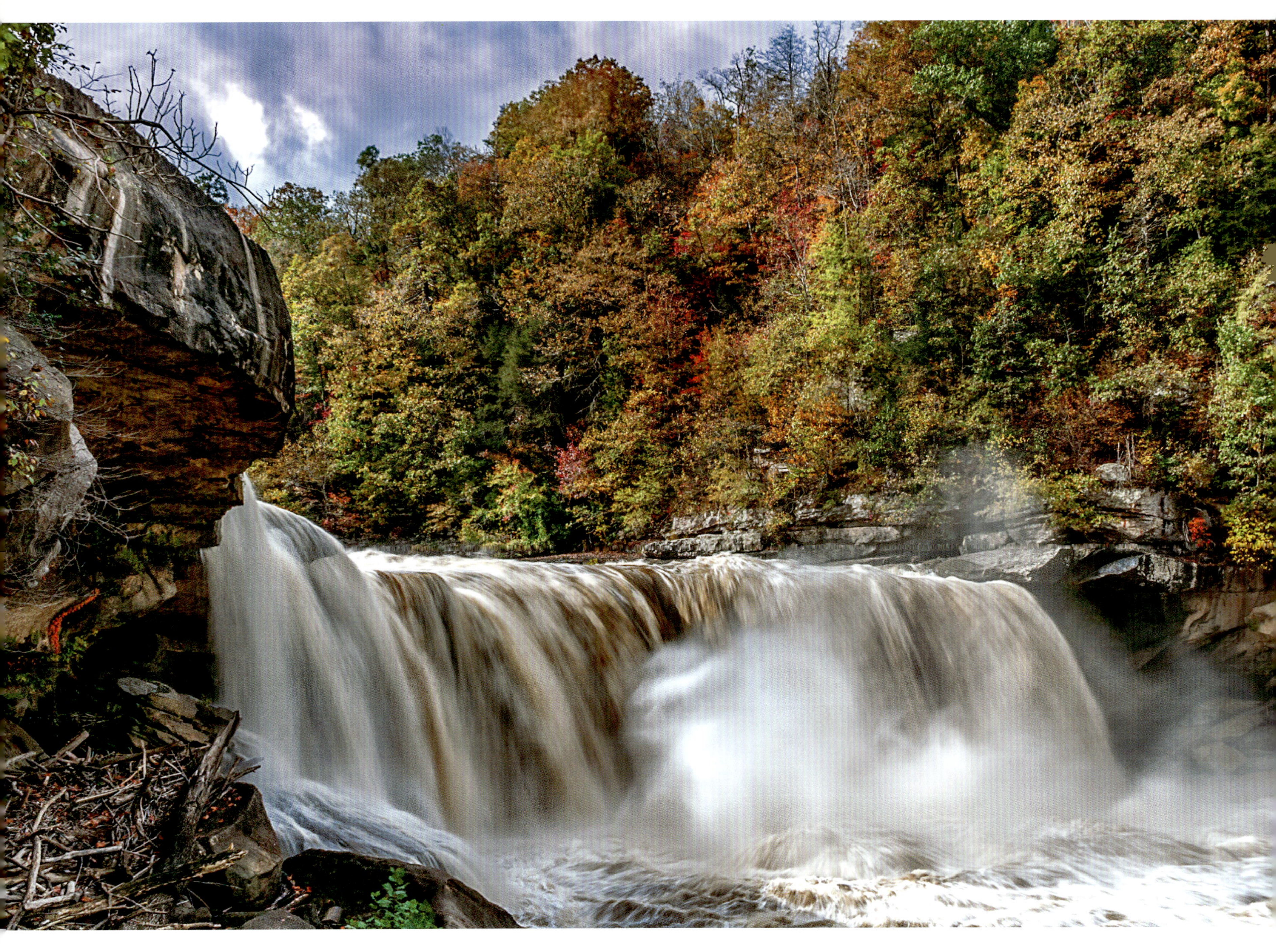

At 125-feet wide, Cumberland Falls is the second largest waterfall east of the Rocky Mountains.

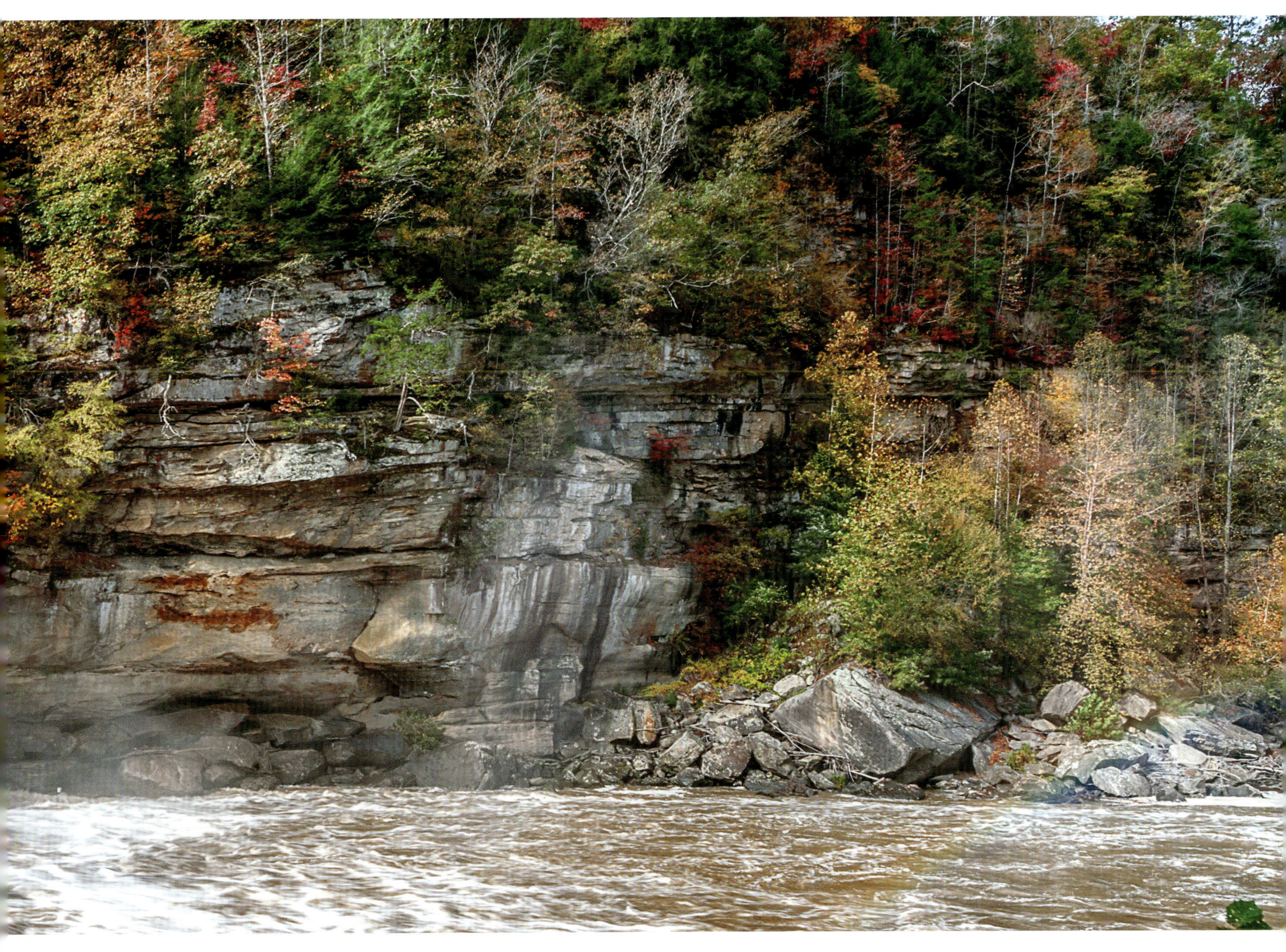

FOLLOWING Even the evergreens are bursting with color in the spring weather.

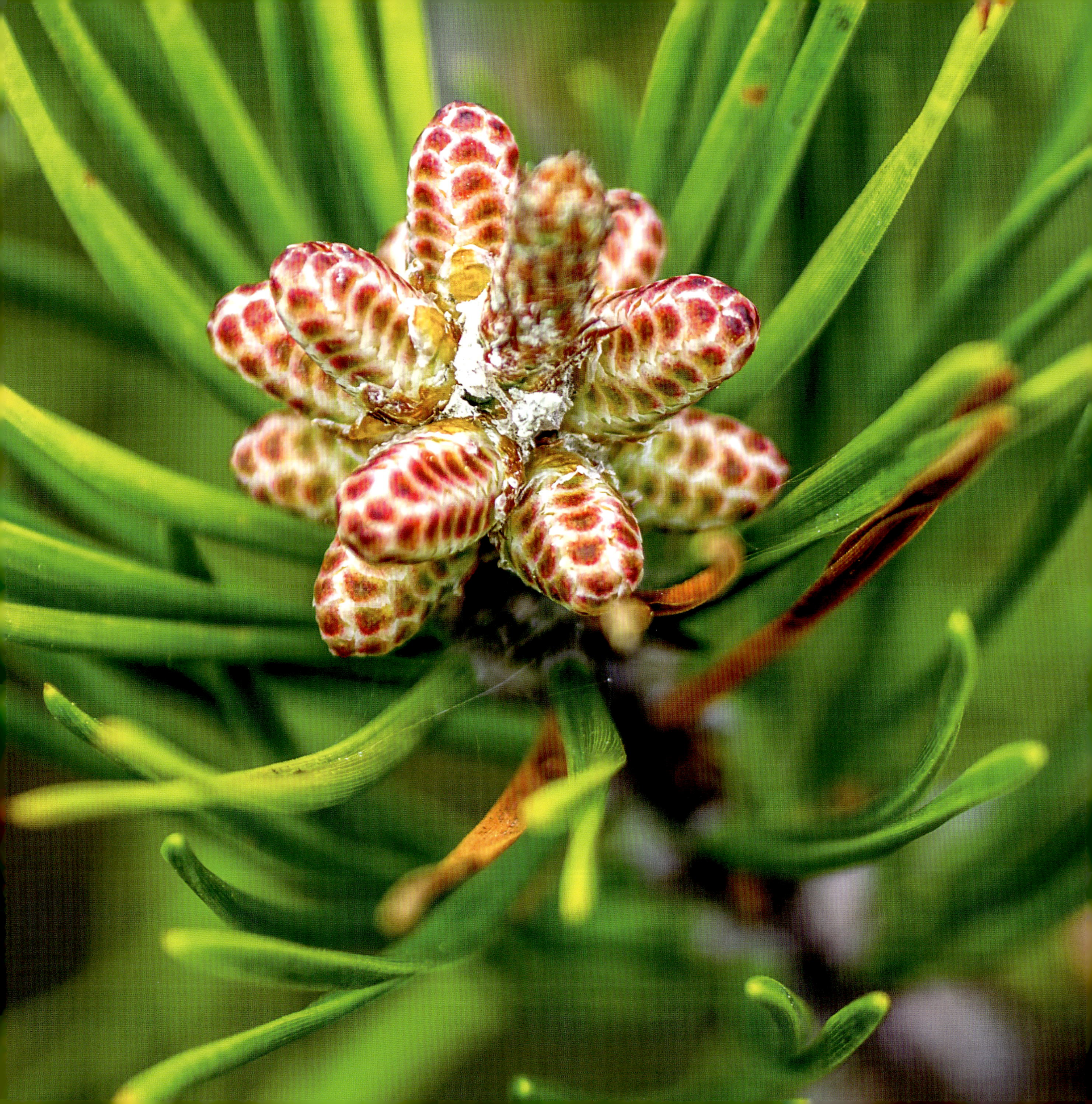

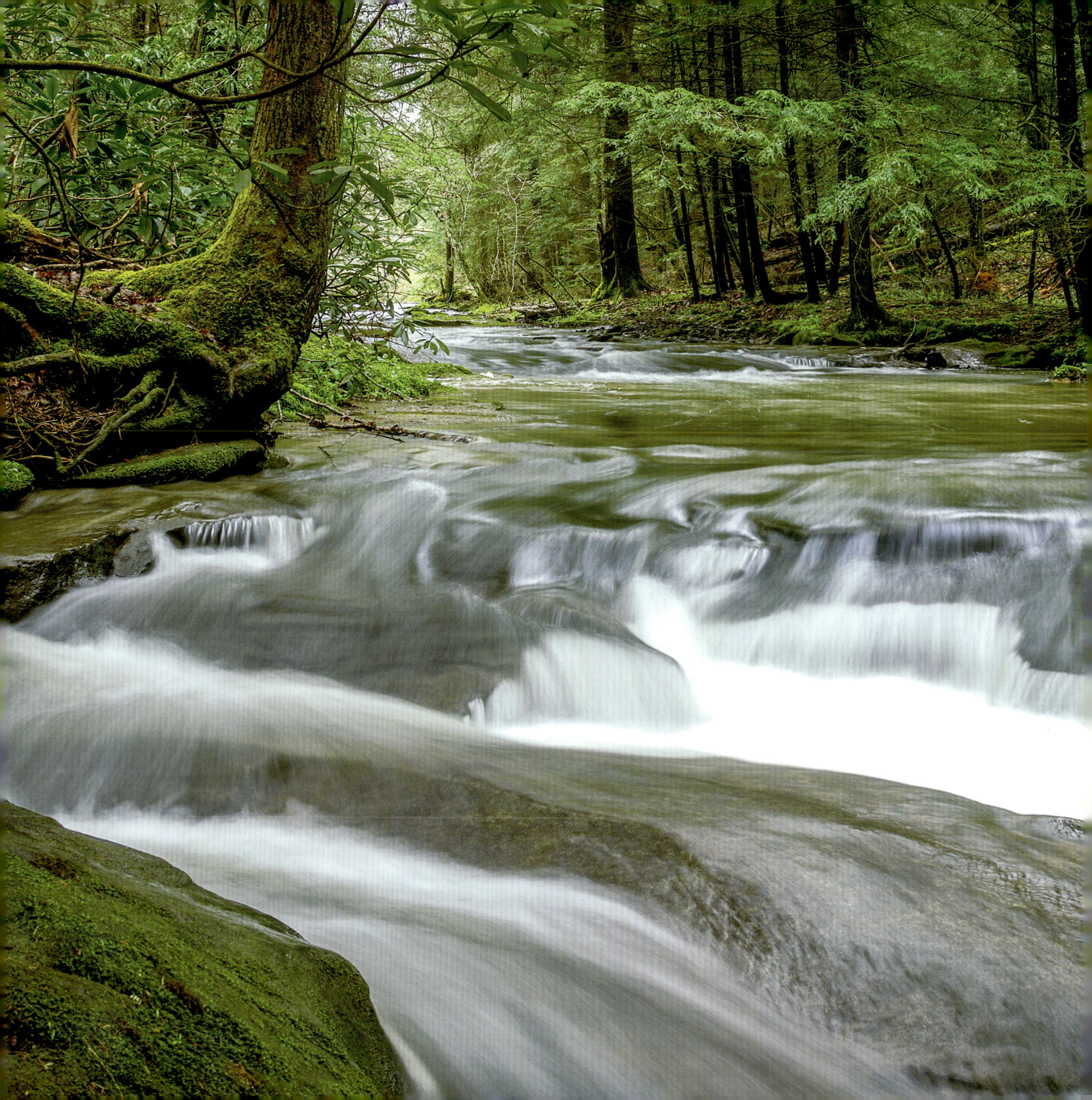

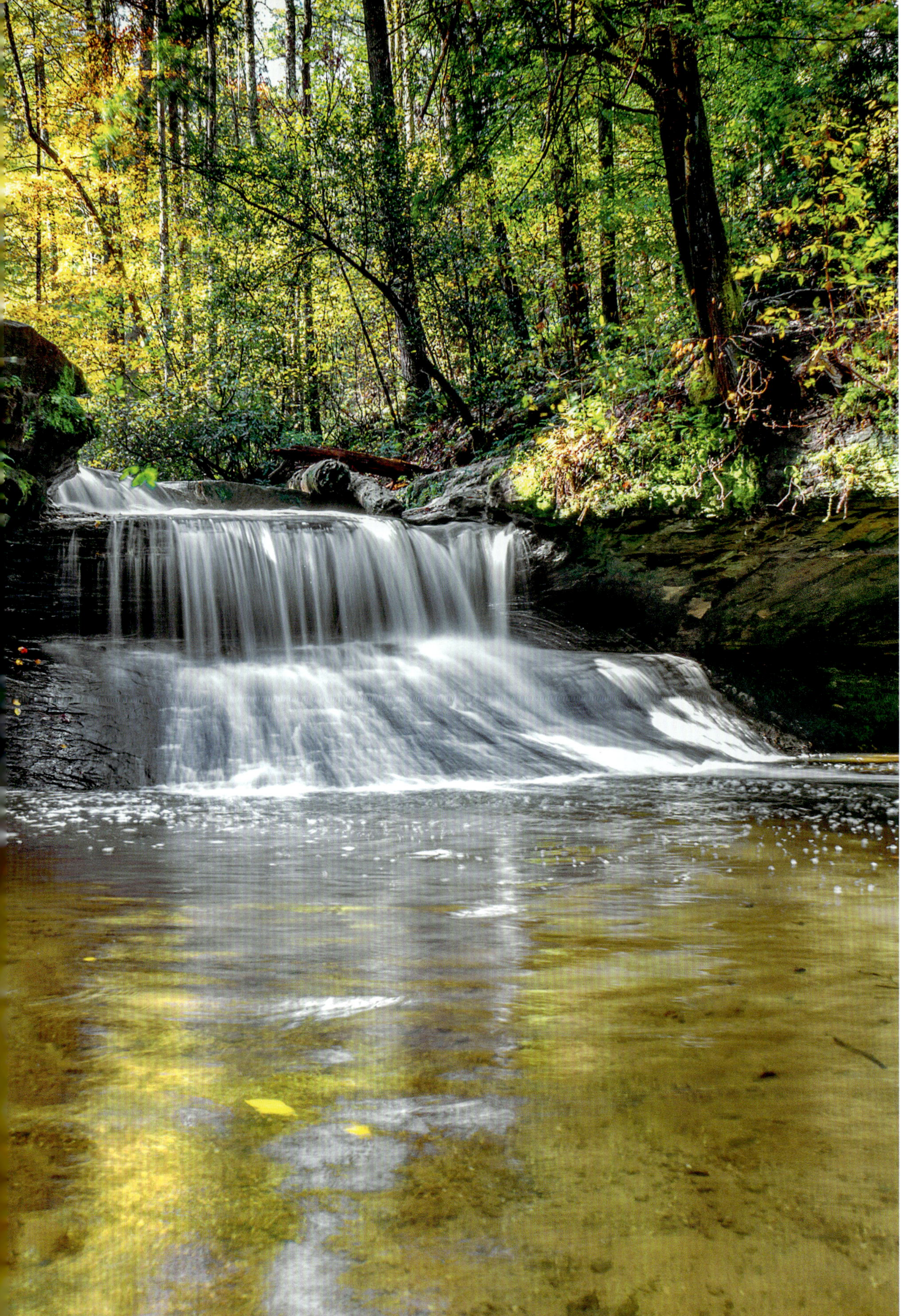

PREVIOUS
Flat Lick Creek flows through clearings and forests toward Flat Lick Falls.

Creation Falls gives interest to Swift Camp Creek in Red River Gorge.

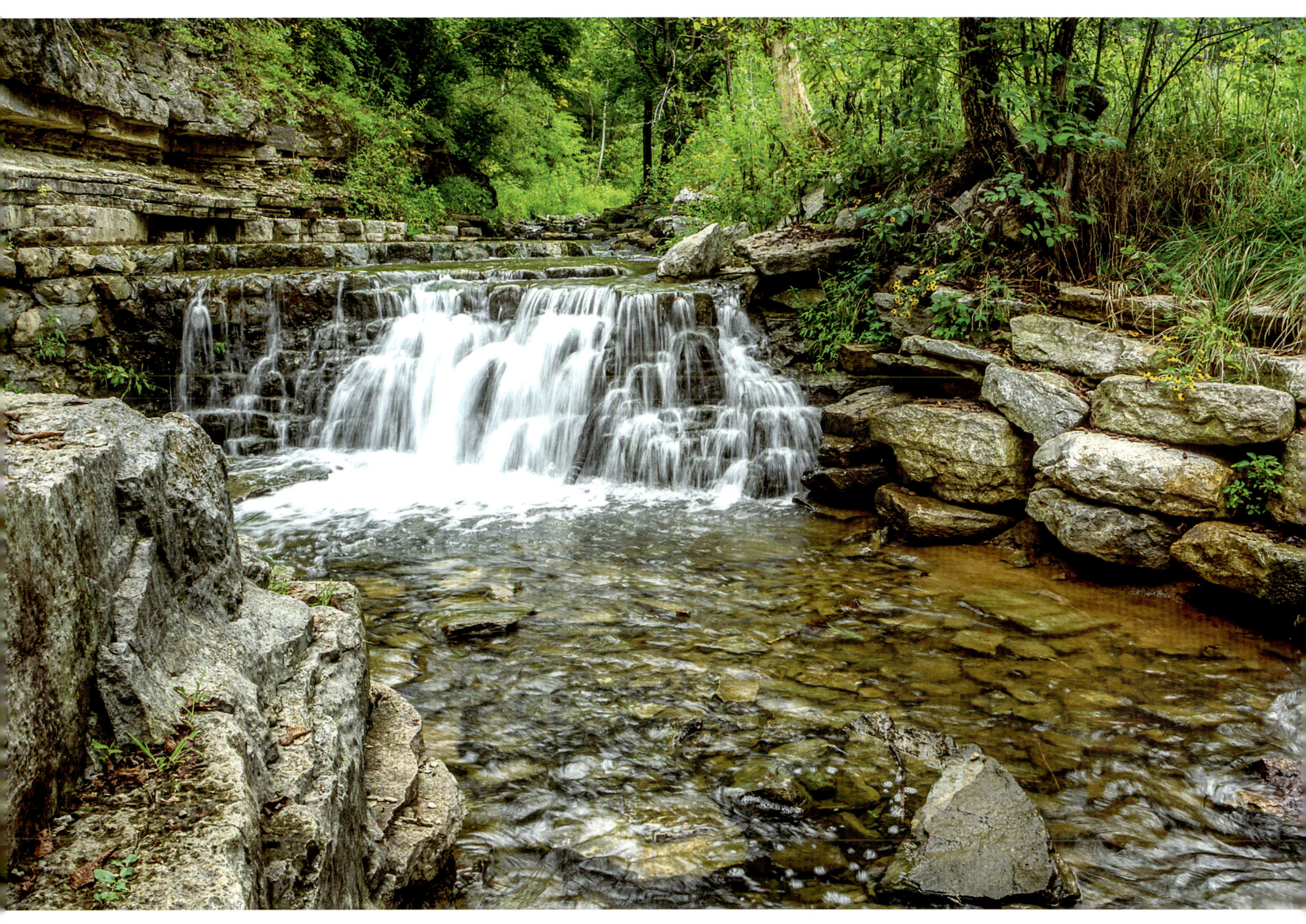

Branching waterfalls on a creek at Cove Spring Park in Frankfort.

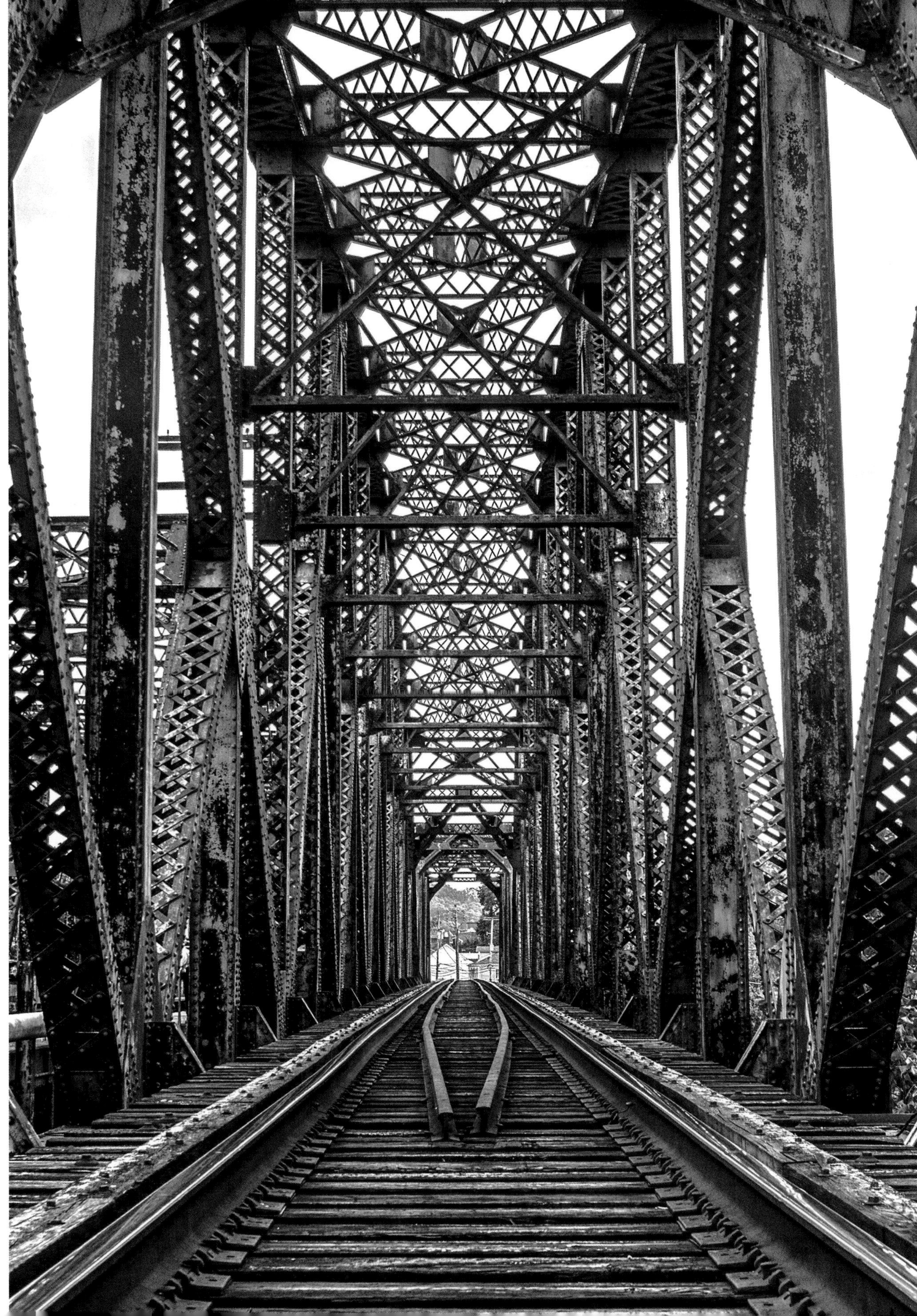

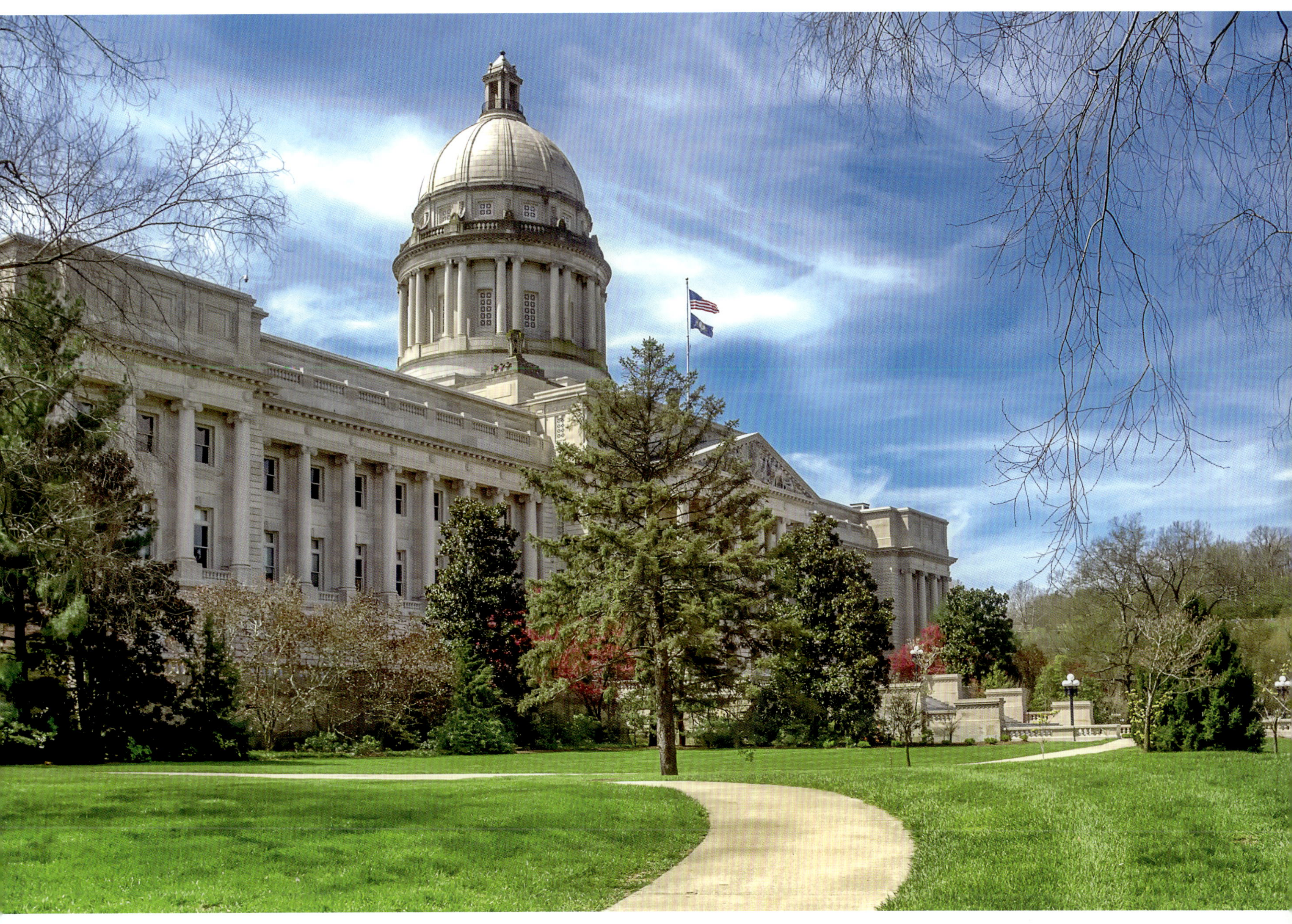

The Kentucky State Capitol building in Frankfort was built starting in 1904.

FACING The Broadway Railroad Bridge spans the Kentucky River at Frankfort.

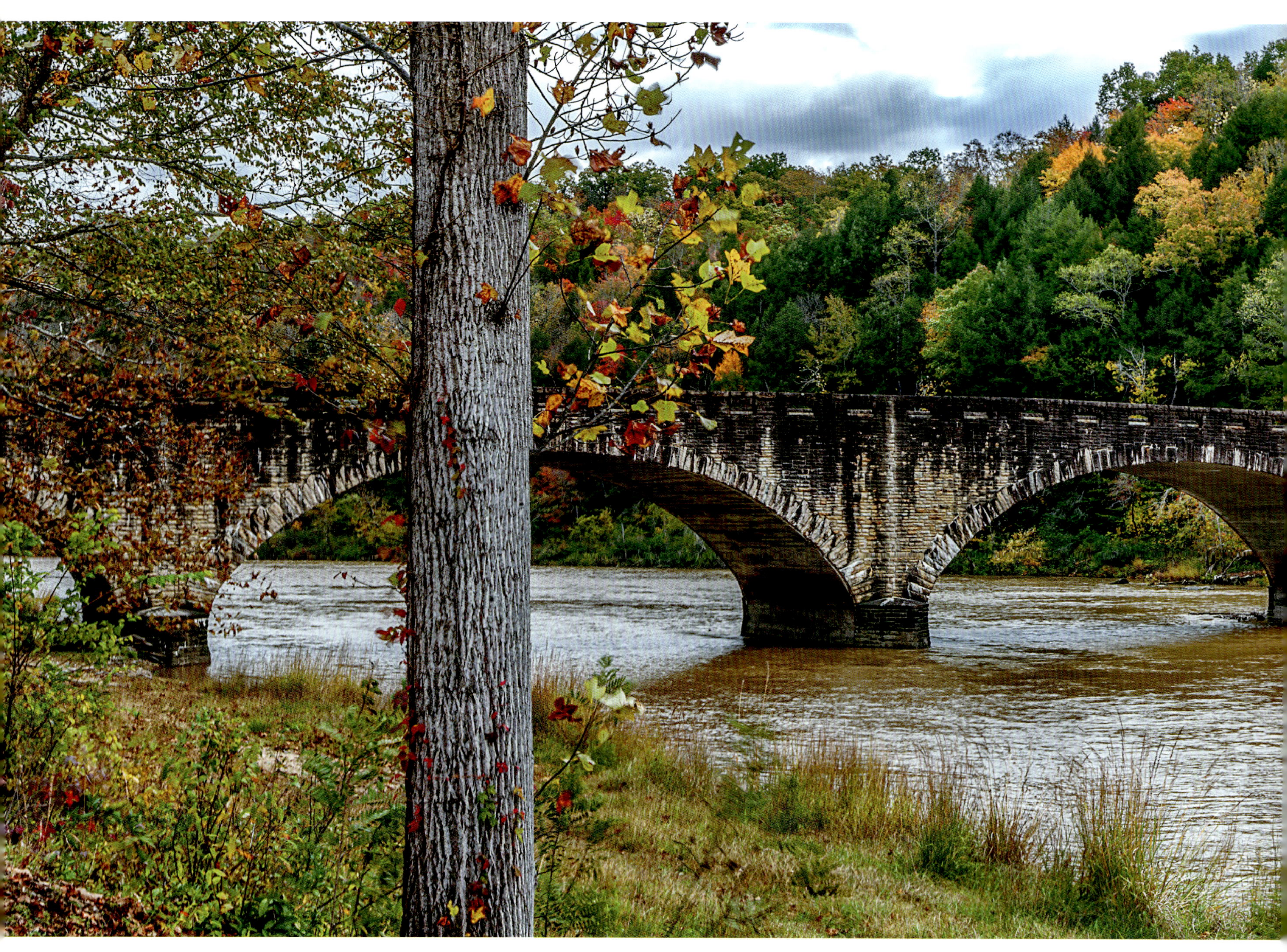

The Edward Moss Gatliff Memorial Bridge at Cumberland Falls State Resort Park.

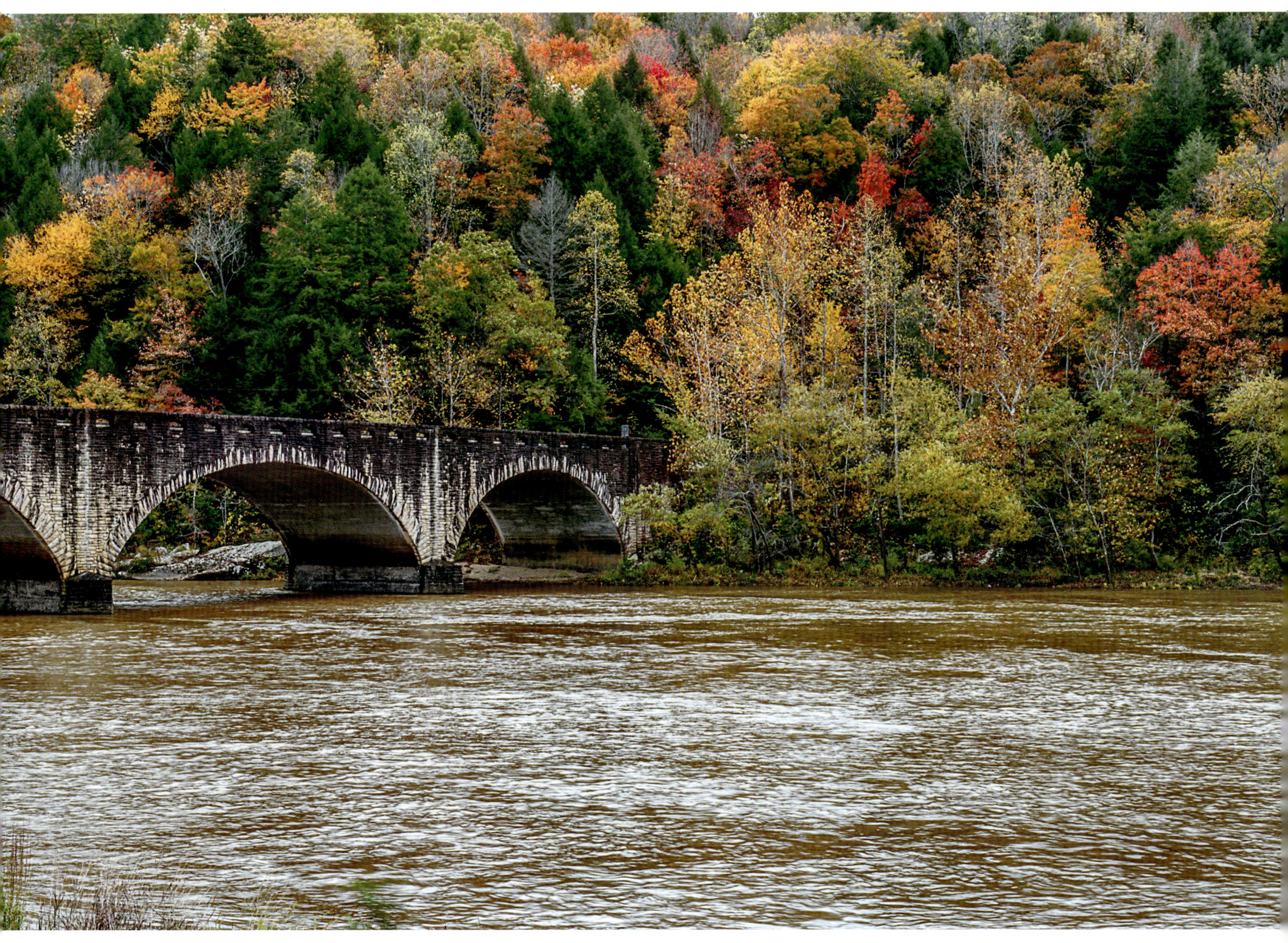

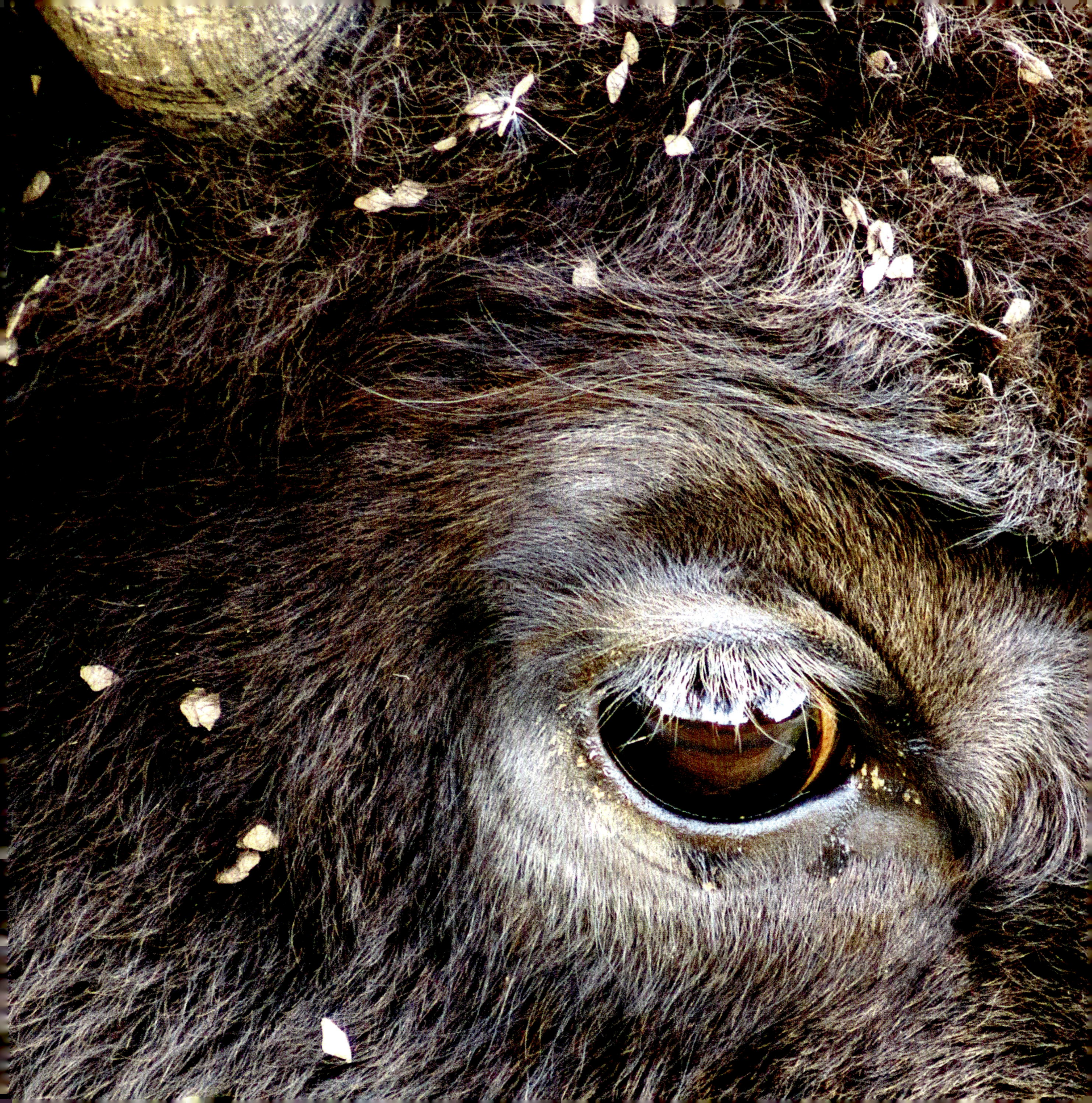

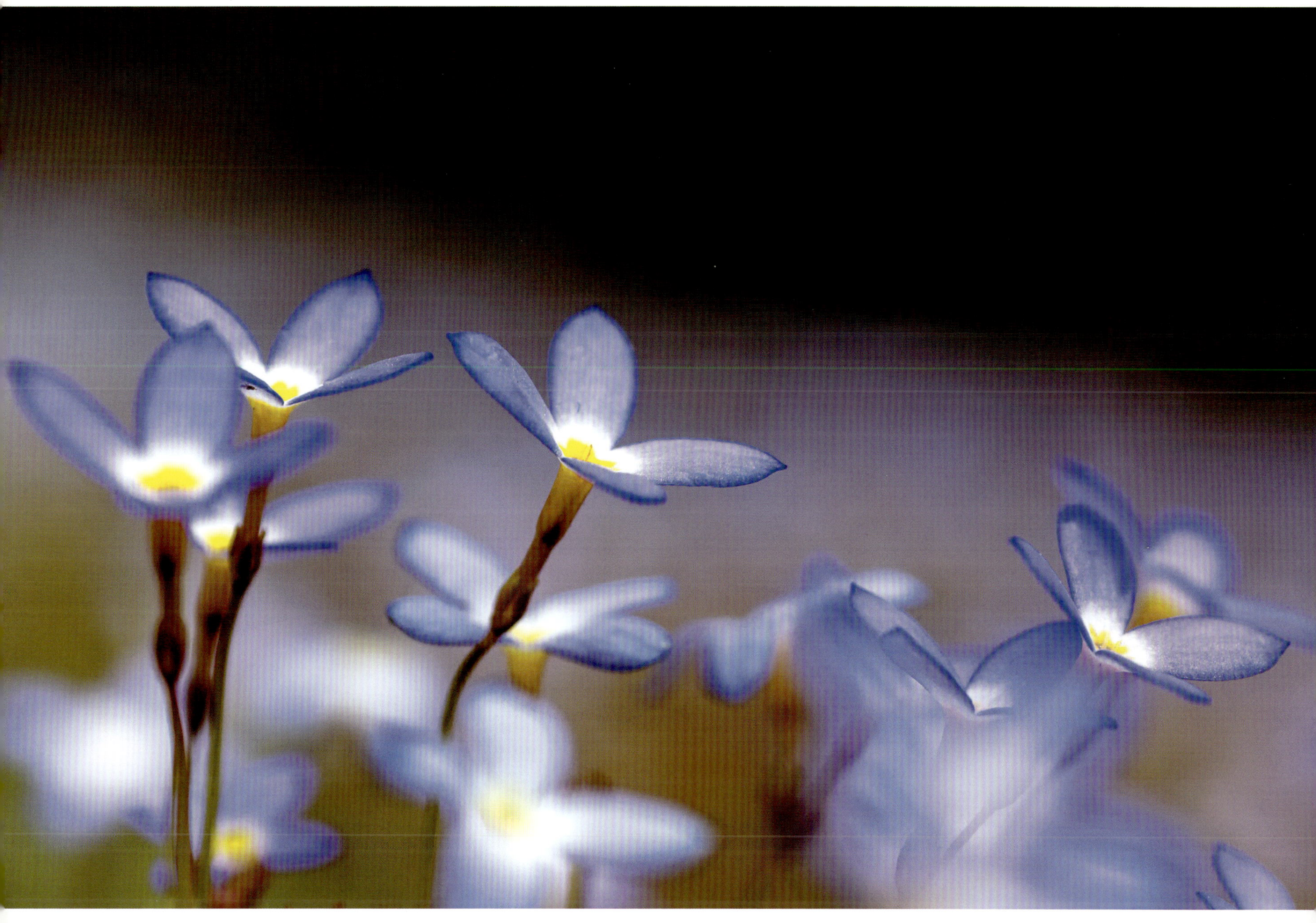

Tiny bluets fill a field with color.

FACING The Elk and Bison Prairie is reflected in a bison's eye at Land Between the Lakes National Recreation Area.

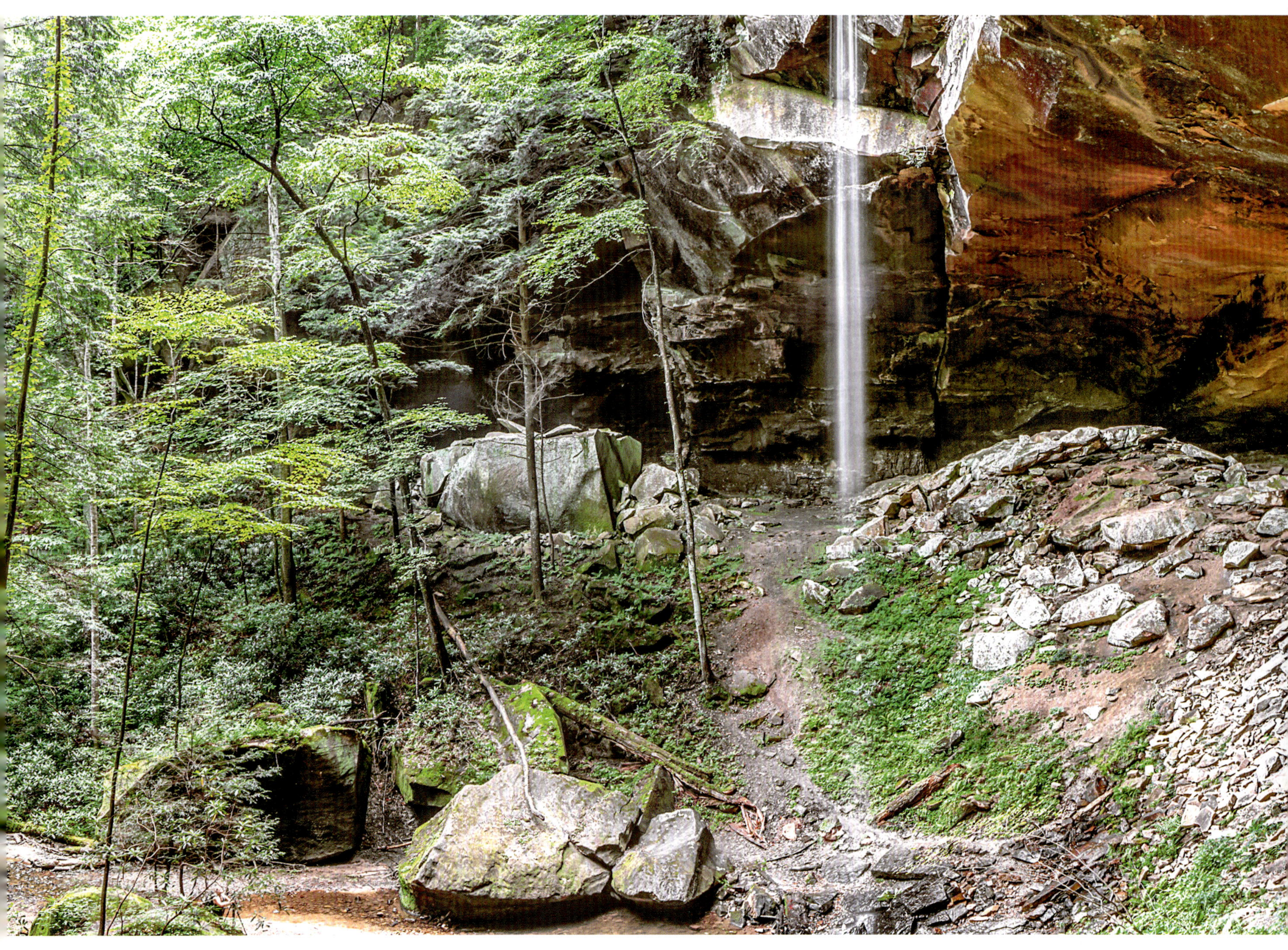

A little piece of paradise at Yahoo Falls.

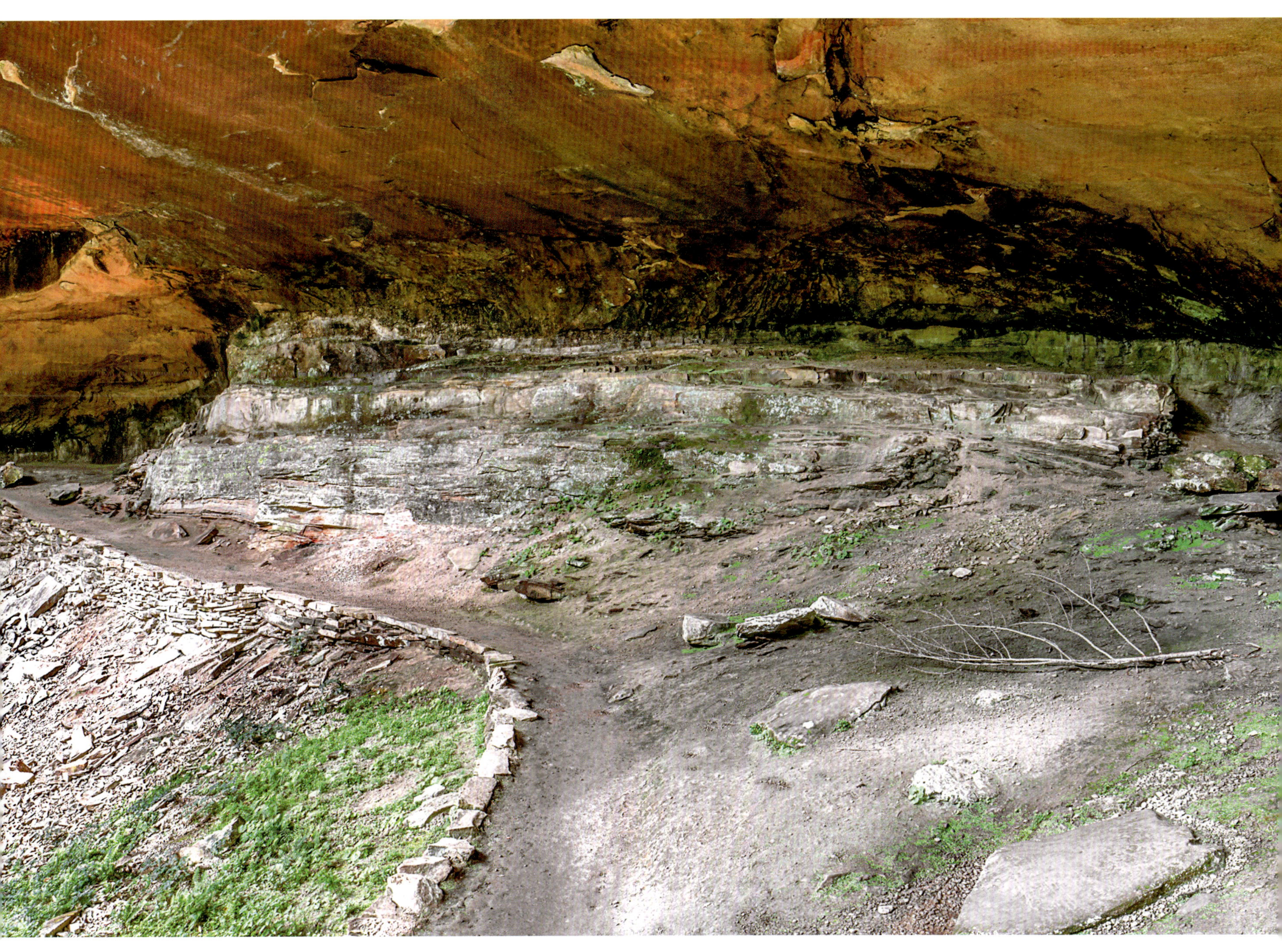

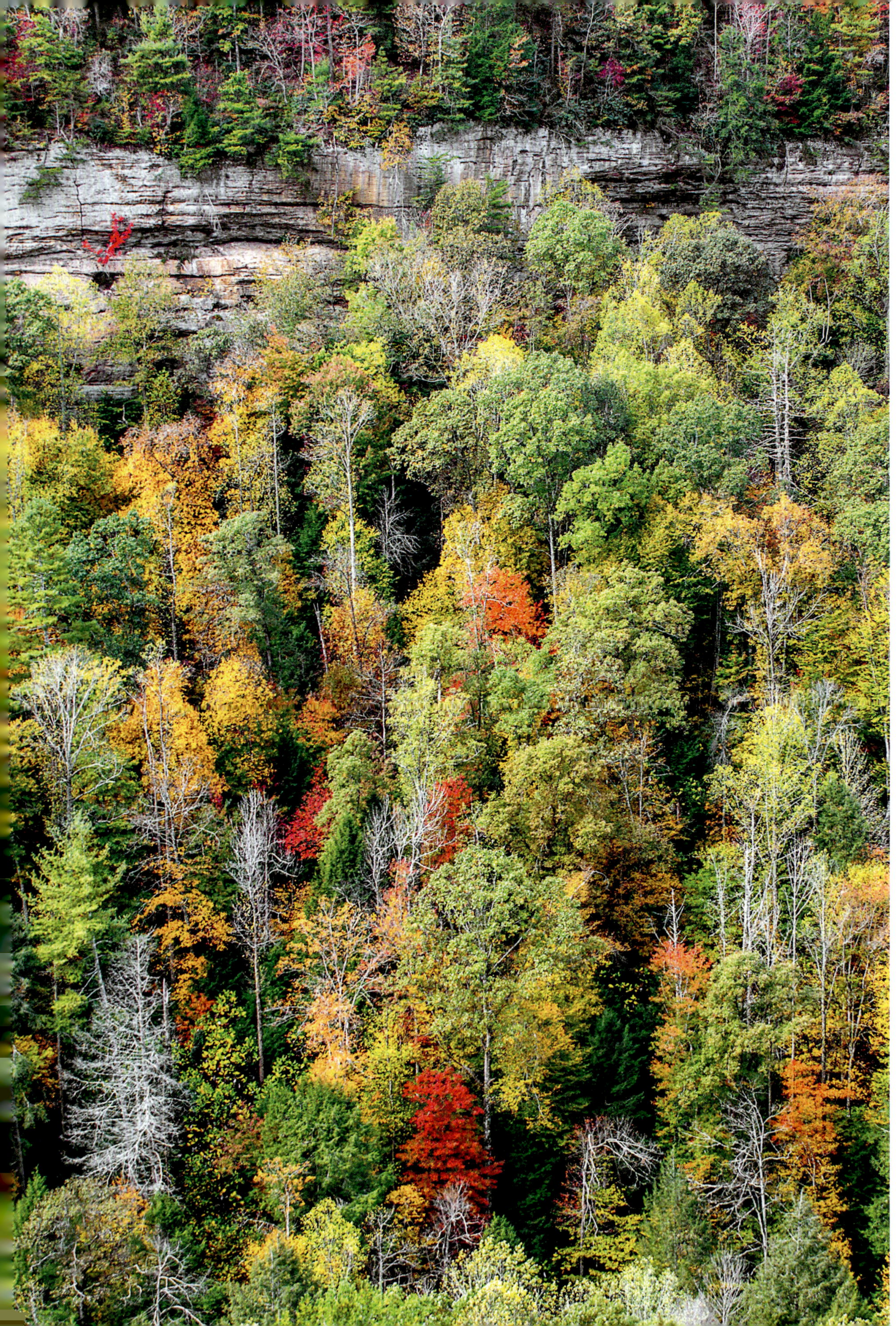

Fall color throughout the hills at Red River Gorge.

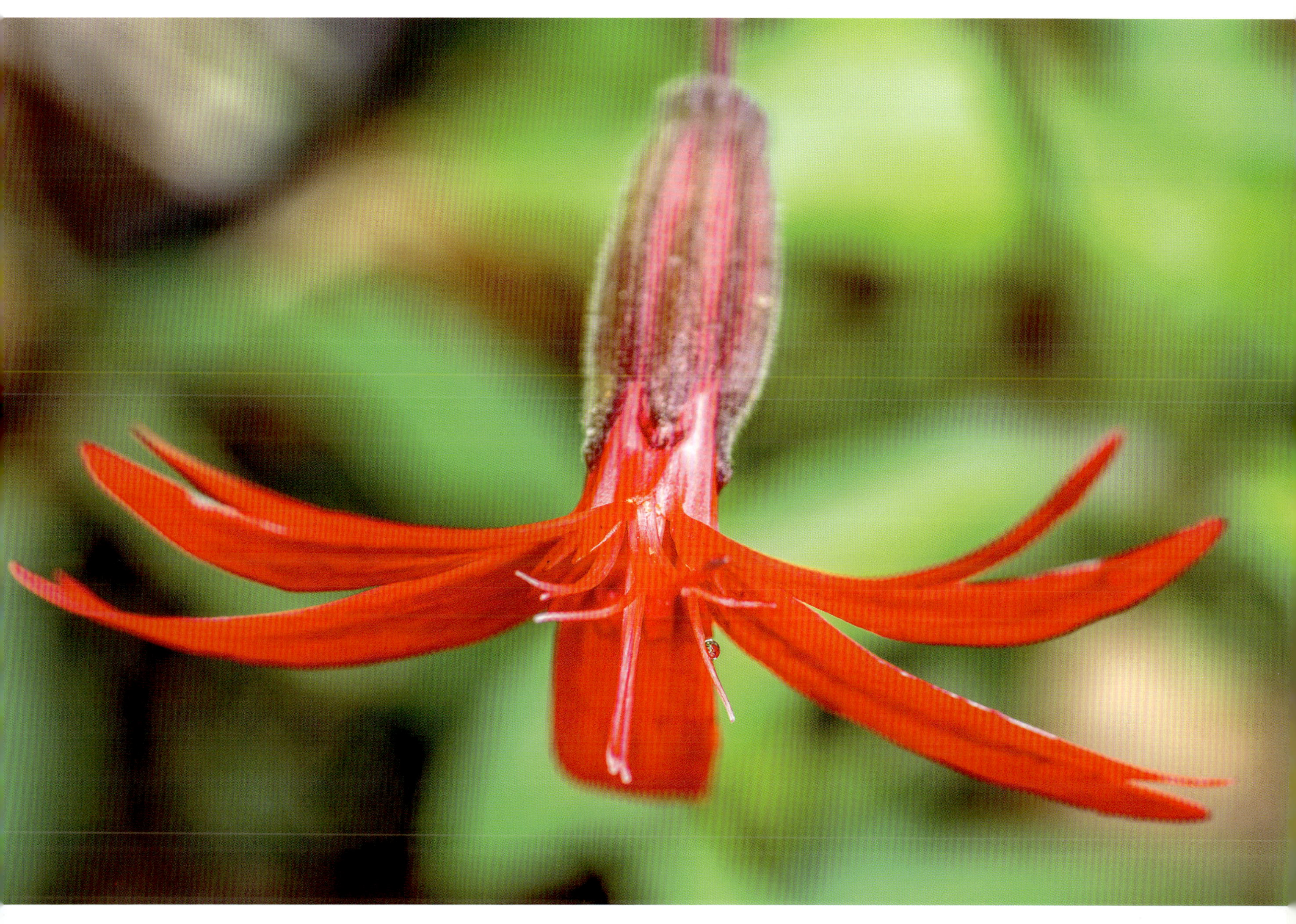

Glowing Fire Pinks along the trail can't be missed.

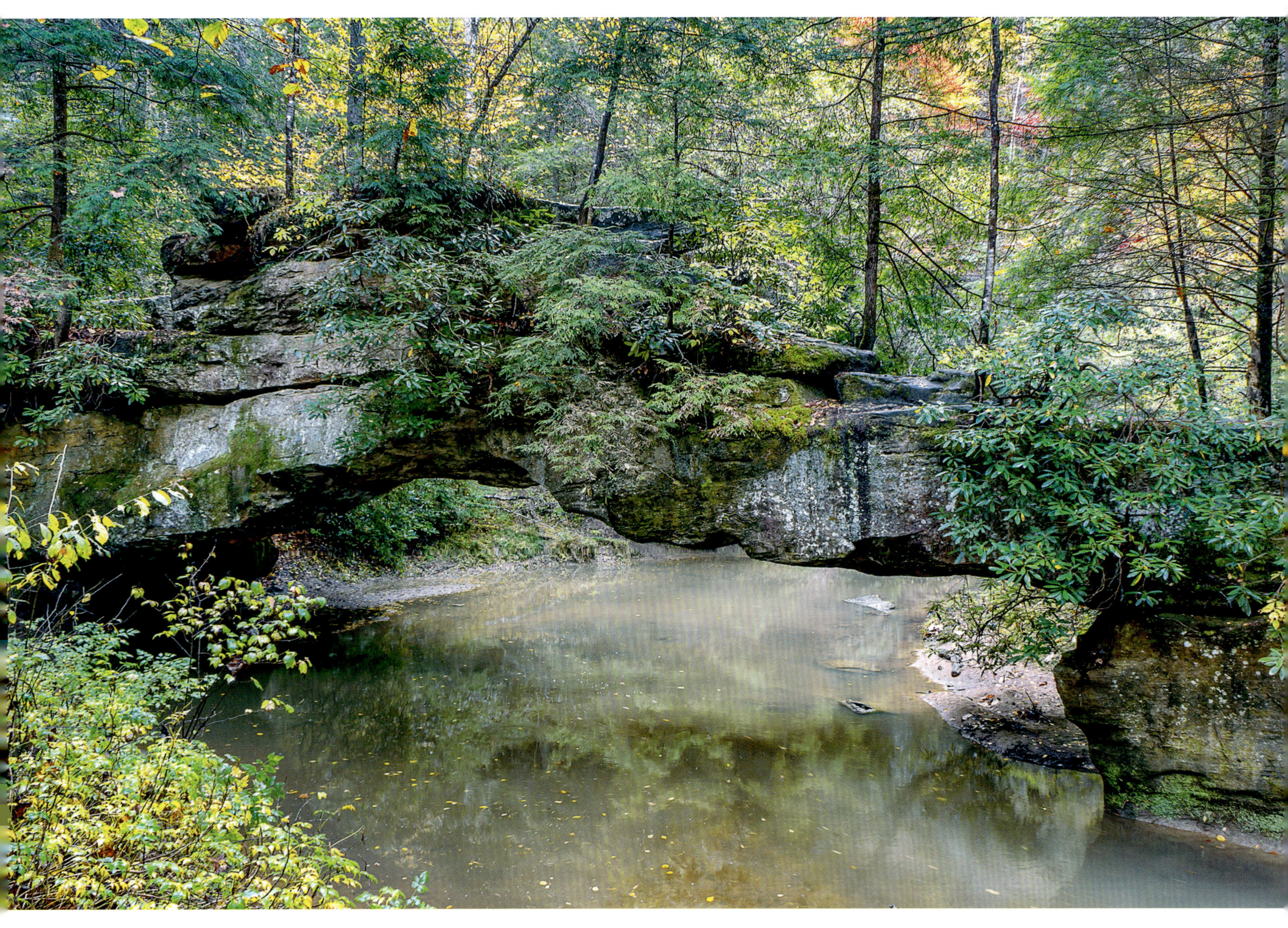

Swift Camp Creek flows under Rock Bridge at Red River Gorge

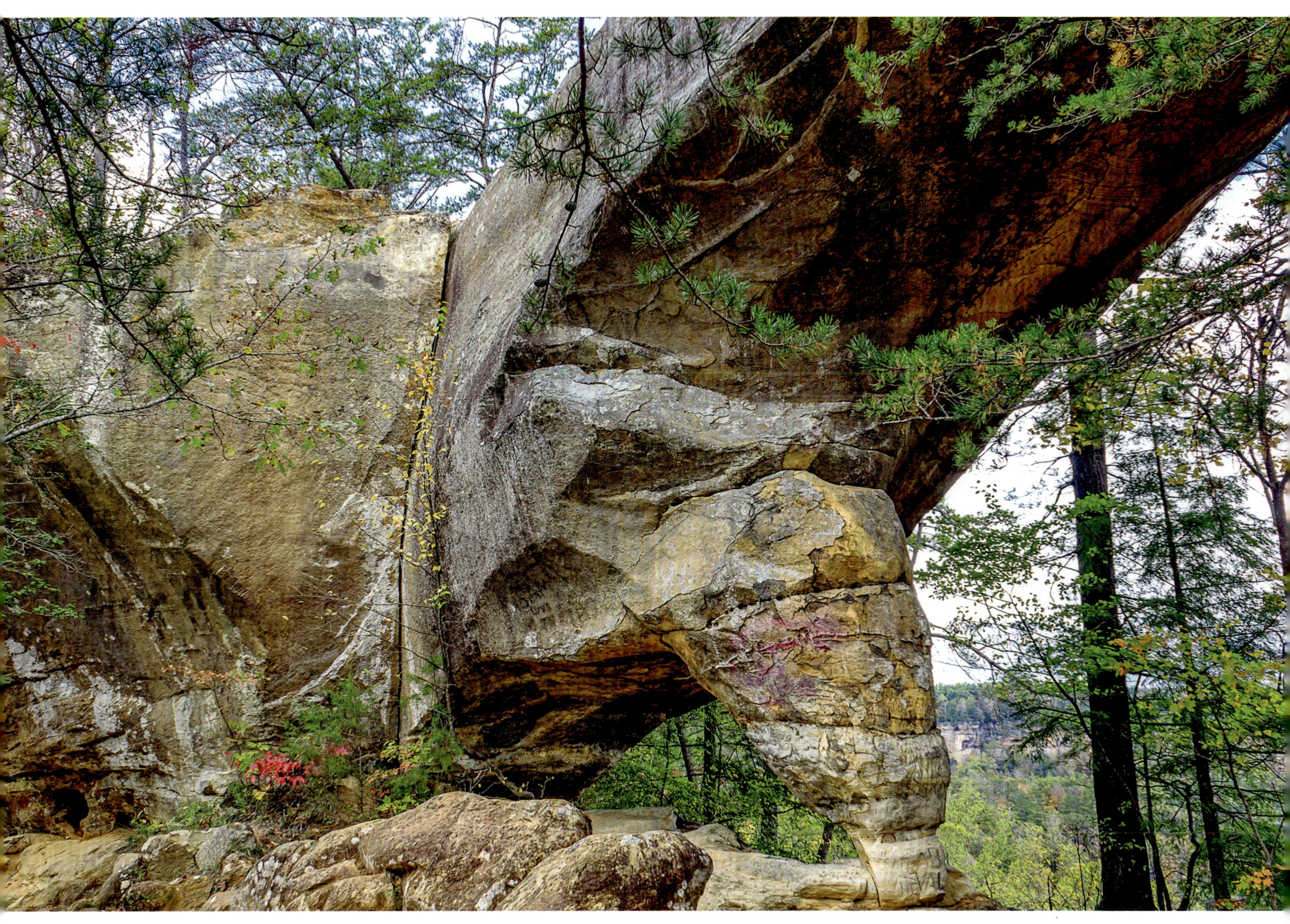

Sky Bridge offers breathtaking views from the top to the bottom of the Red River Gorge.

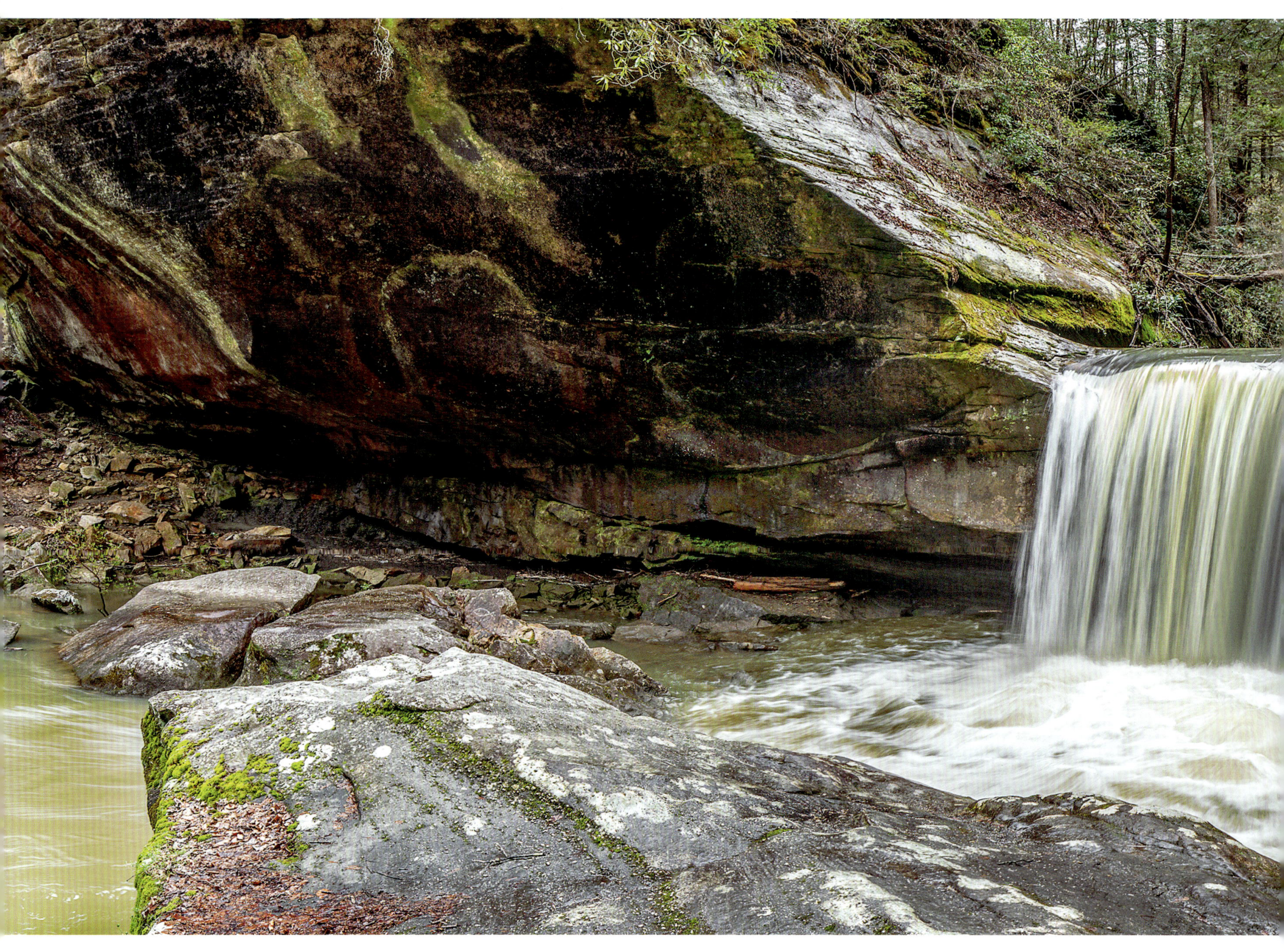

Nestled amid hemlock stands in the London Ranger District of the Daniel Boone National Forest is the scenic beauty of Dog Slaughter Falls.

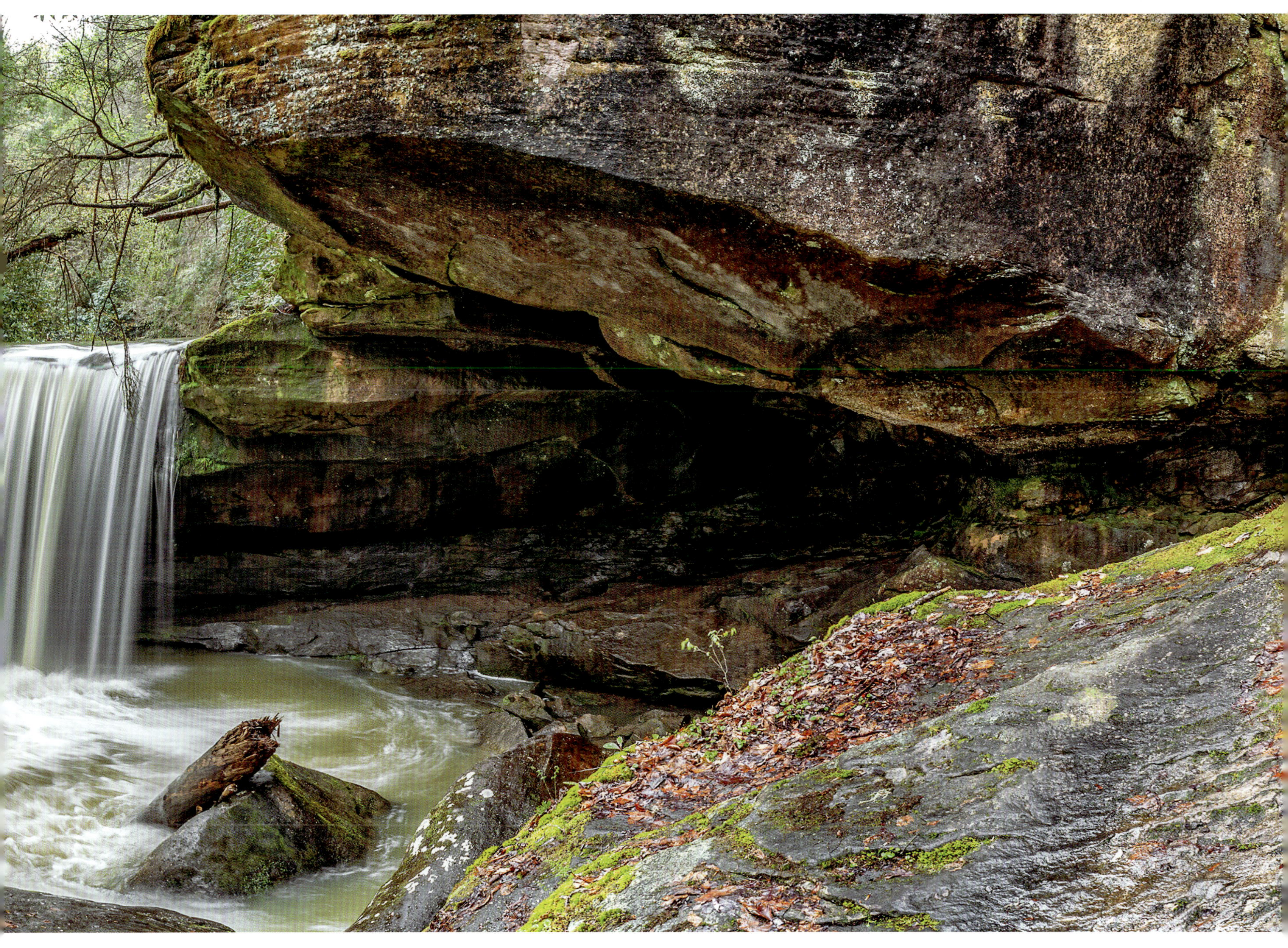

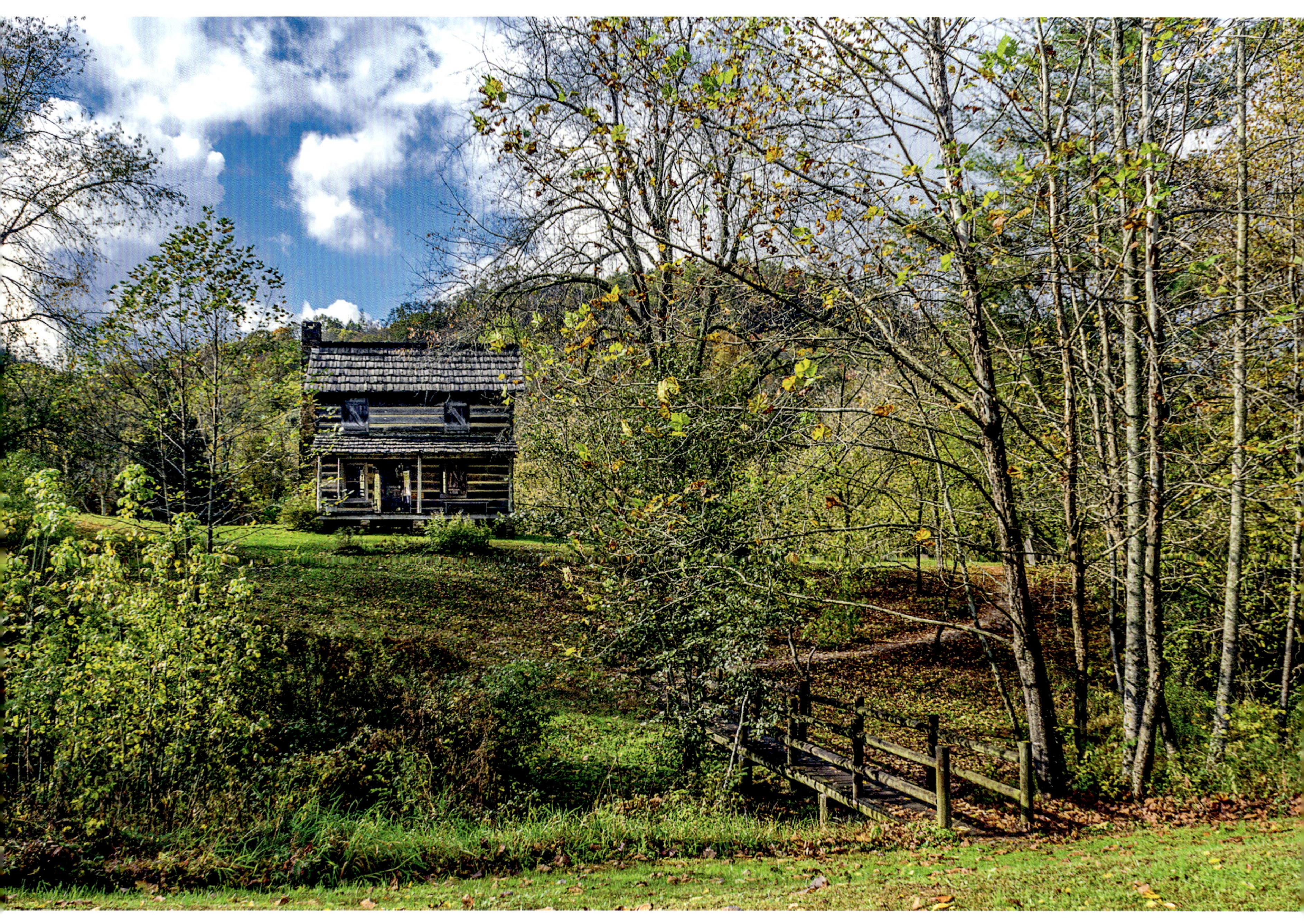

Gladie Cabin shows visitors a way of life that is long past.

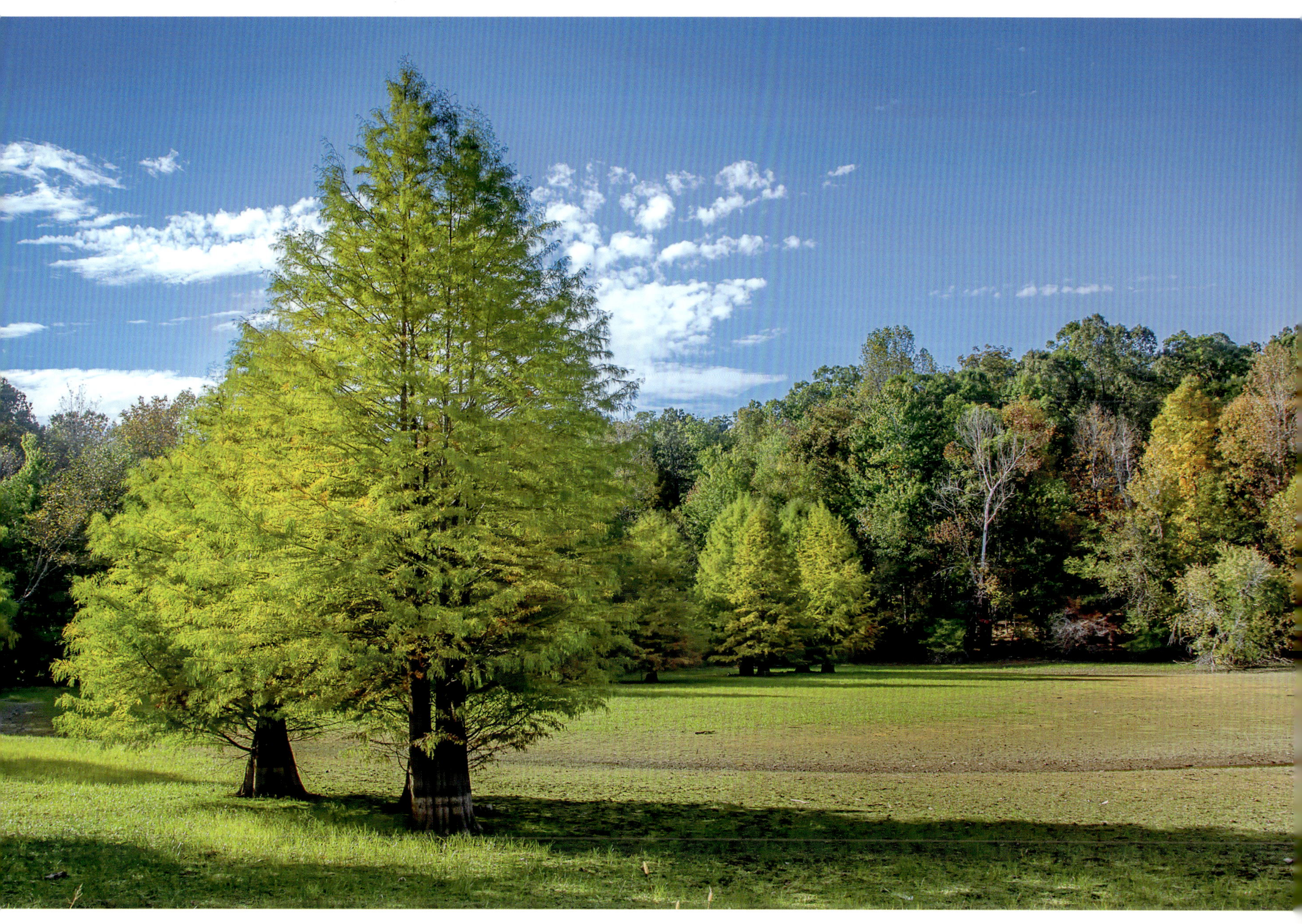

Cypress trees at Land Between the Lakes National Recreation Area.

FOLLOWING Hyssop growing along Clear Creek near Pineville.

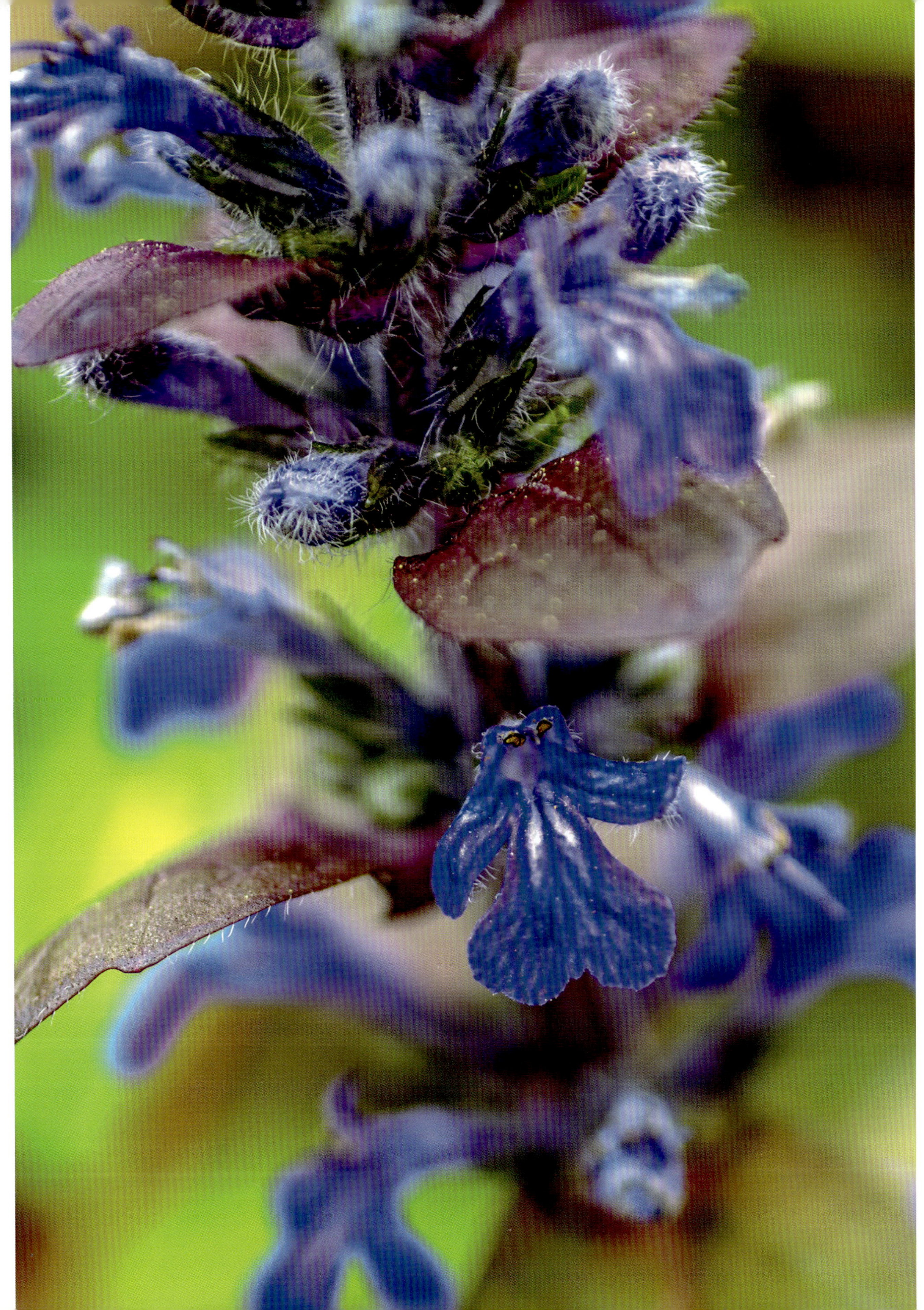

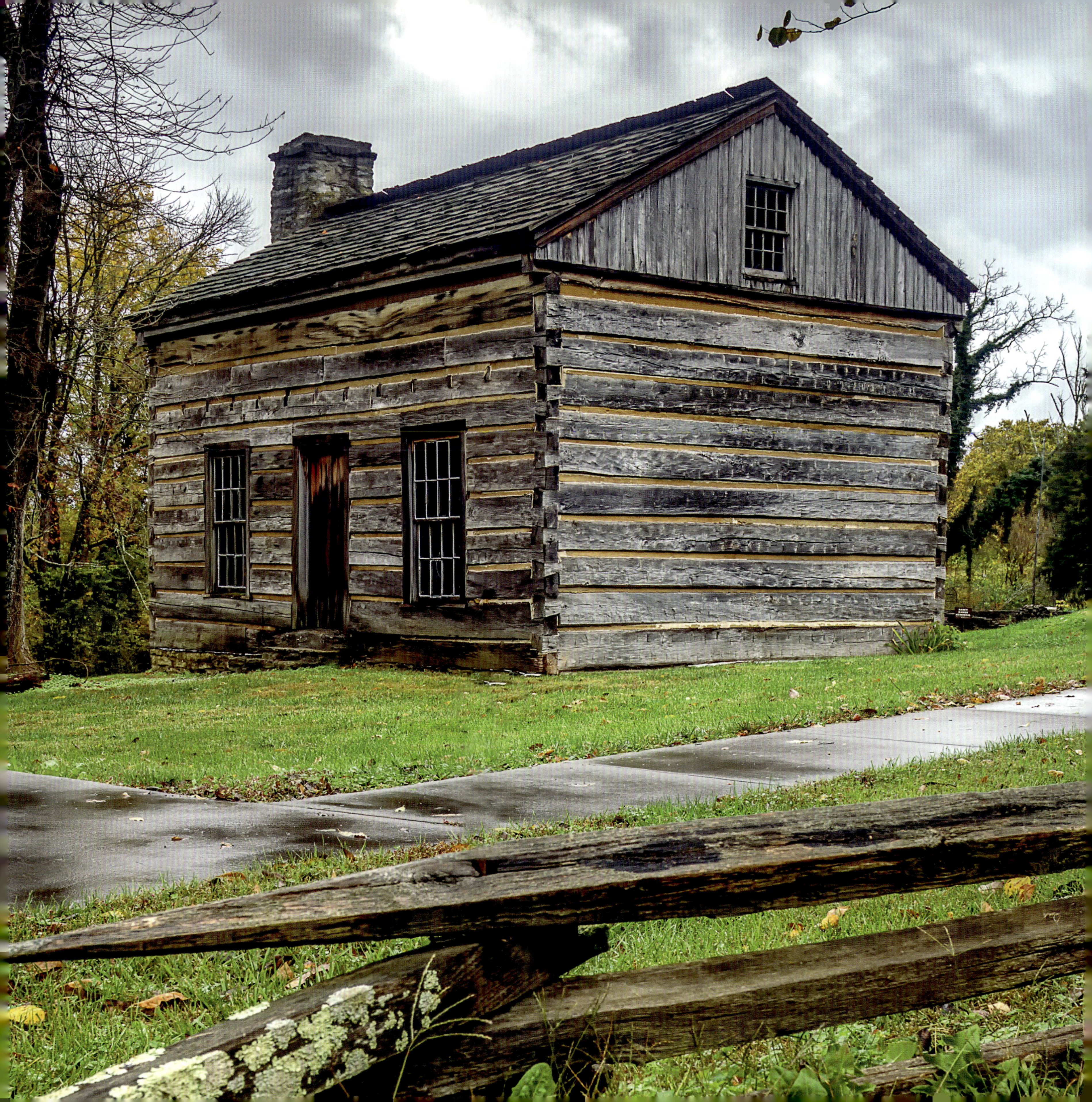

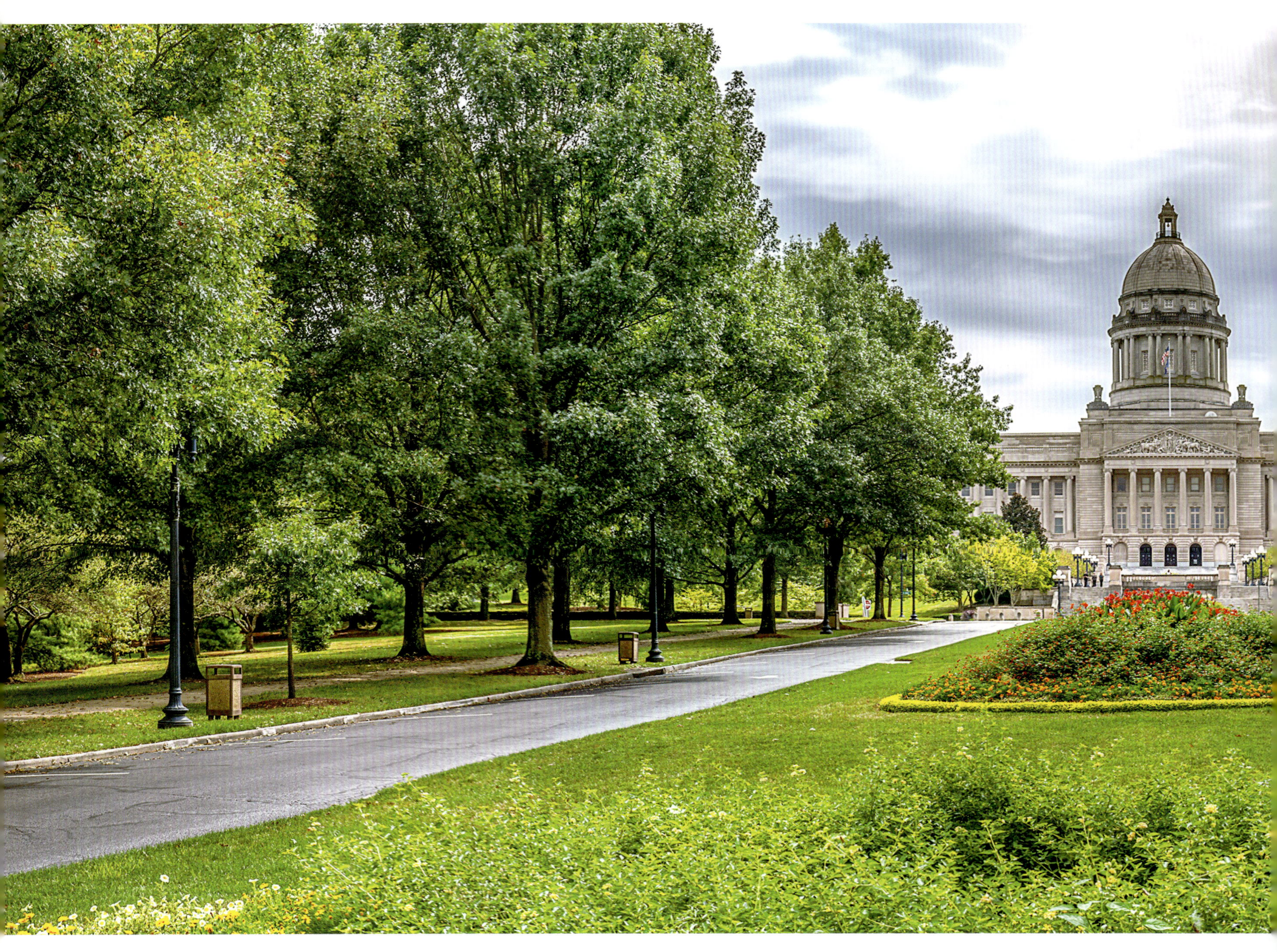

PREVIOUS Experience Lincoln family history at Lincoln Homestead State Park.

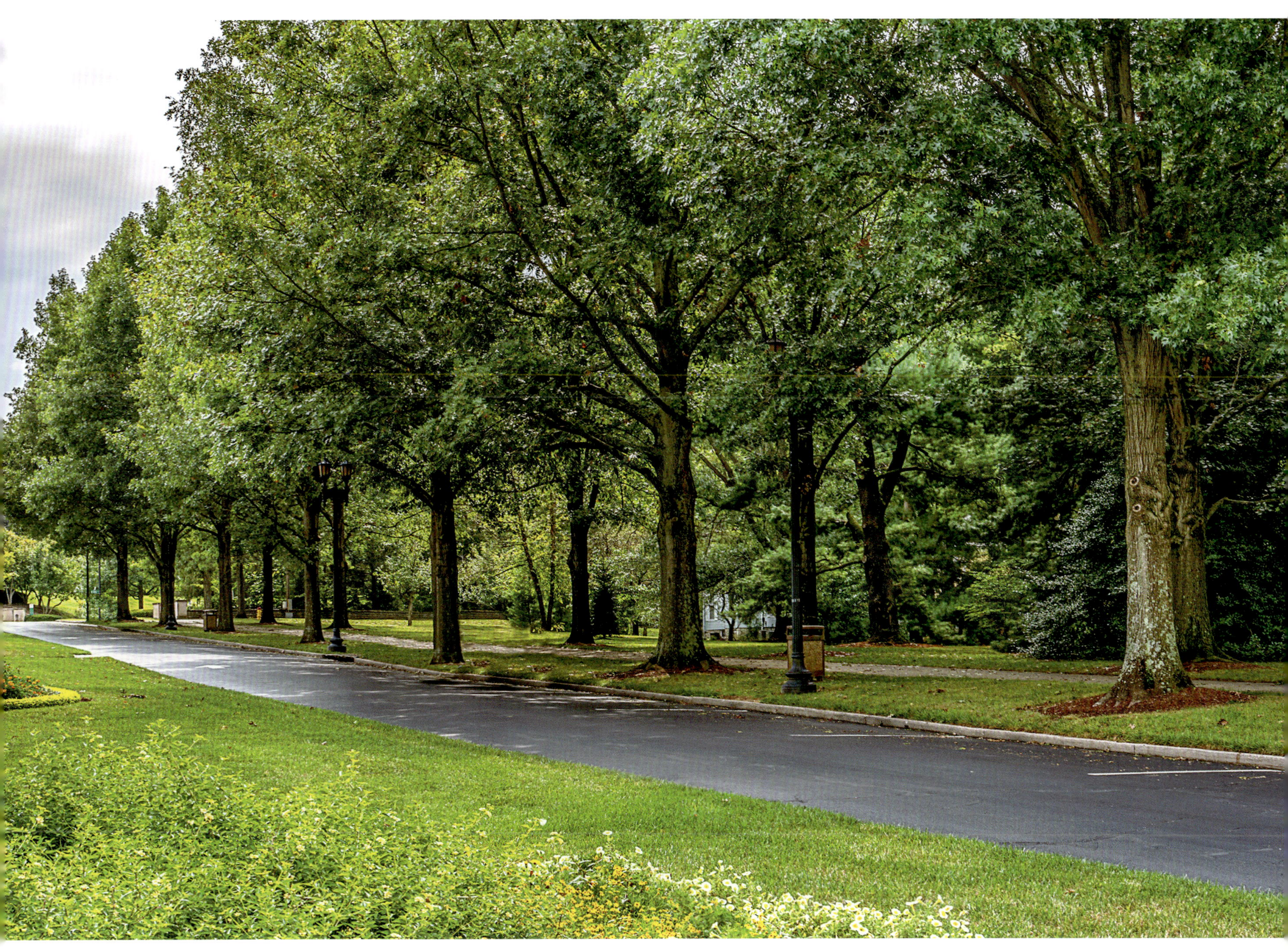

Frankfort has been Kentucky's state capital since 1792.

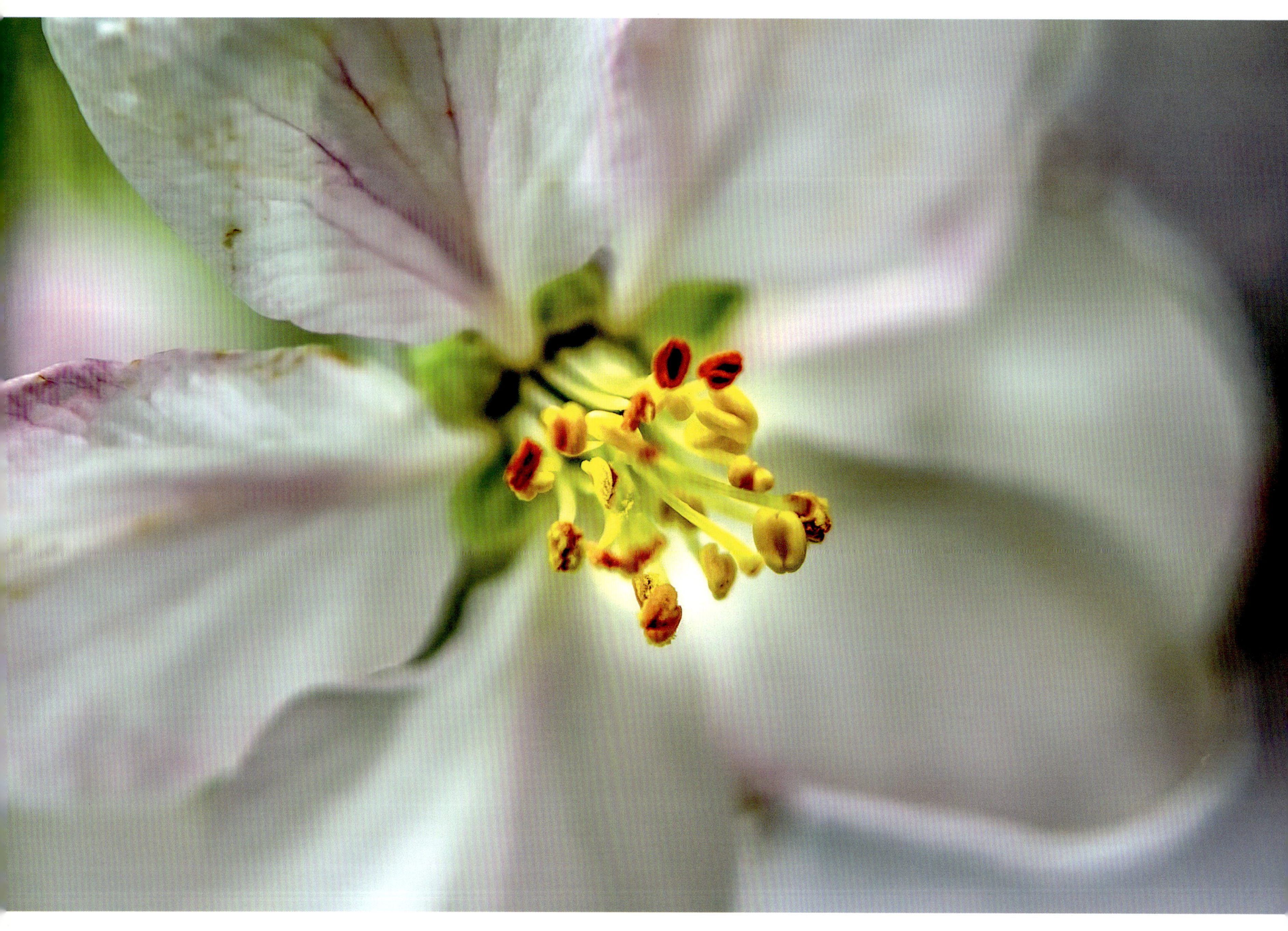

Apple blossom at Laurel River Lake.

Sloan's Crossing Pond at Mammoth Cave National Park is home to an array of wetland plants and creatures.

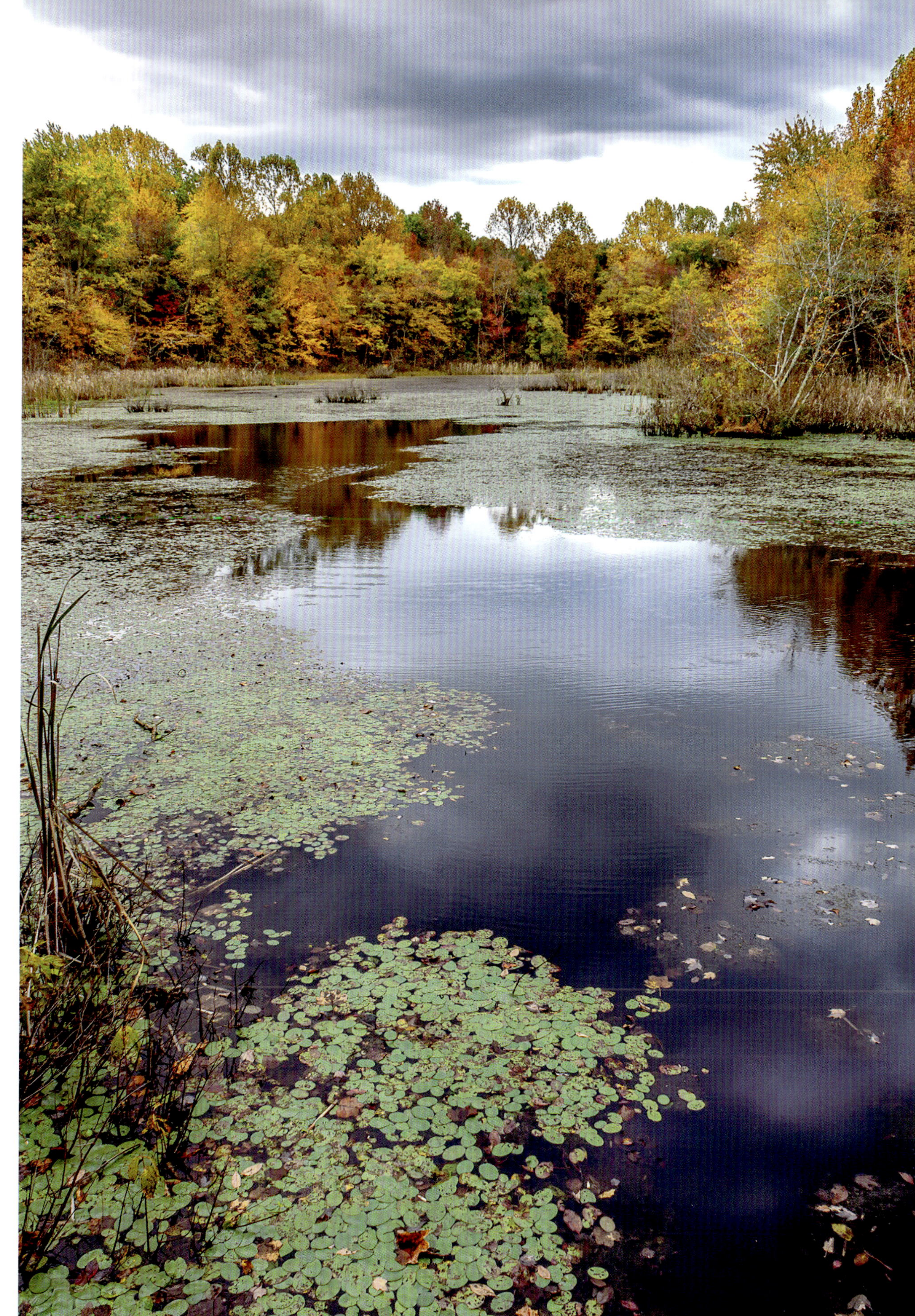

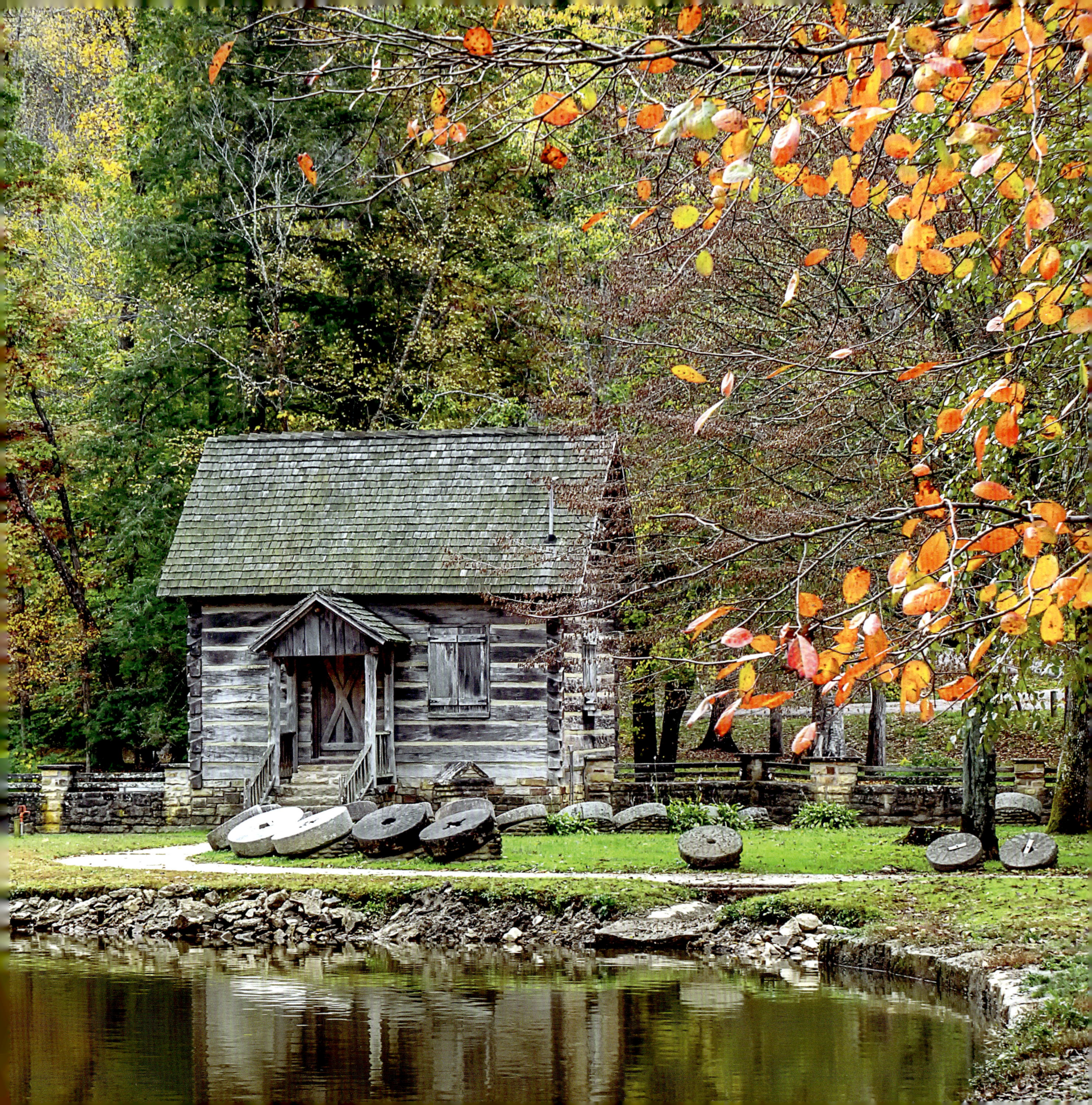

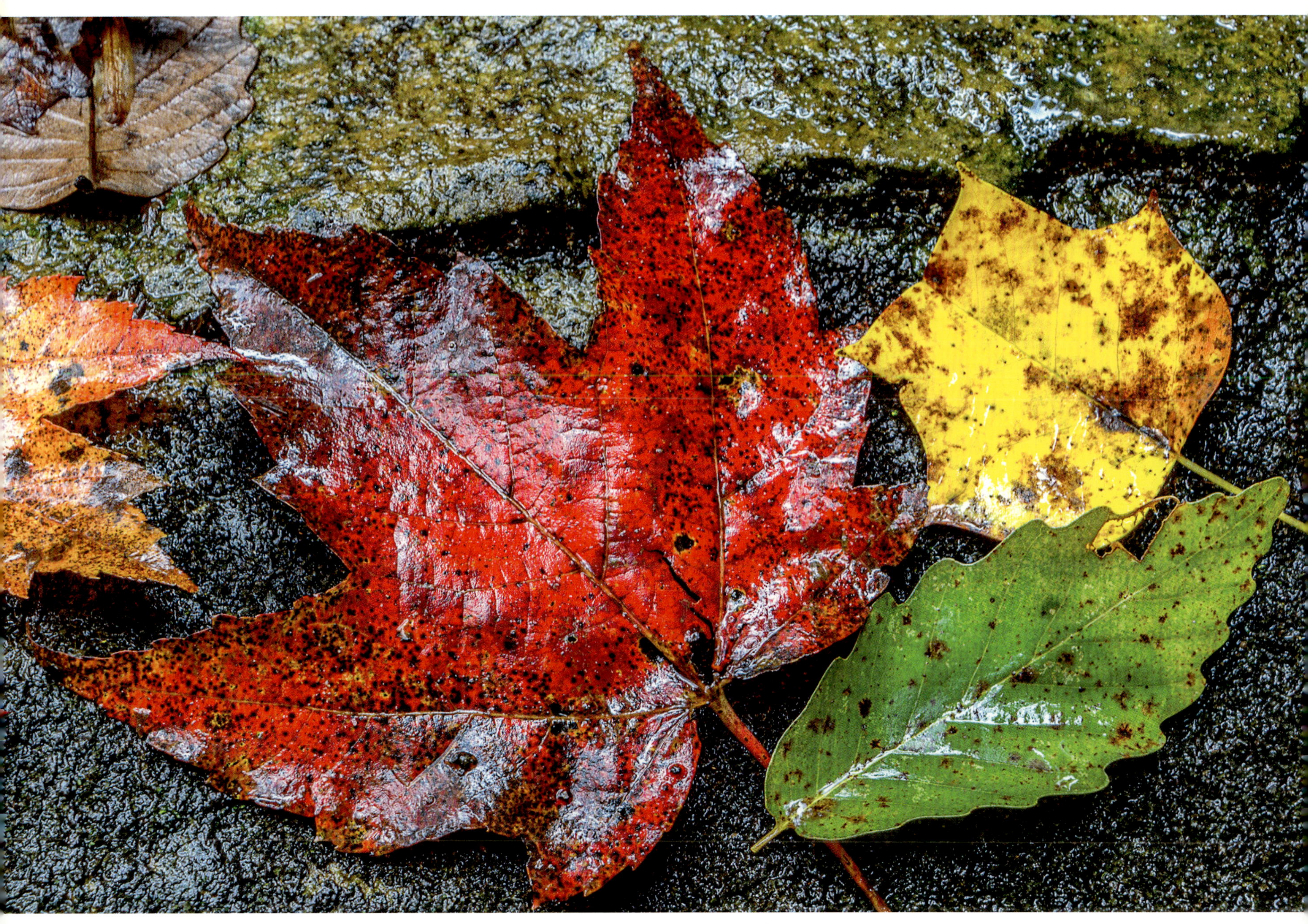

An intimate look at autumn.

FACING McHargue's Mill, an attraction in Levi Jackson Wilderness Road State Park, features one of the largest collections of authentic millstones in the country.

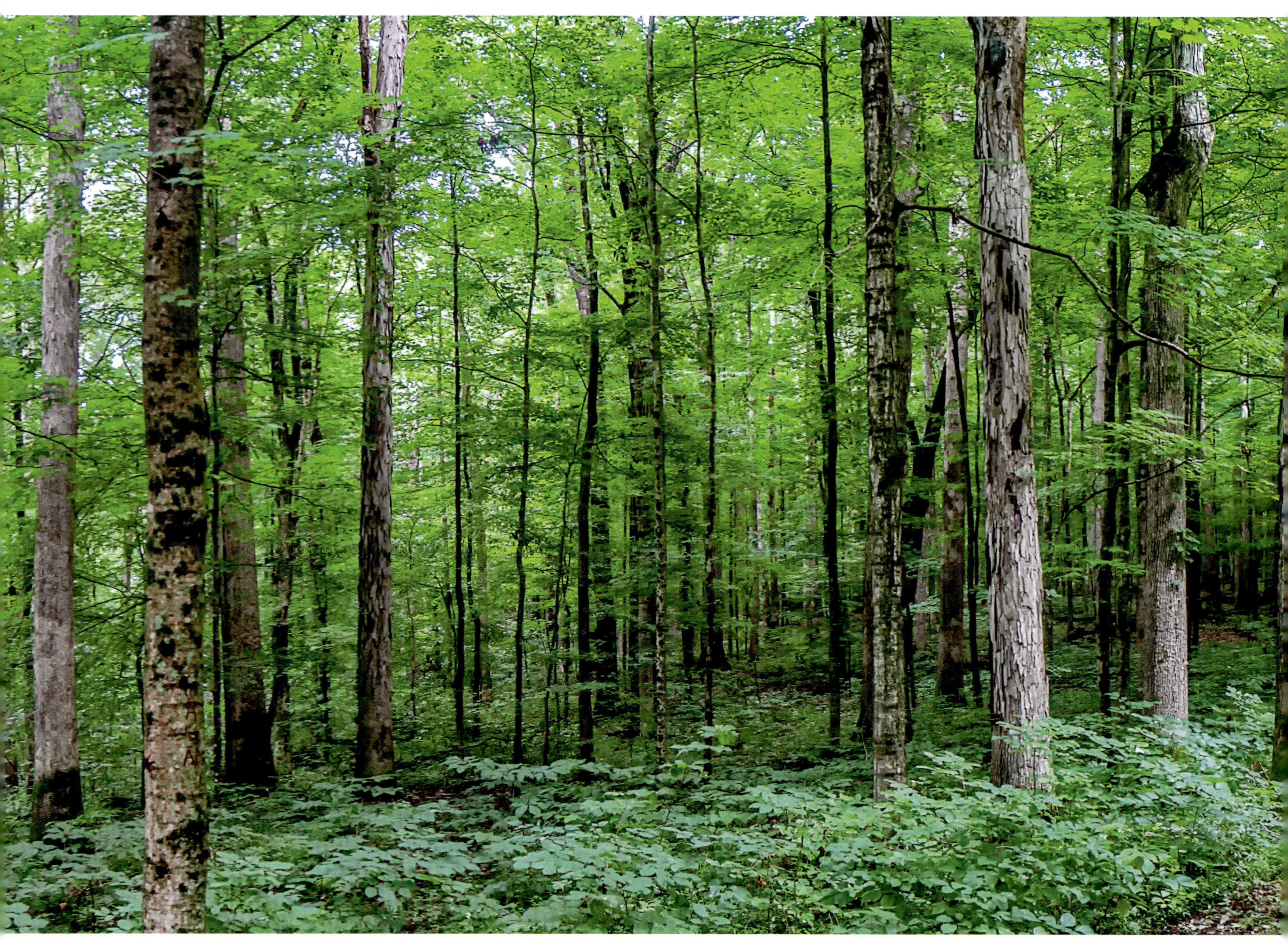

The forest invites visitors to explore.

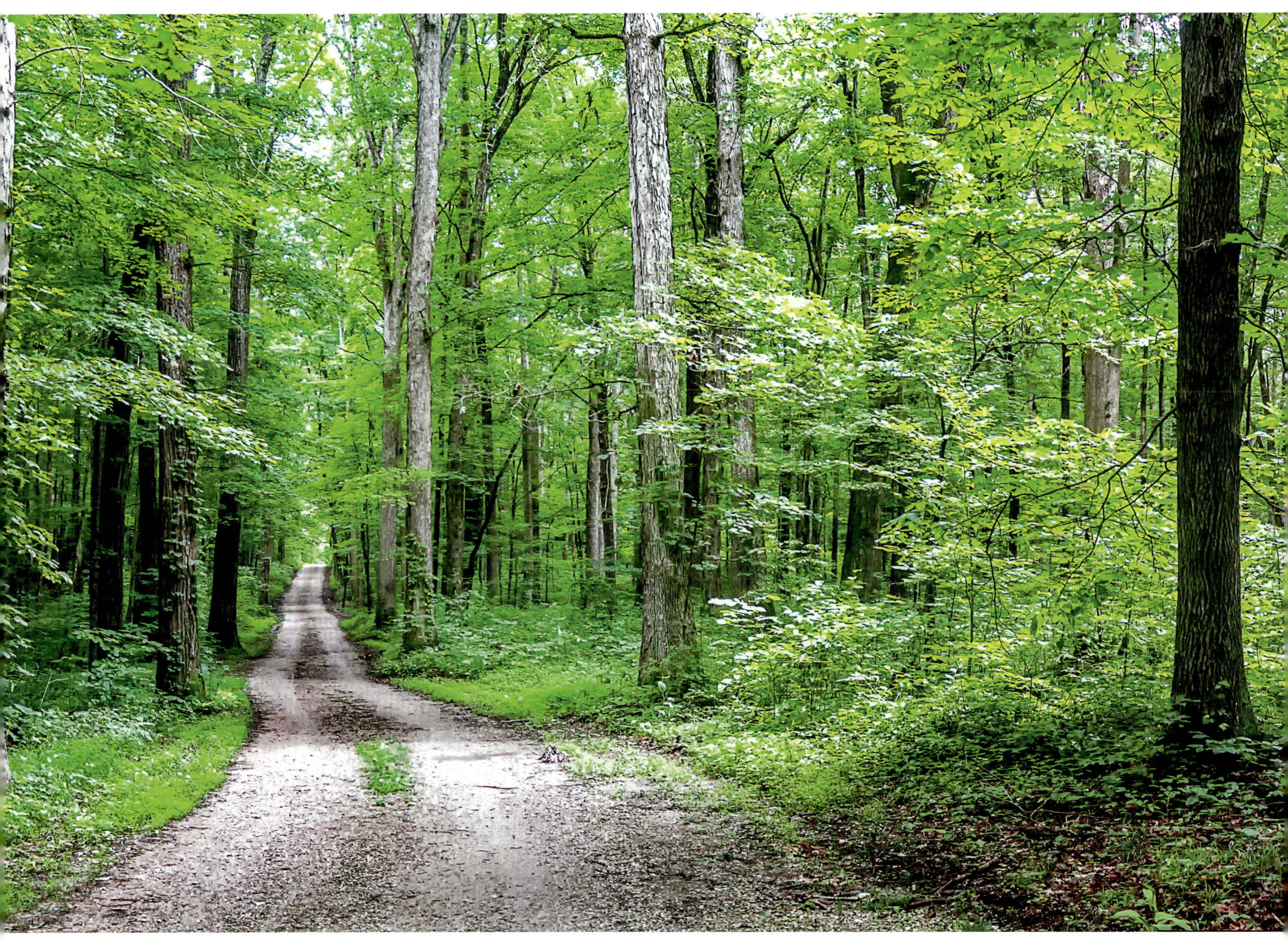

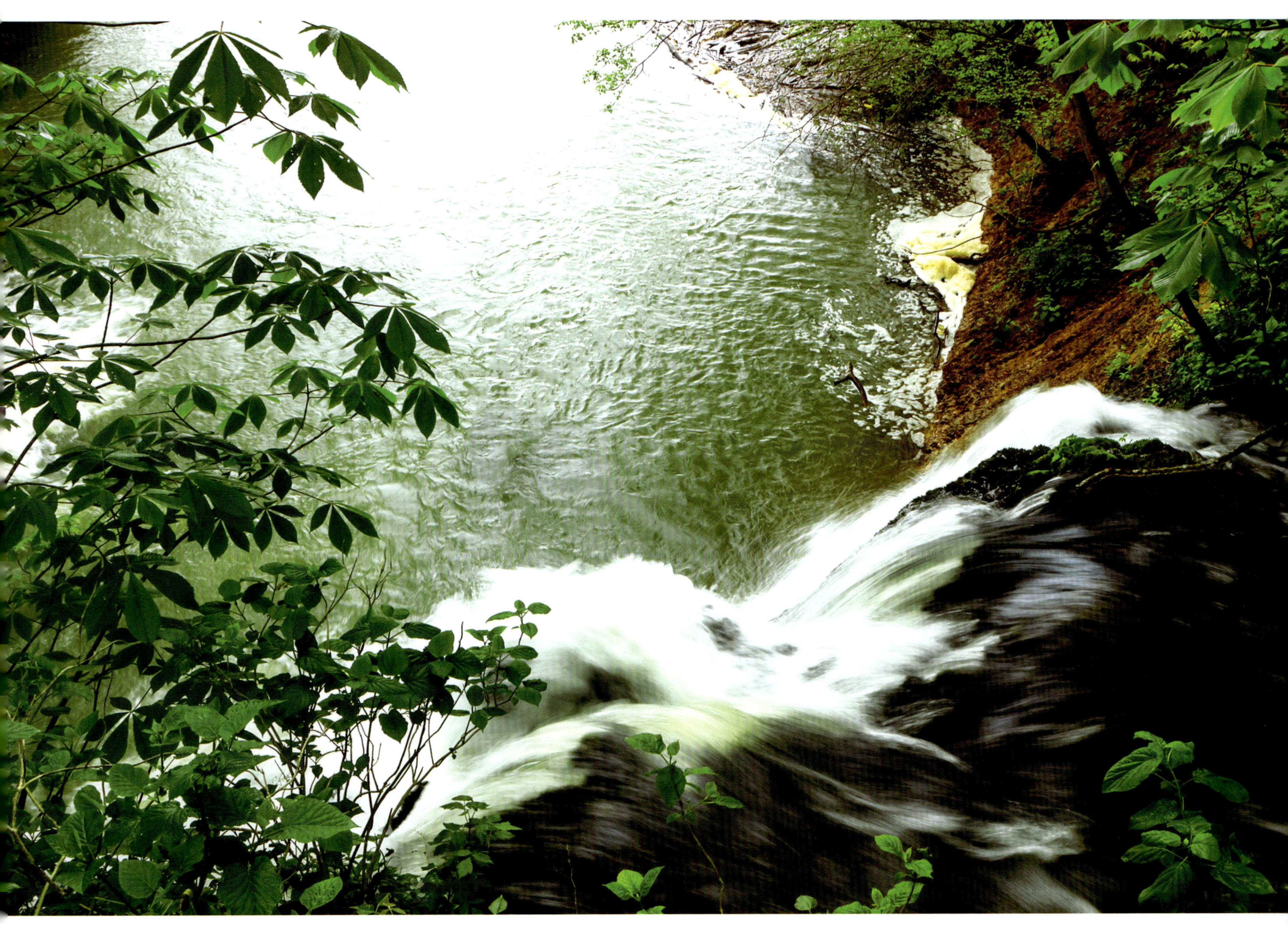

The moment when the water falls. Mill Springs Park.

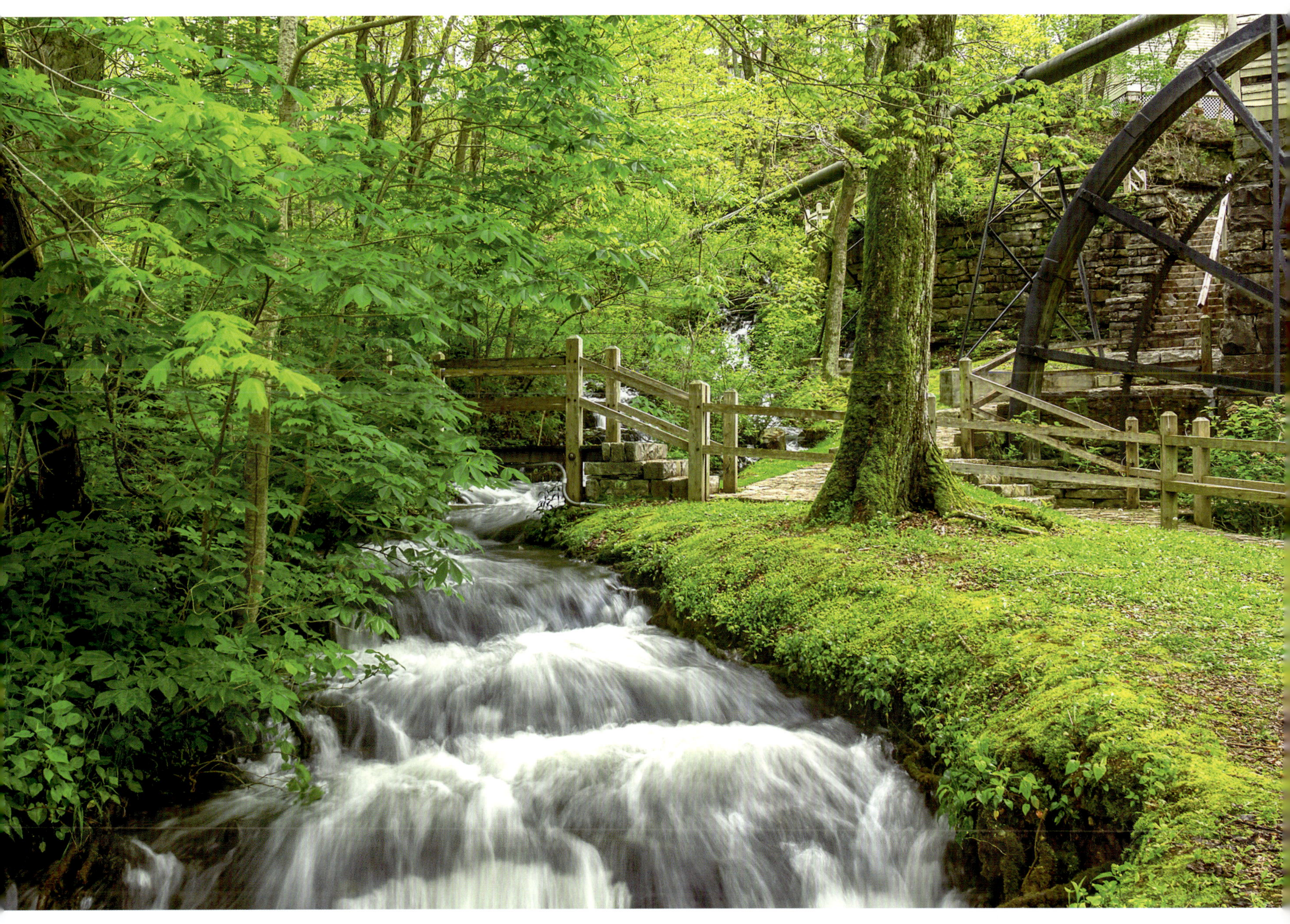

Water flows everywhere through Mill Springs Park.

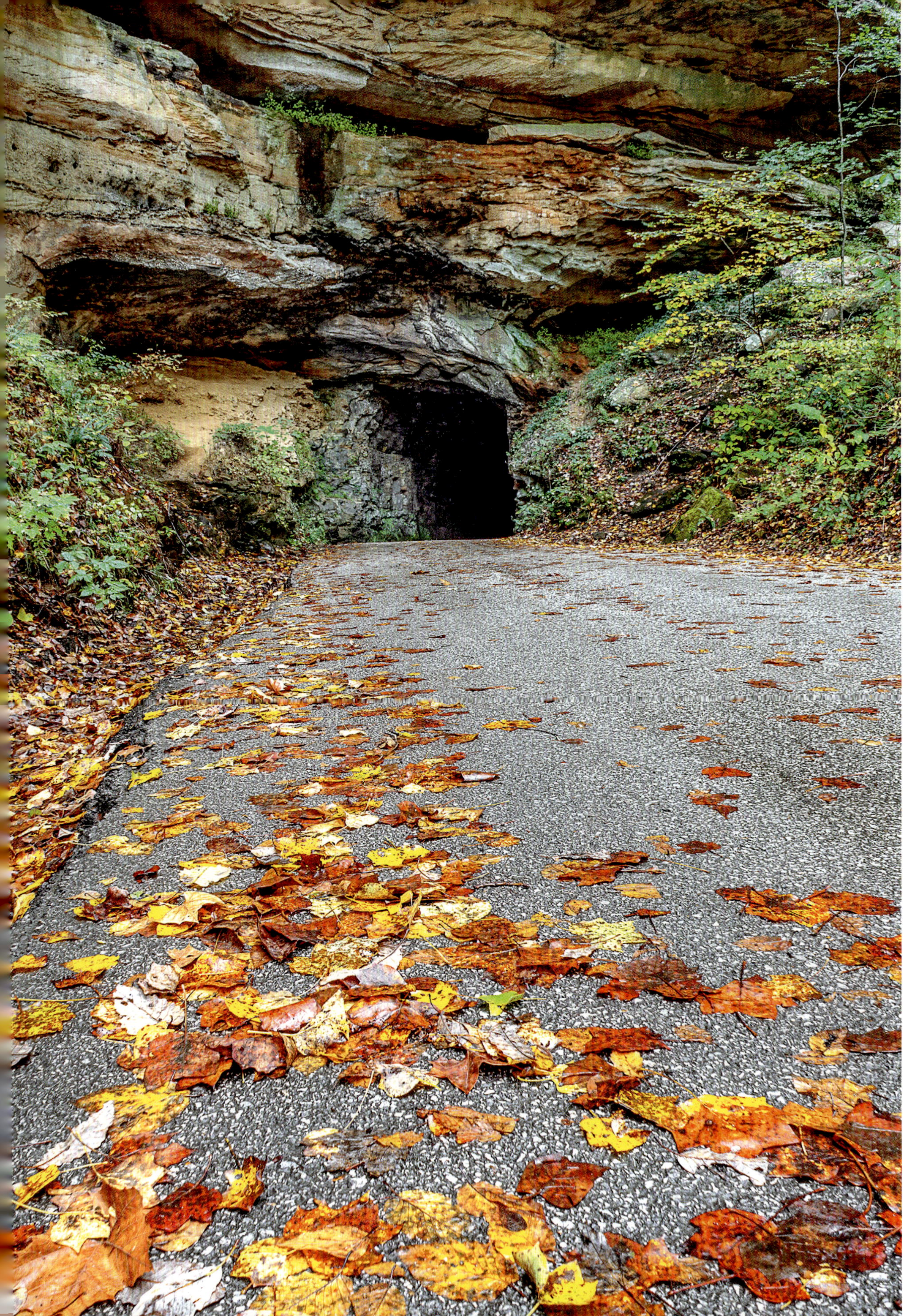

Fall color brightens the roadway at Nada Tunnel near Red River Gorge.

FACING Visitors can see how life as a coal miner might have been at Blue Heron Mining Community.

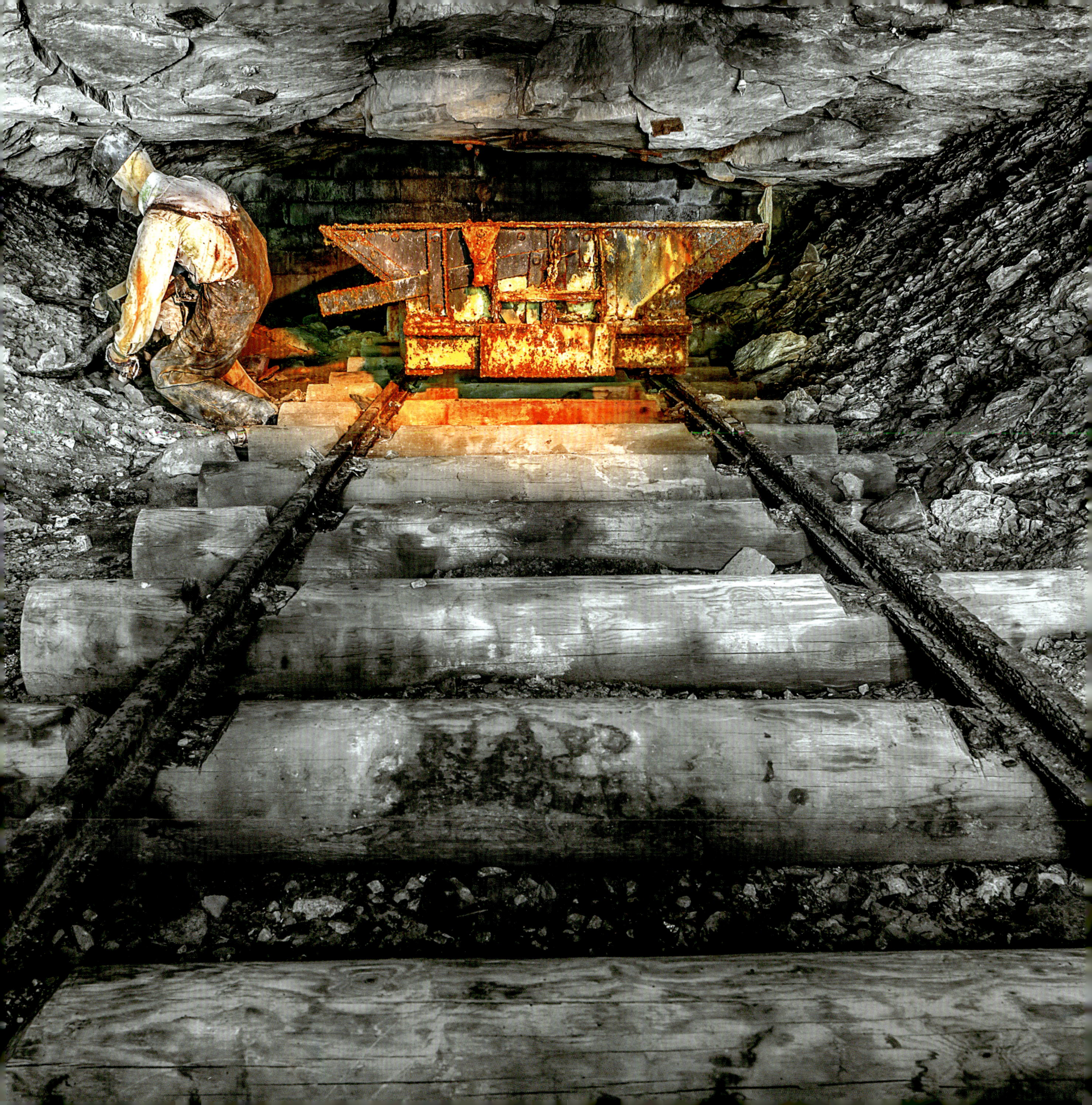

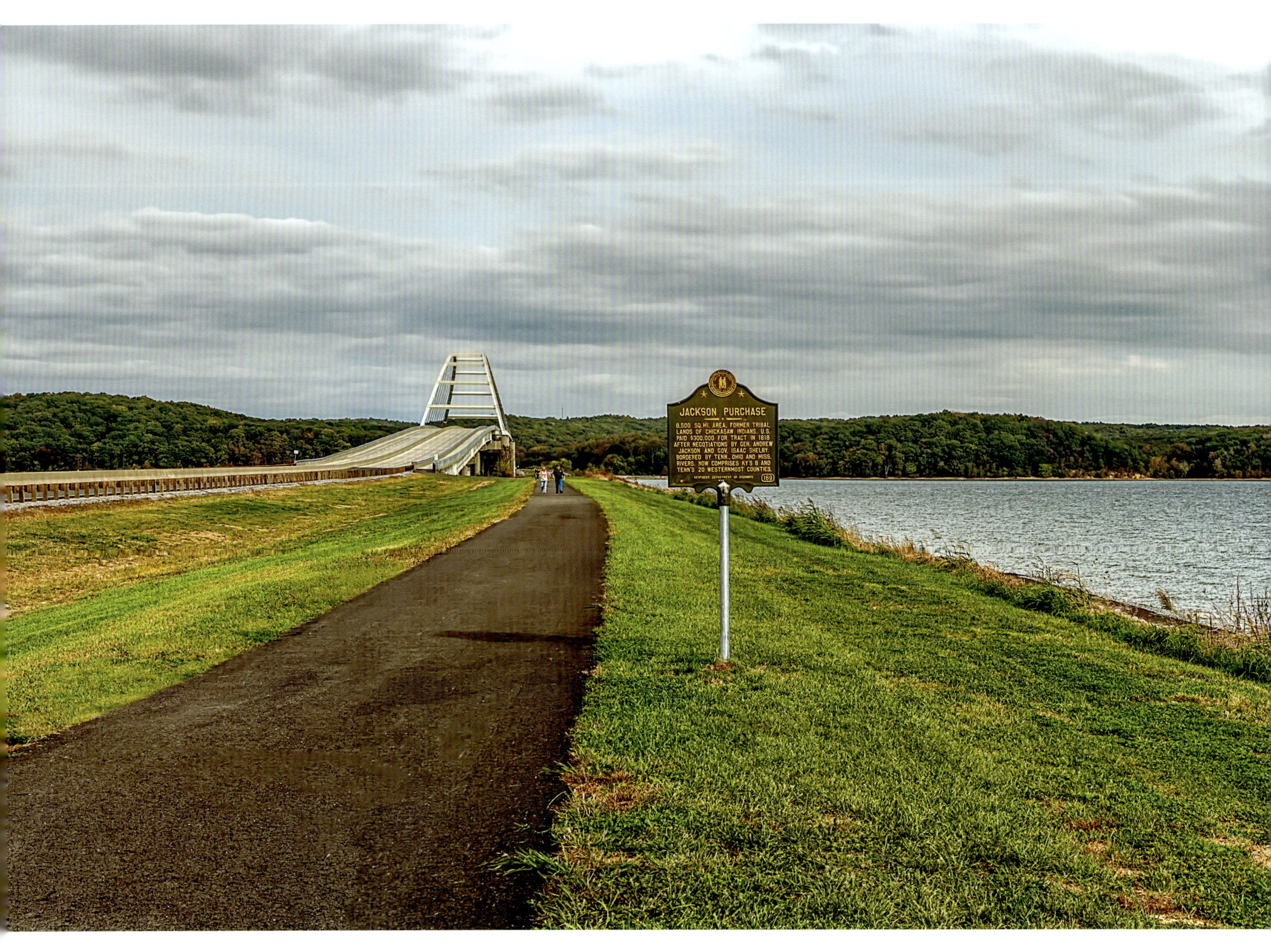

The Eggner Ferry Bridge gives drivers a 360-degree view of Kentucky Lake.

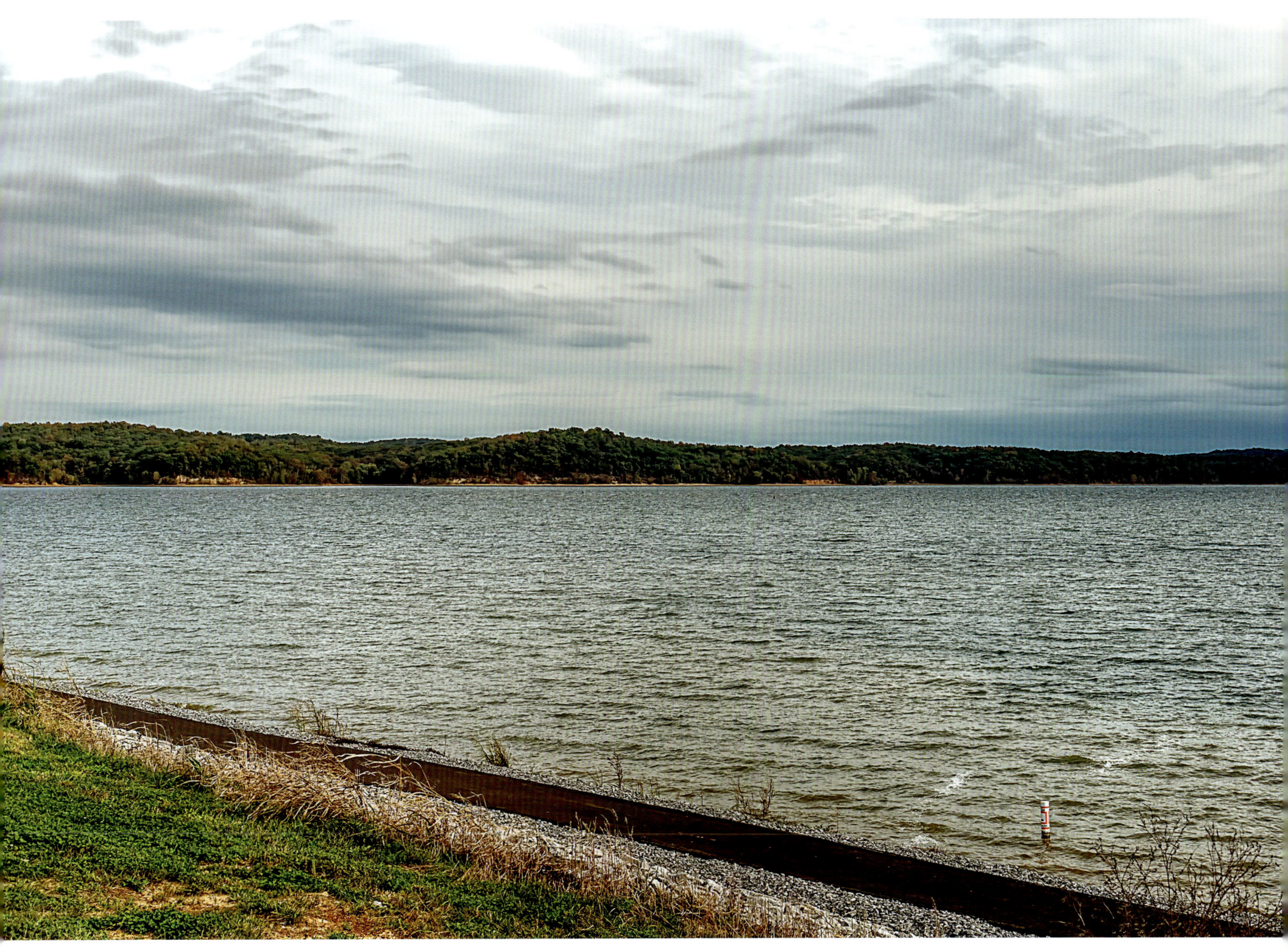

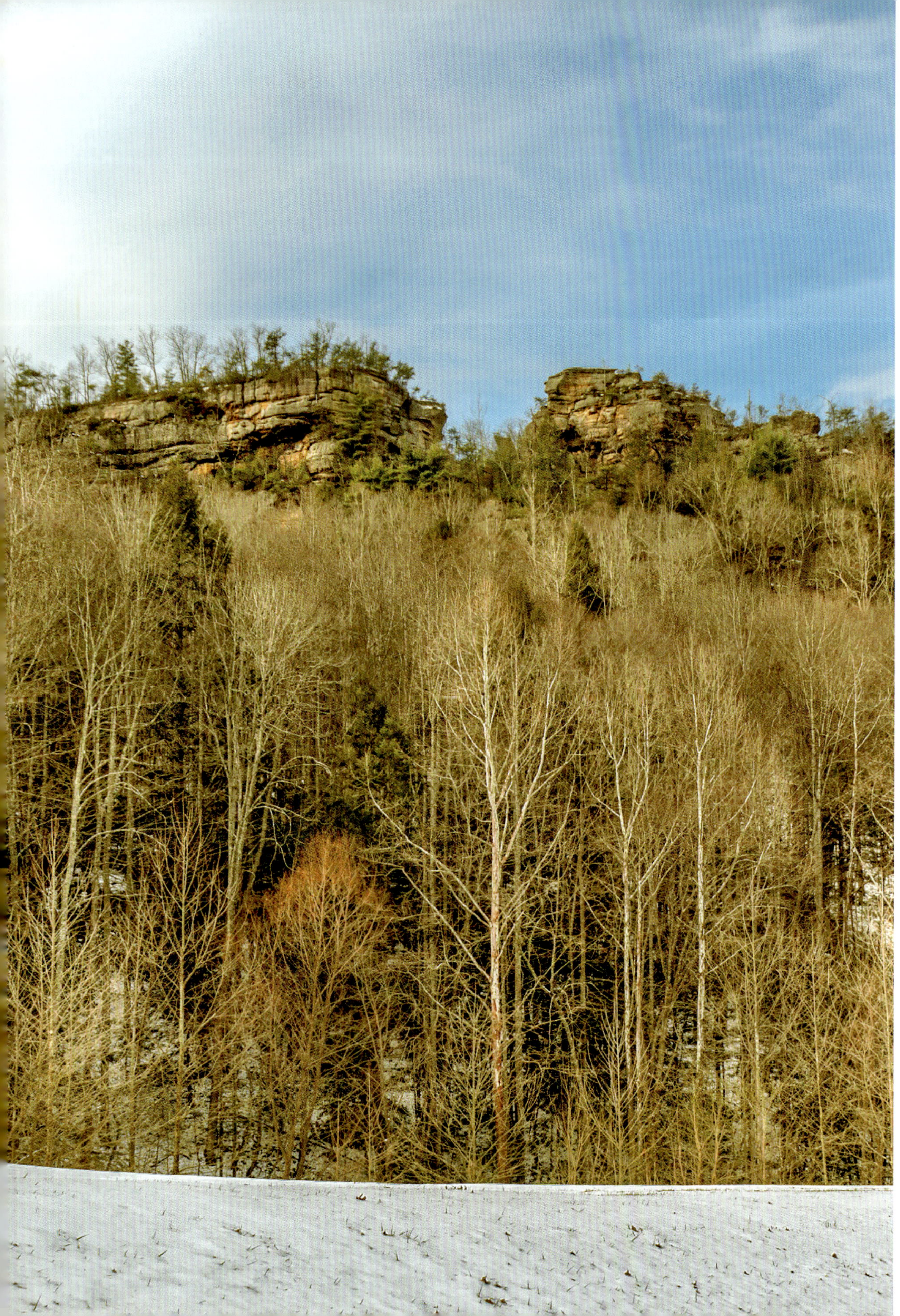

A dusting of snow at Natural Bridge Resort State Park.

The last remnants of winter at Natural Bridge State Resort Park.

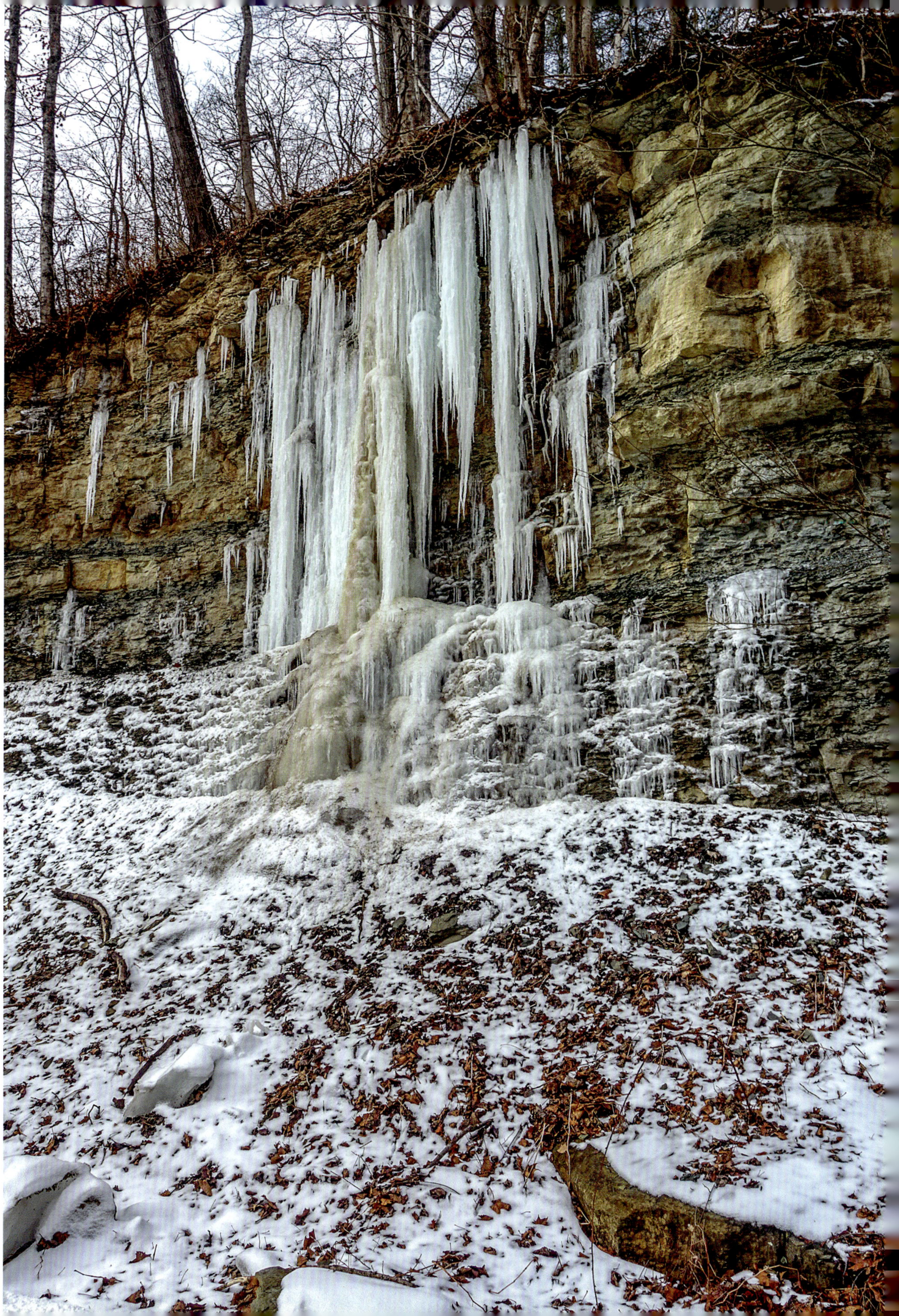

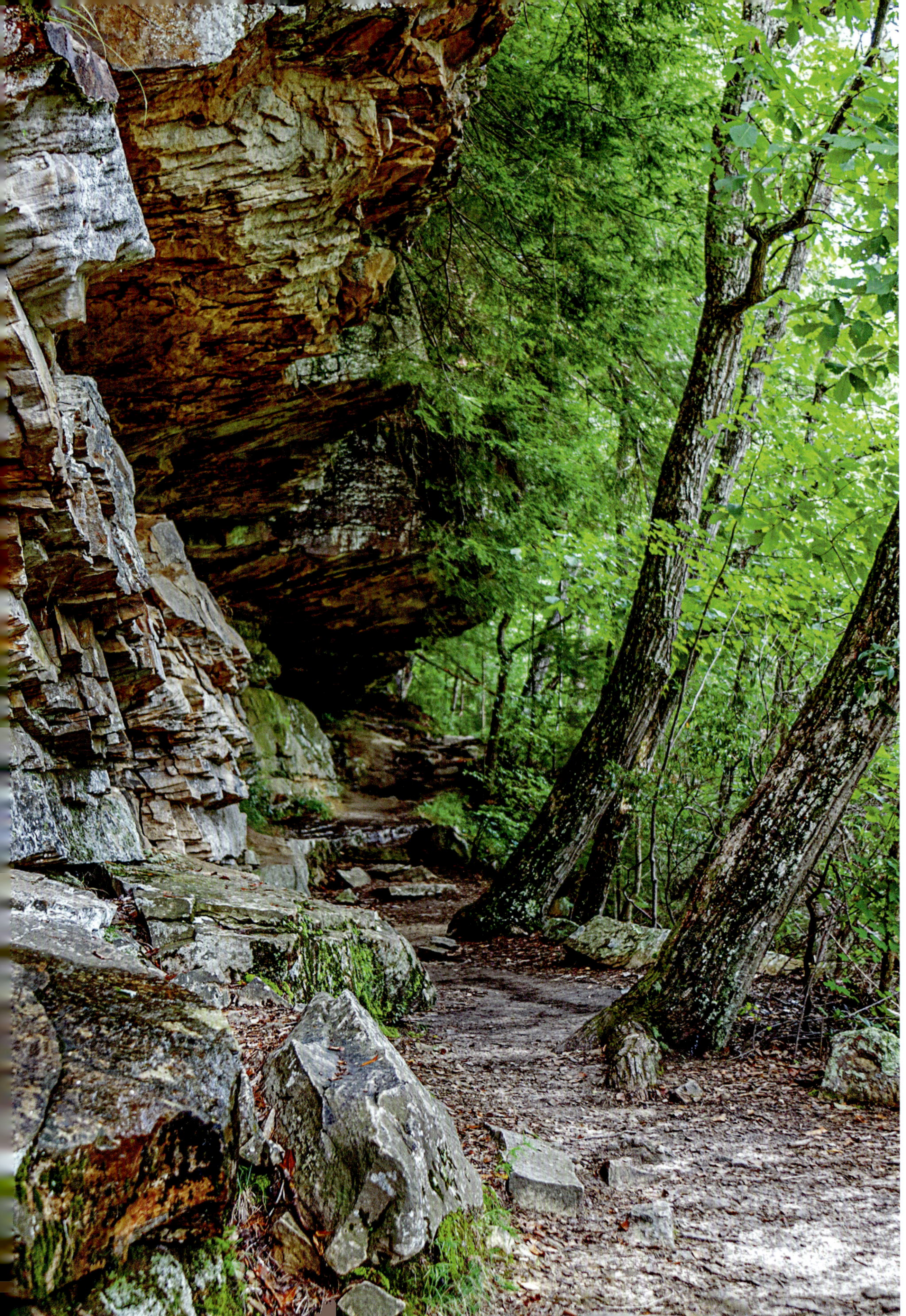

The trail to Natural Bridge winds around interesting sights and formations.

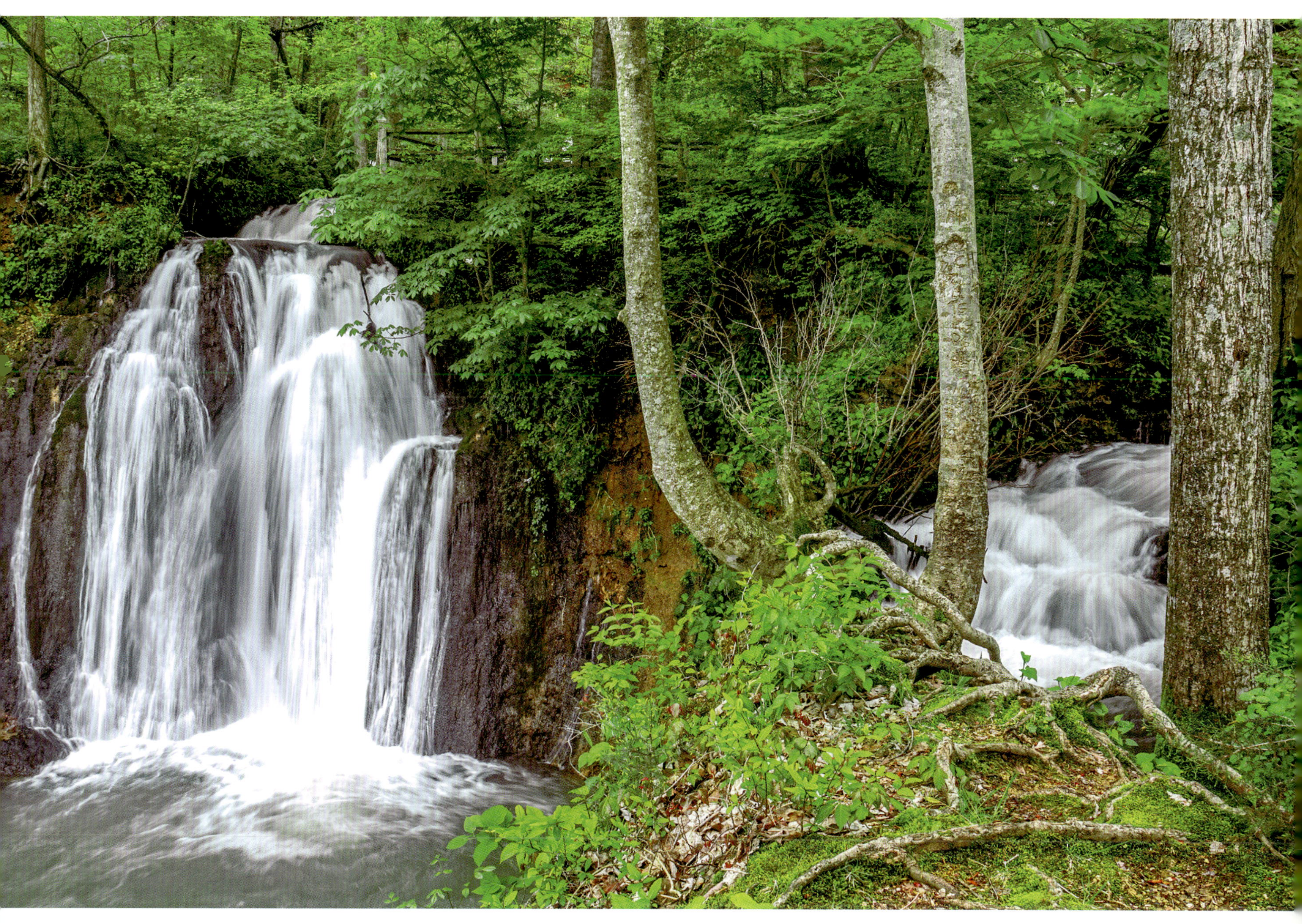

The waterfall at Mill Springs Park makes its way into the Cumberland River

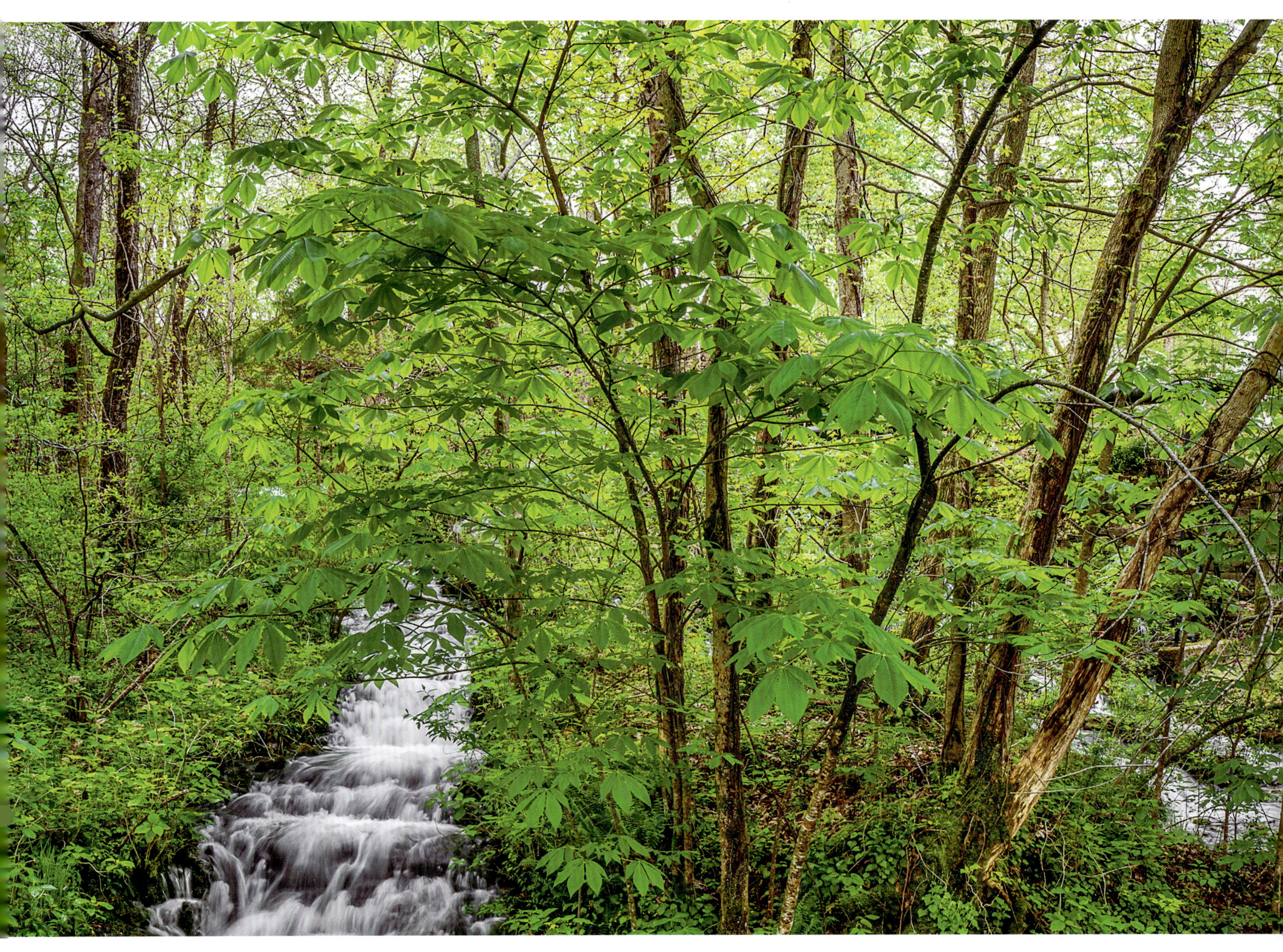

Interpretive signs at Mill Springs Park commemorate the Battle of Mill Springs, a decisive Union victory and a close escape for Confederate troops in the Civil War.

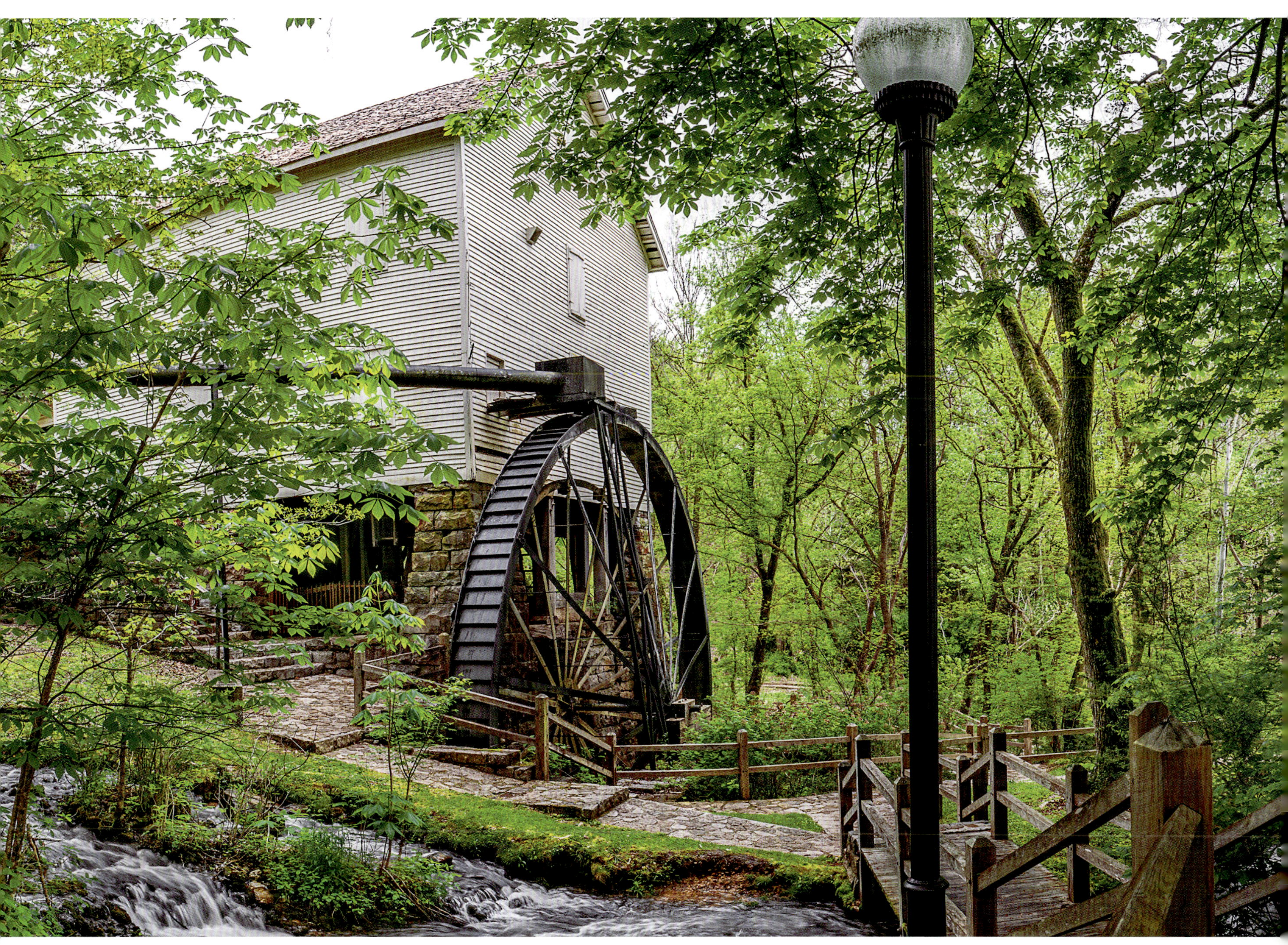

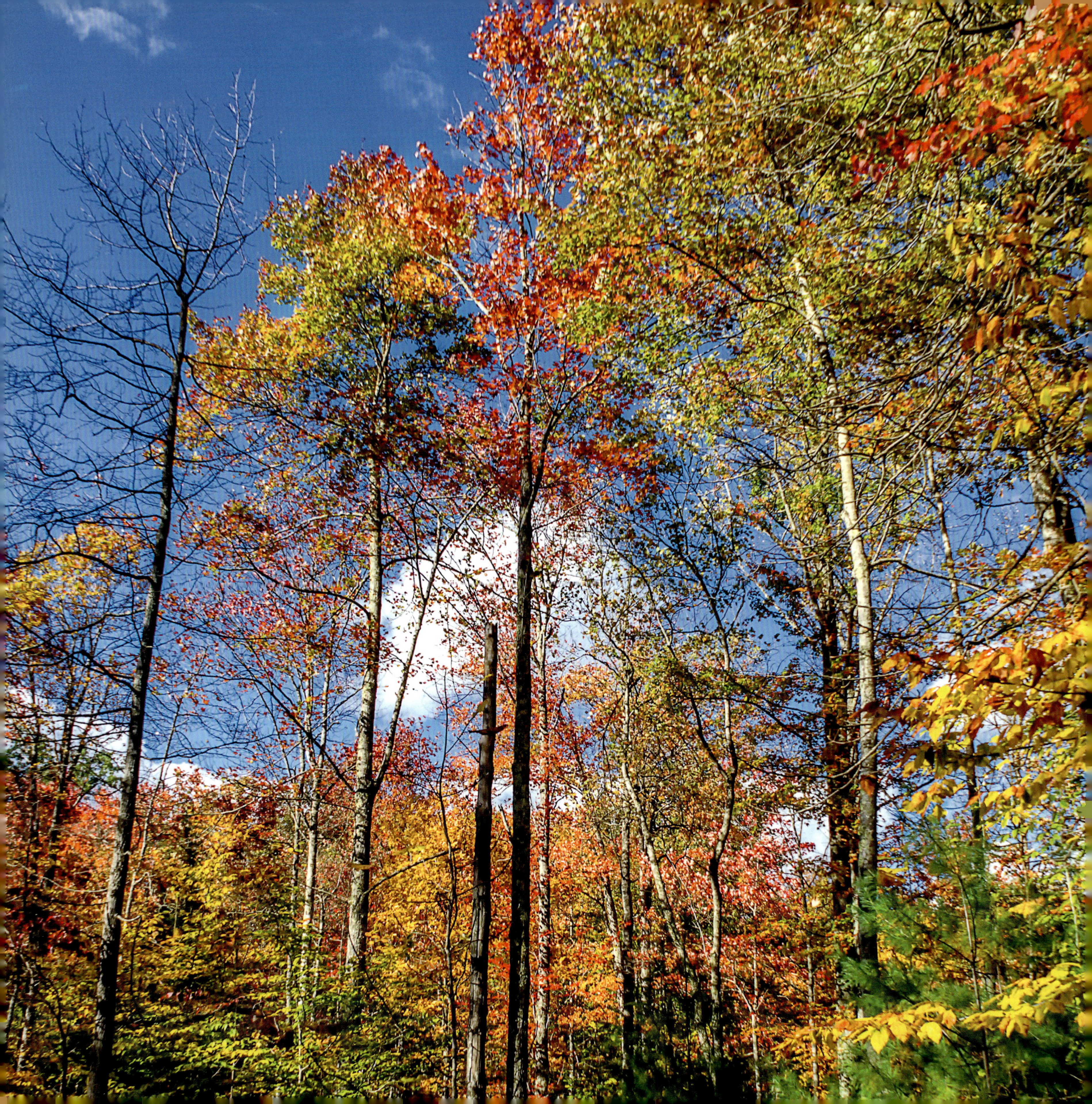

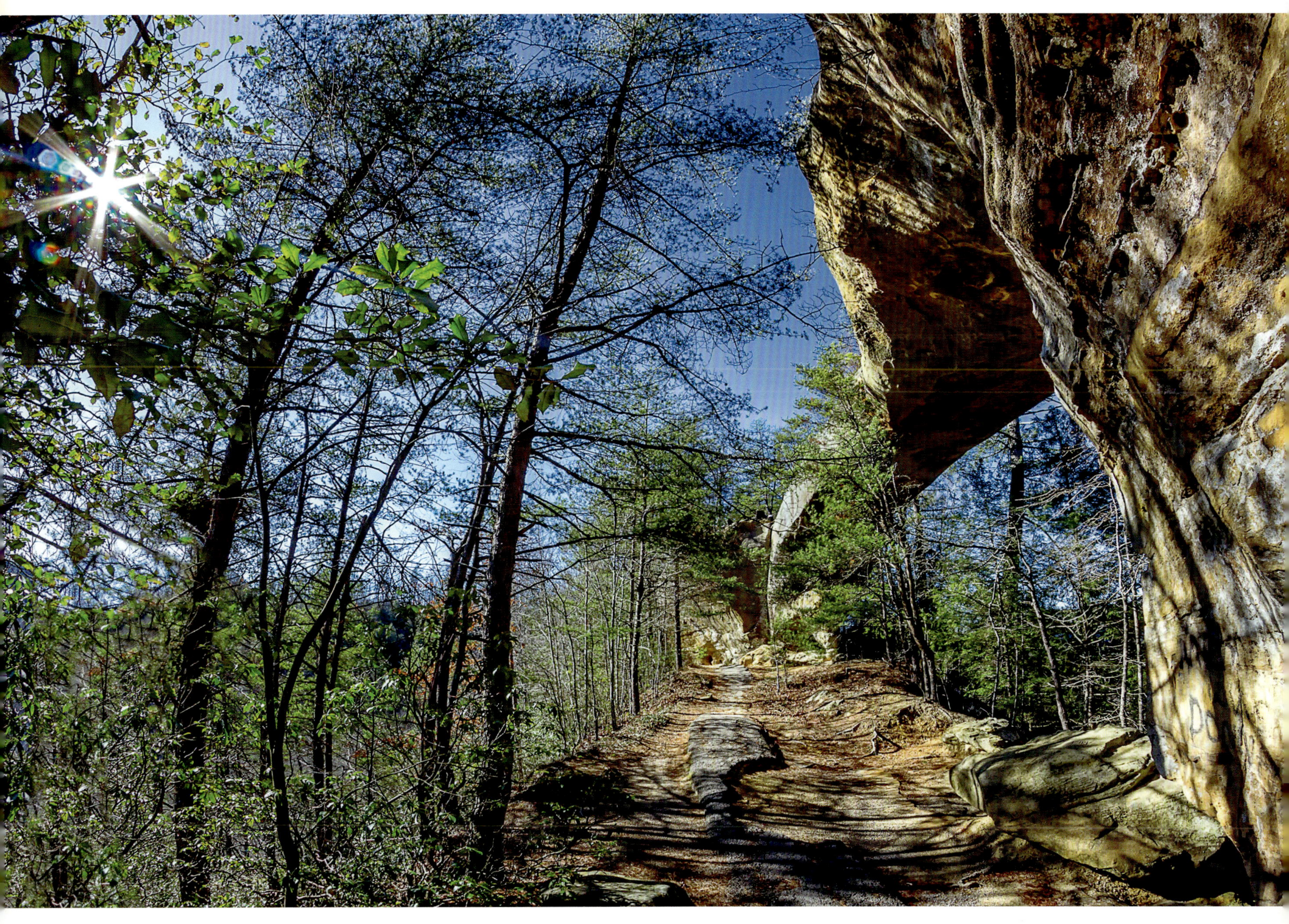

Sky Bridge stretches through the landscape at Red River Gorge.

FACING Autumn leaves catch the sunlight at Red River Gorge

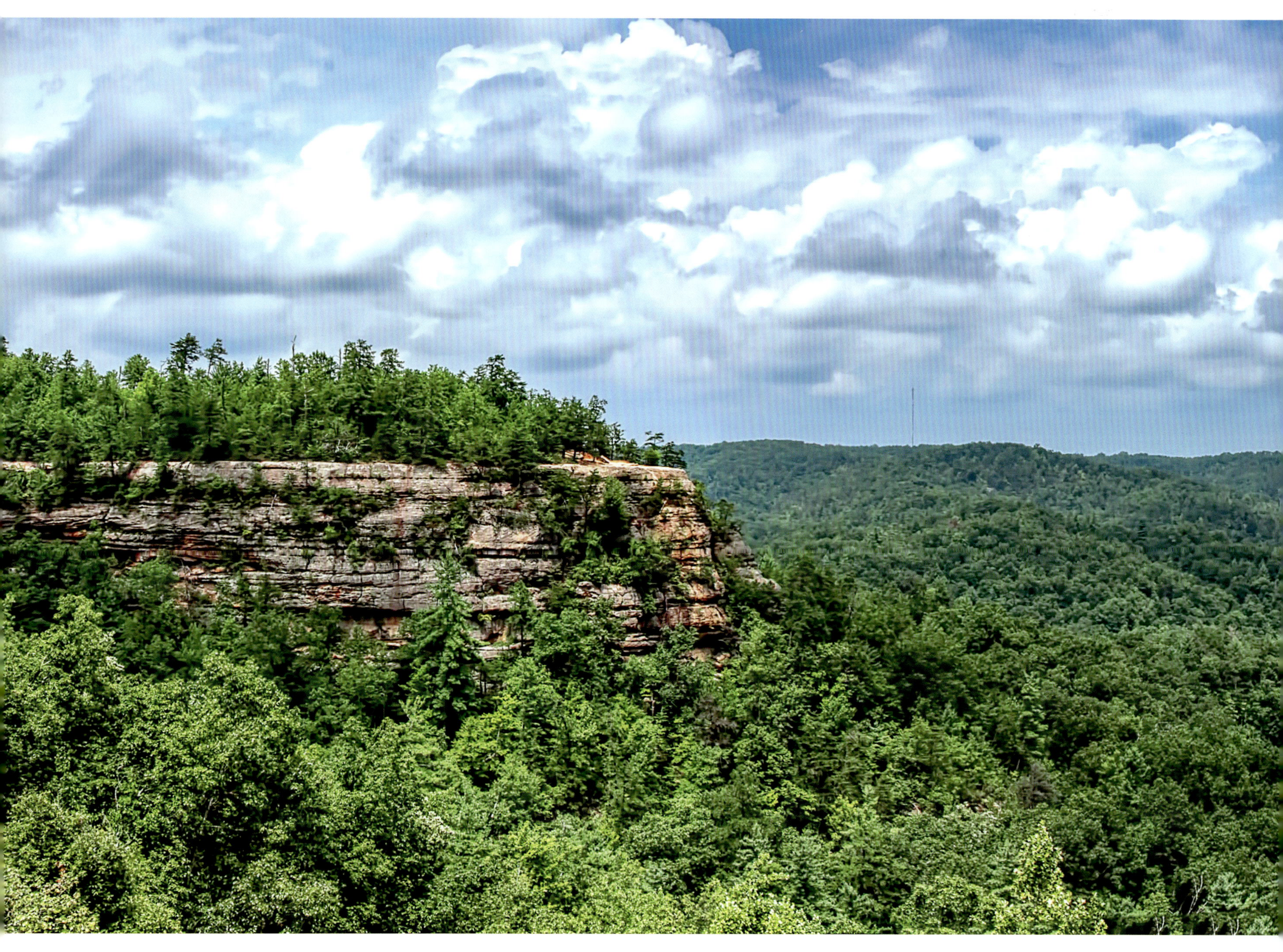

A view to remember from the top of Natural Bridge.

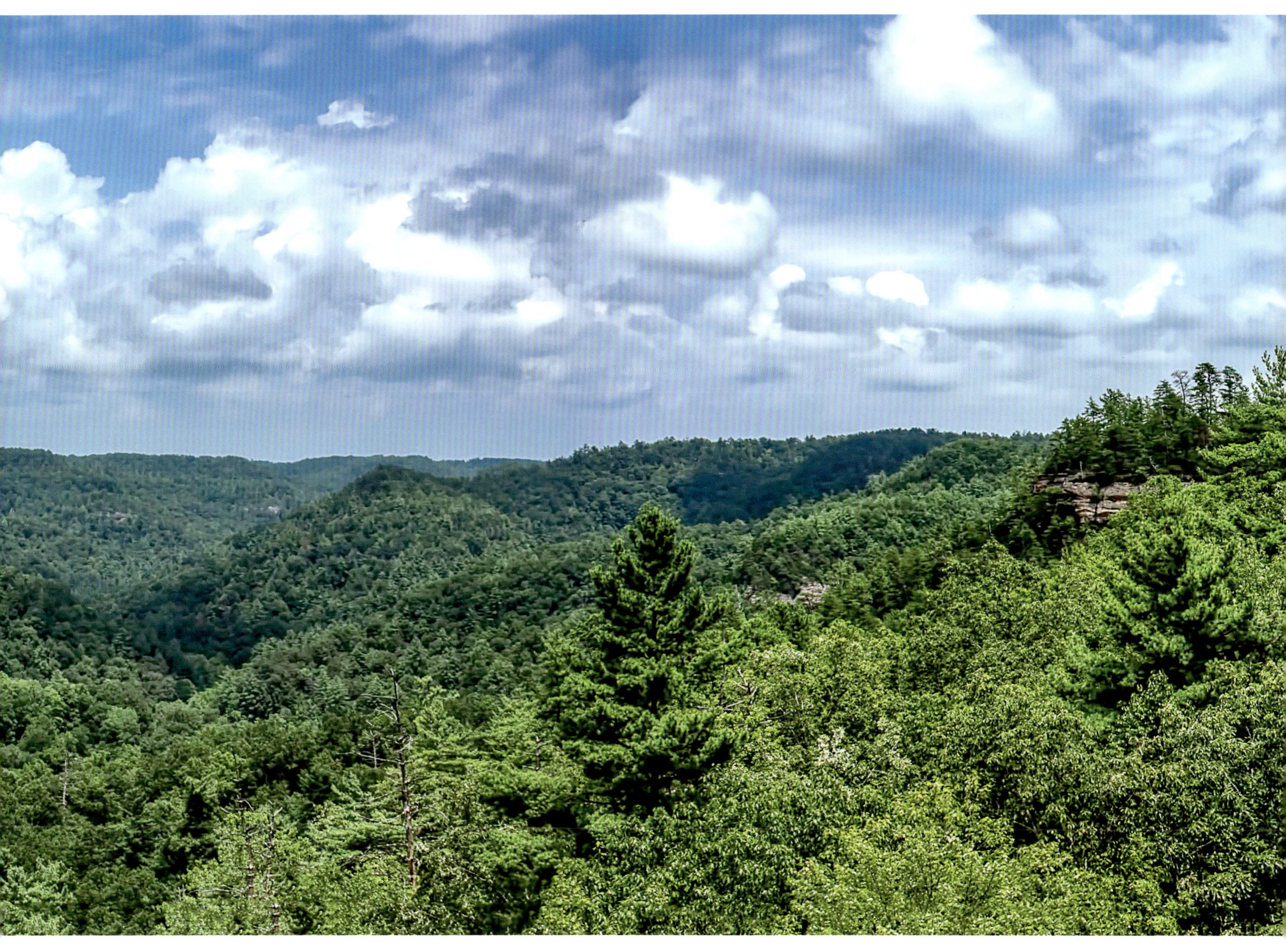

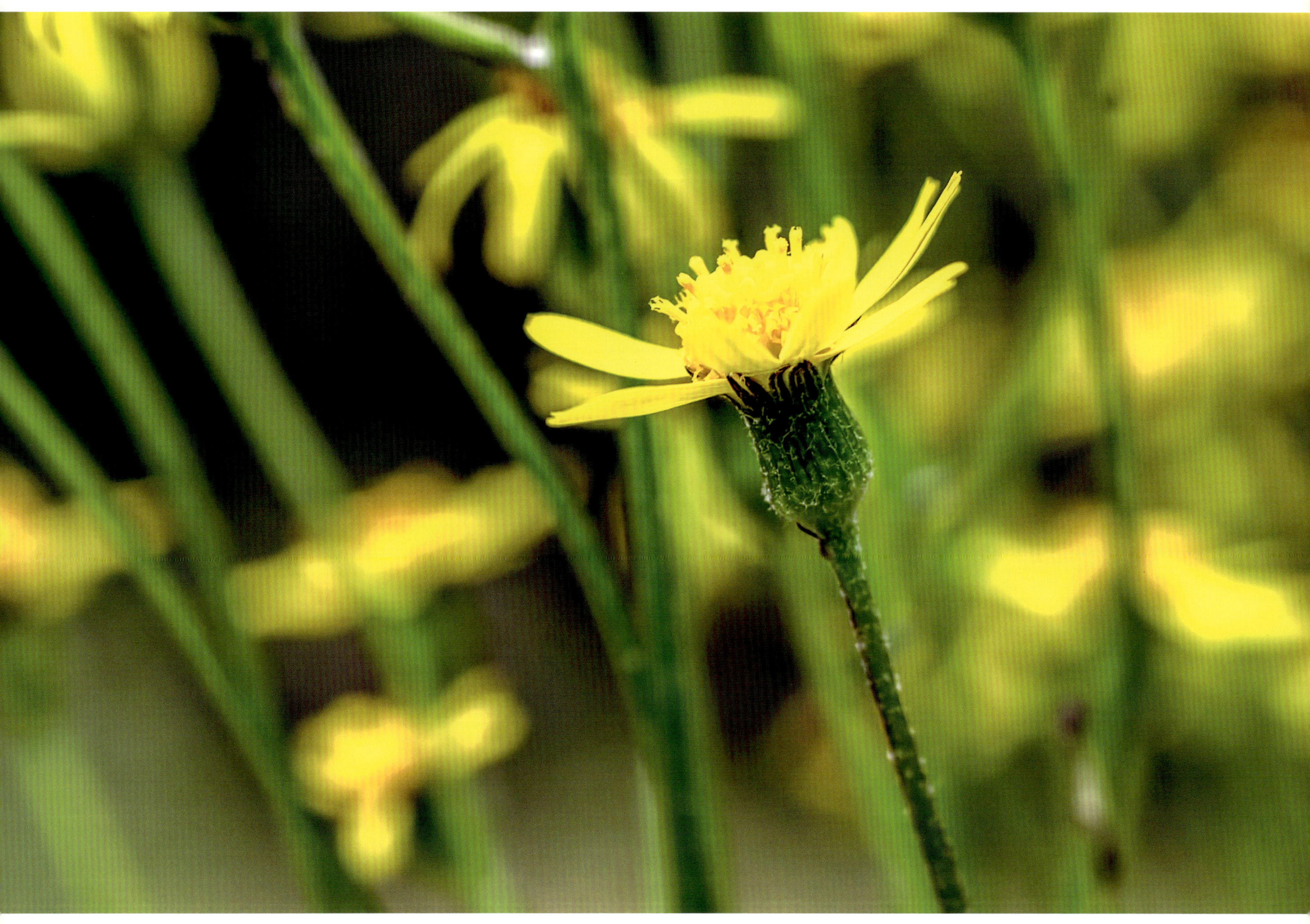

The sunny disposition of a ragwort calls to be photographed.

FACING A stop on one of Kentucky's quilt barn trails, close to the Gladie Cabin at Red River Gorge.

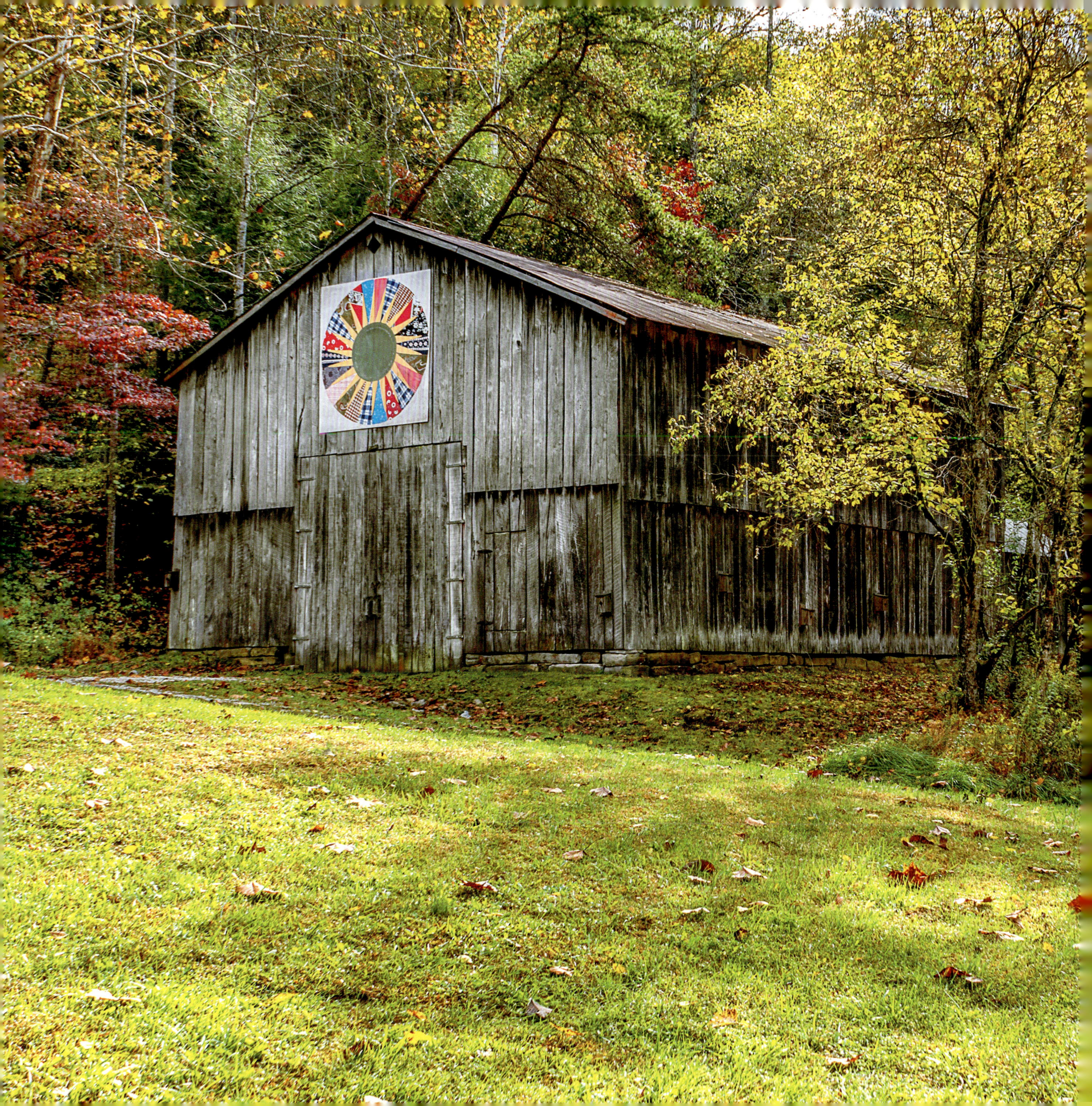

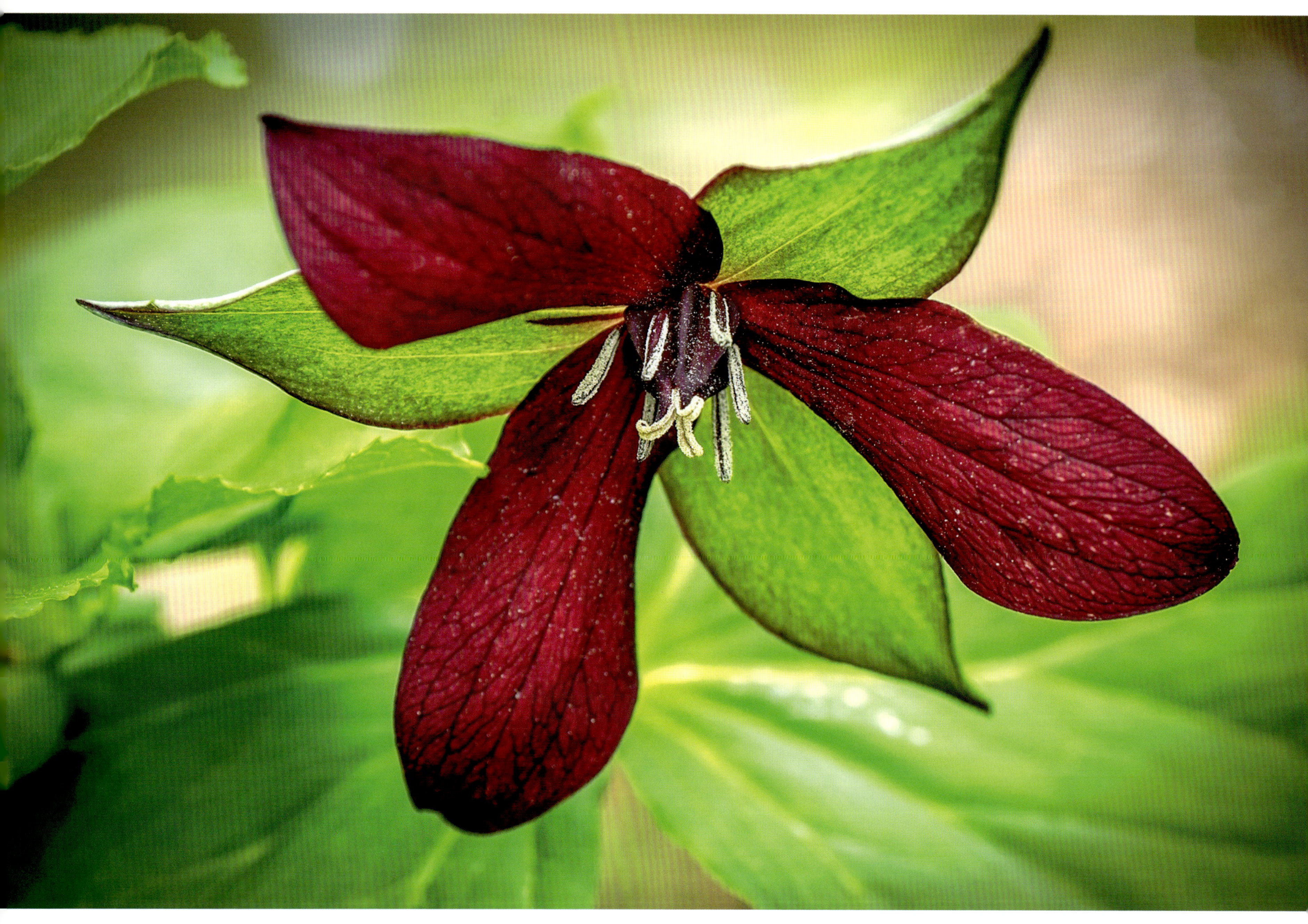

Red Trilliums are a wildflower treasure.

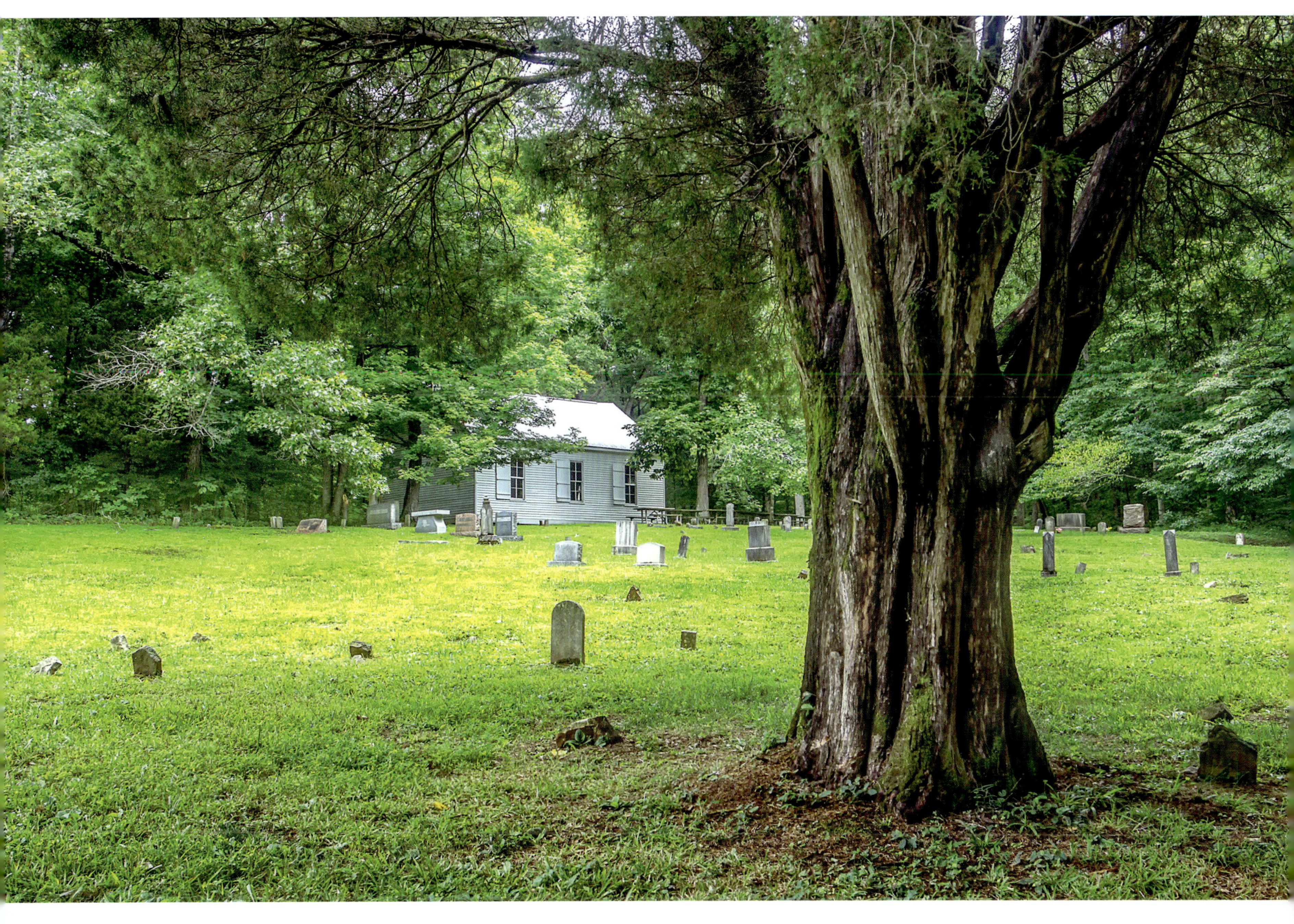

Mammoth Cave National Park Baptist Church and Cemetery offers a peaceful place to reflect.

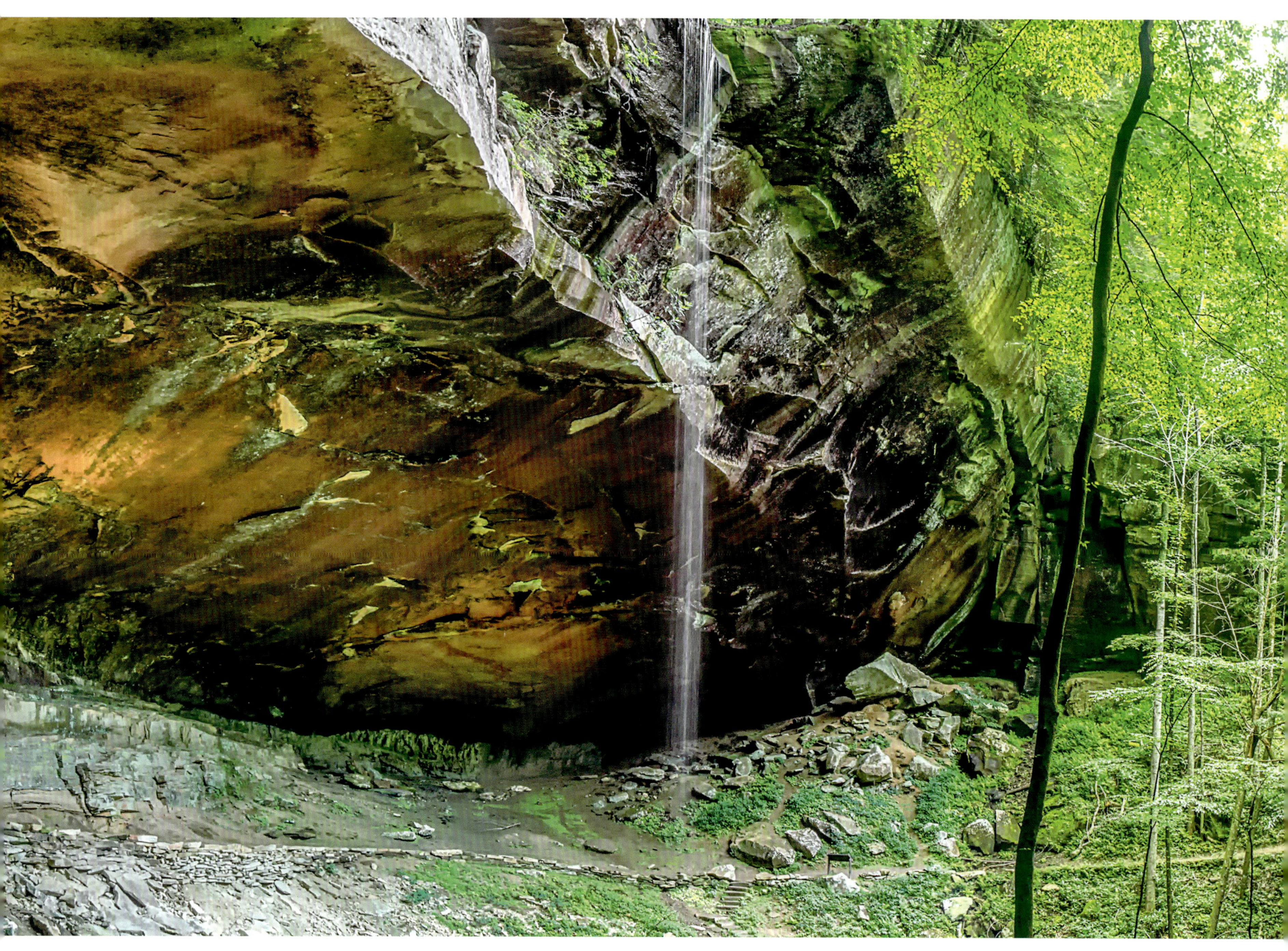

Yahoo Falls seems as tall as the trees.

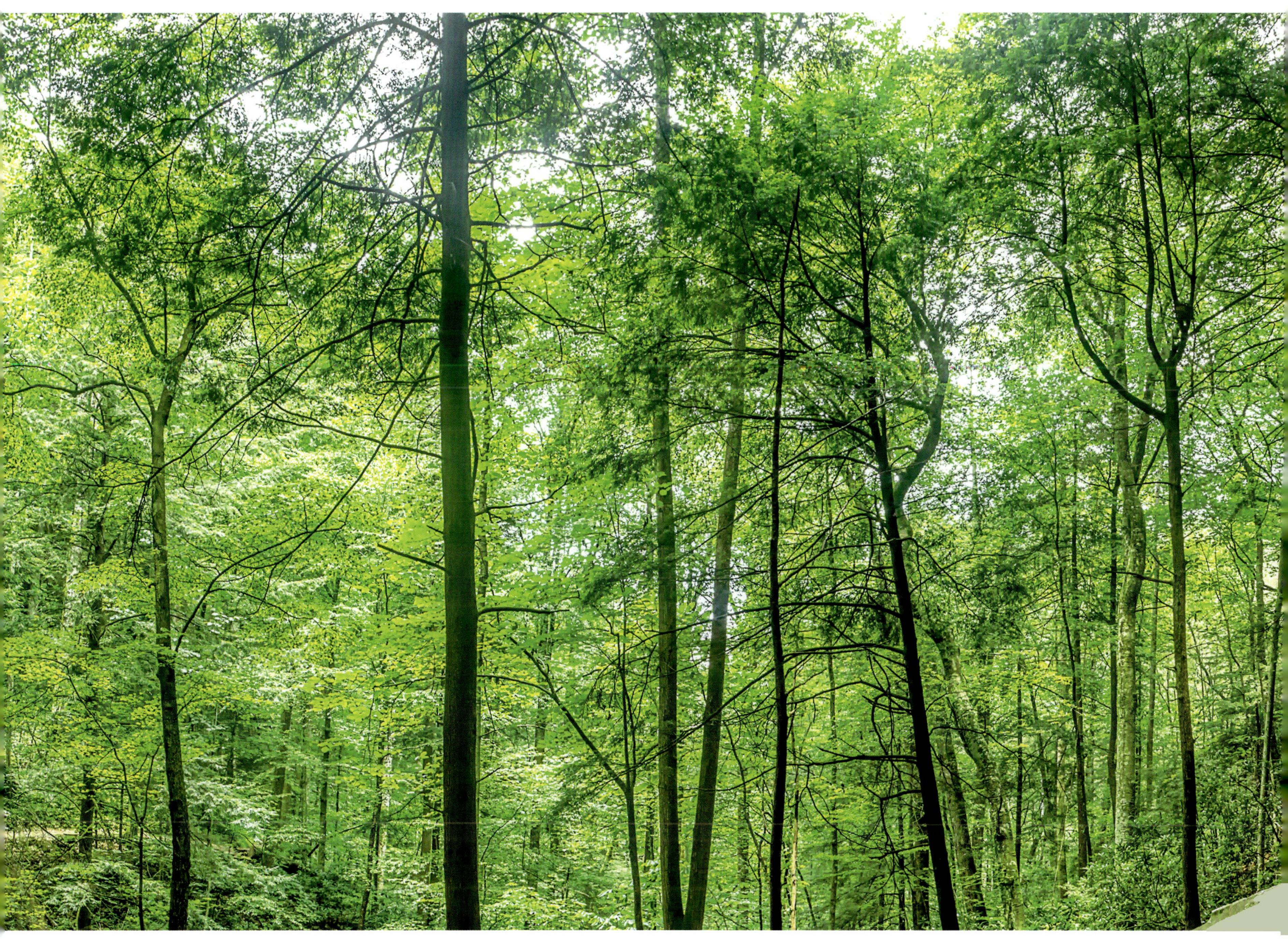

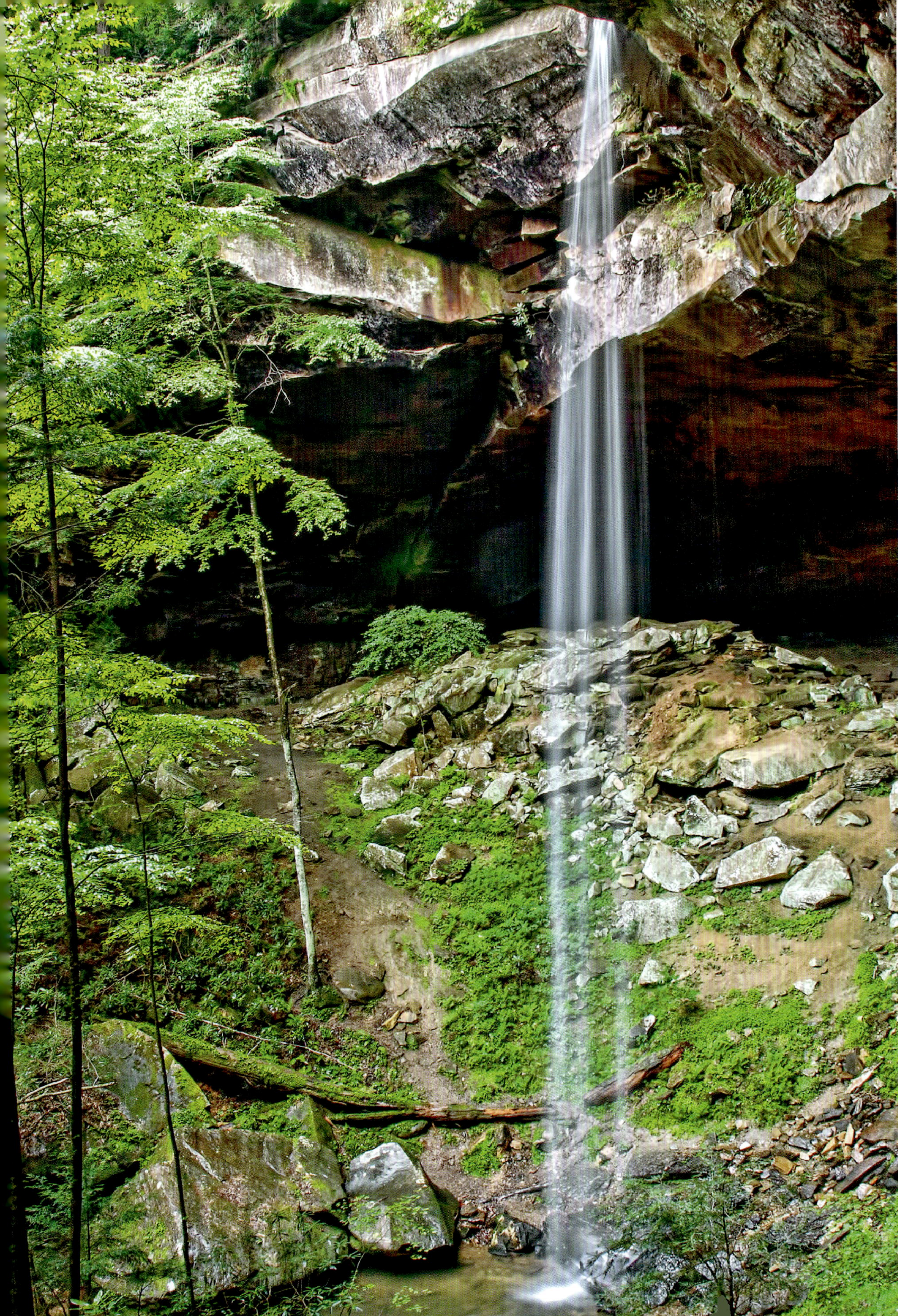

Yahoo Falls drops 113 feet into a clear forest stream.

FACING

Visitors commonly see a variety of wildlife at the Elk and Bison Prairie at Land Between the Lakes National Recreation Area.

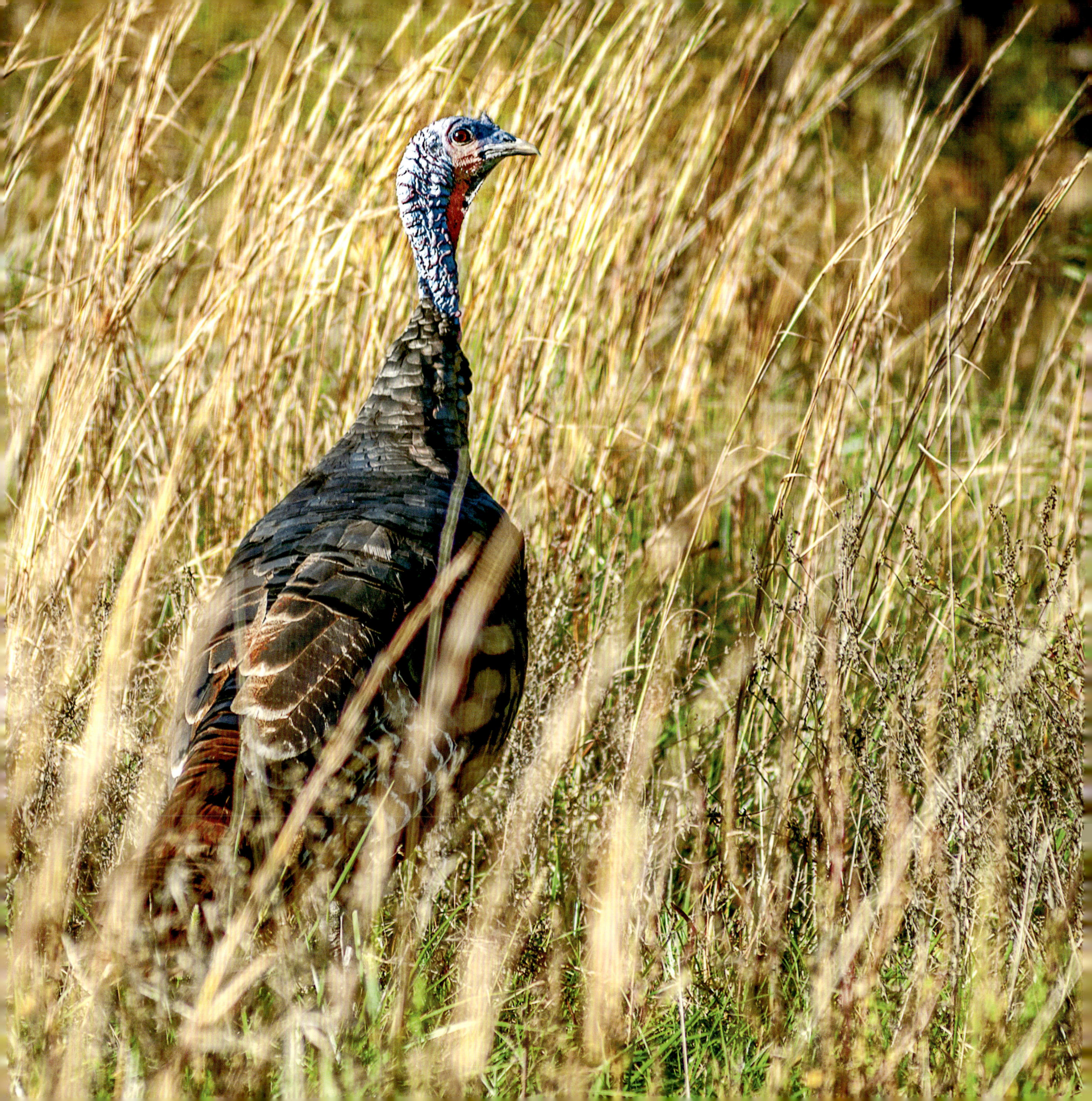

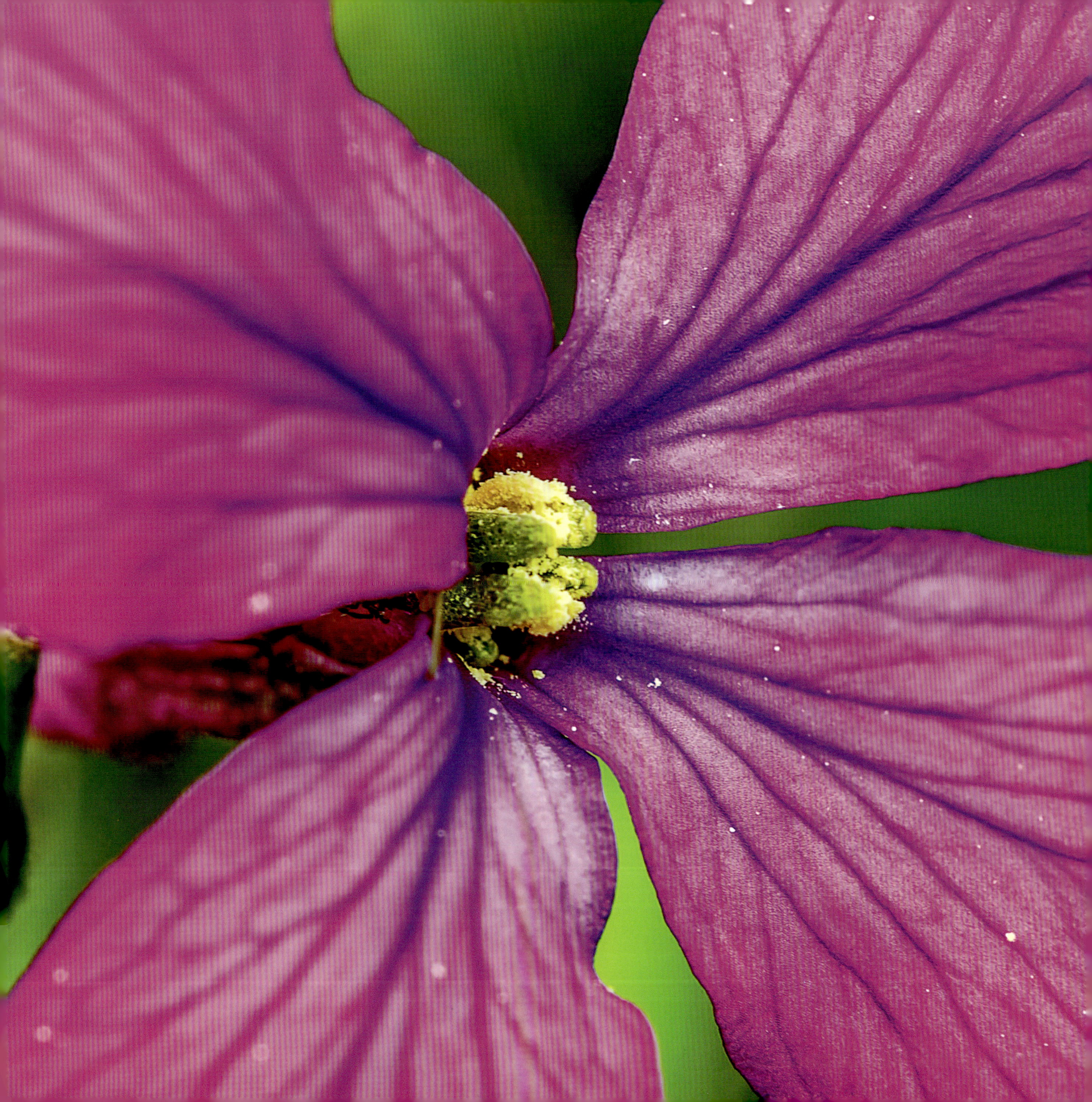

The peaceful gardens at Buffalo Trace Distillery are beautiful all year around.

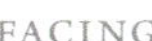

FACING

Wildflowers like this pink money plant add spring color all over Kentucky.

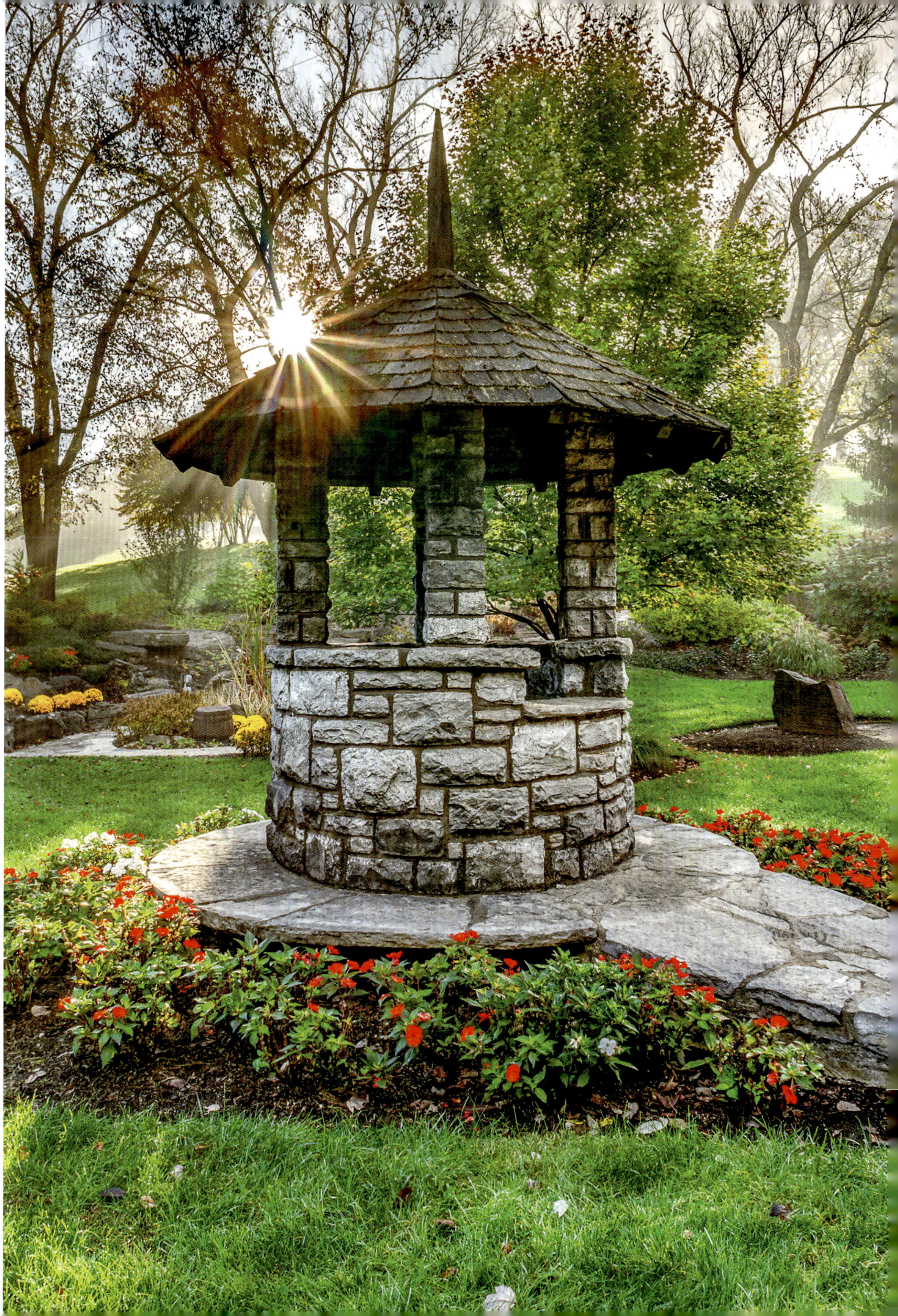

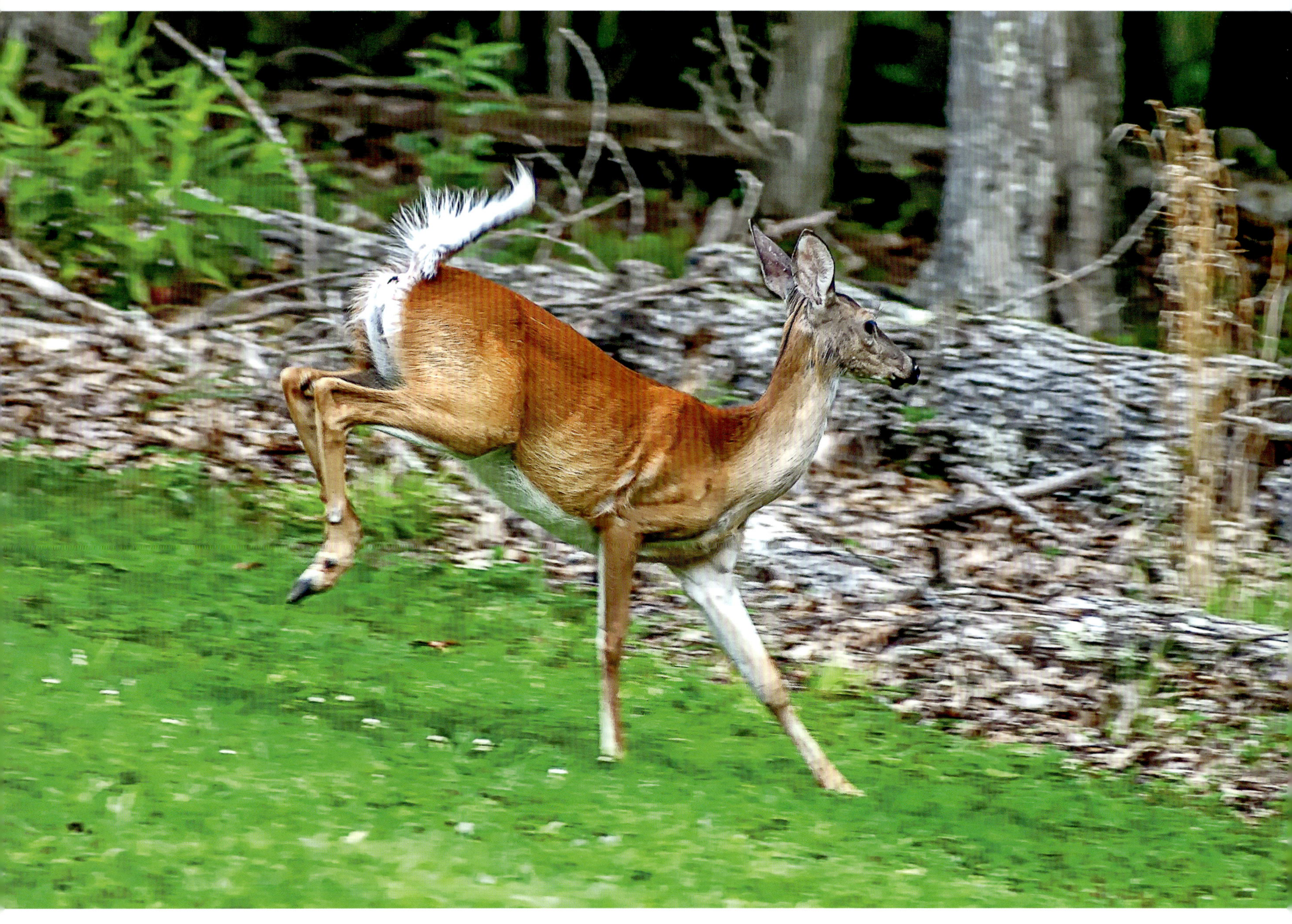

Deer and other wildlife can be seen throughout the parks and wooded landscapes.

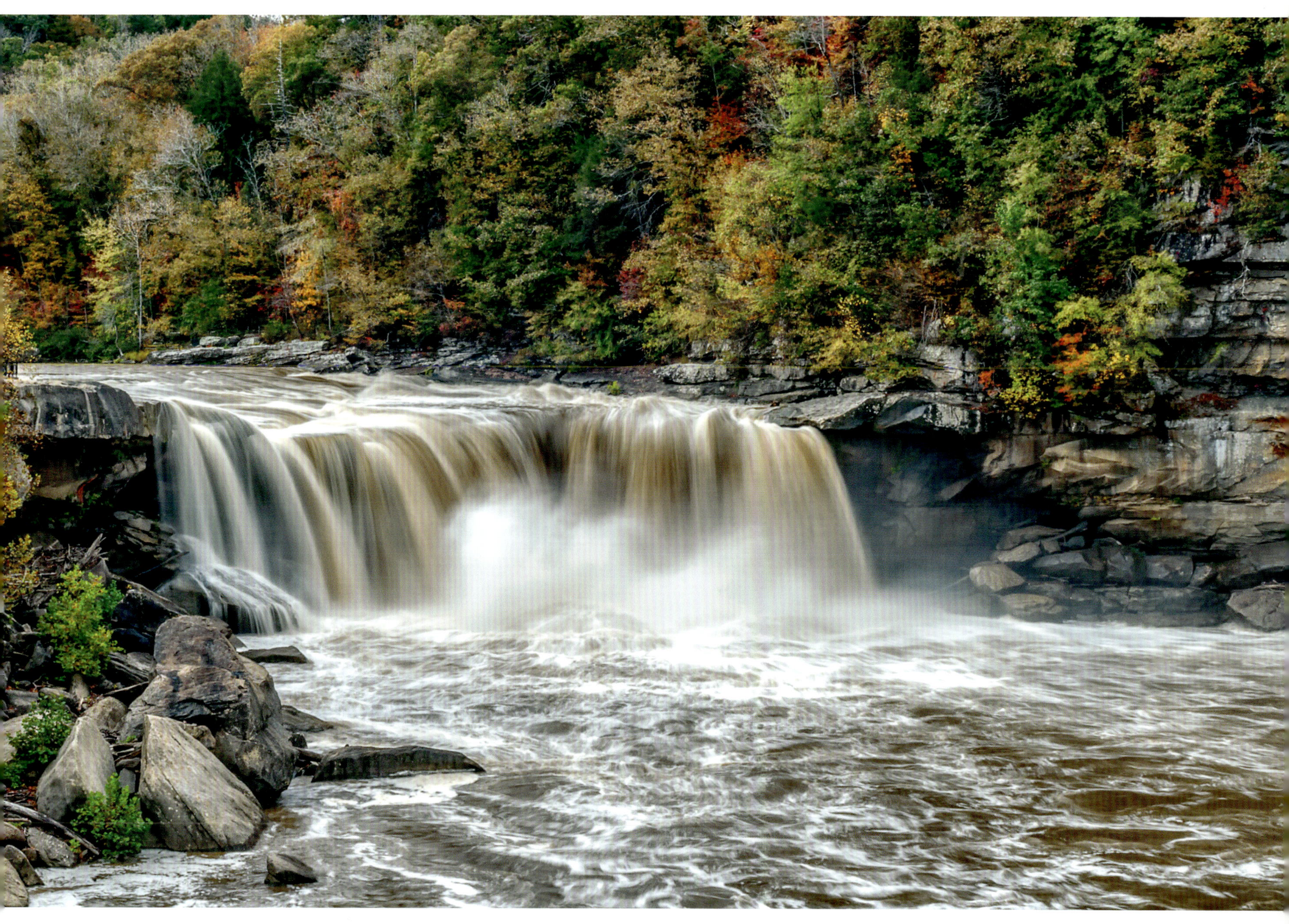

The rushing waters of Cumberland Falls draw more than seven hundred thousand visitors a year. The Falls is one of the few places in the world where a moonbow can be seen when conditions are right.

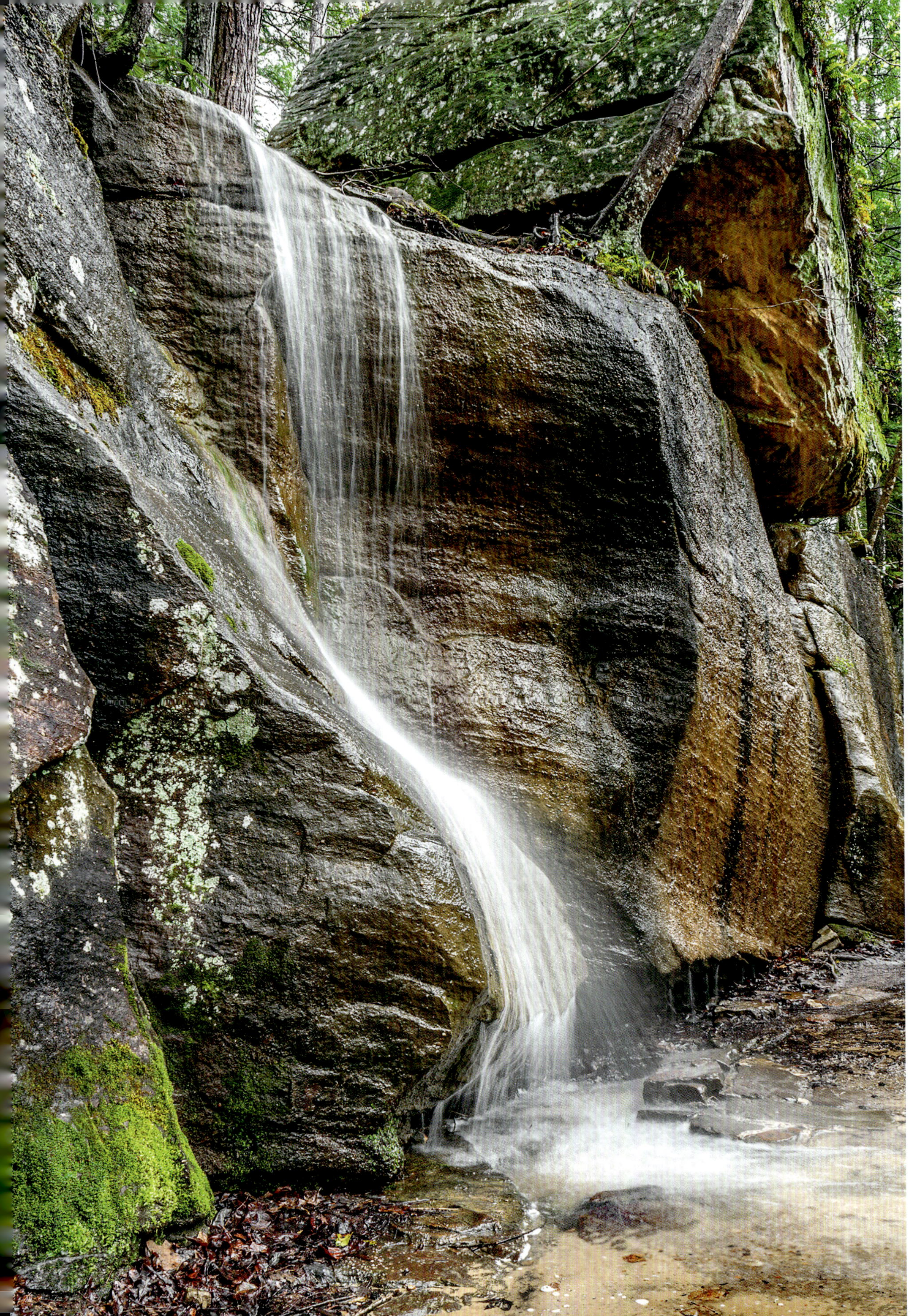

Water is overflowing and creating new waterfalls throughout the park with the spring rains.

FACING
Bright fire pinks add pops of color along the trails and on the hillsides.

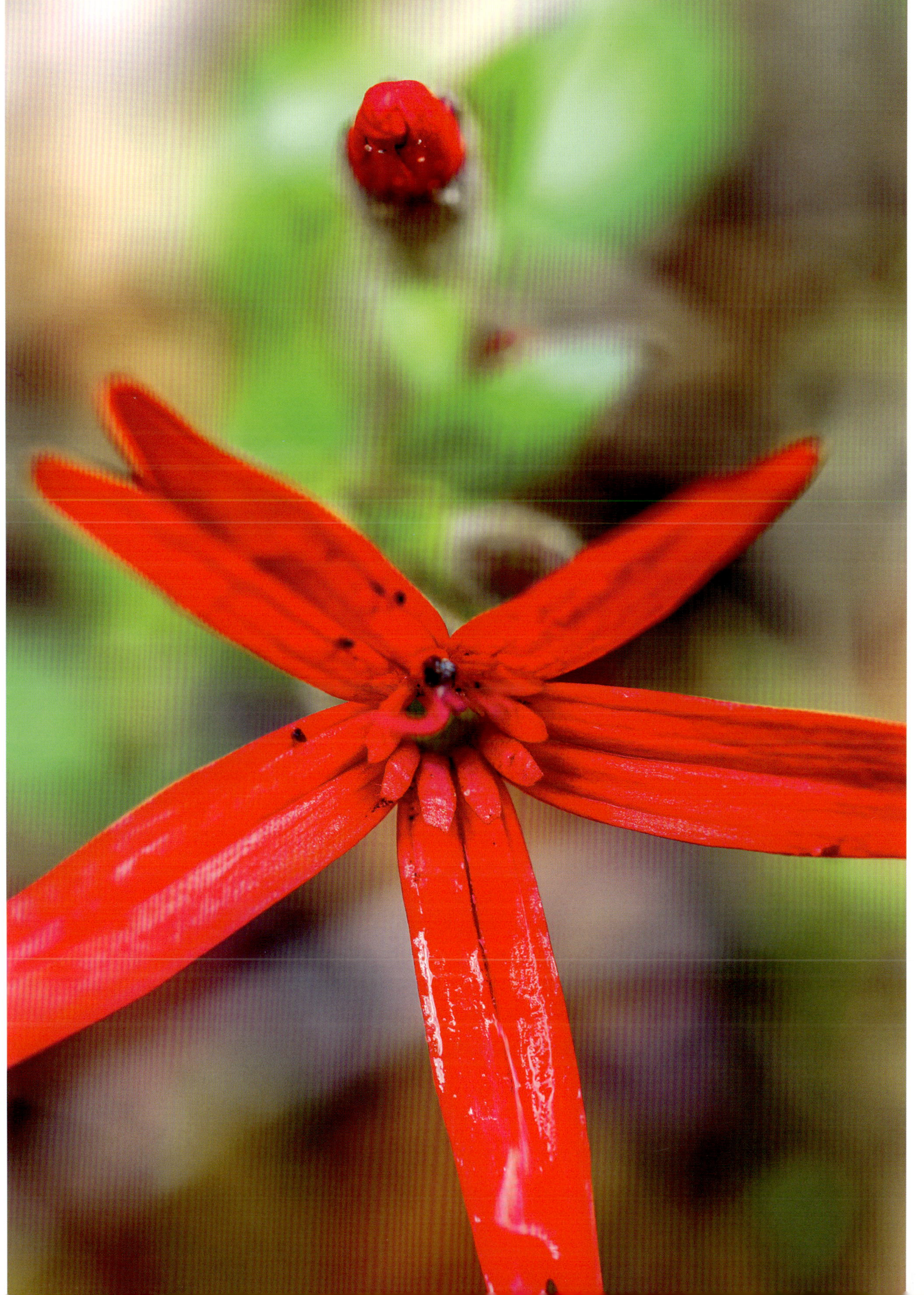

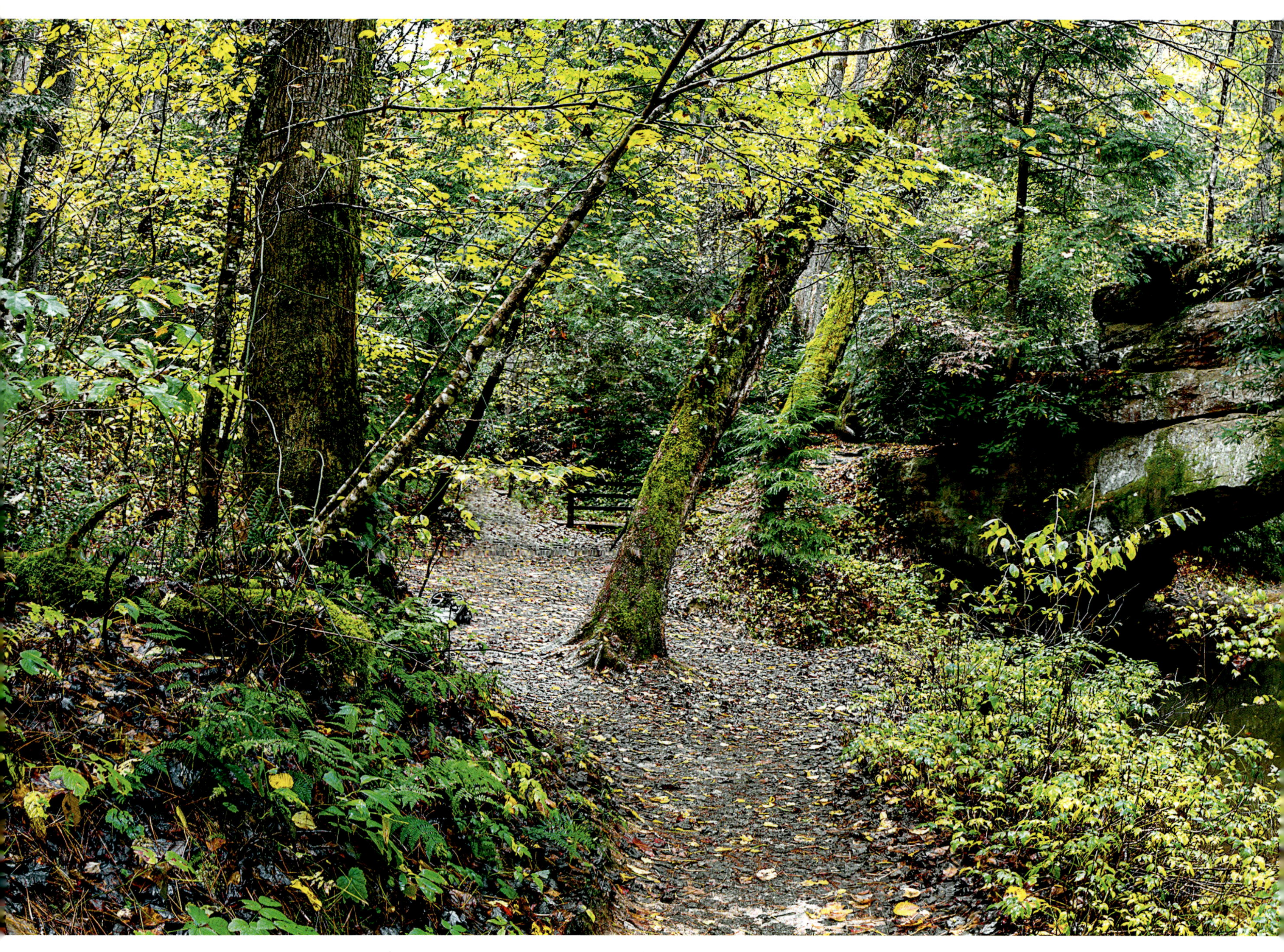

Rock Bridge is just one reason to visit Red River Gorge.

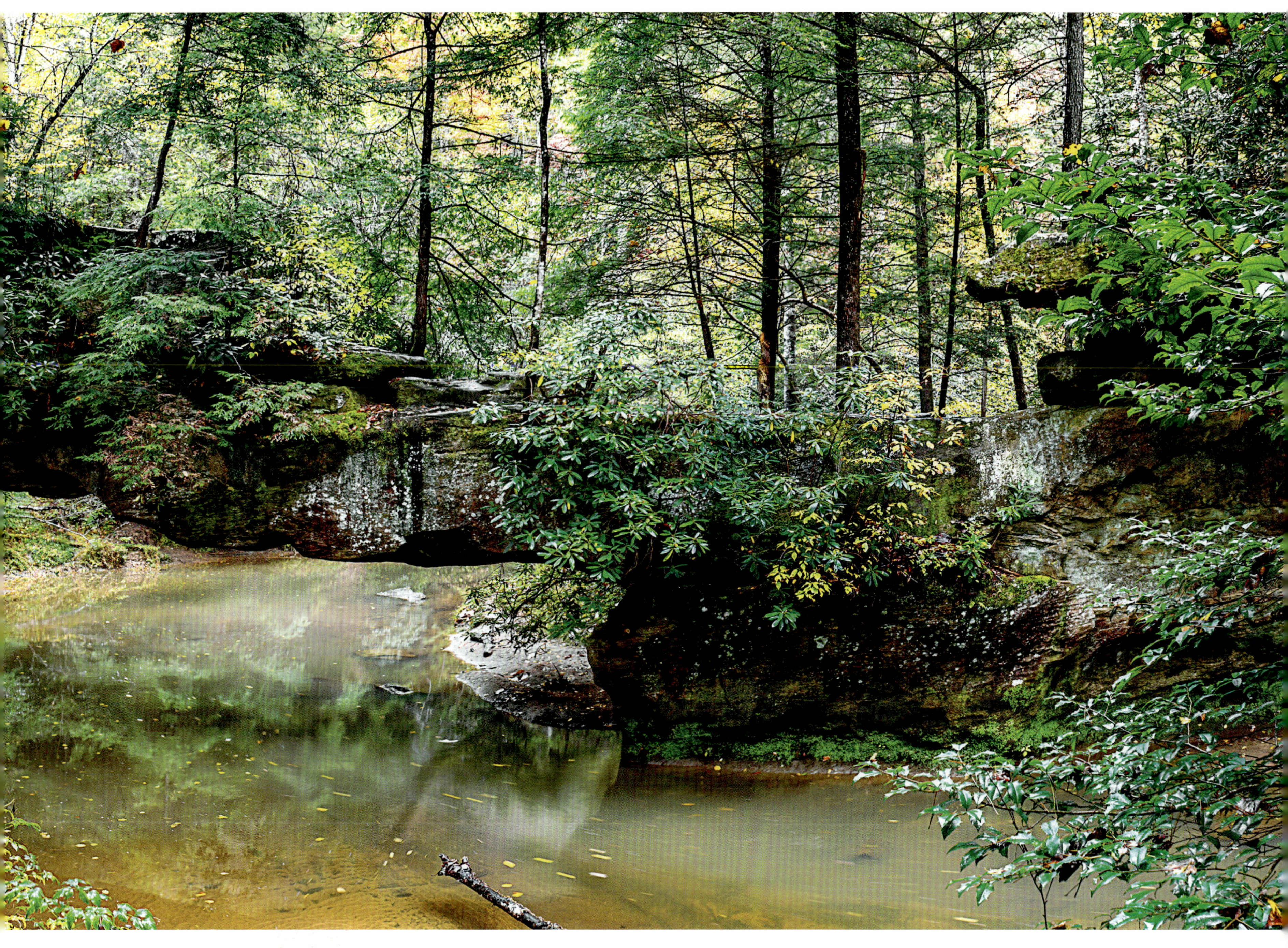

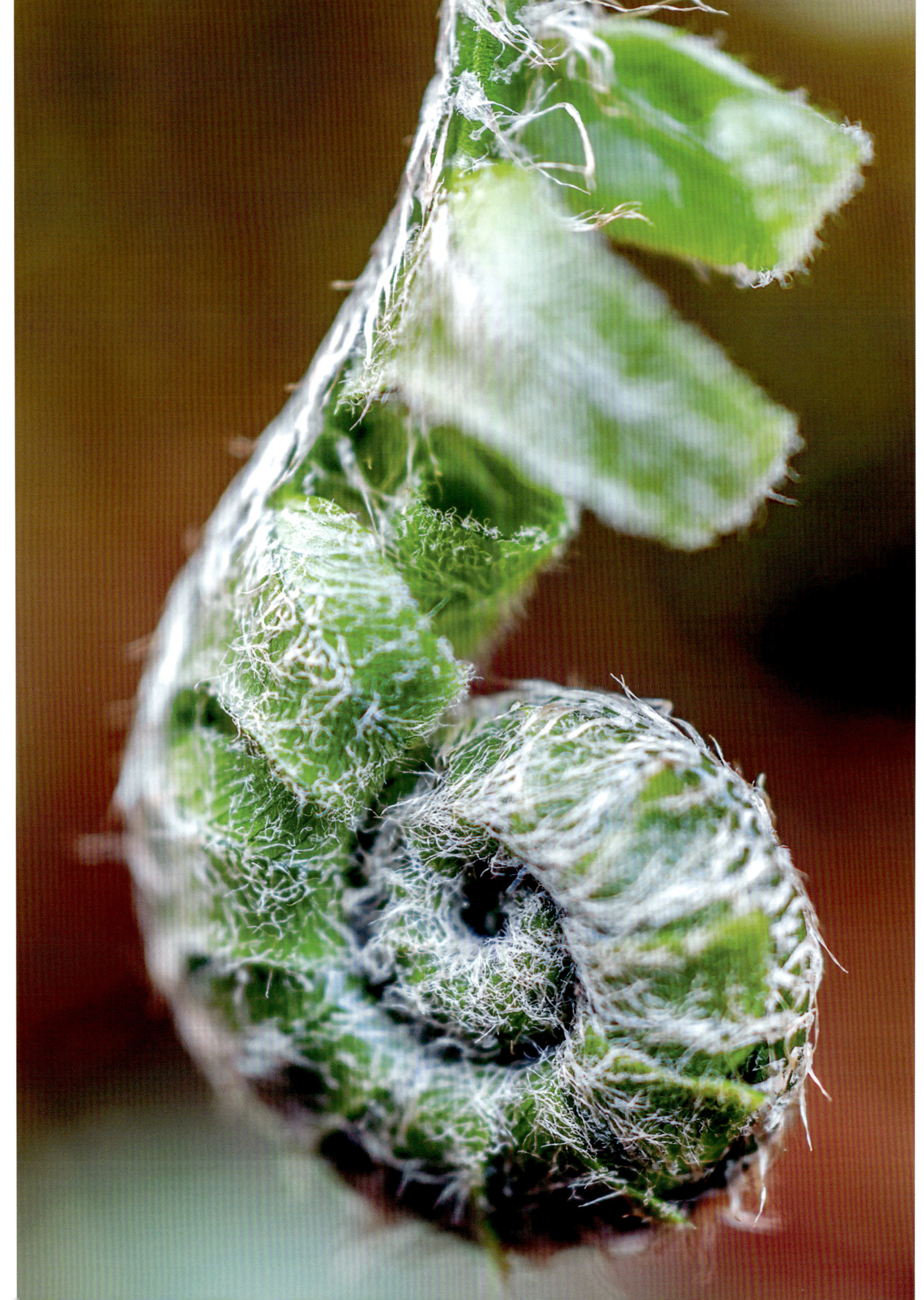

Interesting rock formations are forms of art at Cumberland Gap National Historical Park.

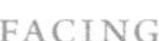

FACING

Along with wildflowers, spring brings fiddlehead ferns unrolling their fronds in the sunlight.

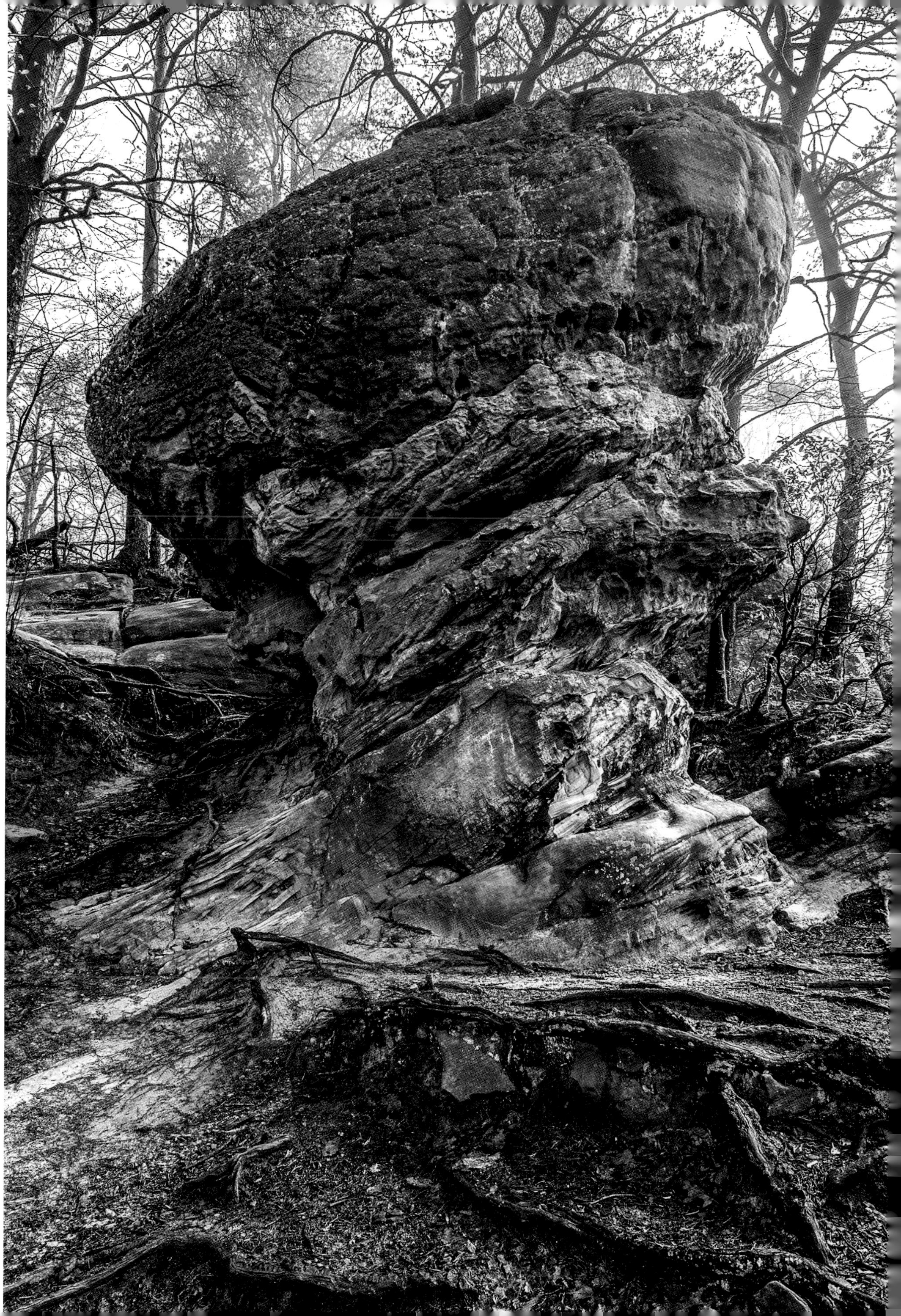

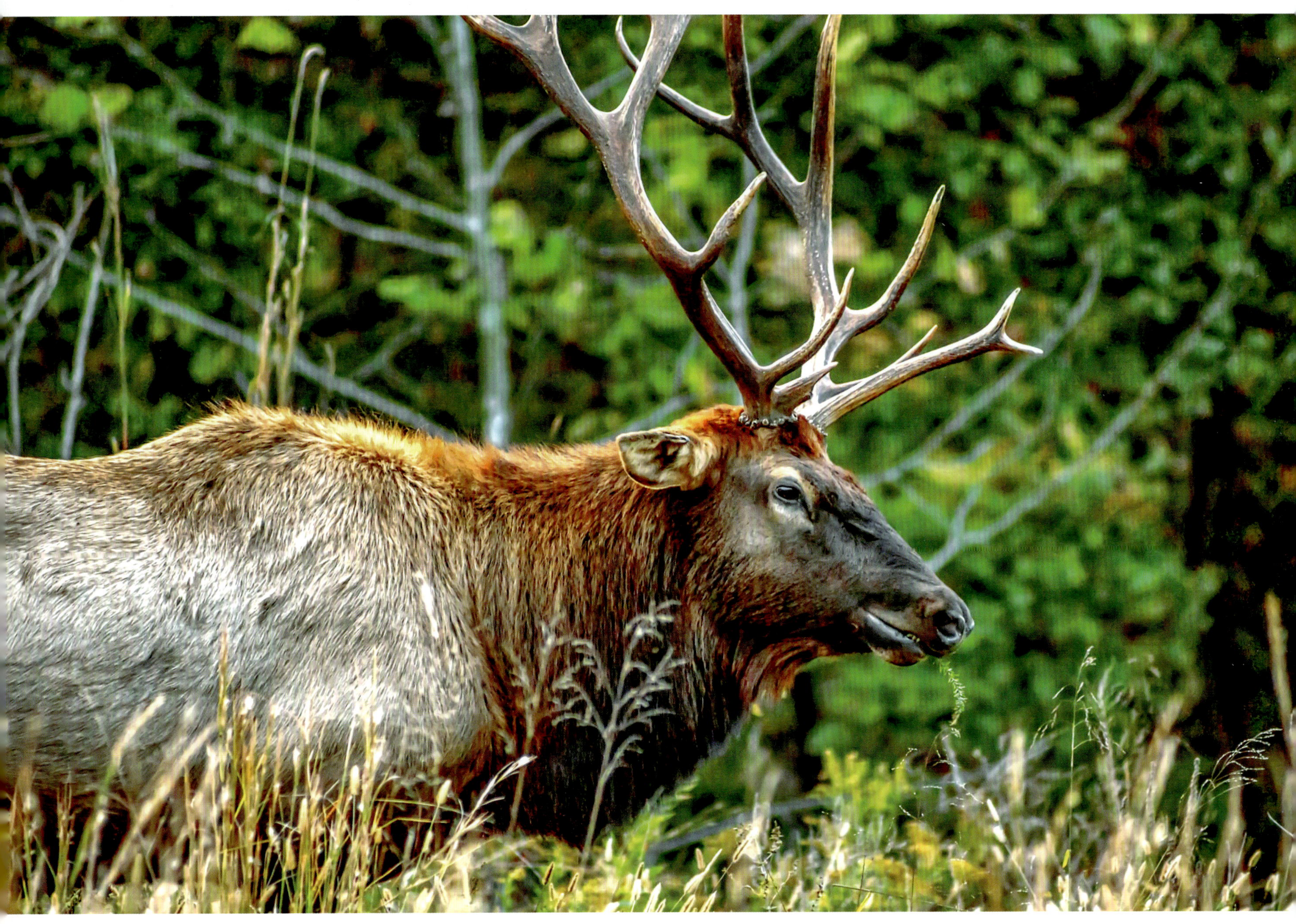

The Elk and Bison Prairie allows visitors to have a close look at the majestic elk.

The Elk and
Bison Prairie
provides a safe
and natural refuge
for the animals.

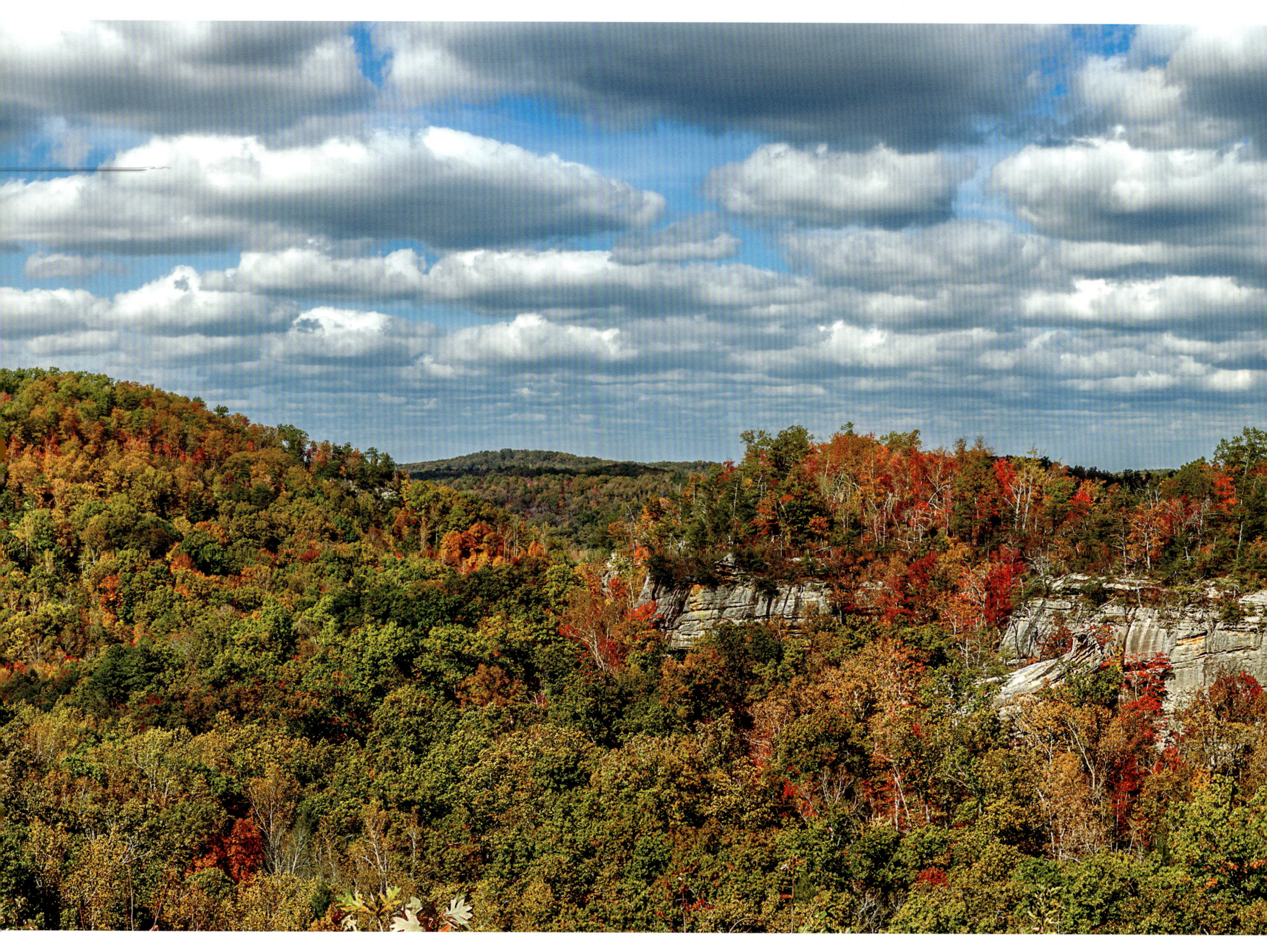

Spanning nearly 100 feet, Natural Arch is a popular site to see in the Daniel Boone National Forest.

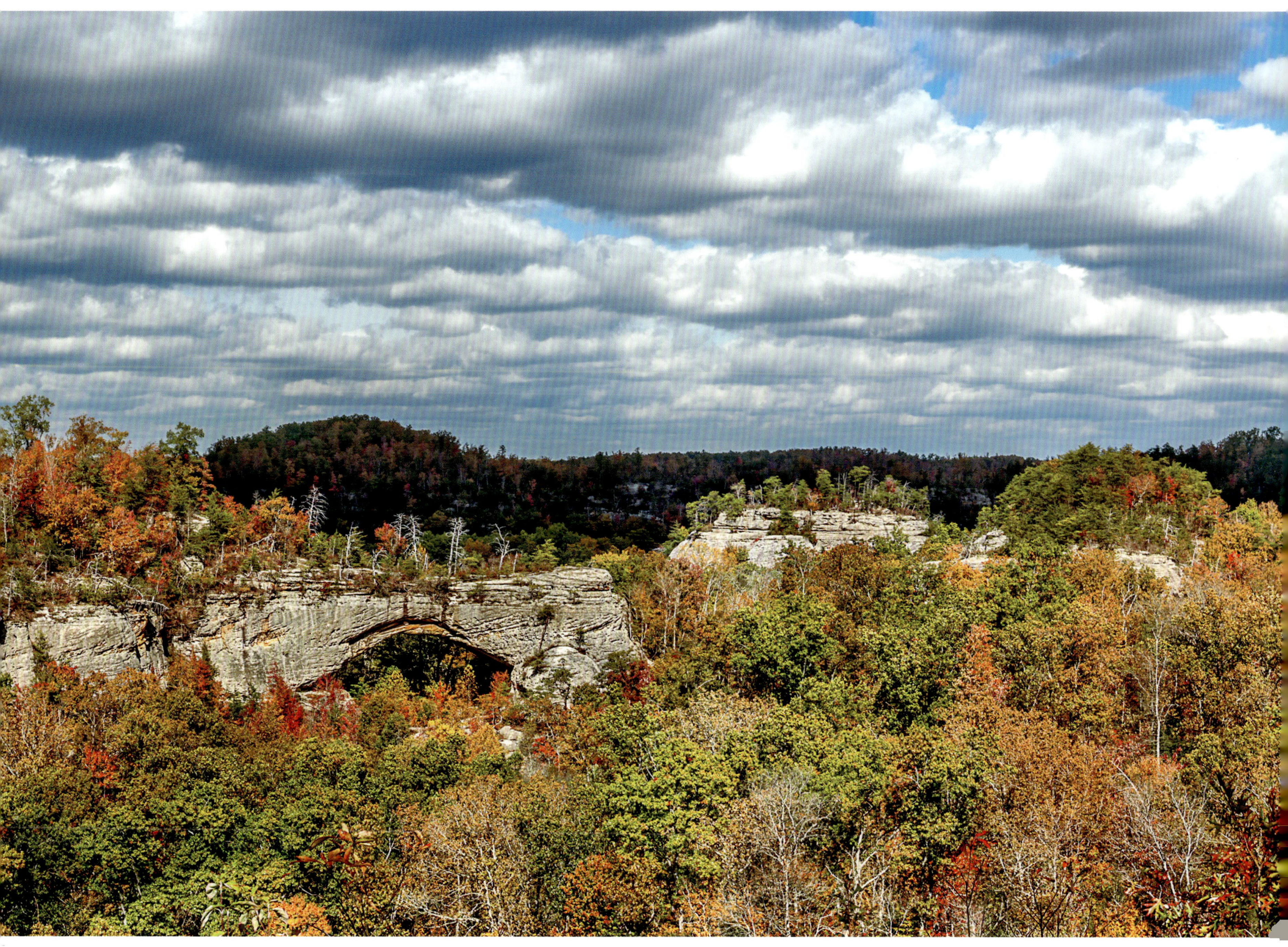

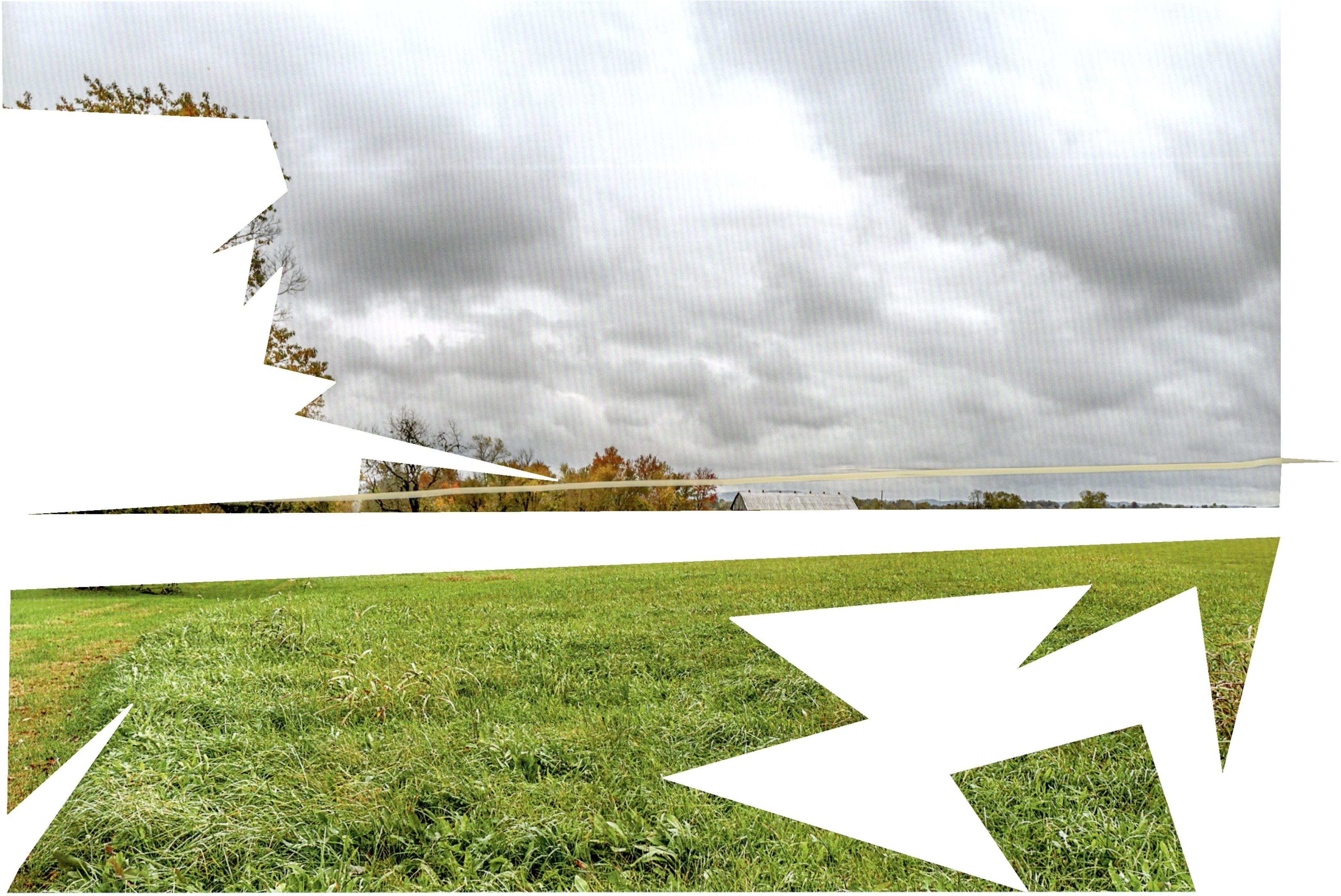

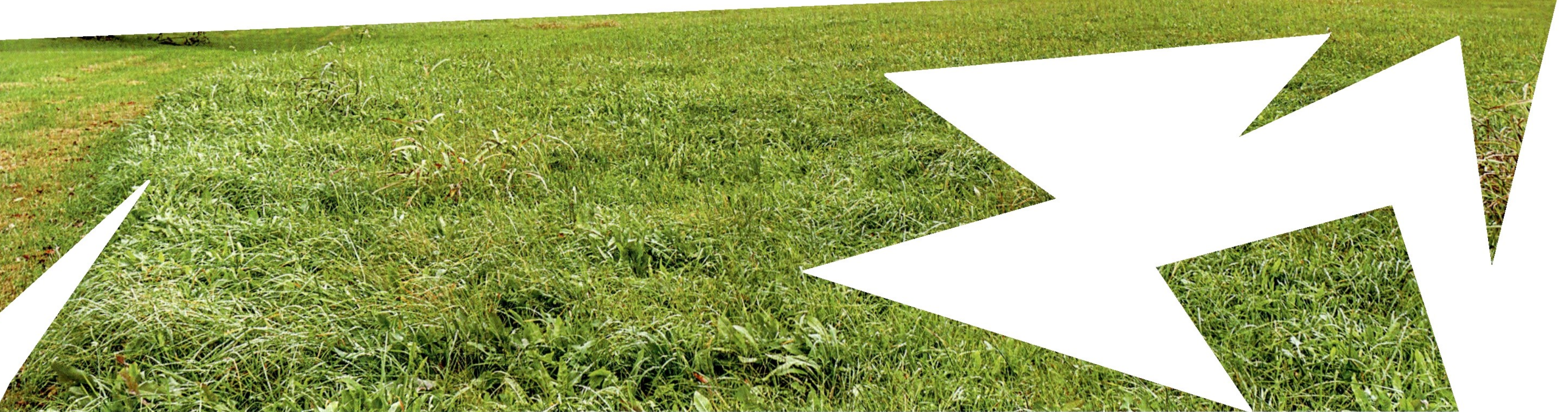

Civil War history comes alive at Perryville Battlefield State Historic Park.

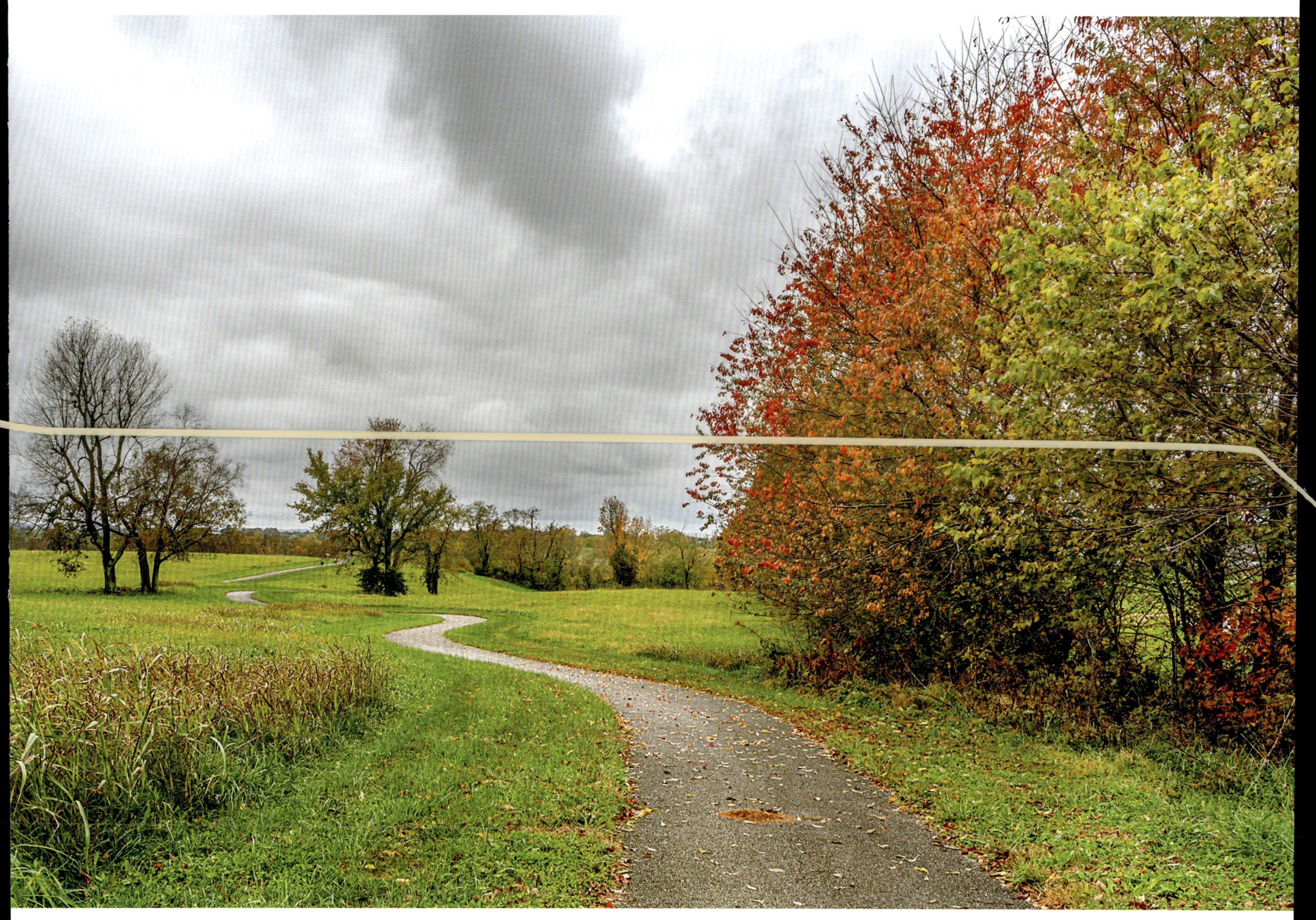

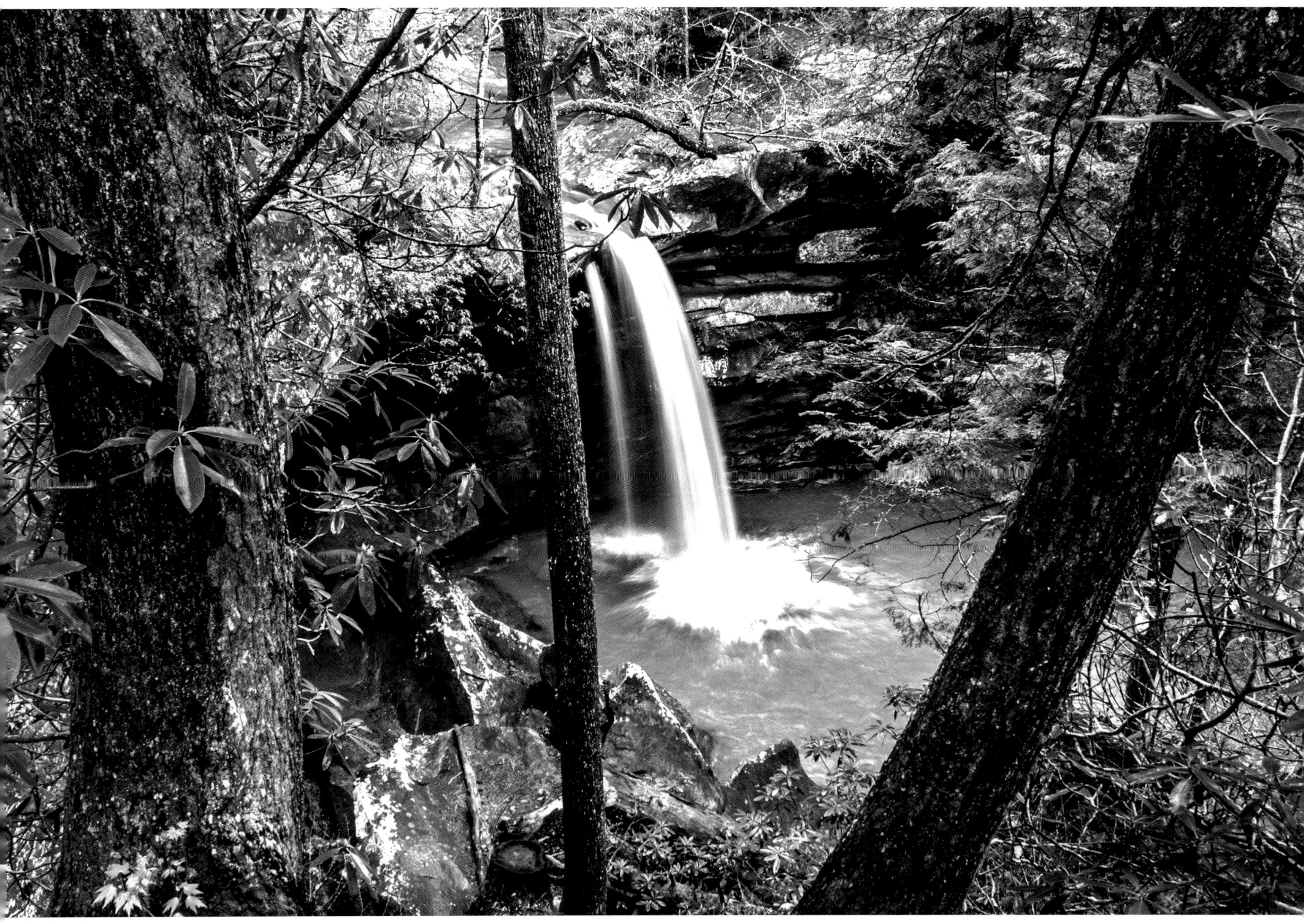

Glowing traces left by Kentucky travelers under a sunset sky.

FACING

Pack a picnic and spend the day at Flat Lick Falls.

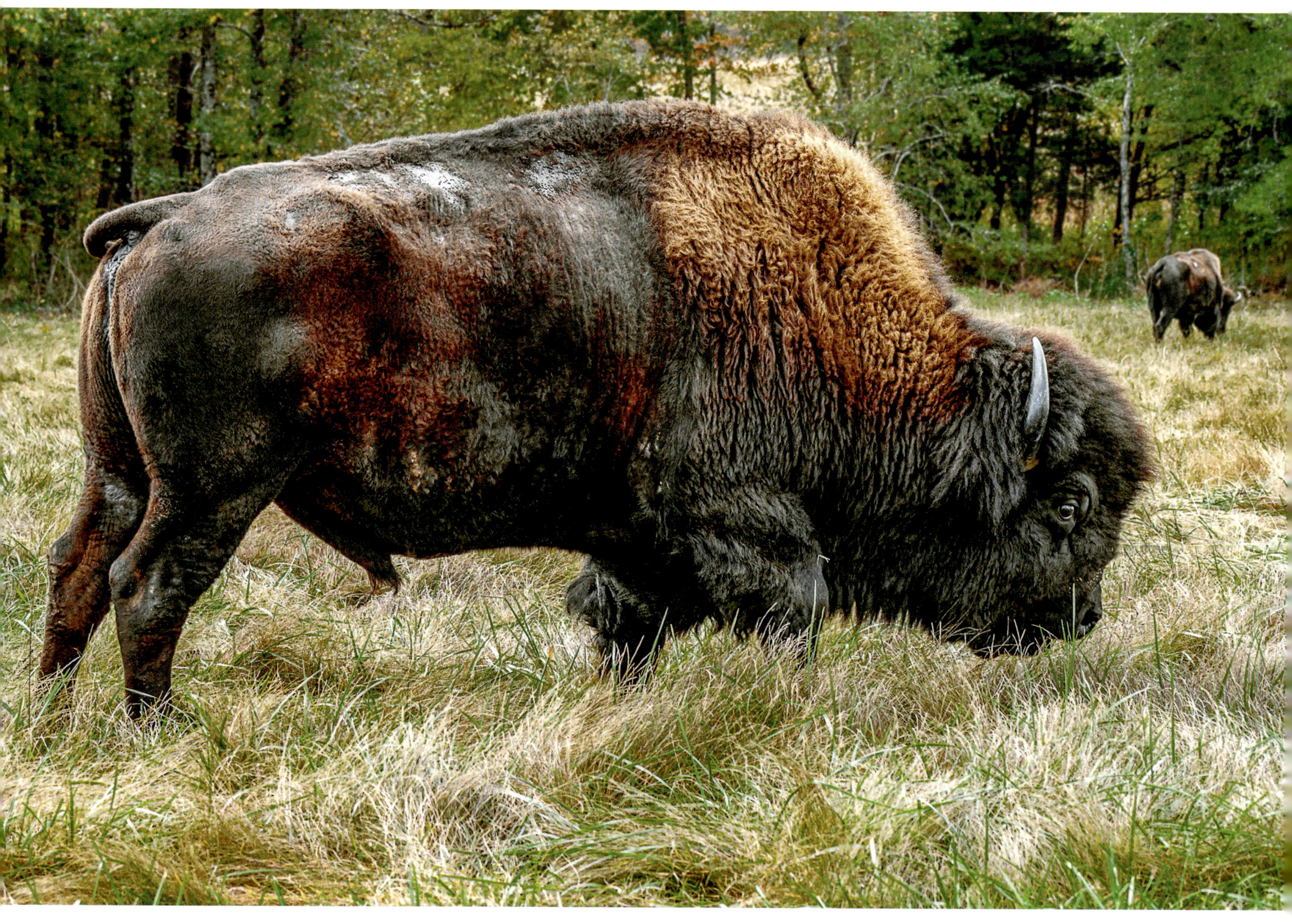

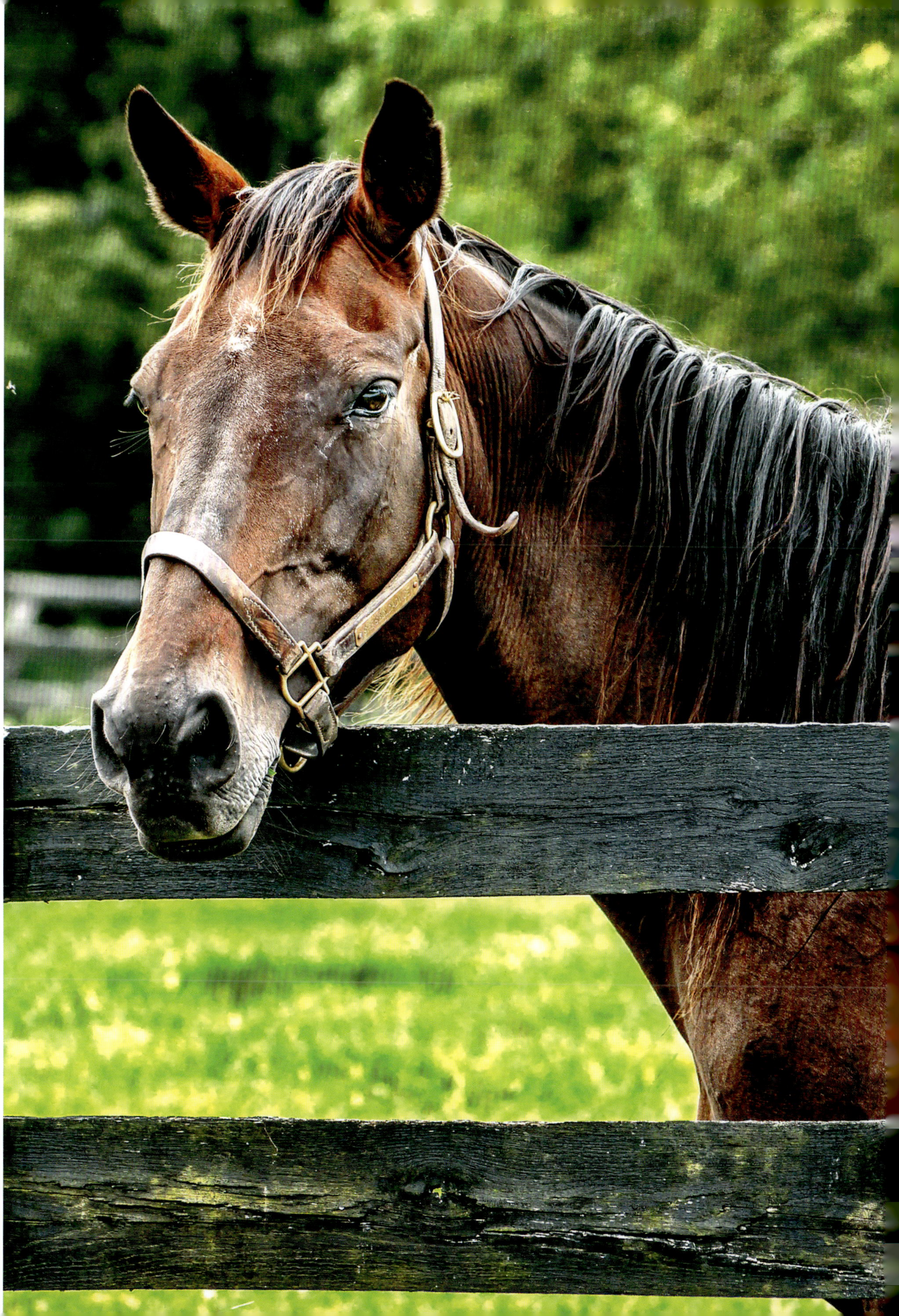

There is no shortage of horses around Lexington and the Kentucky Horse Park.

FACING

The largest bison of the herd seems to be respected by the rest at the Elk and Bison Prairie.

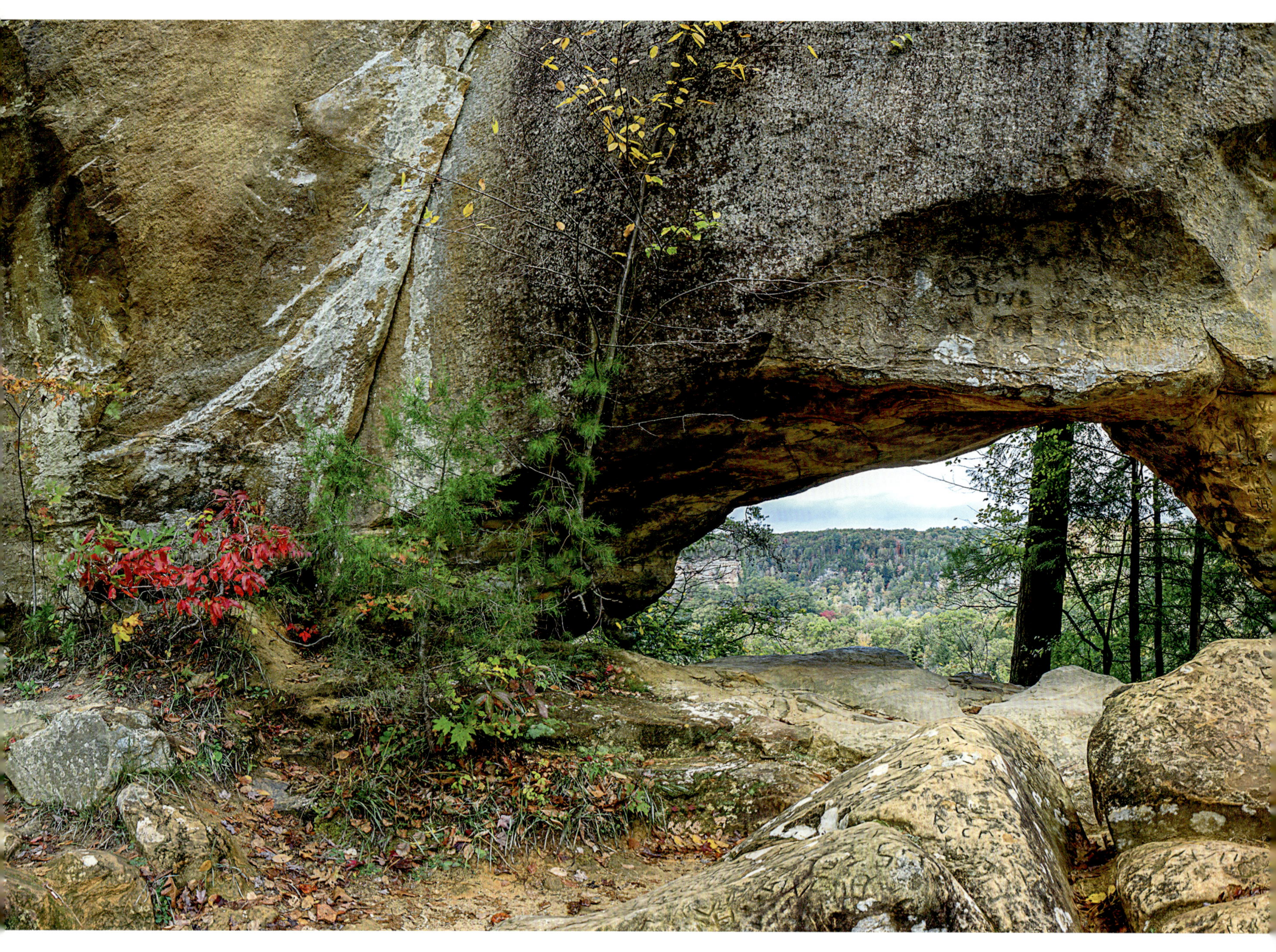

Sky Bridge invites visitors to explore the Red River Gorge from every angle.

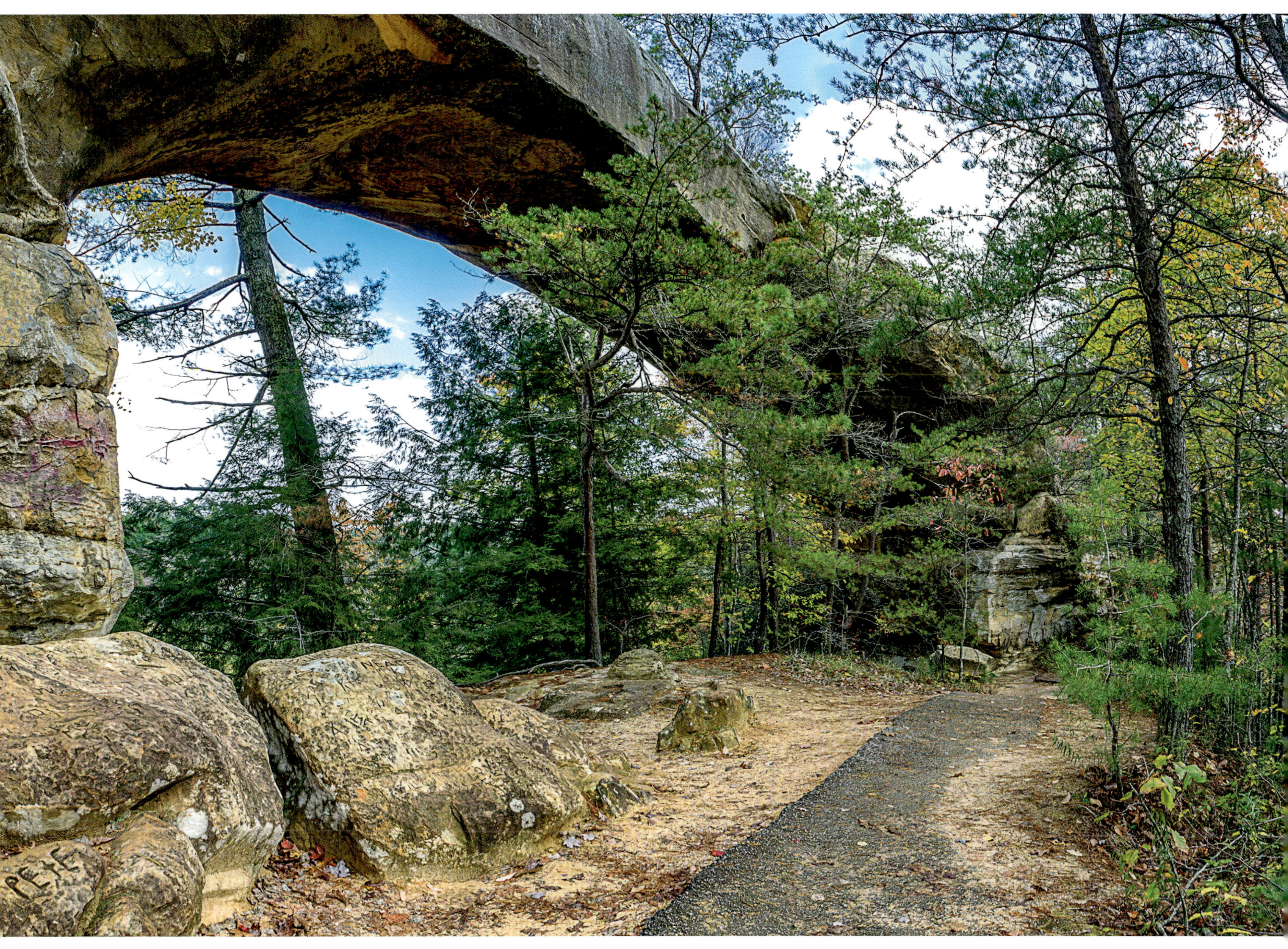

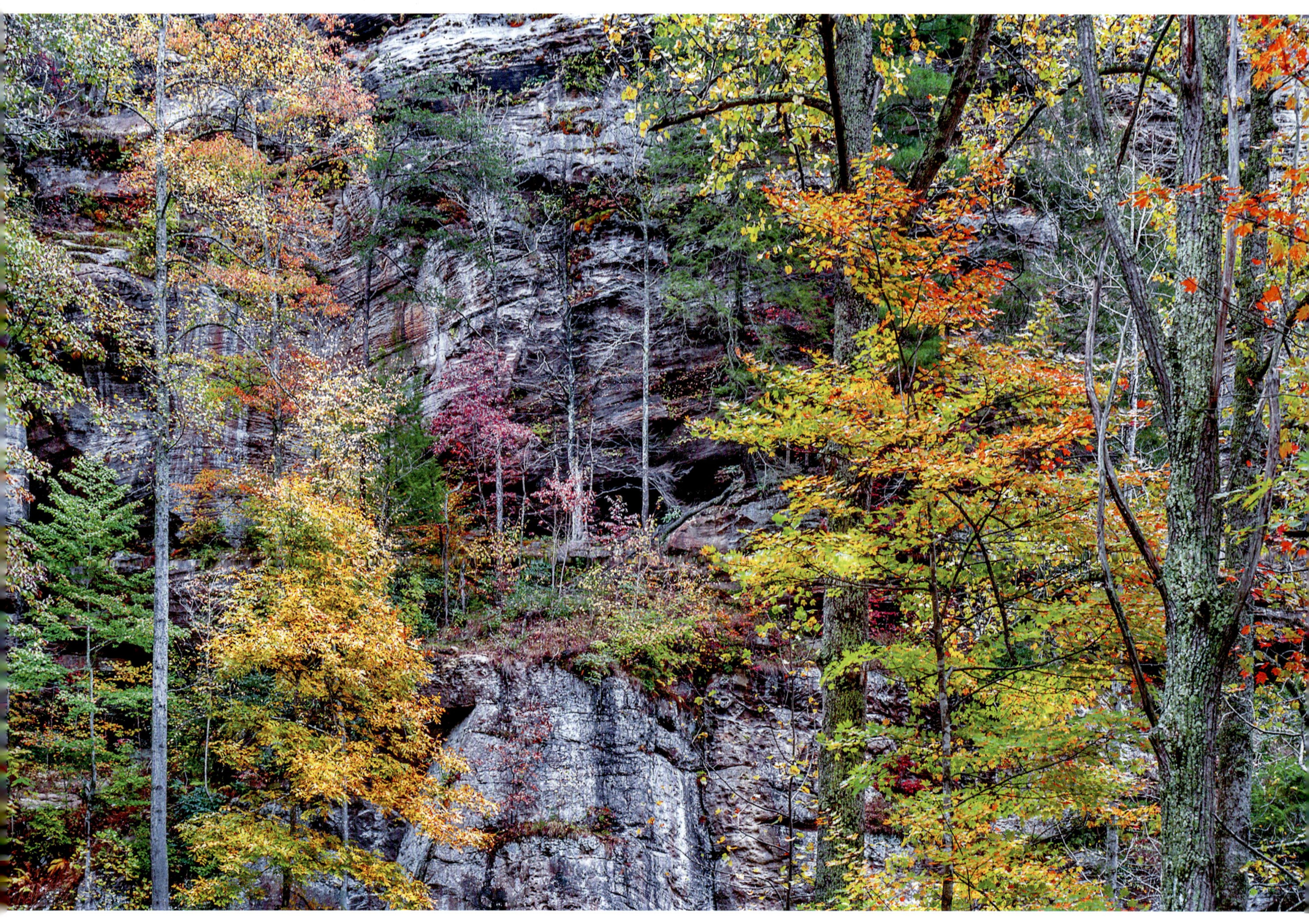

Autumn color paints the landscape at Red River Gorge.

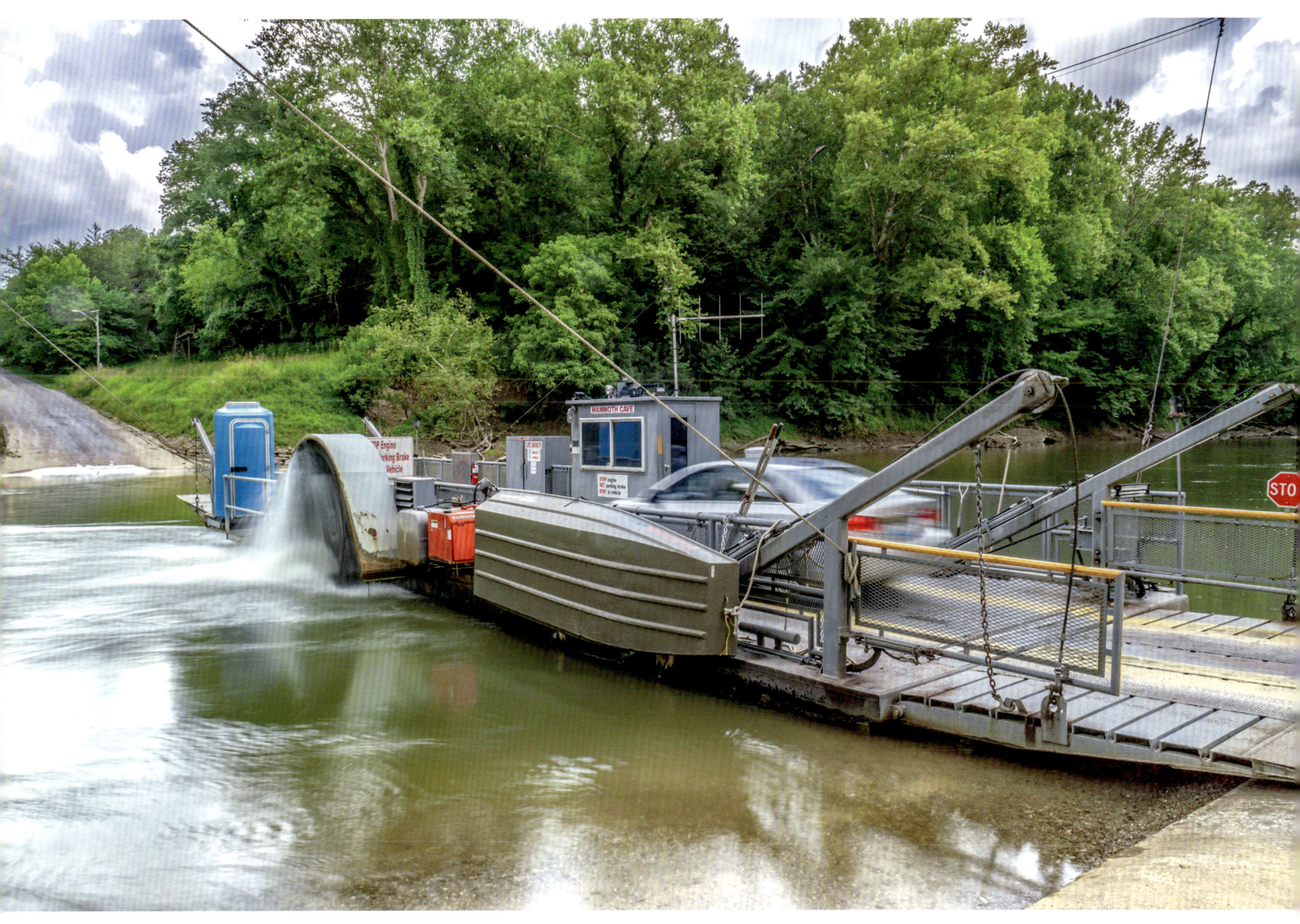

If the water levels are right, the Green River Ferry can carry you across the river at Mammoth Cave National Park.

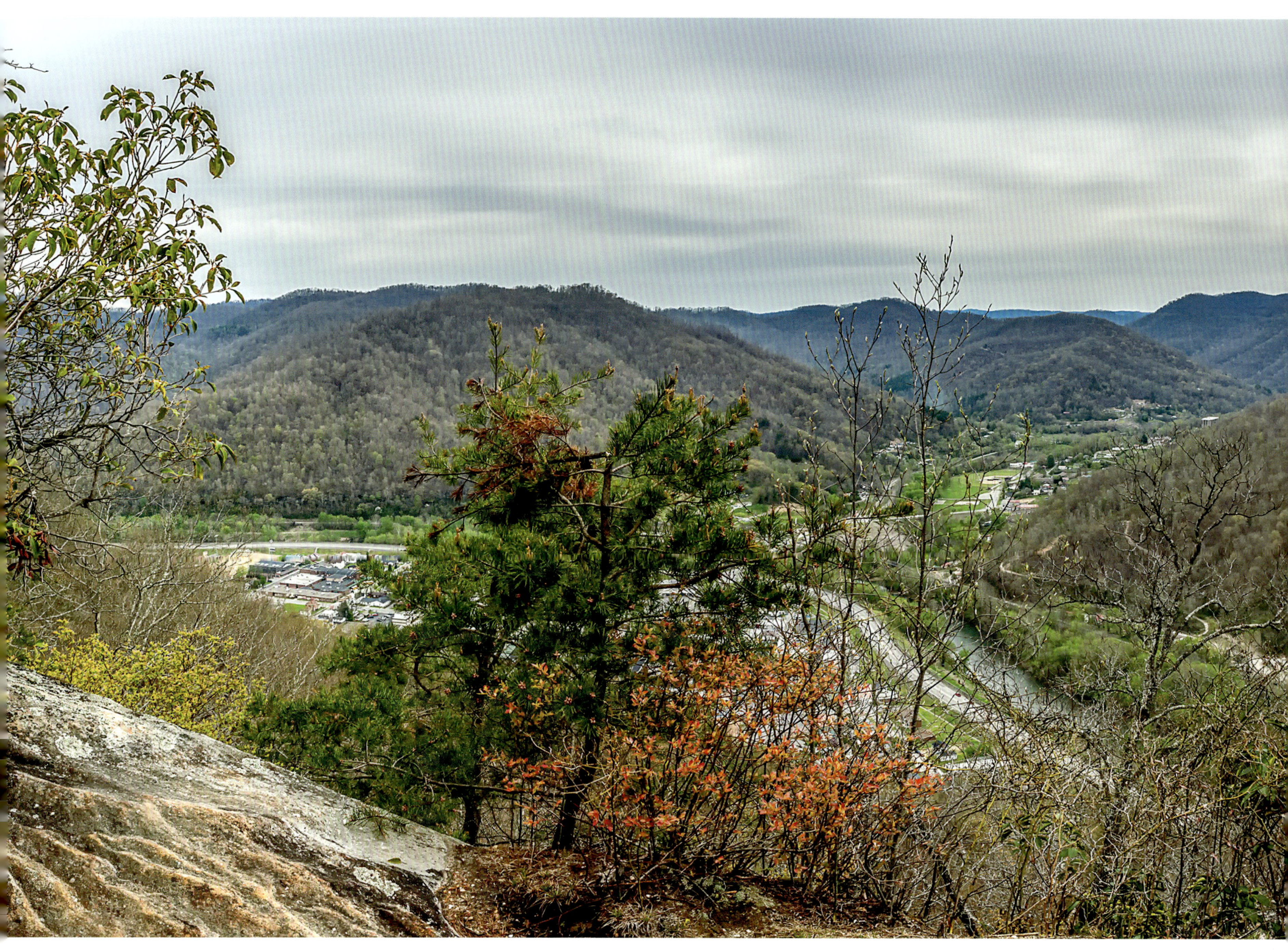

Mountain folklore says that Chained Rock is secured from tumbling down onto Pineville, Kentucky, by the enormous chain bolted to the rock in 1932.

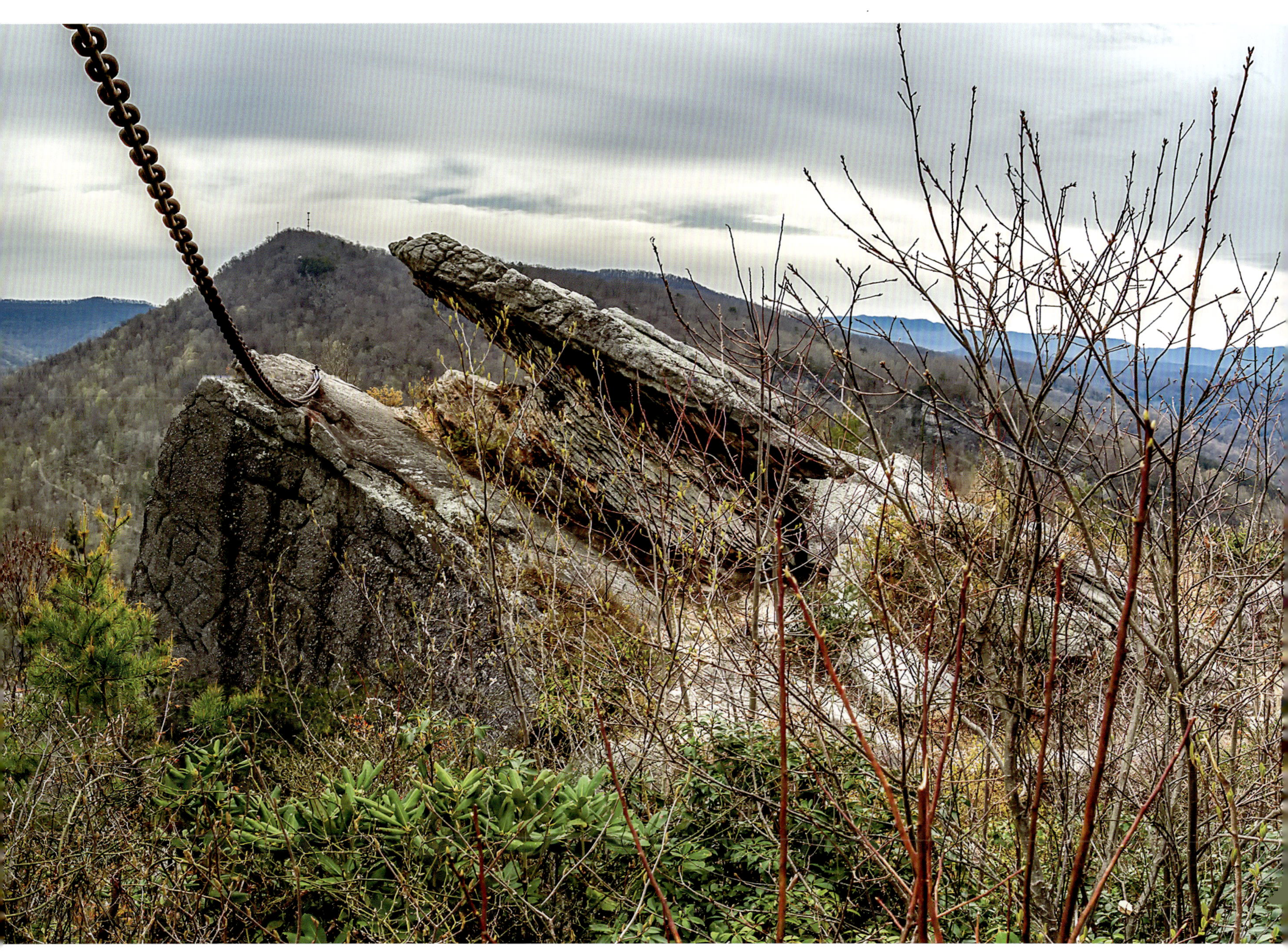

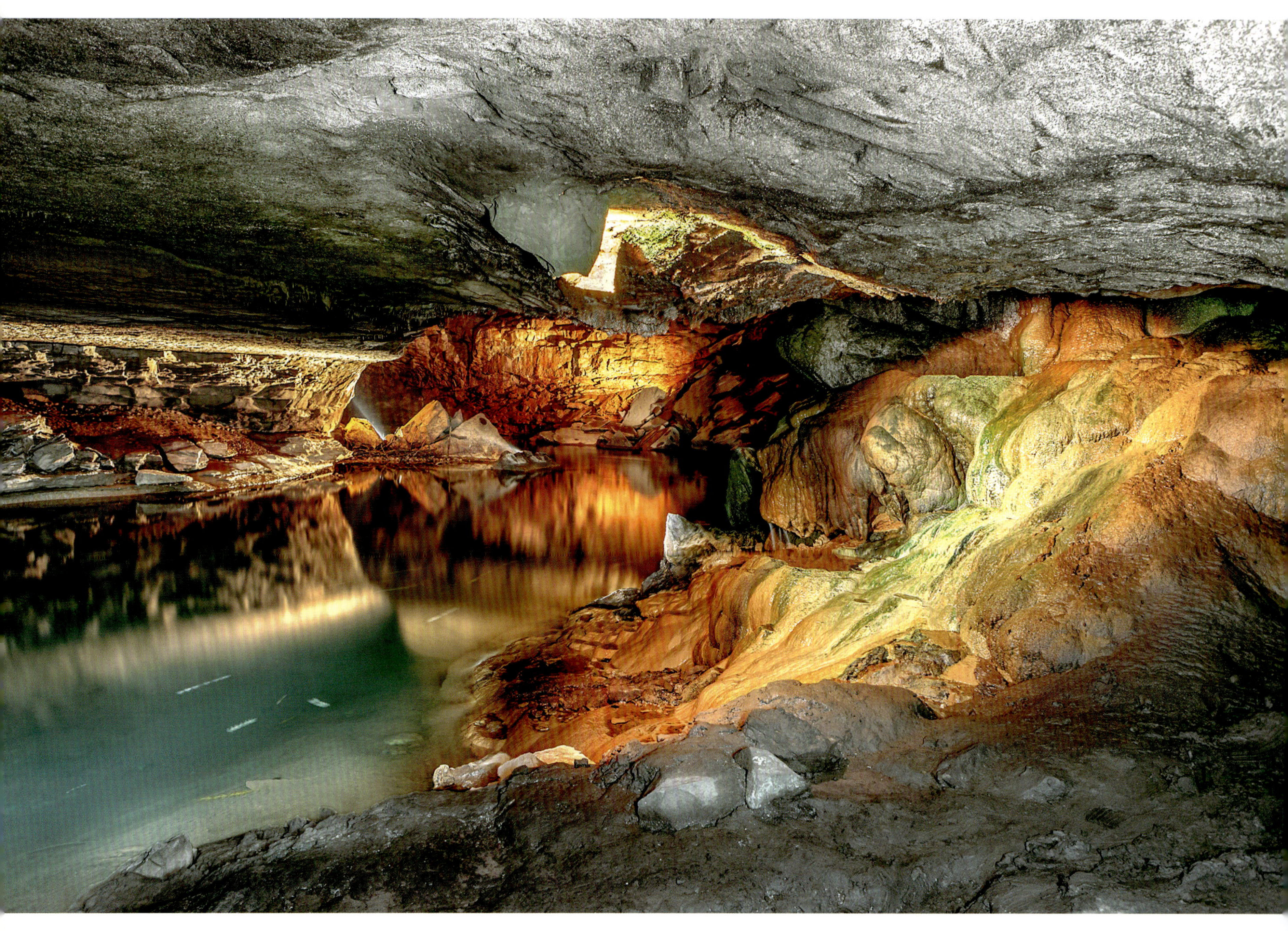

Lost River Cave is best experienced on the underground boat tour.

Simple historical Baptist church at Mammoth Cave National Park.

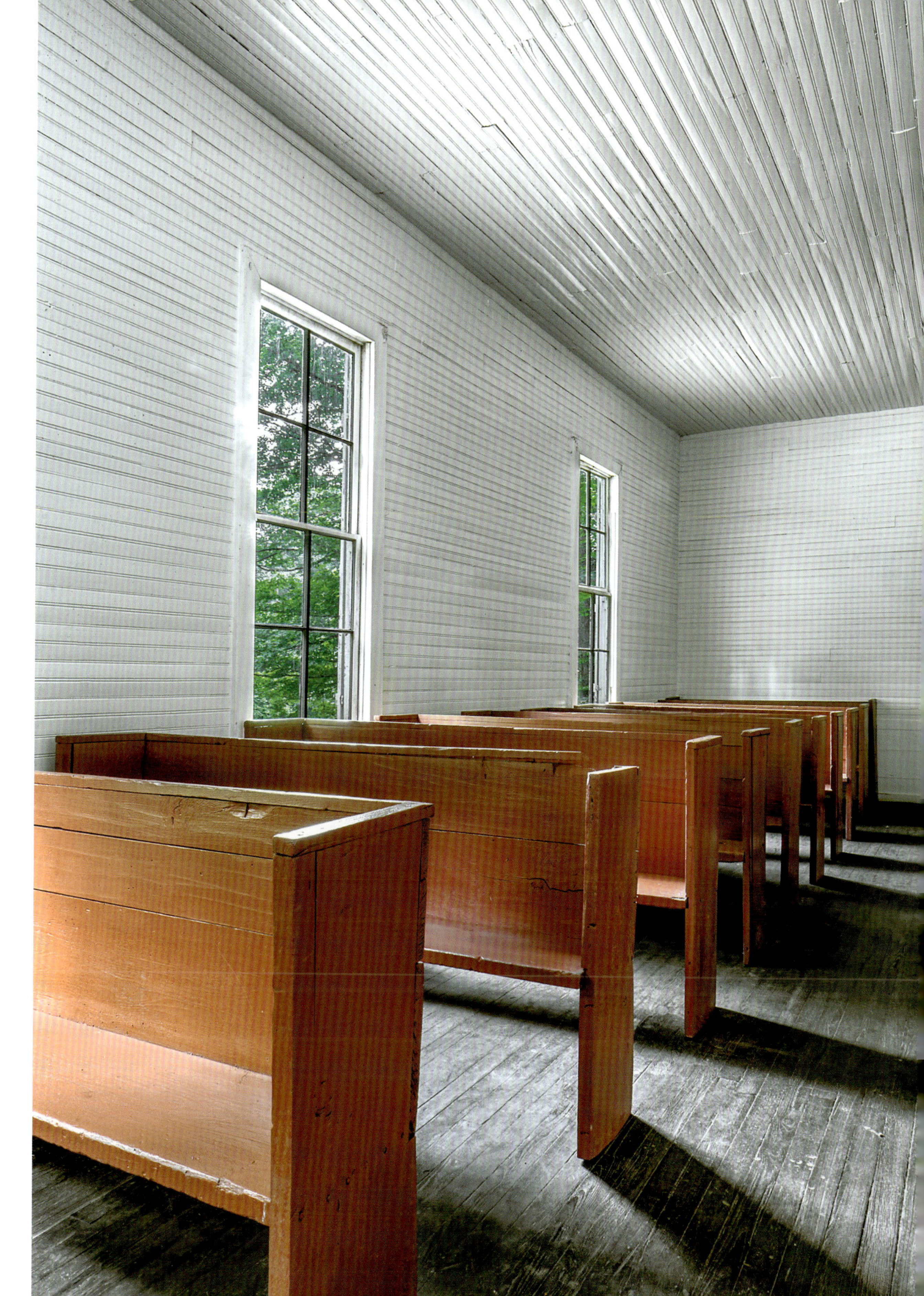

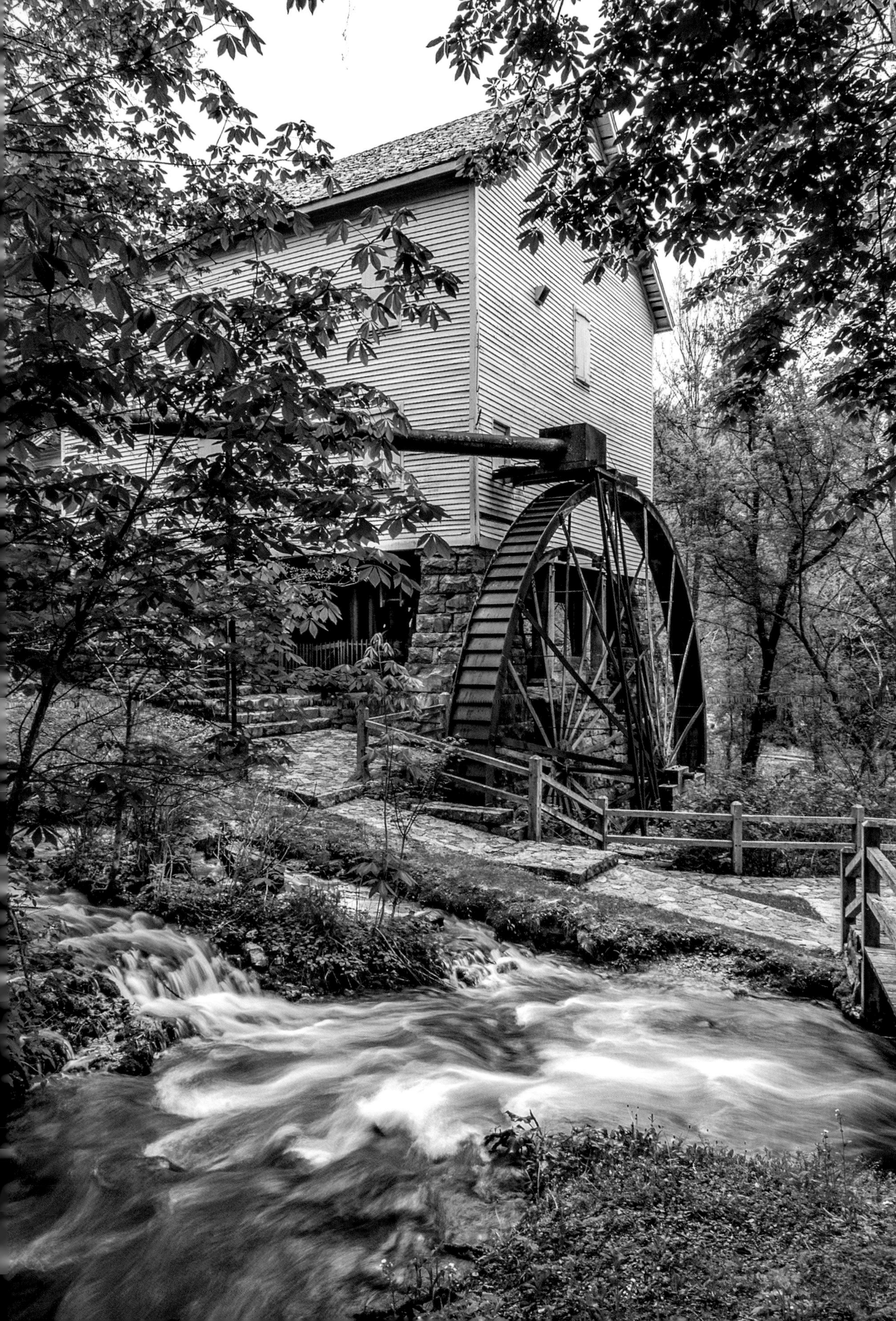

Mill Springs Mill offers Civil War history exhibits as well as the world's largest water wheel at forty-feet tall.

FACING
Trillium is a springtime favorite all over Kentucky.

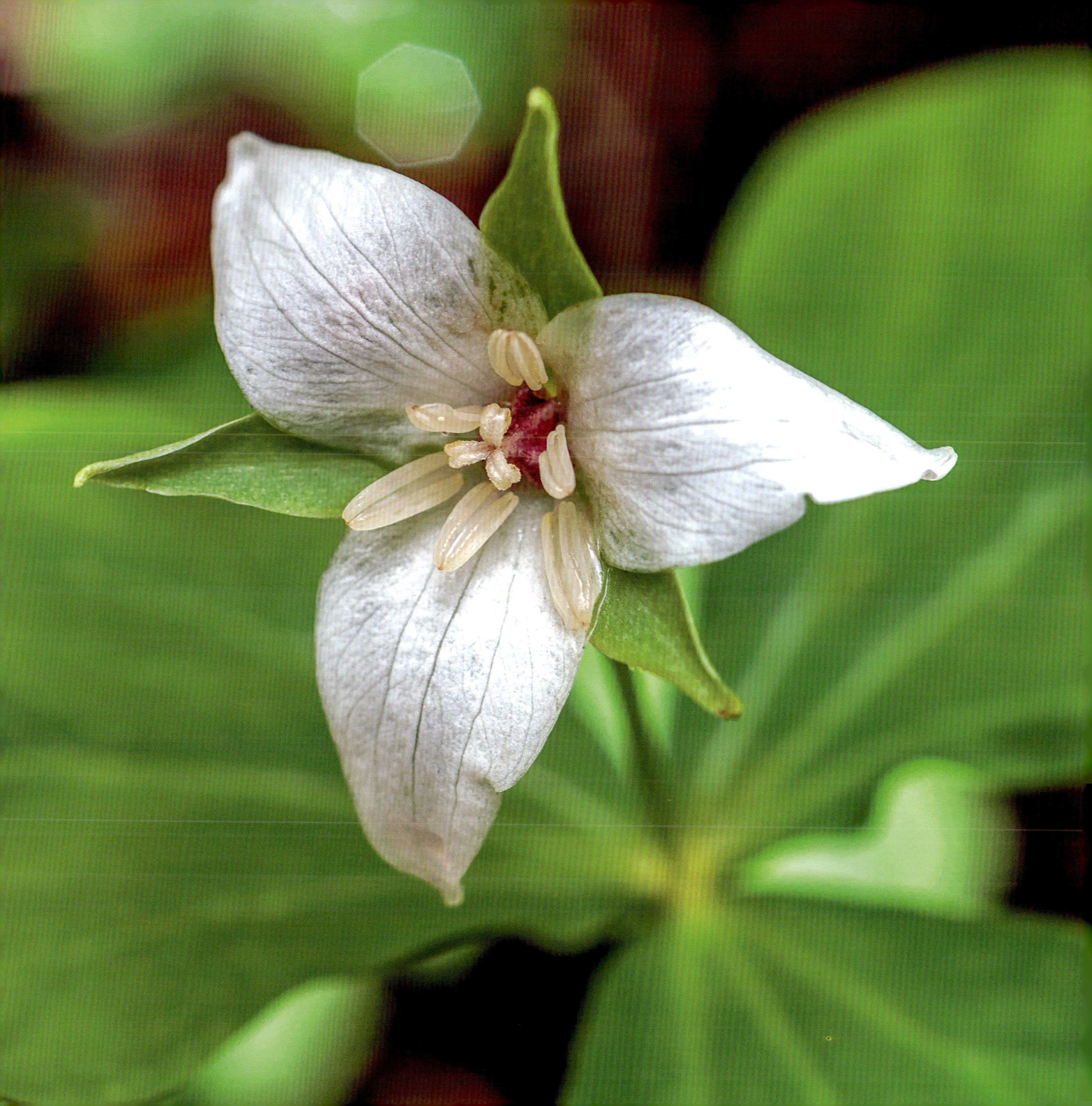

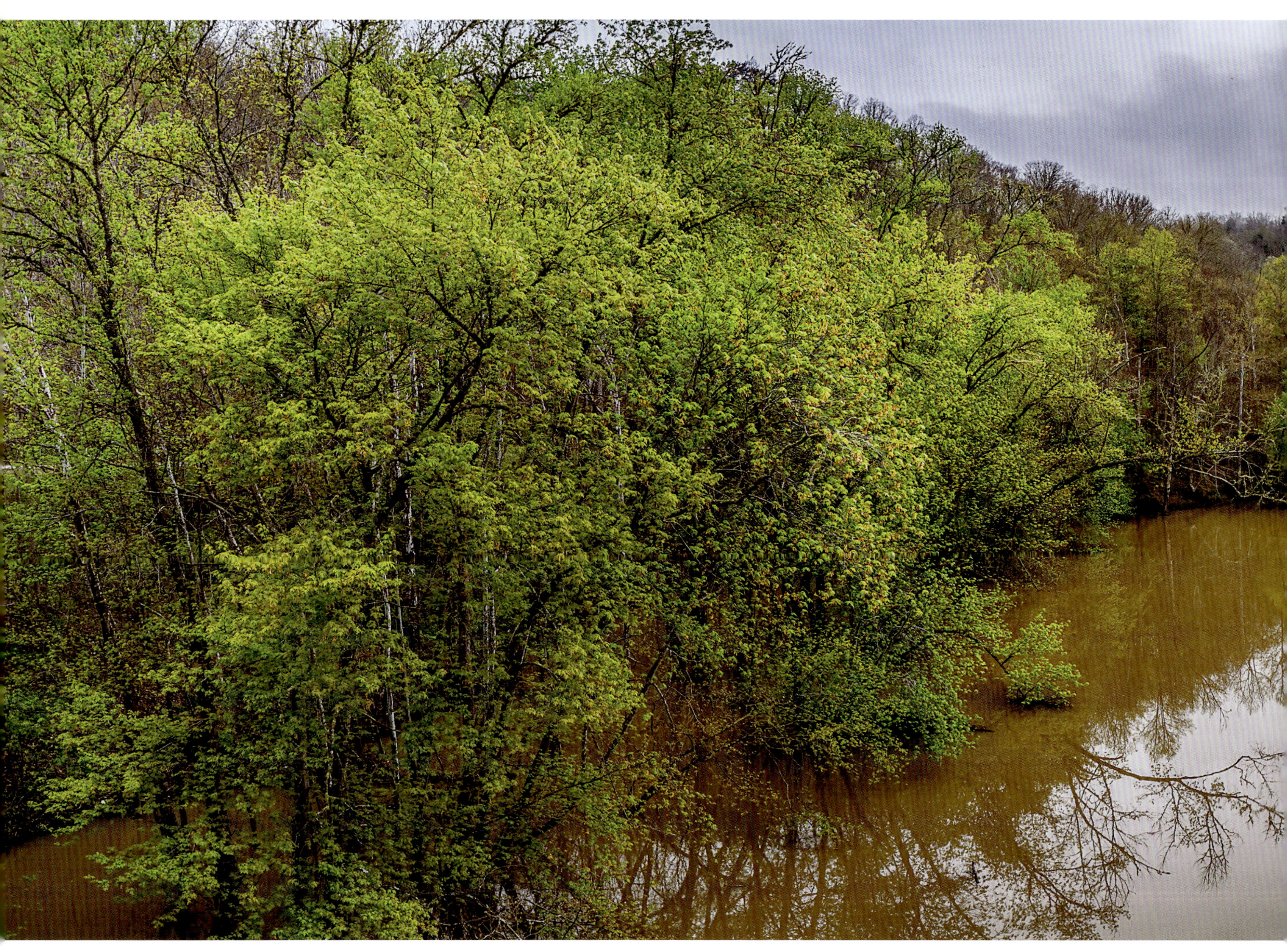

Rockcastle River on an early spring morning.

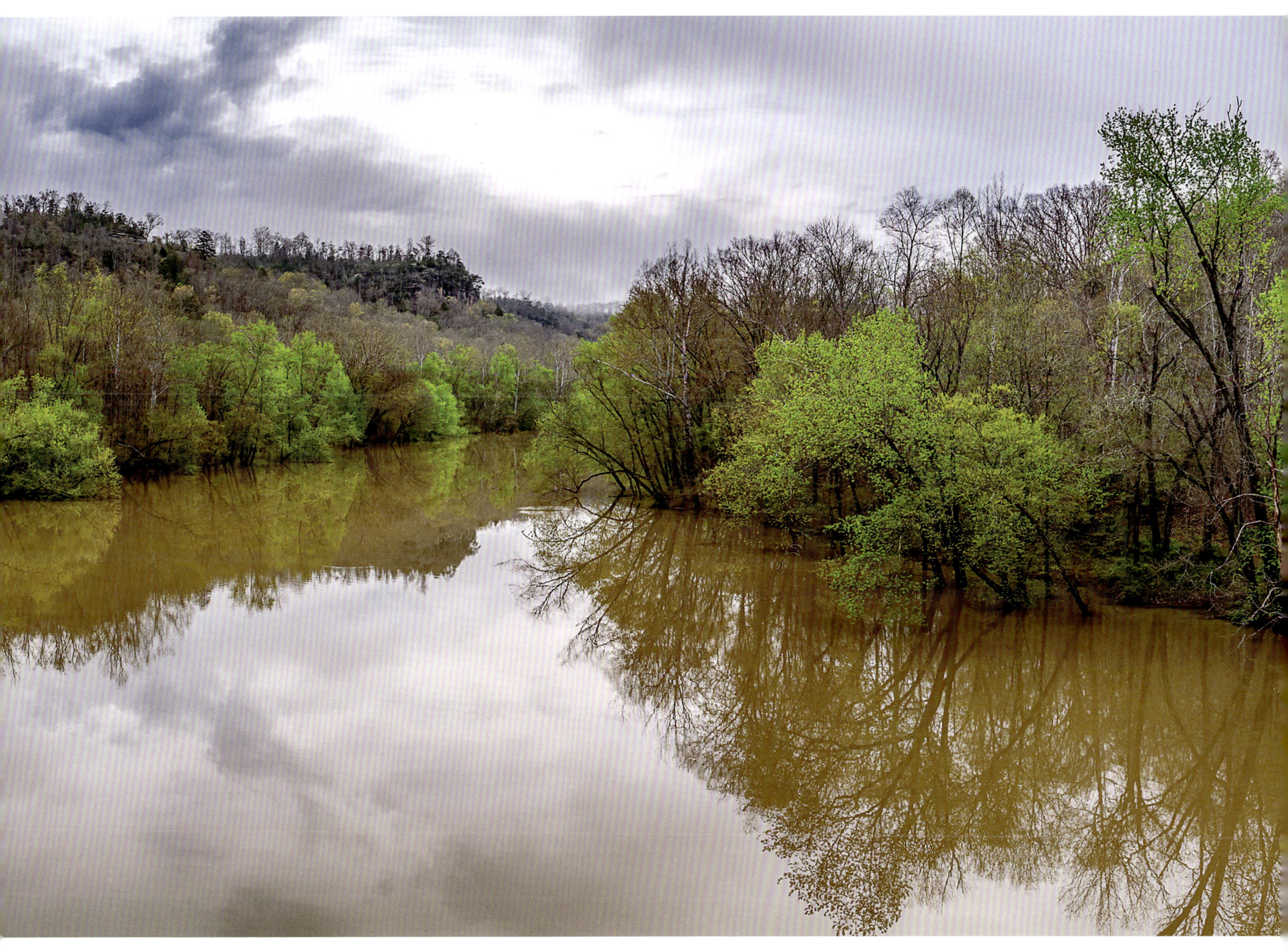

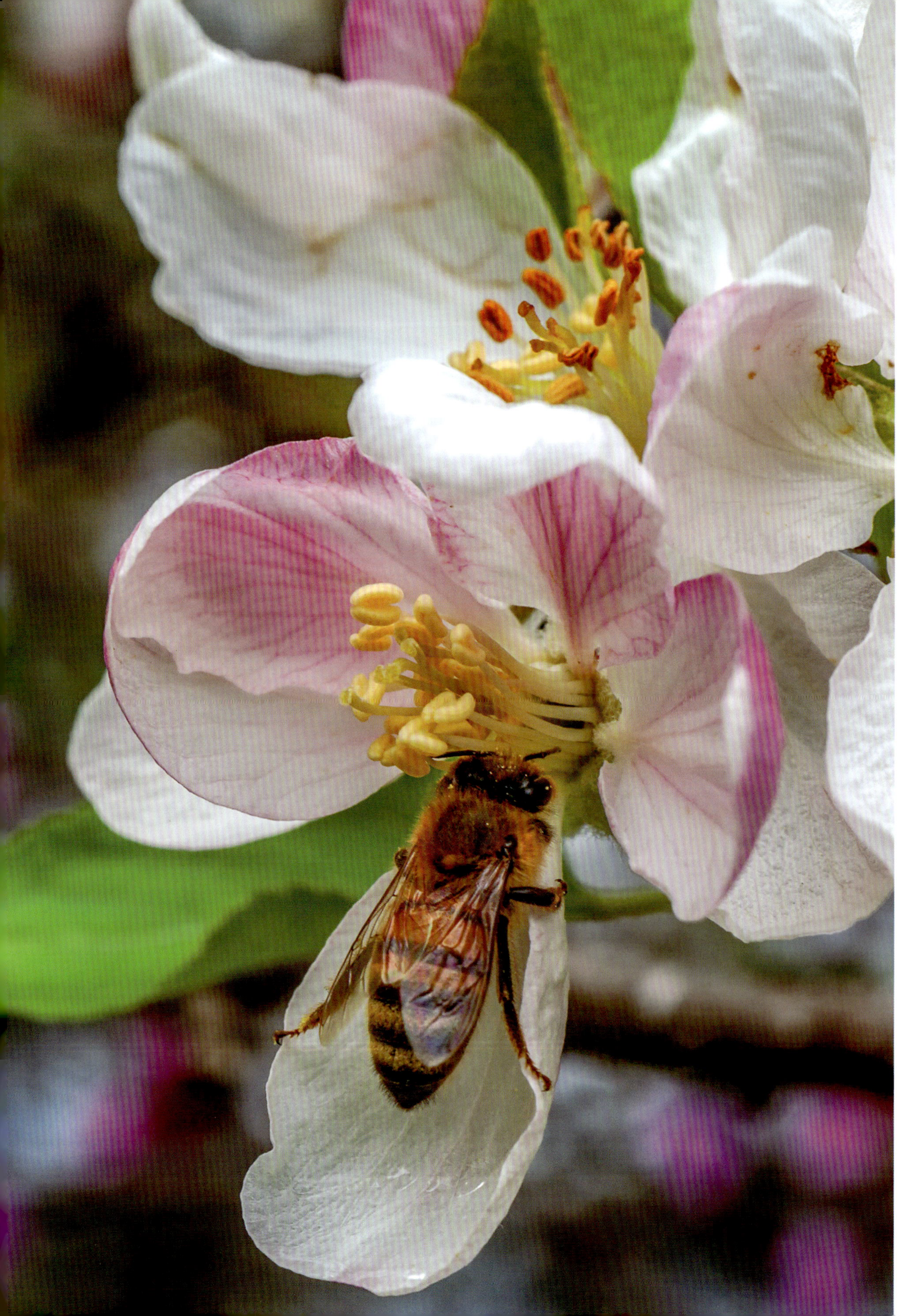

Pollinating the apple blossoms at Laurel River Lake.

Ice formations at Nada Tunnel near the Red River Gorge.

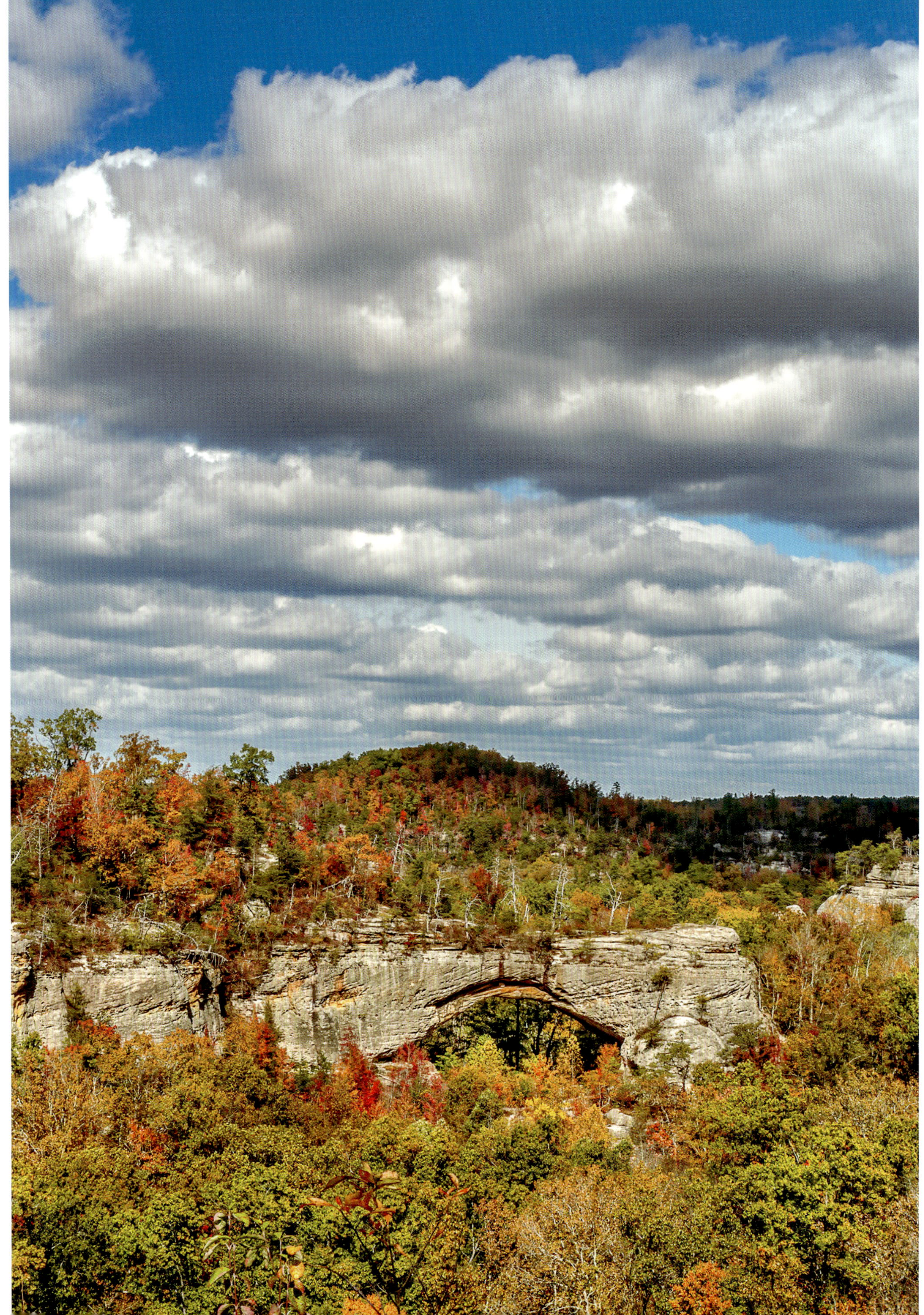

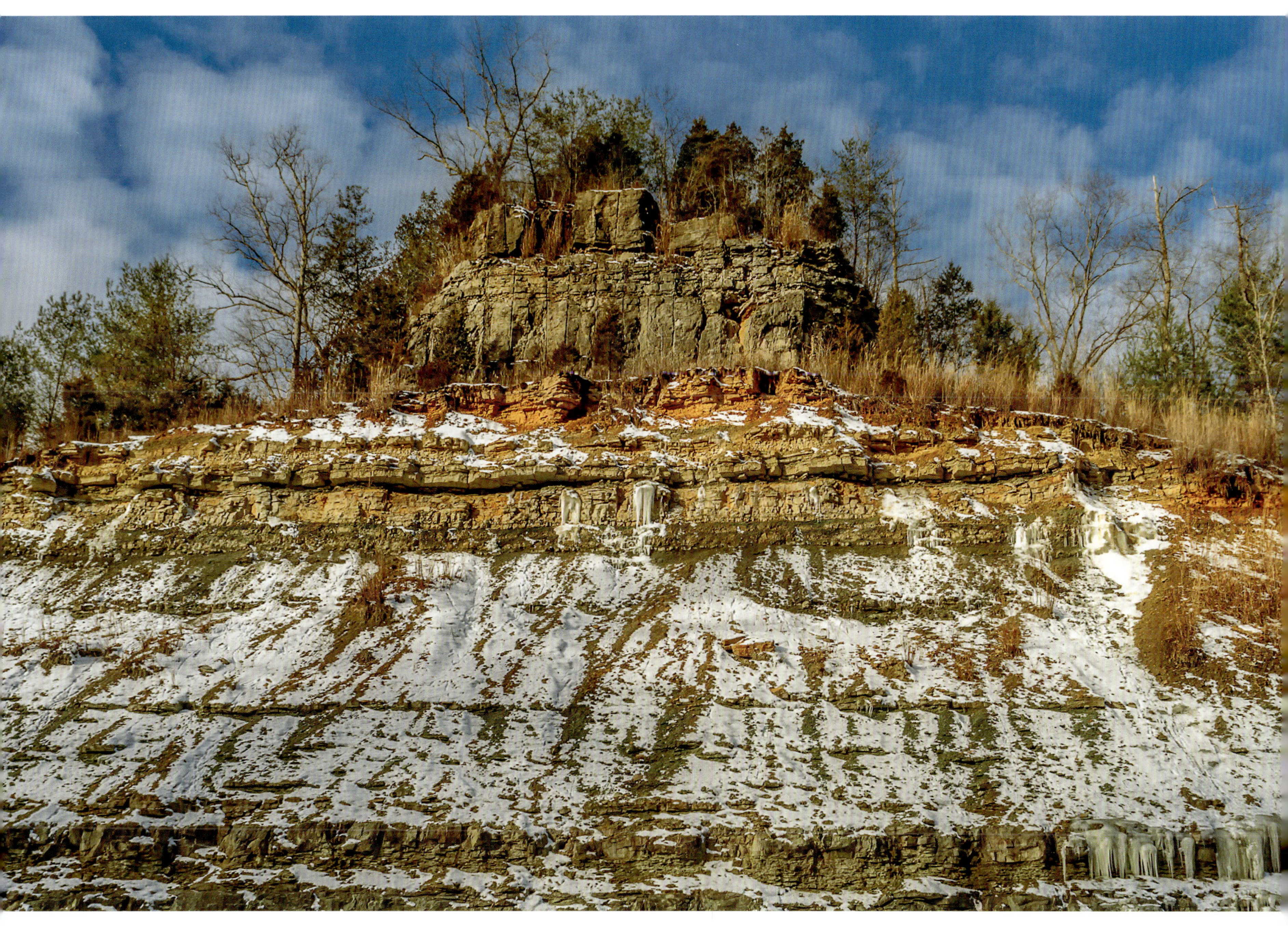

Spectacular rock formations are abundant at Natural Bridge State Resort Park.

FACING Natural Arch stands out amid early fall colors at the Daniel Boone National Forest.

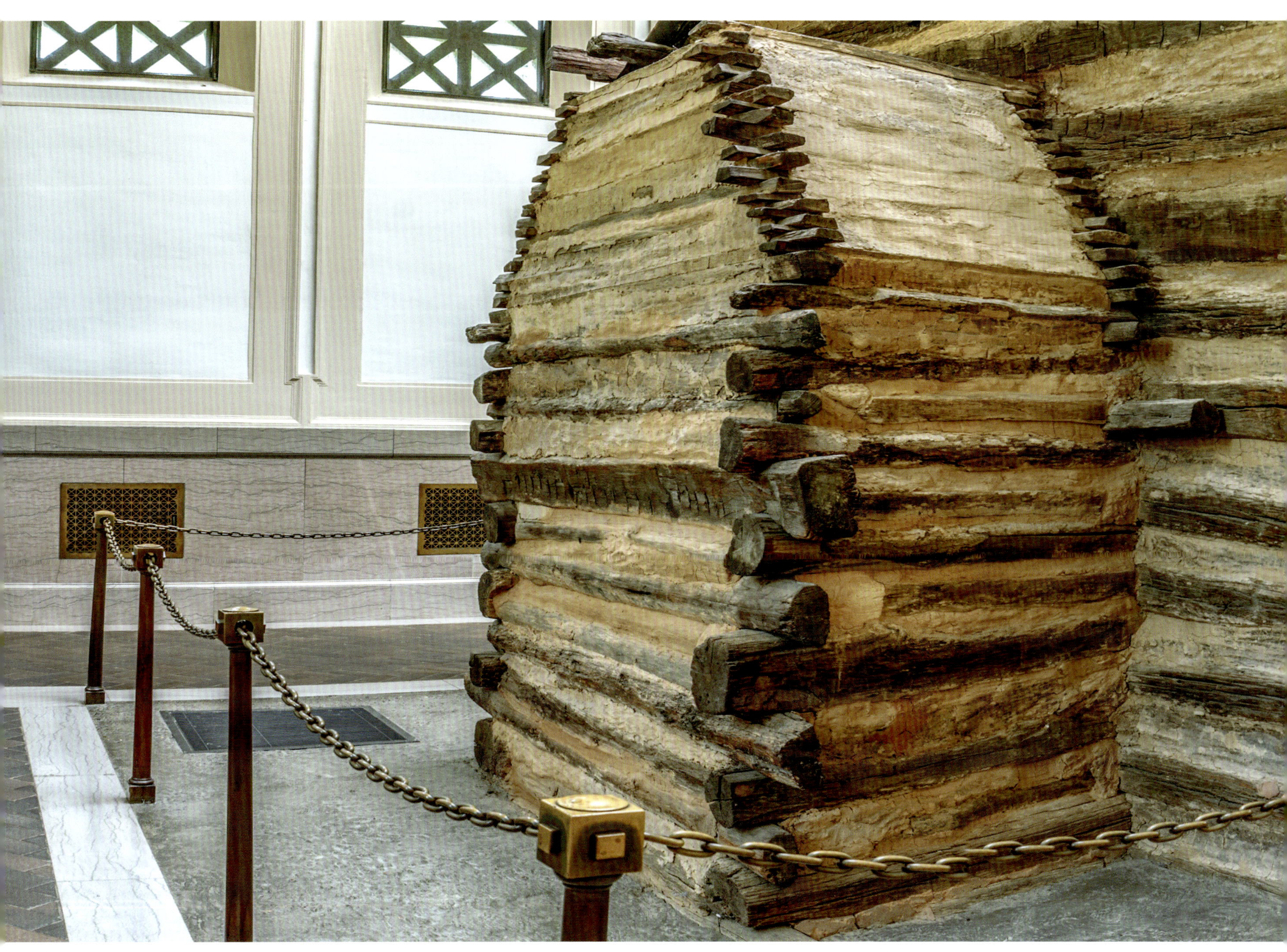

At the Abraham Lincoln Birthplace National Historical Park visitors can see a symbolic replica of a cabin erected where Abraham Lincoln was thought to be born.

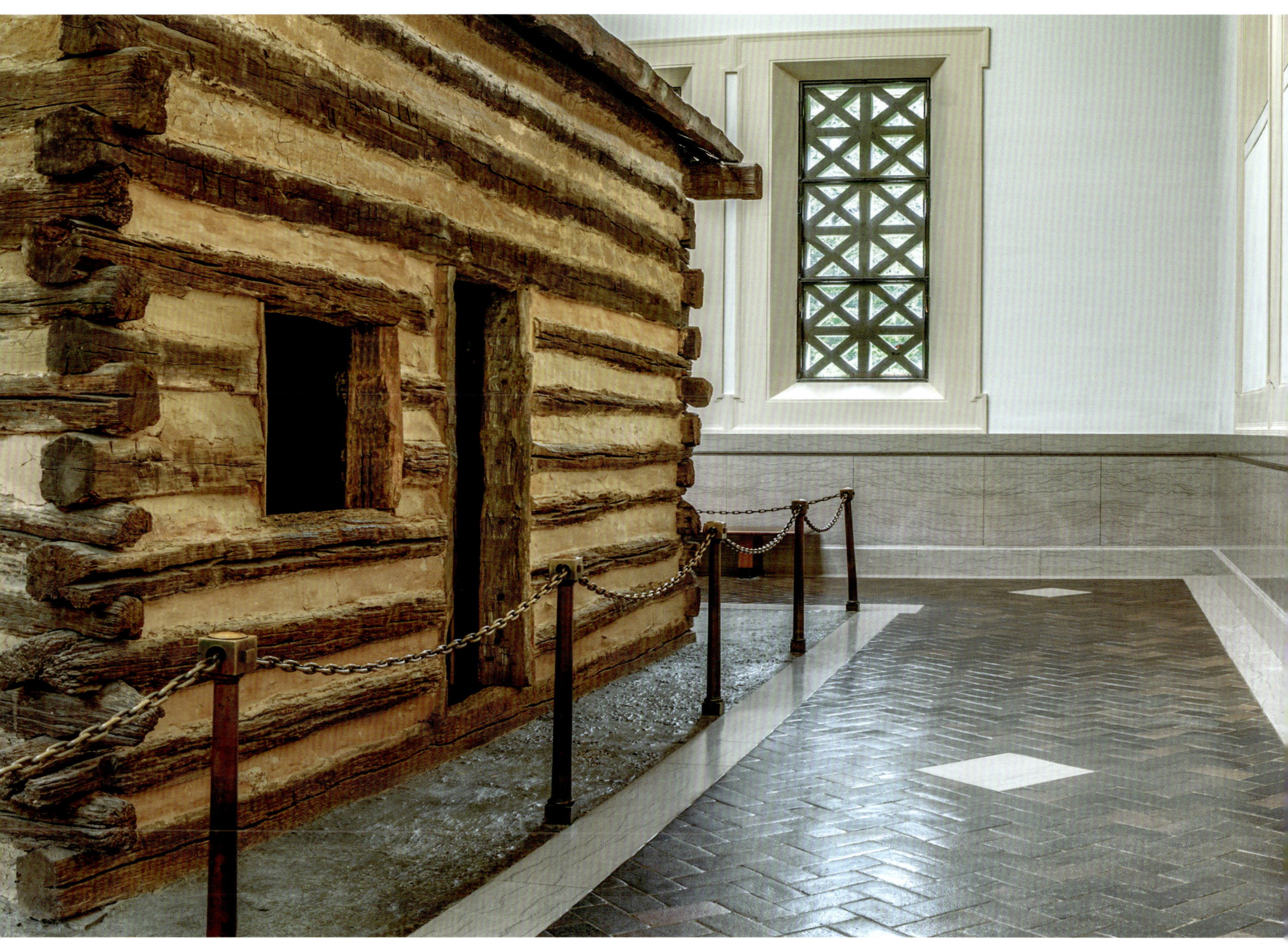

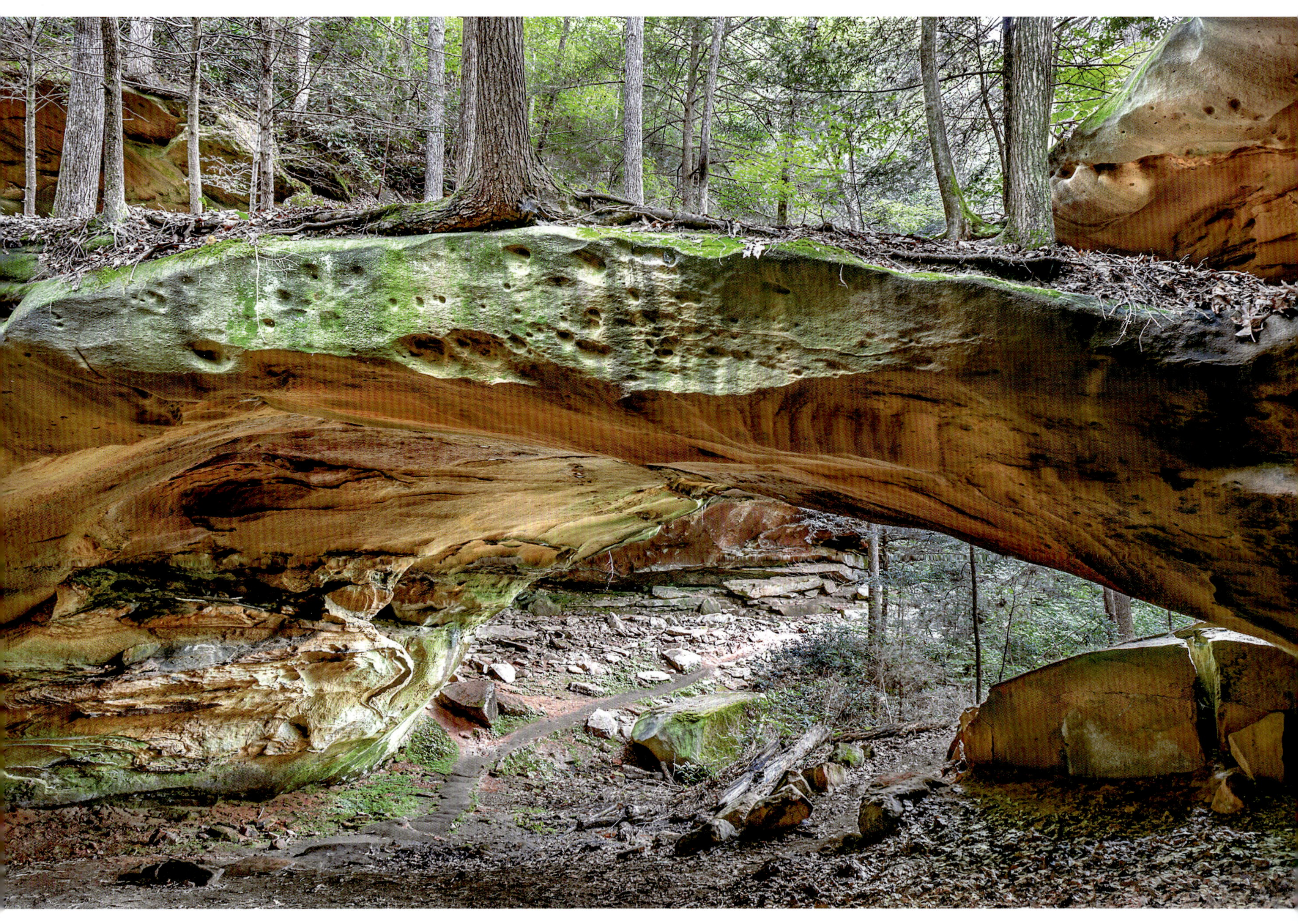

Springtime at Yahoo Arch is nature's way of showing off.

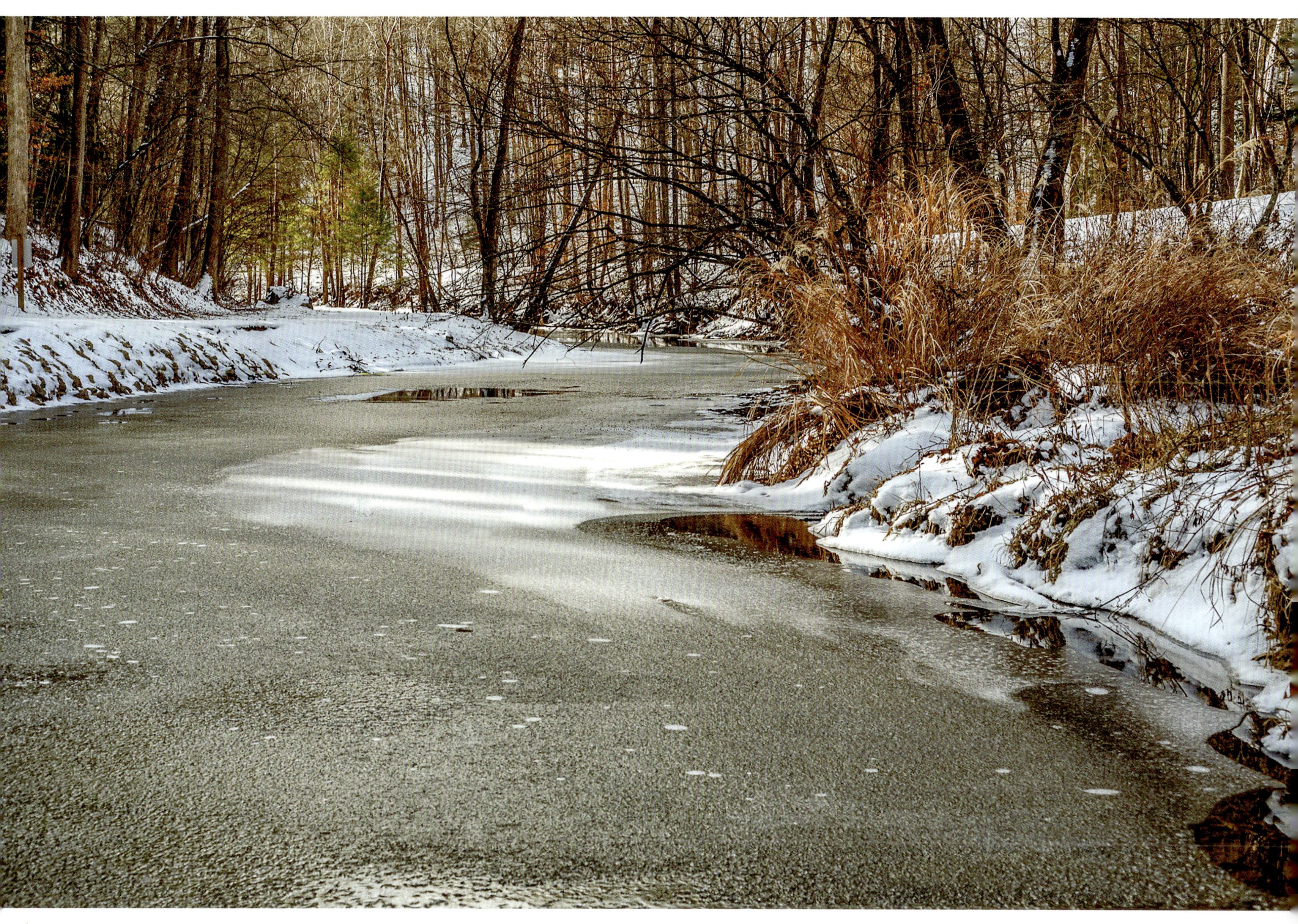

Ice covers the creek at Natural Bridge State Resort Park.

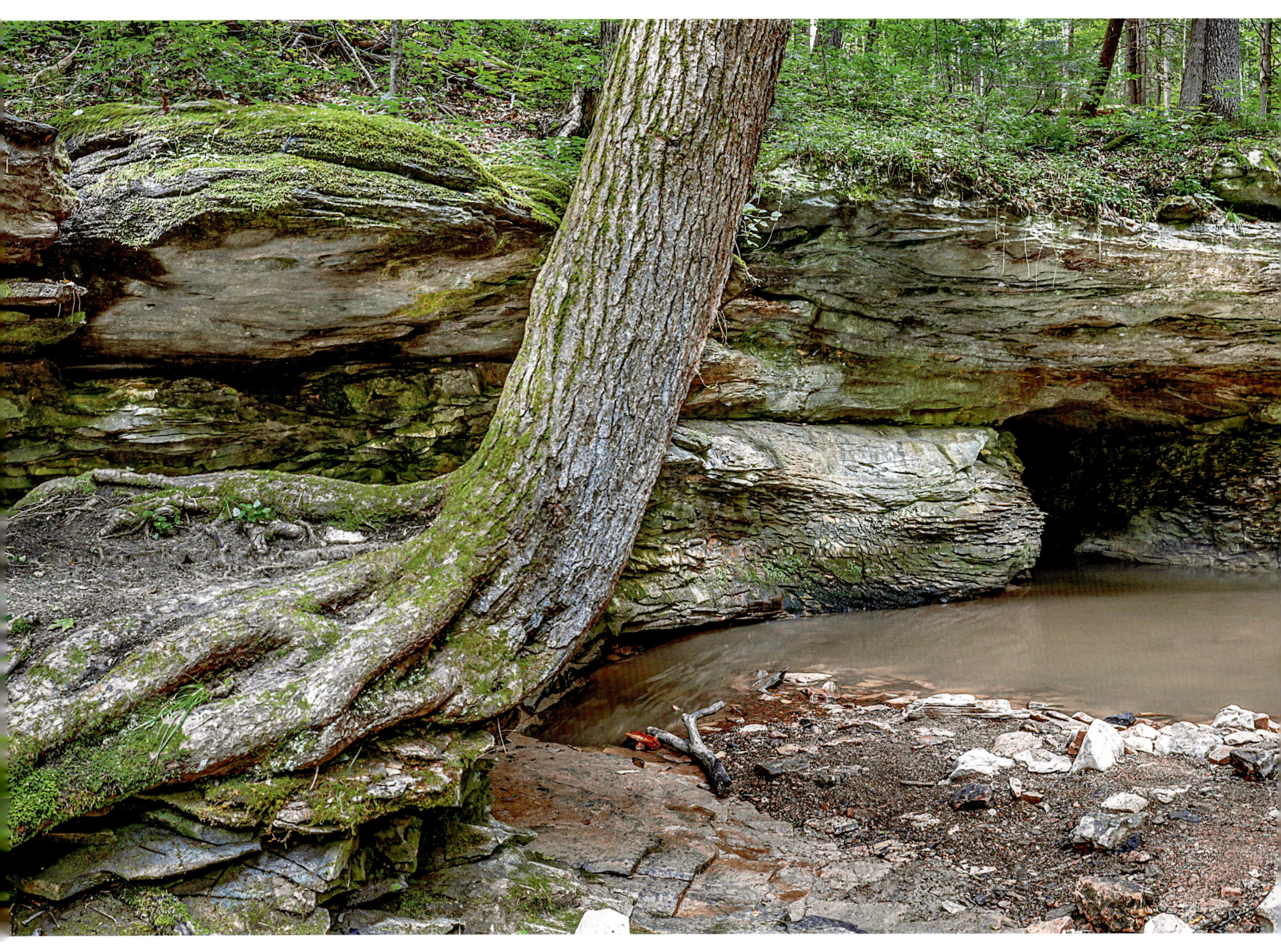

Horn Hollow Cave is one of the many caves for visitors to explore at Carter Caves State Resort Park.

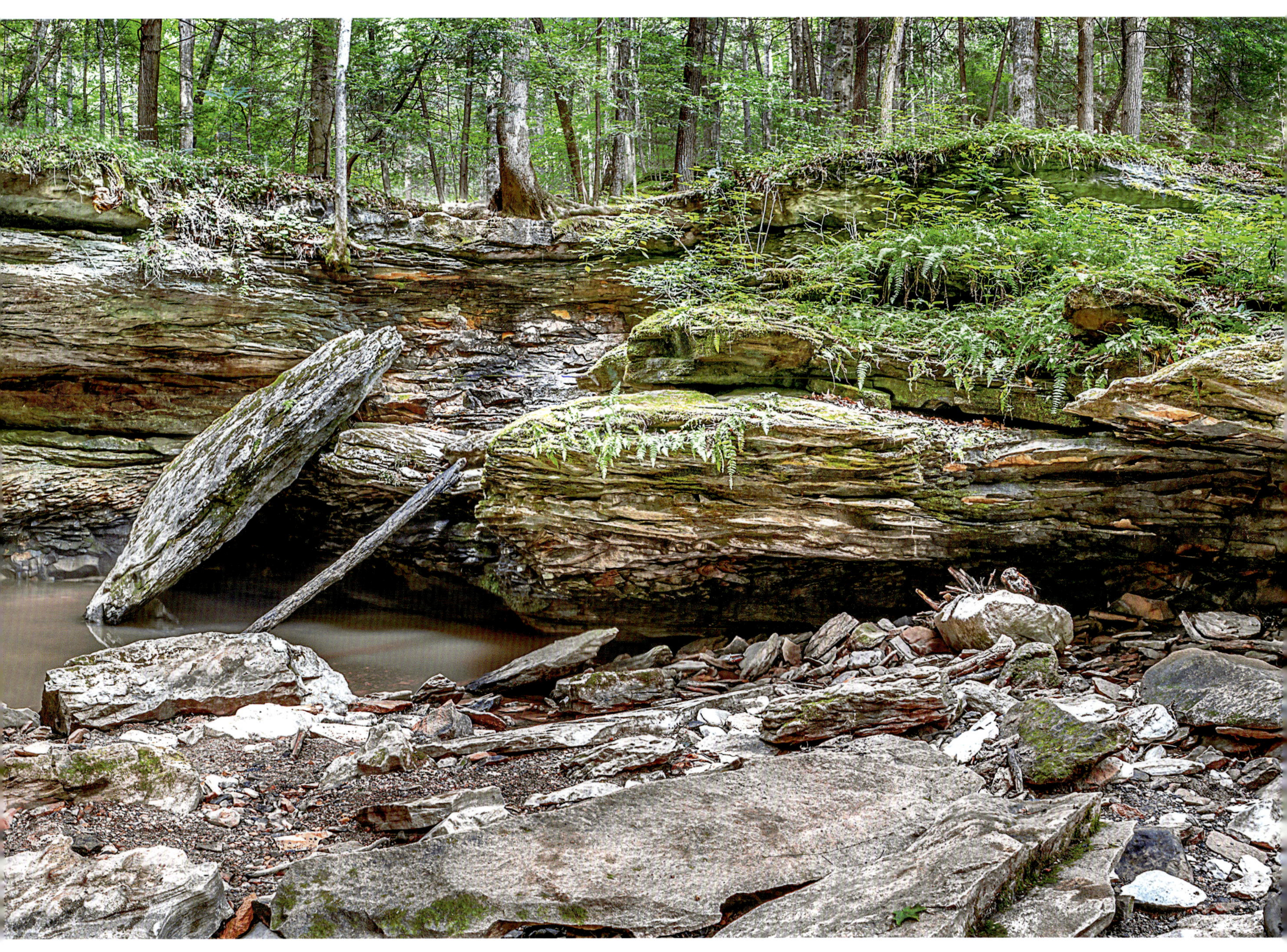

FOLLOWING Snow and ice formations along a creek start to melt in the morning sun.

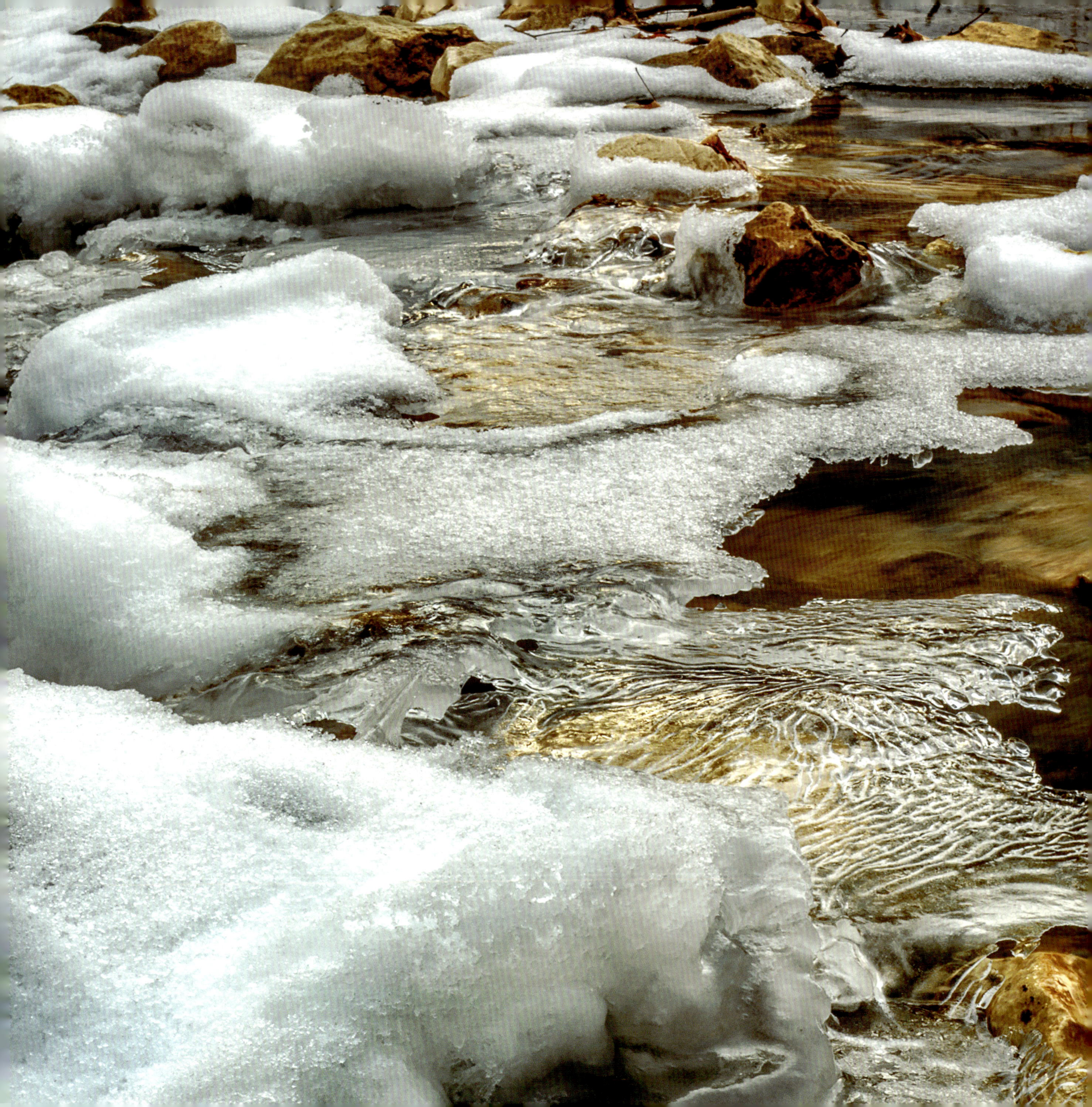

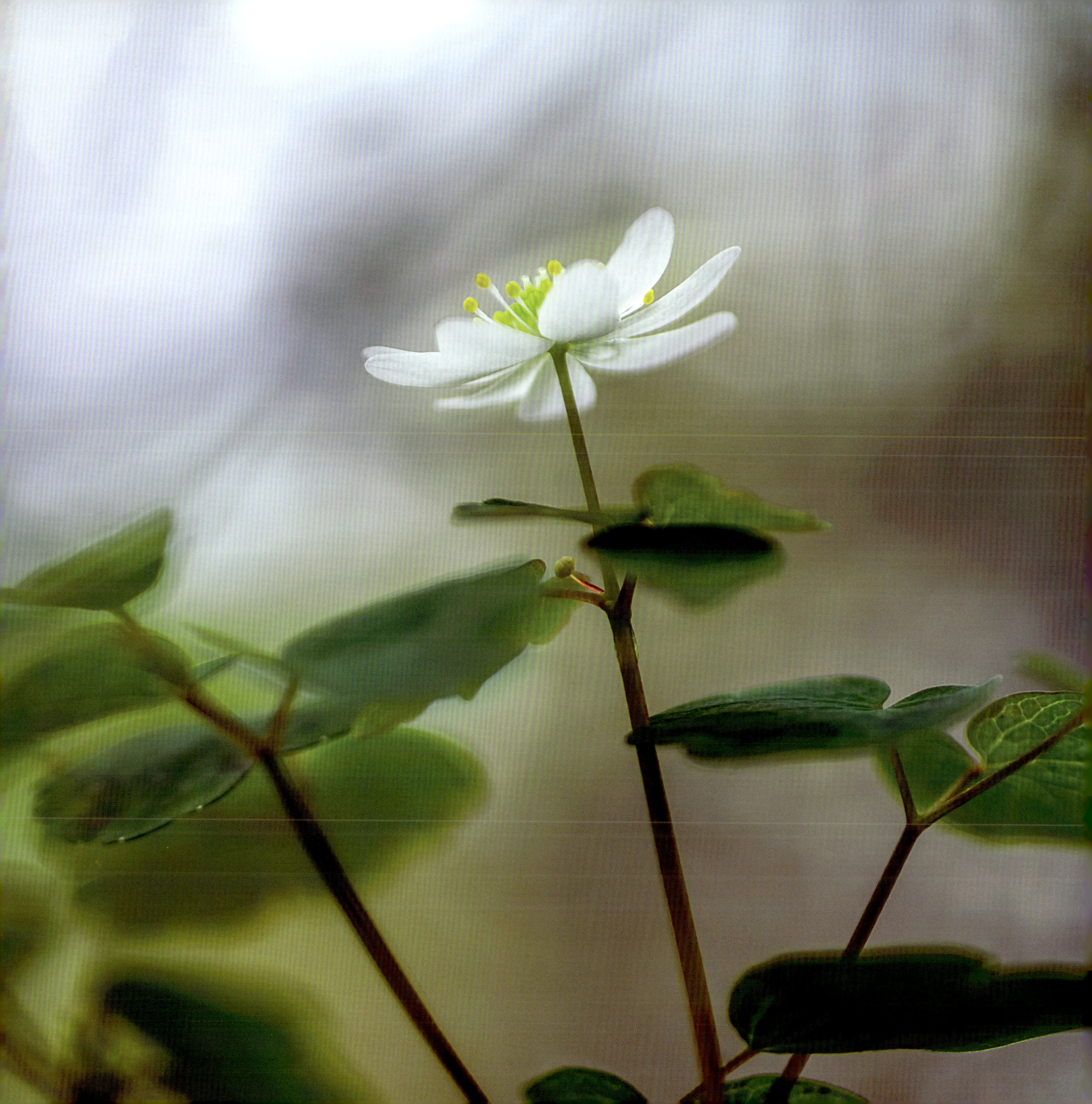

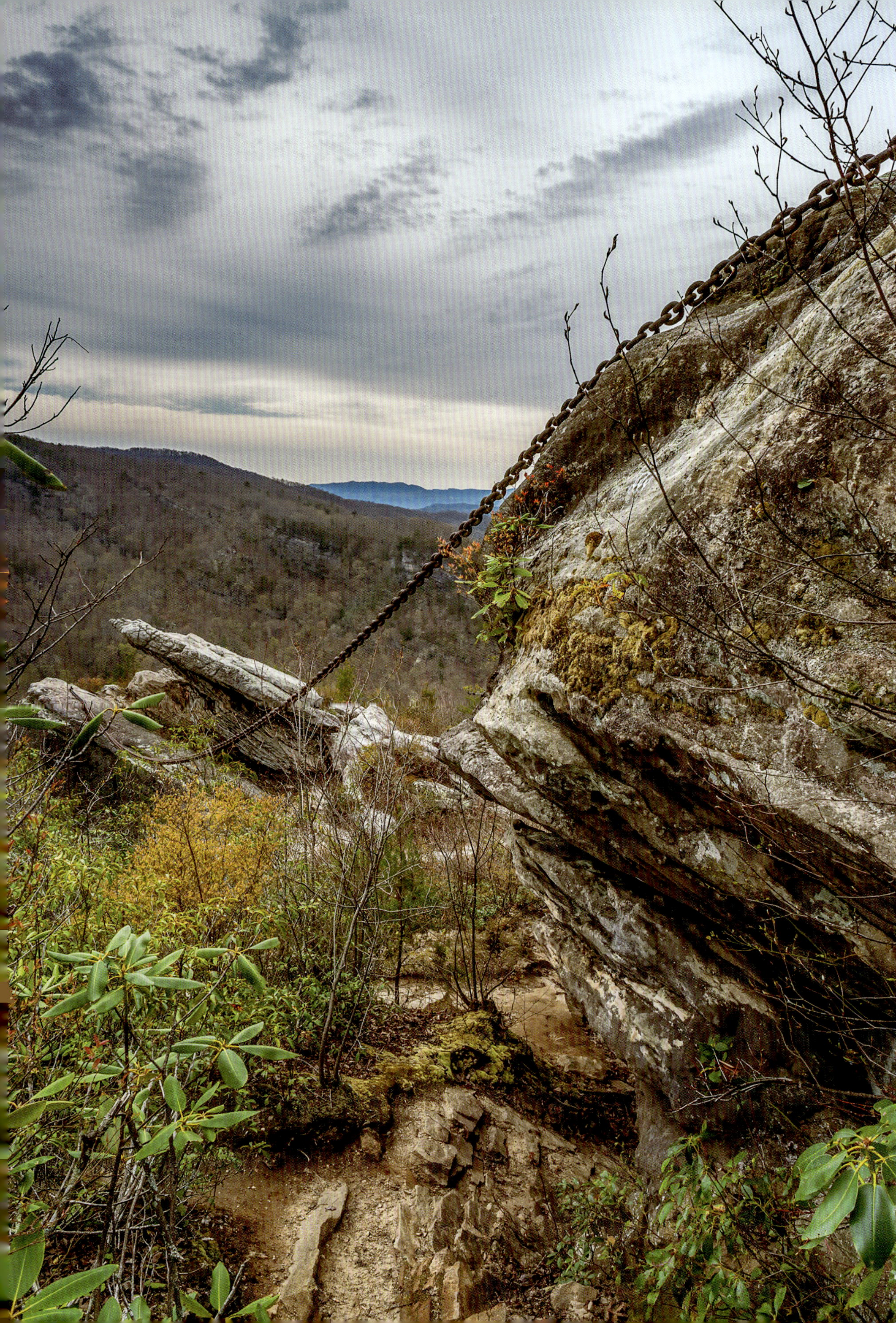

PREVIOUS
Rue Anemones spring up in the Kentucky landscape.

Pine Mountain State Resort Park is home to the legendary Chained Rock.

Beauty around every curve in the road at Red River Gorge.

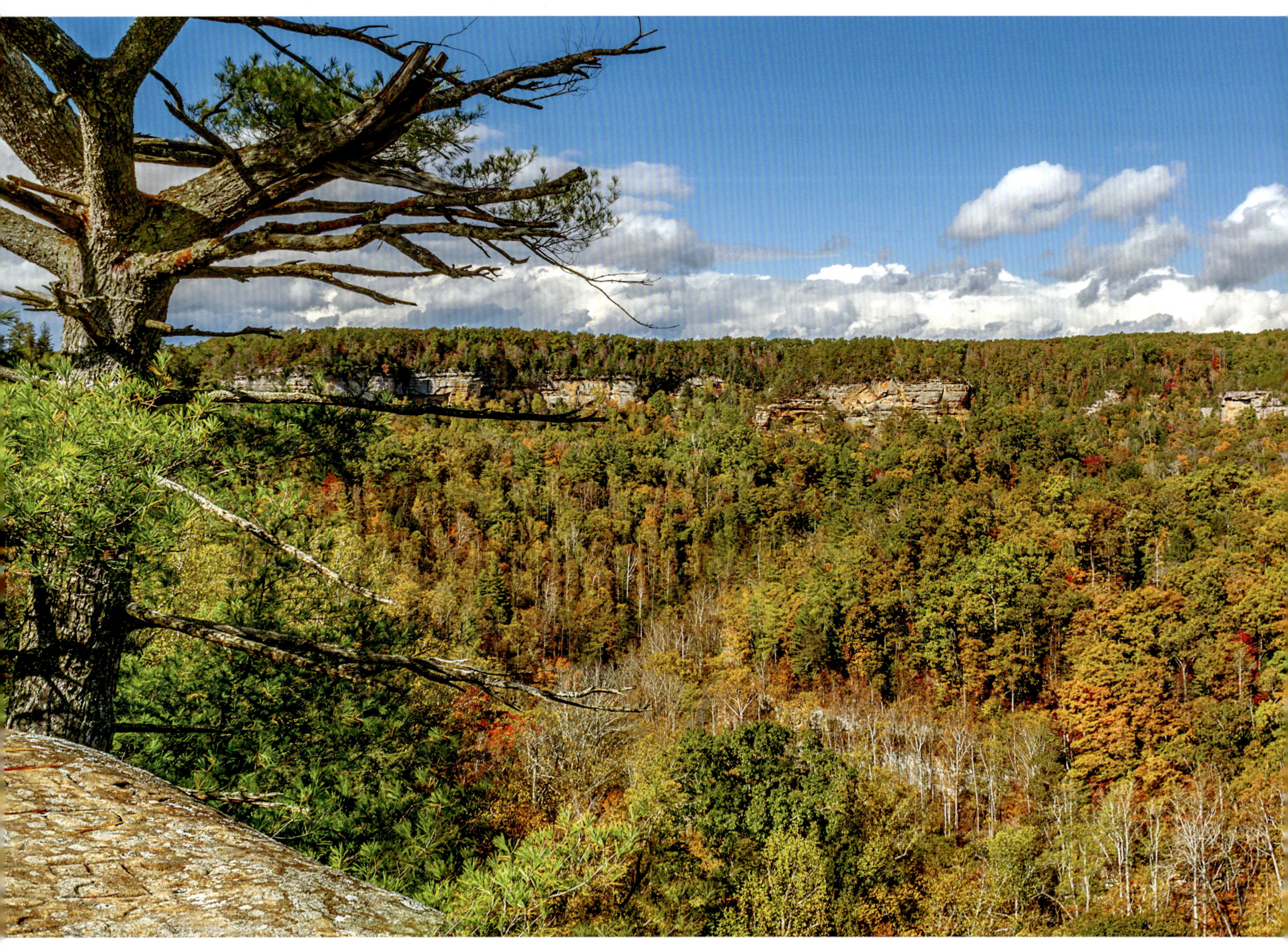

Red River Gorge showing off its fall color.

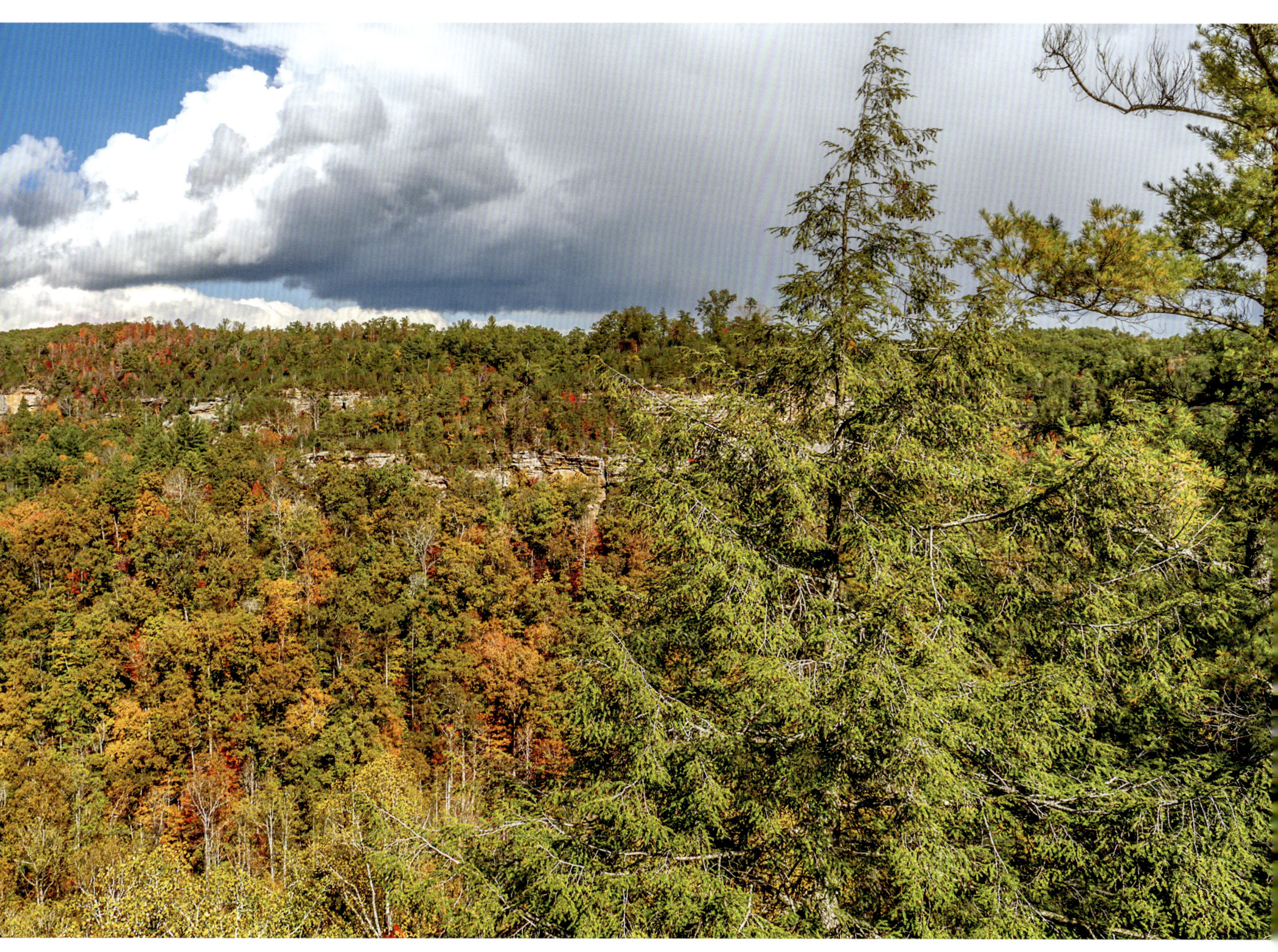

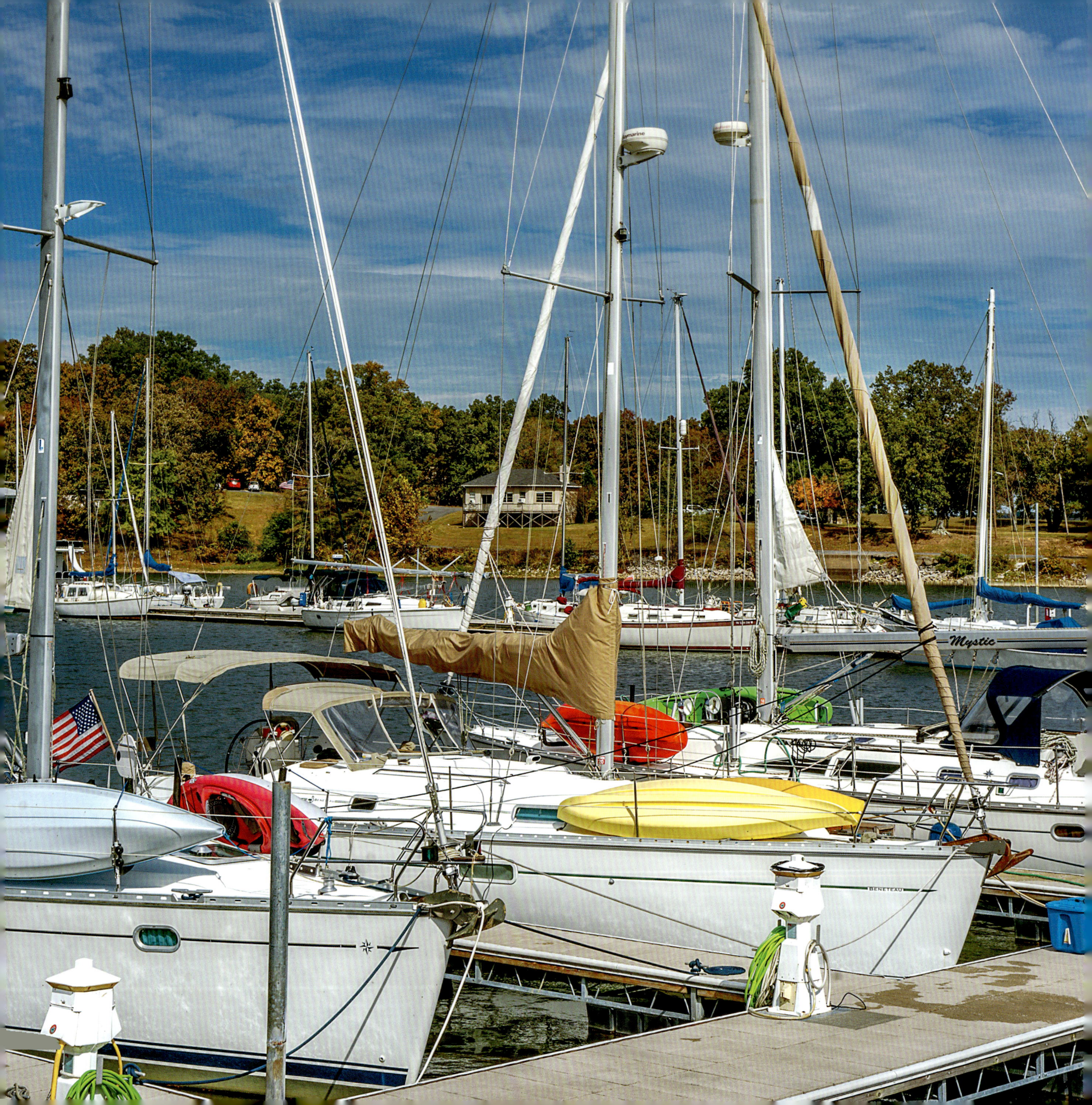
Mystic

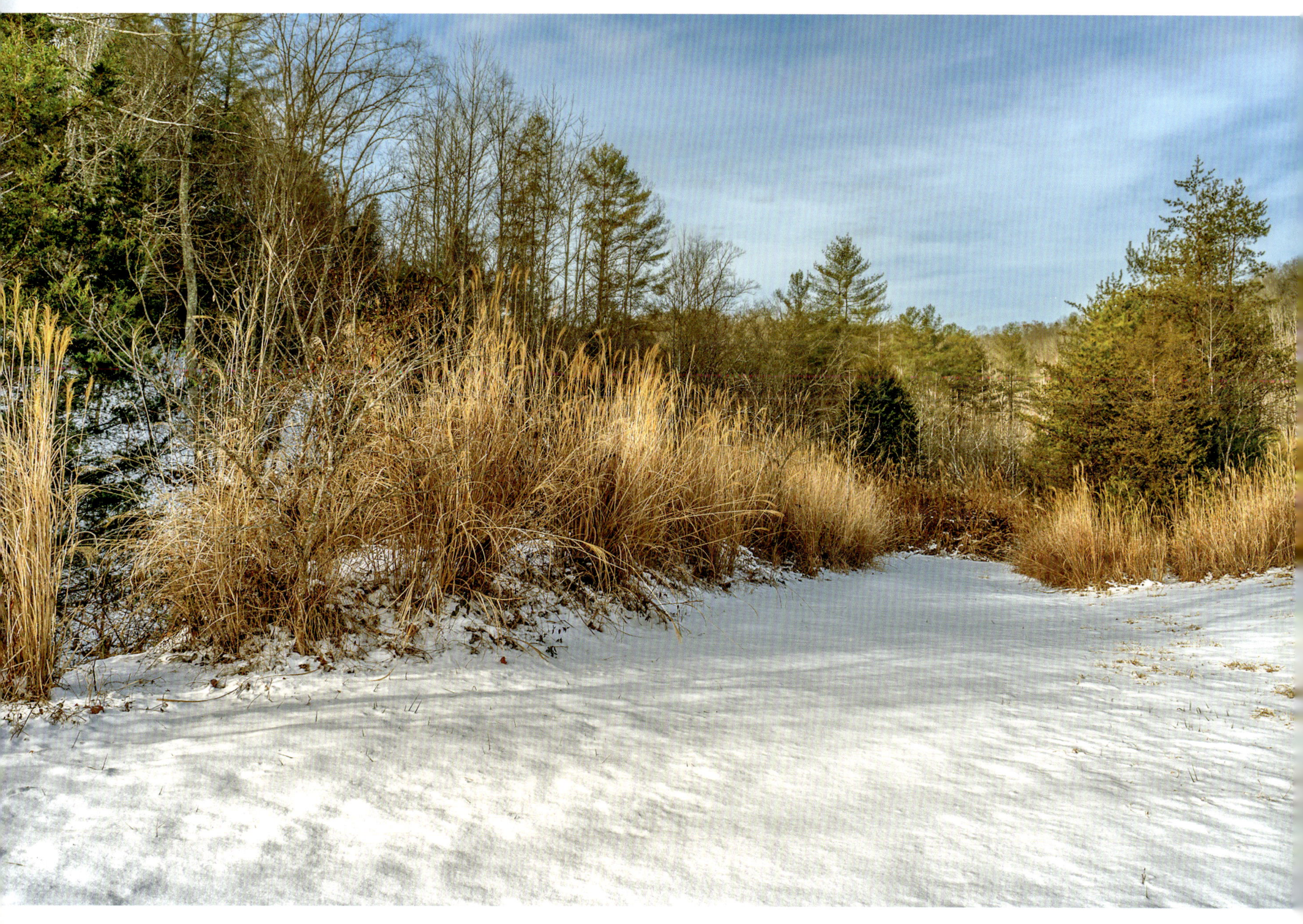

Fresh snow on a trail beckons at Natural Bridge State Resort Park.

FACING The Kenlake Marina hosts sailboats for residents and weekend visitors from cities near and far.

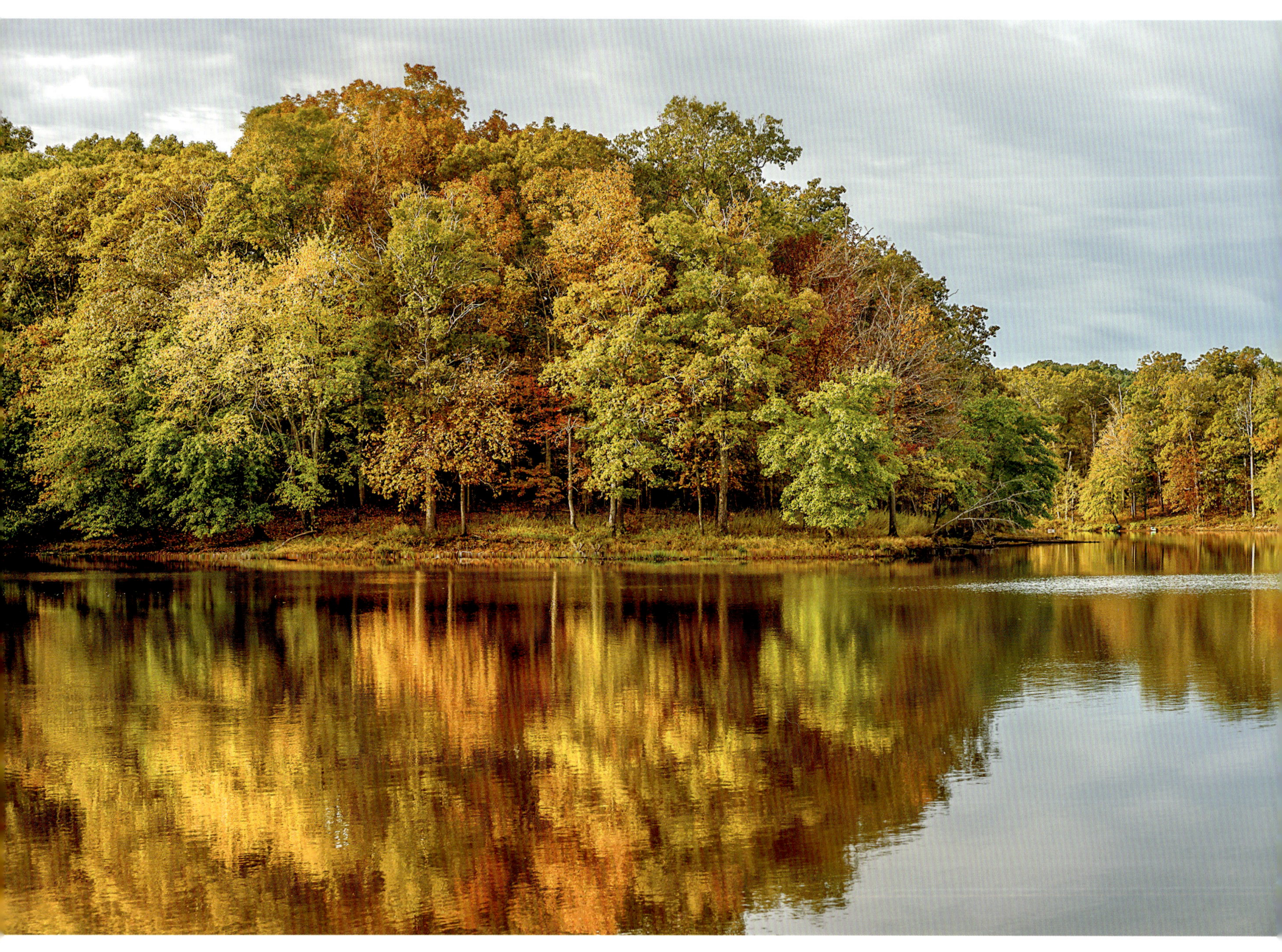

Peak fall color reflected in Energy Lake at Land Between the Lakes National Recreation Area.

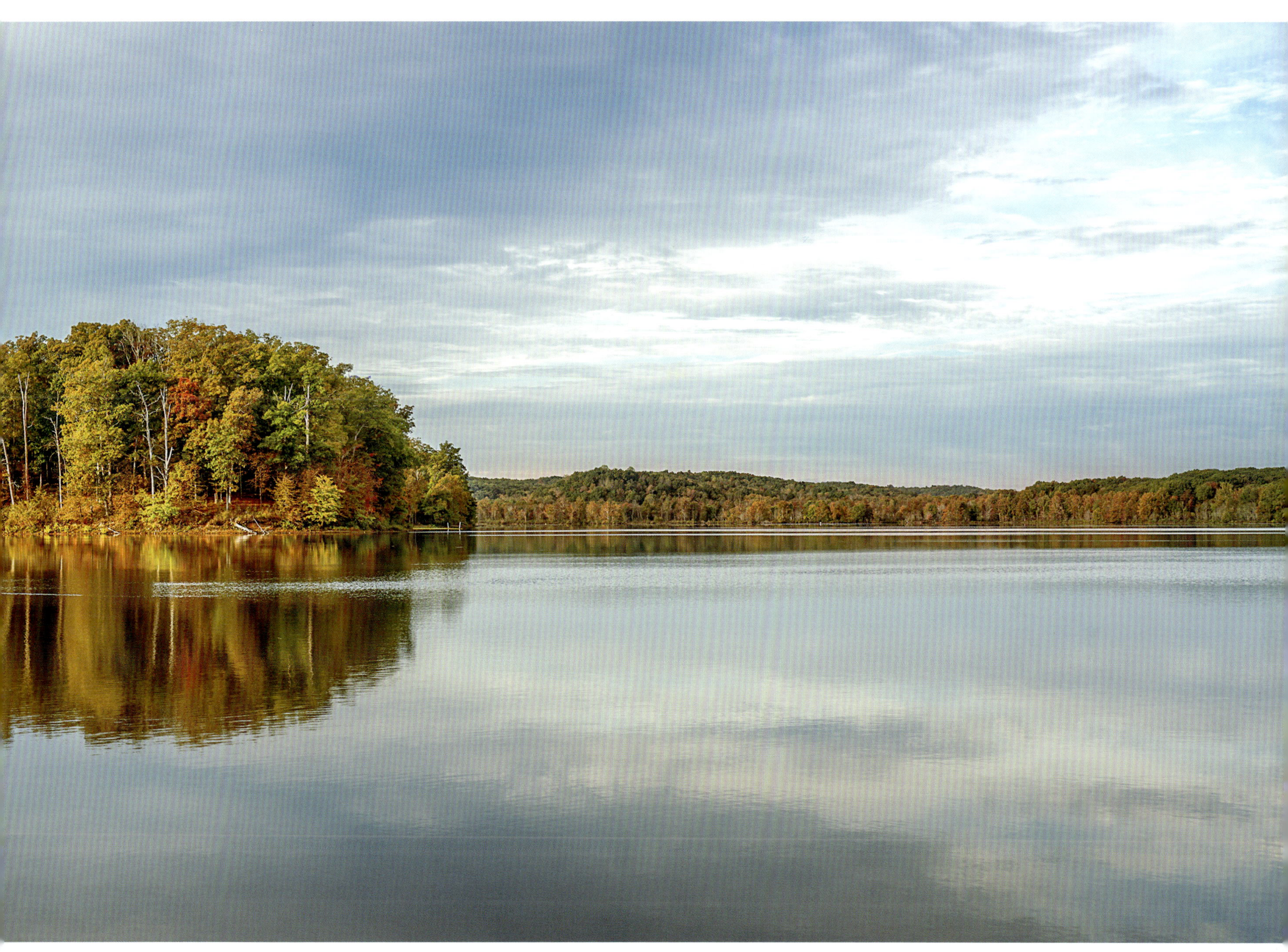

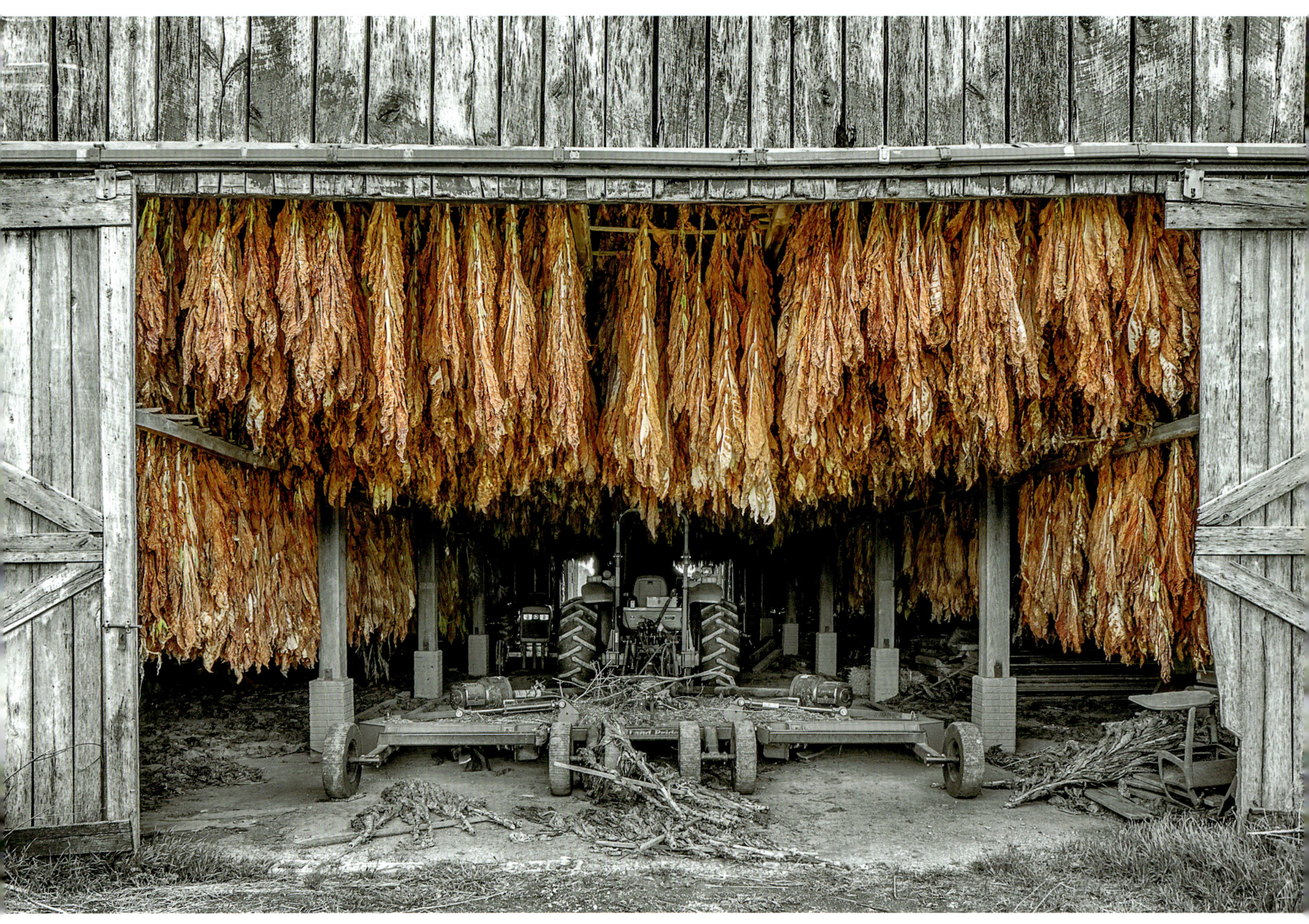

Tobacco is still cured to a rich brown in tobacco barns all over the state of Kentucky.

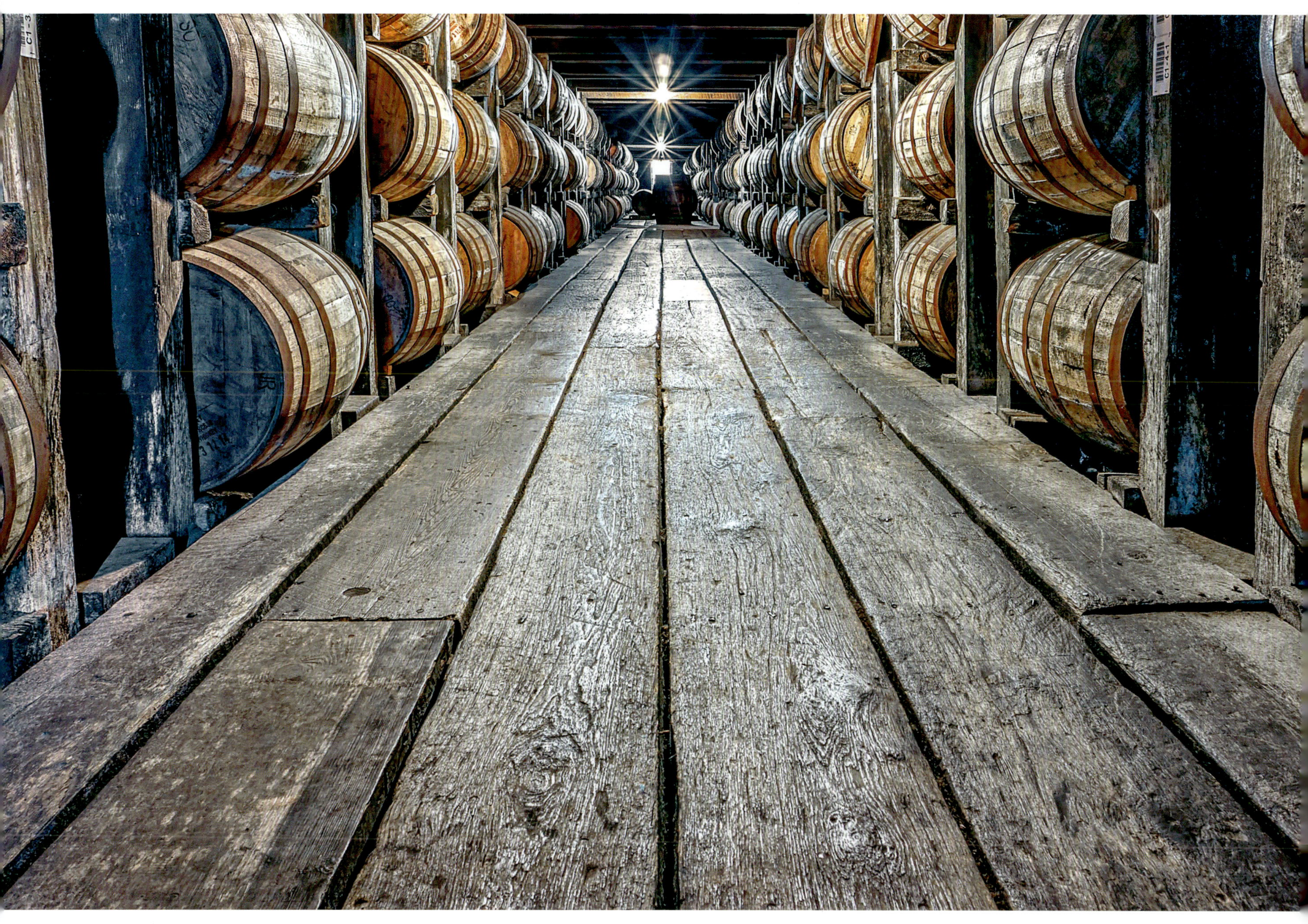

A few years of aging gracefully at Buffalo Trace Distillery.

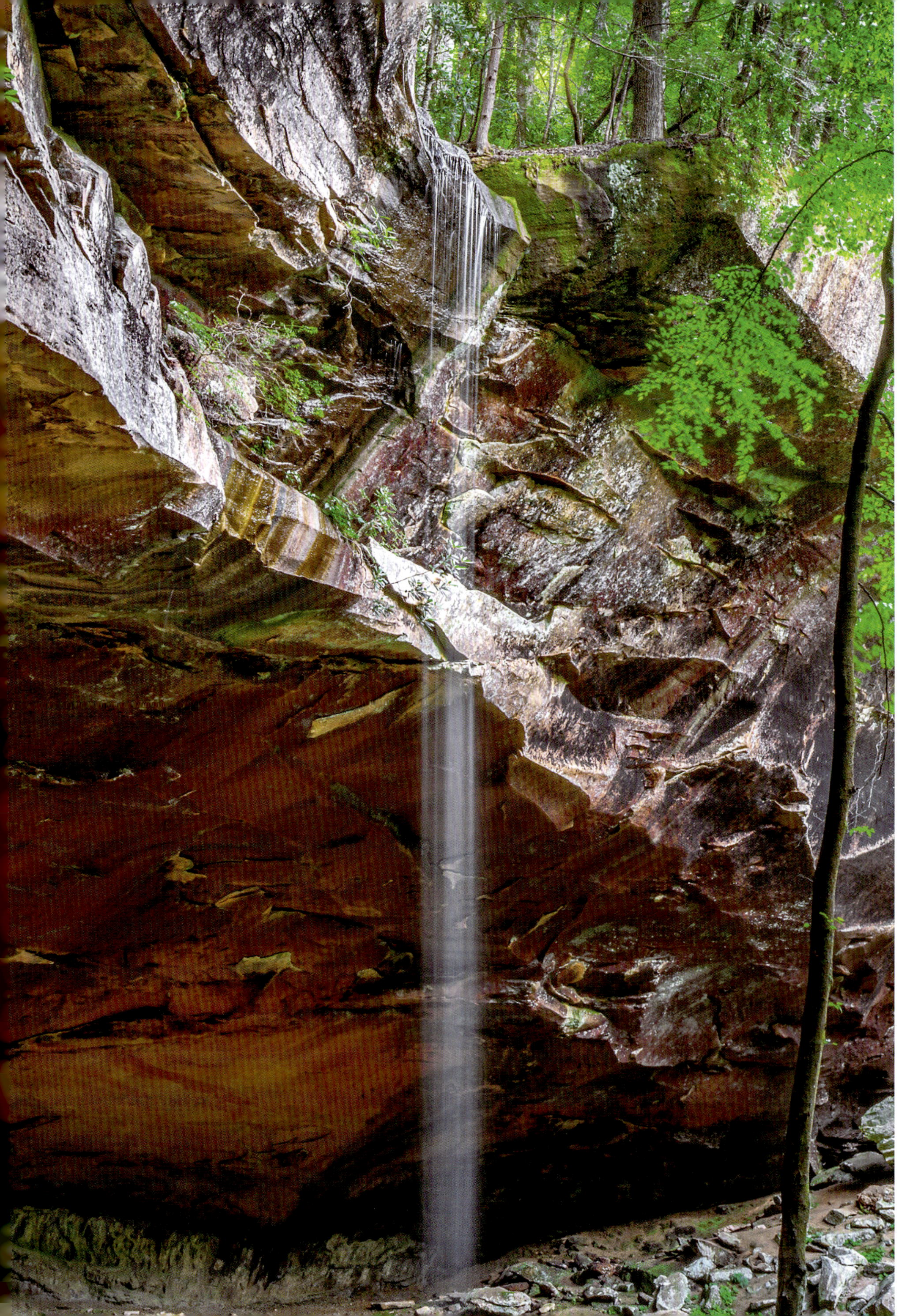

Big South Fork National River and Recreation Area is home to Yahoo Falls.

Nature's art can be seen all around Kentucky.

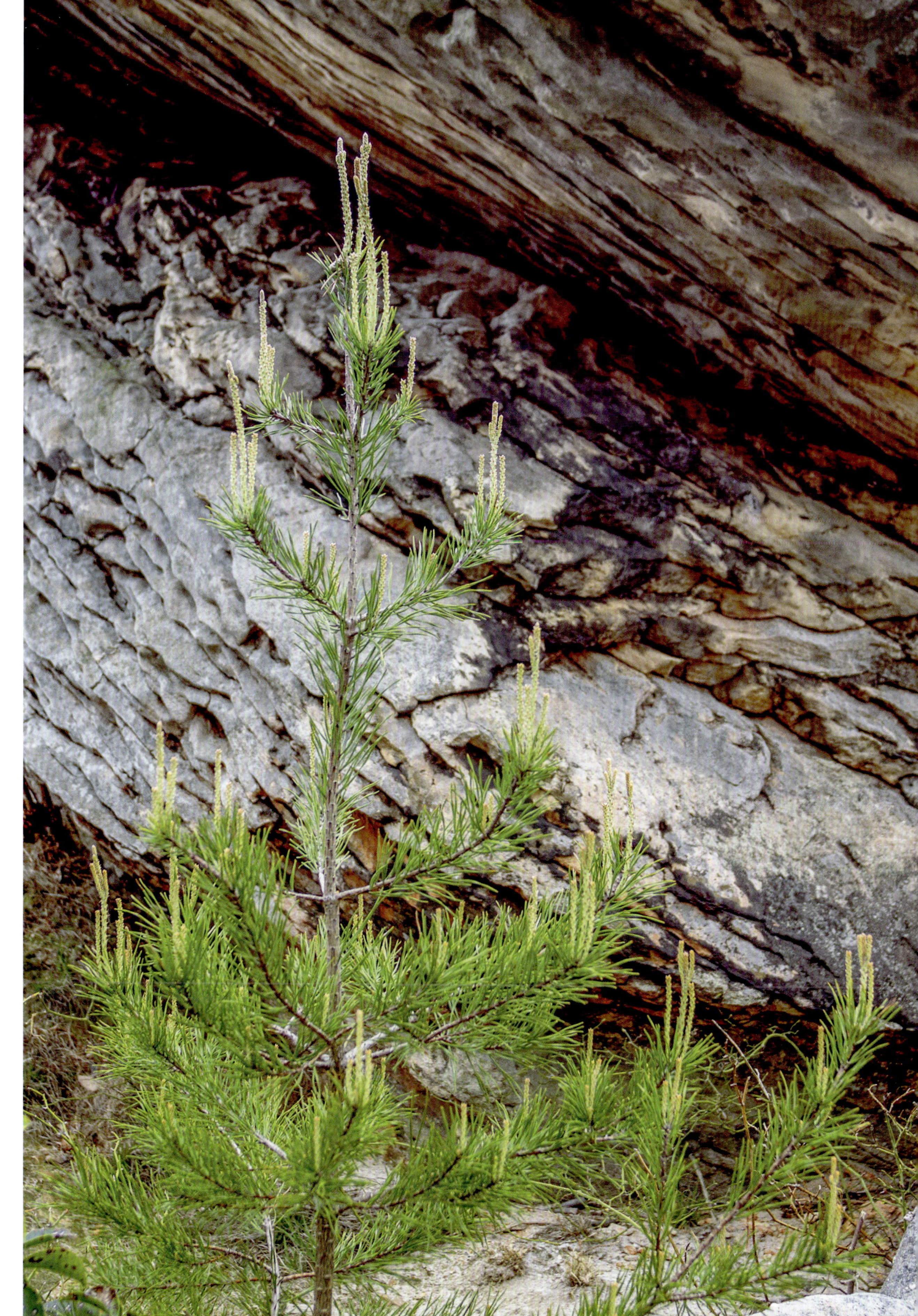

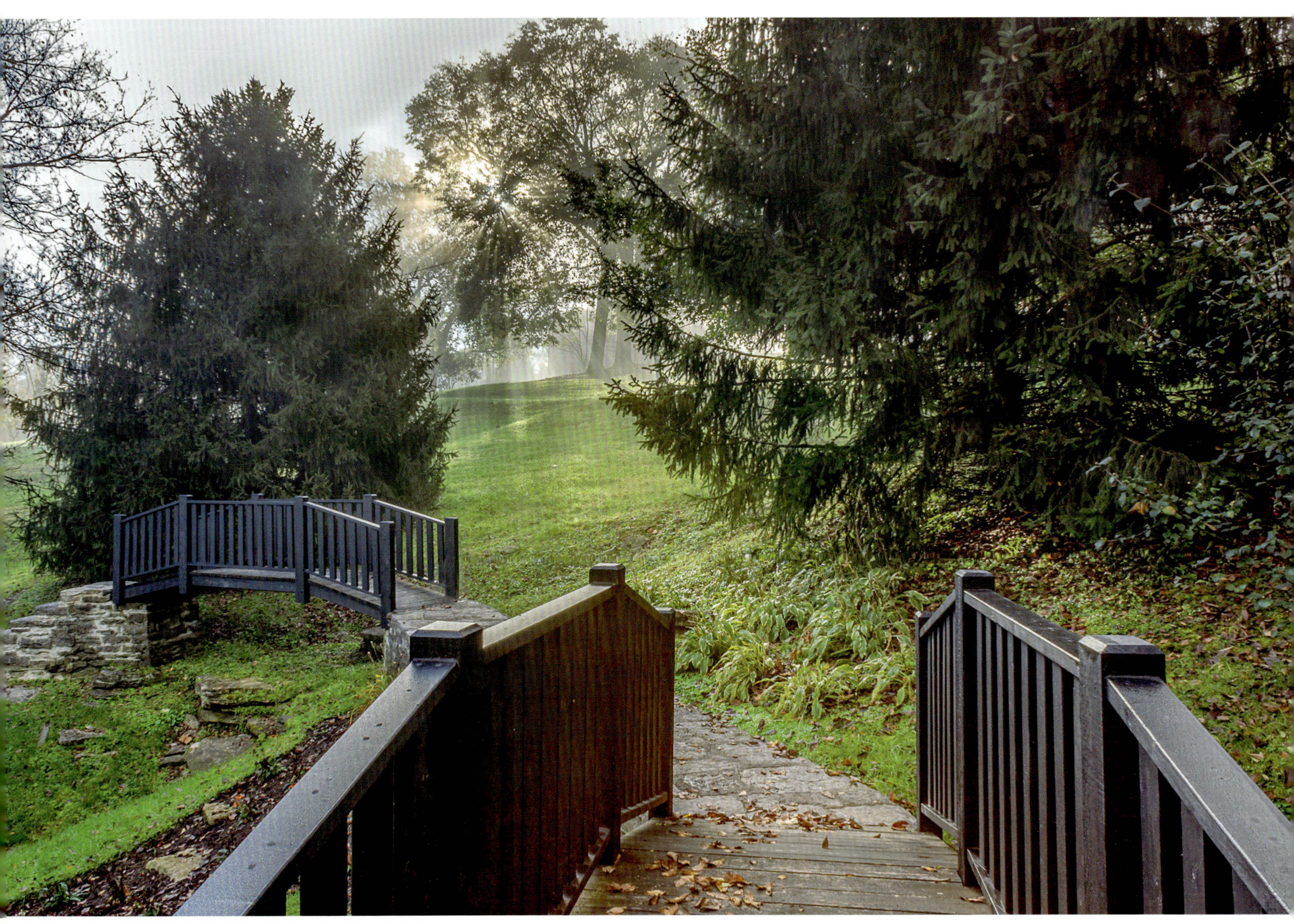

A walk through the gardens at Buffalo Trace Distillery is one more way guests can enjoy their visit.

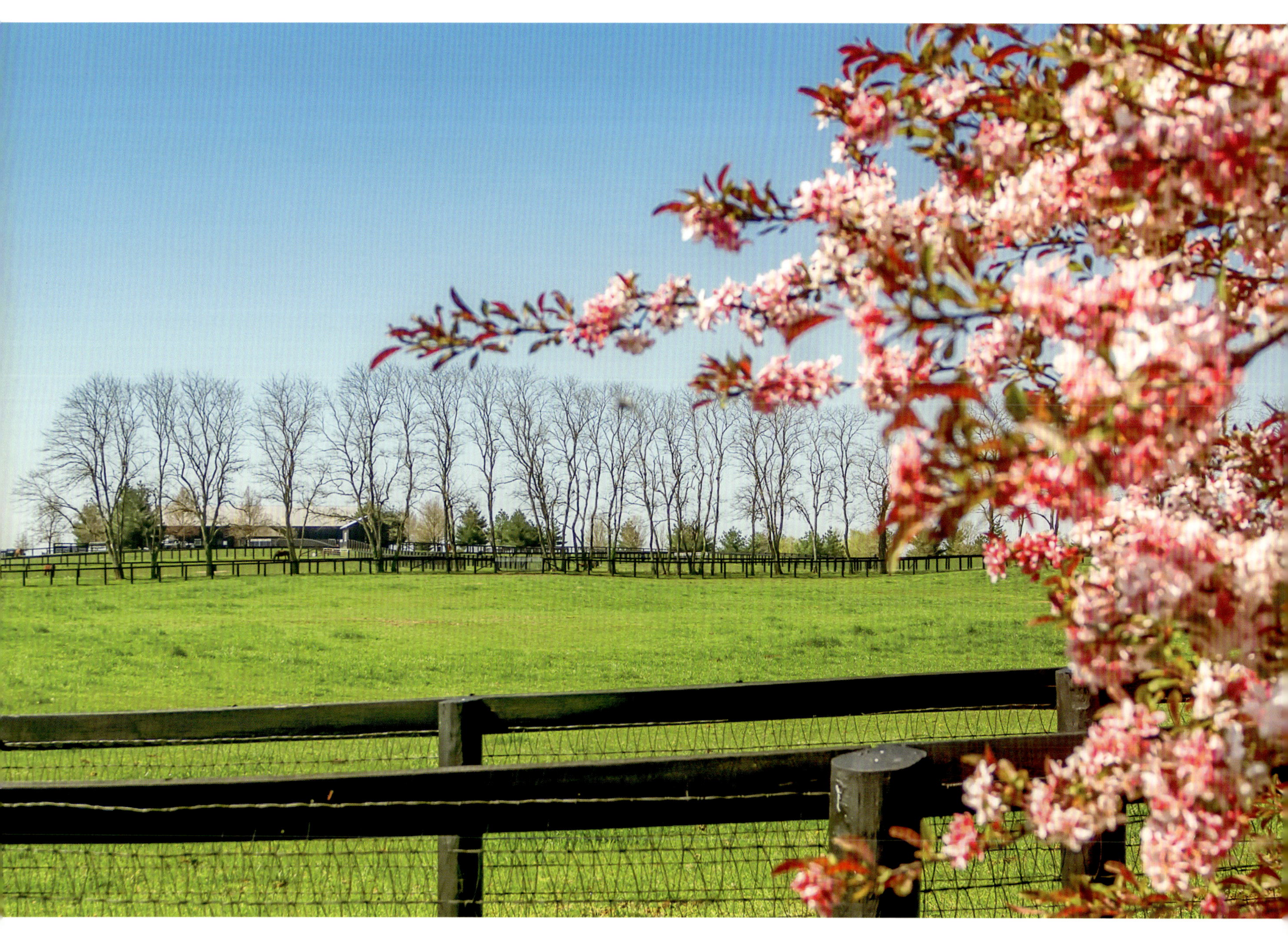

Miles of equestrian fencing run through the bluegrass landscape near the Kentucky Horse Park.

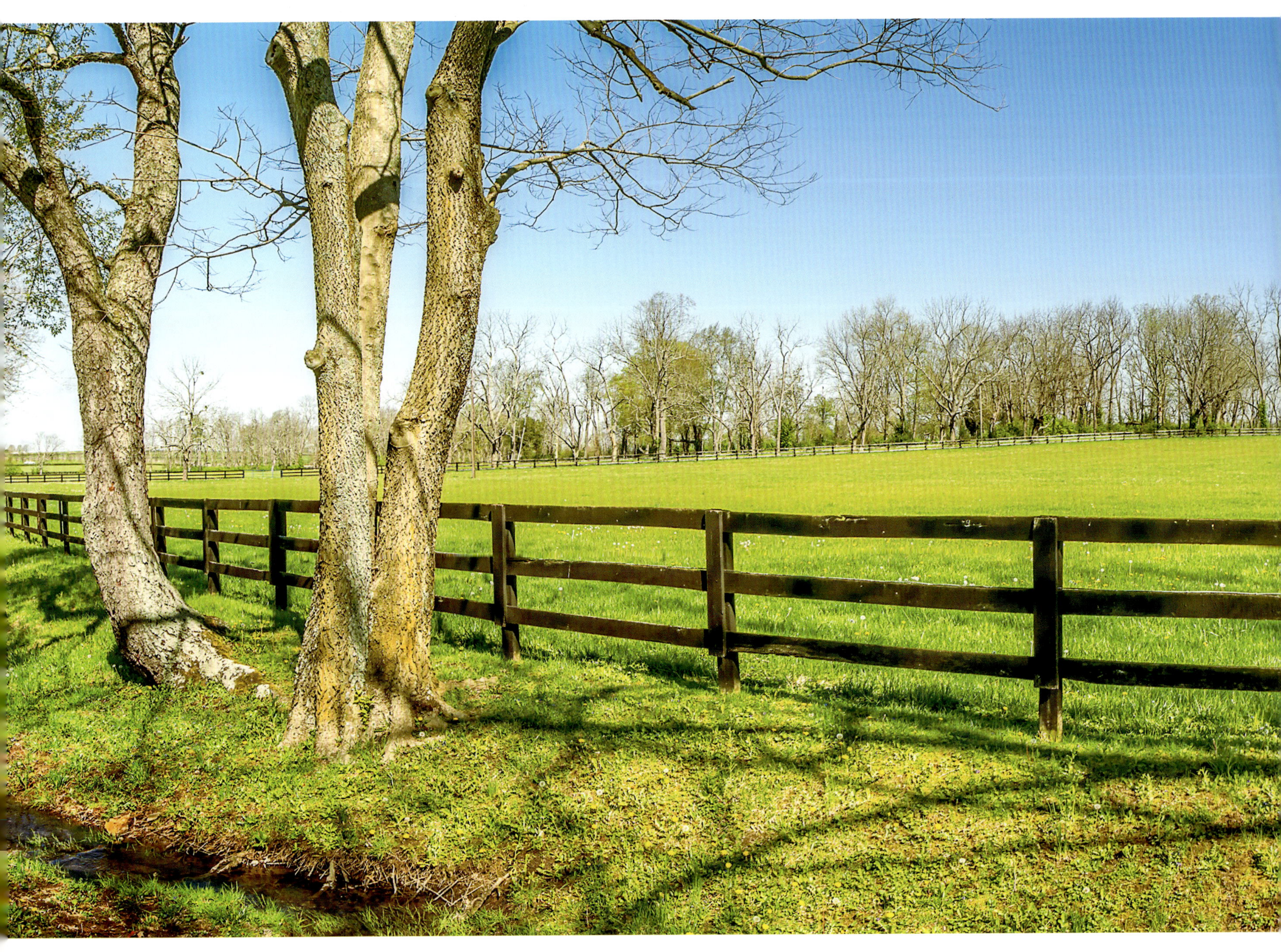

Bluegrass and equestrian fencing are everywhere around Lexington and the Kentucky Horse Park.

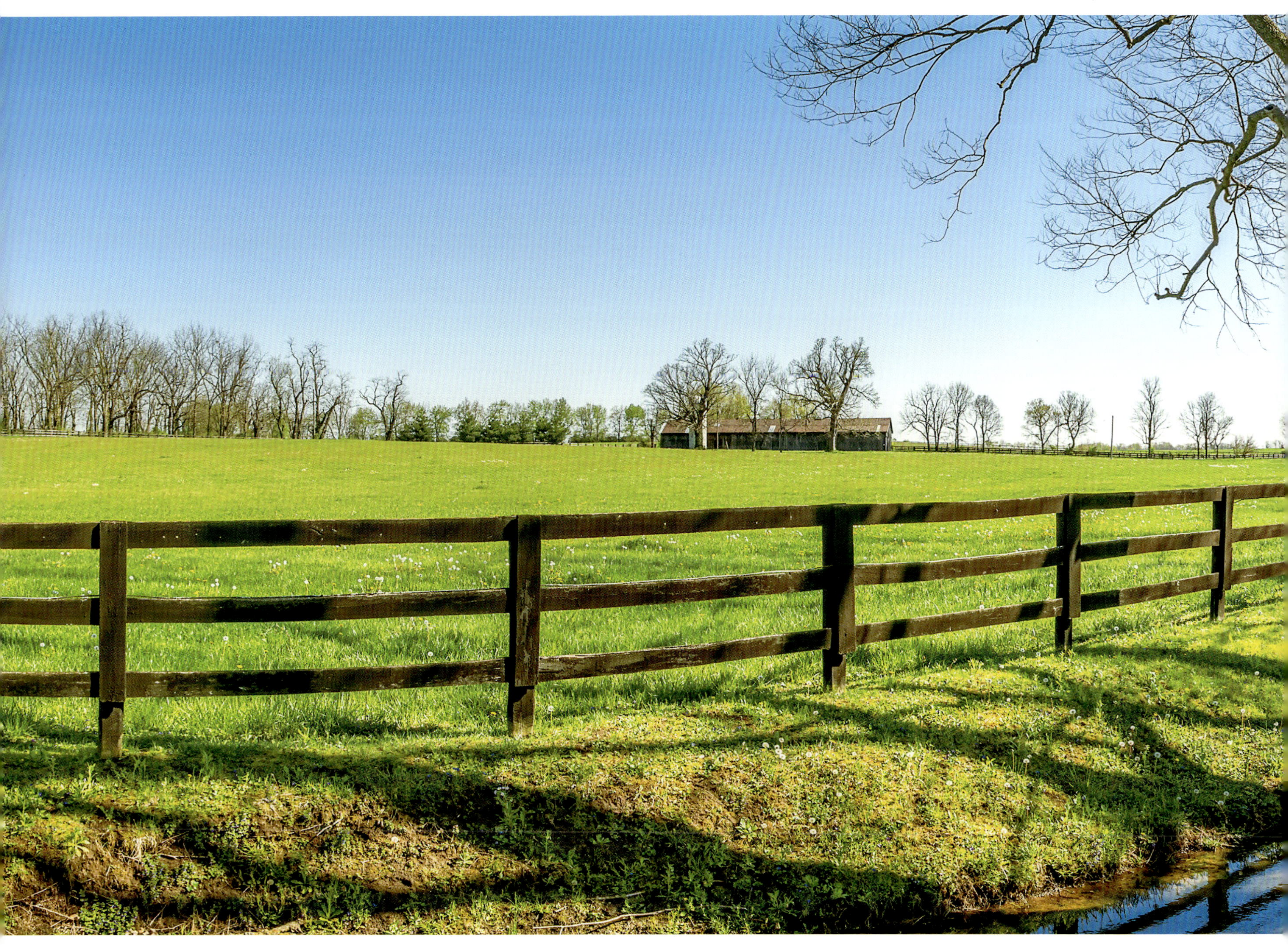

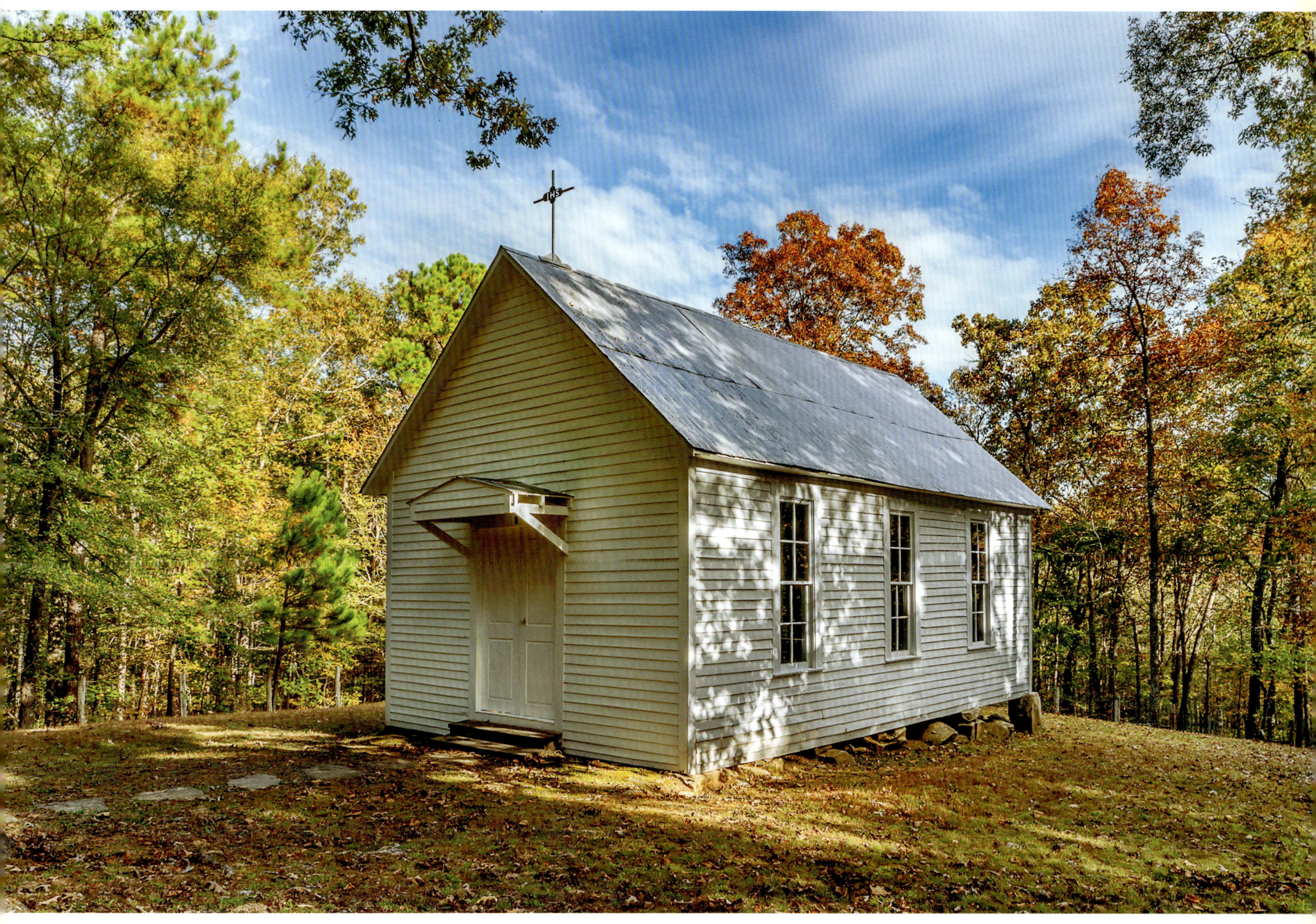

Historical St Stephen's Church is a peaceful haven in the woods at Red River Gorge.

FACING Rich fall color in Red River Gorge begs you to travel farther down the road.

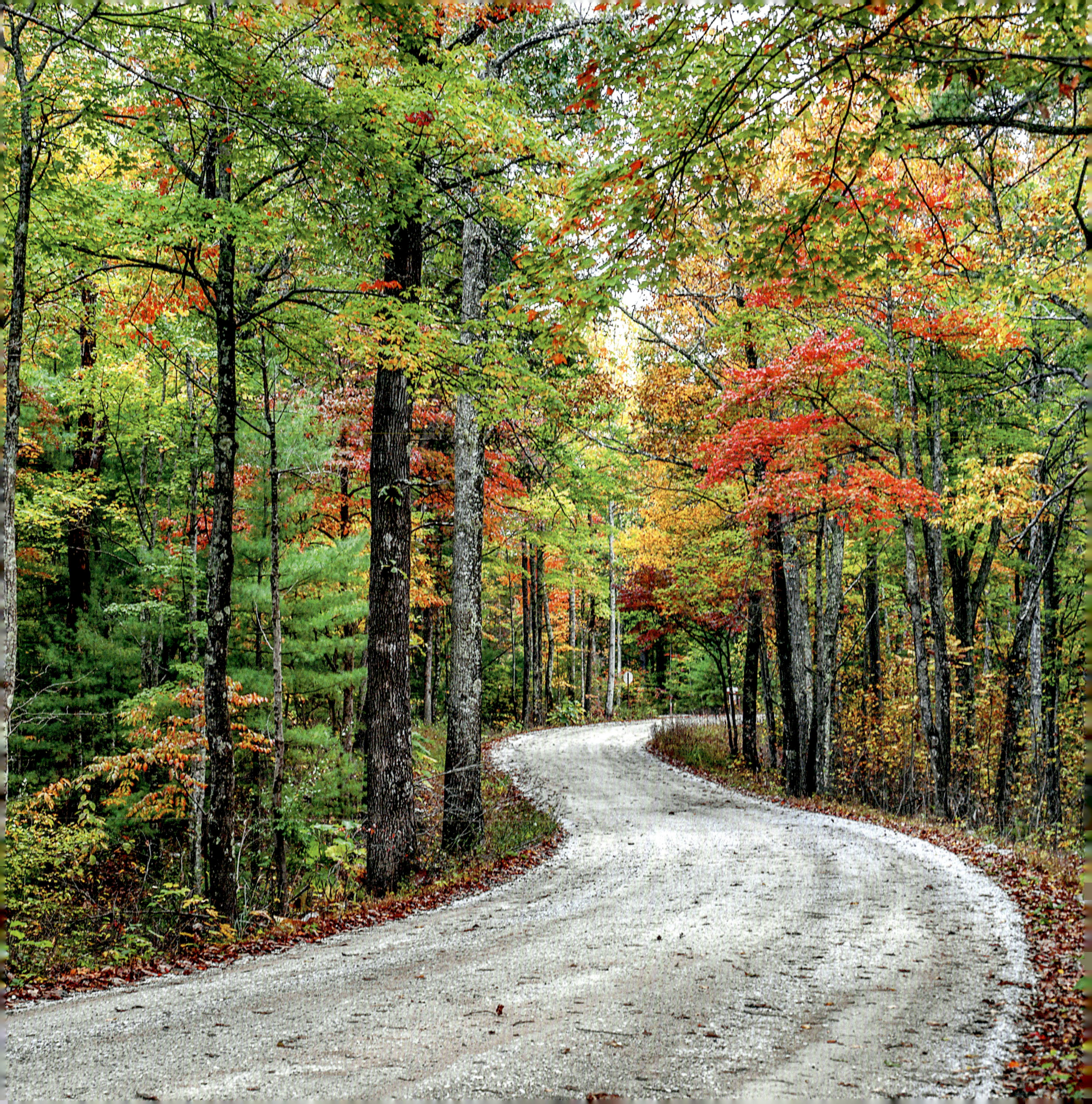

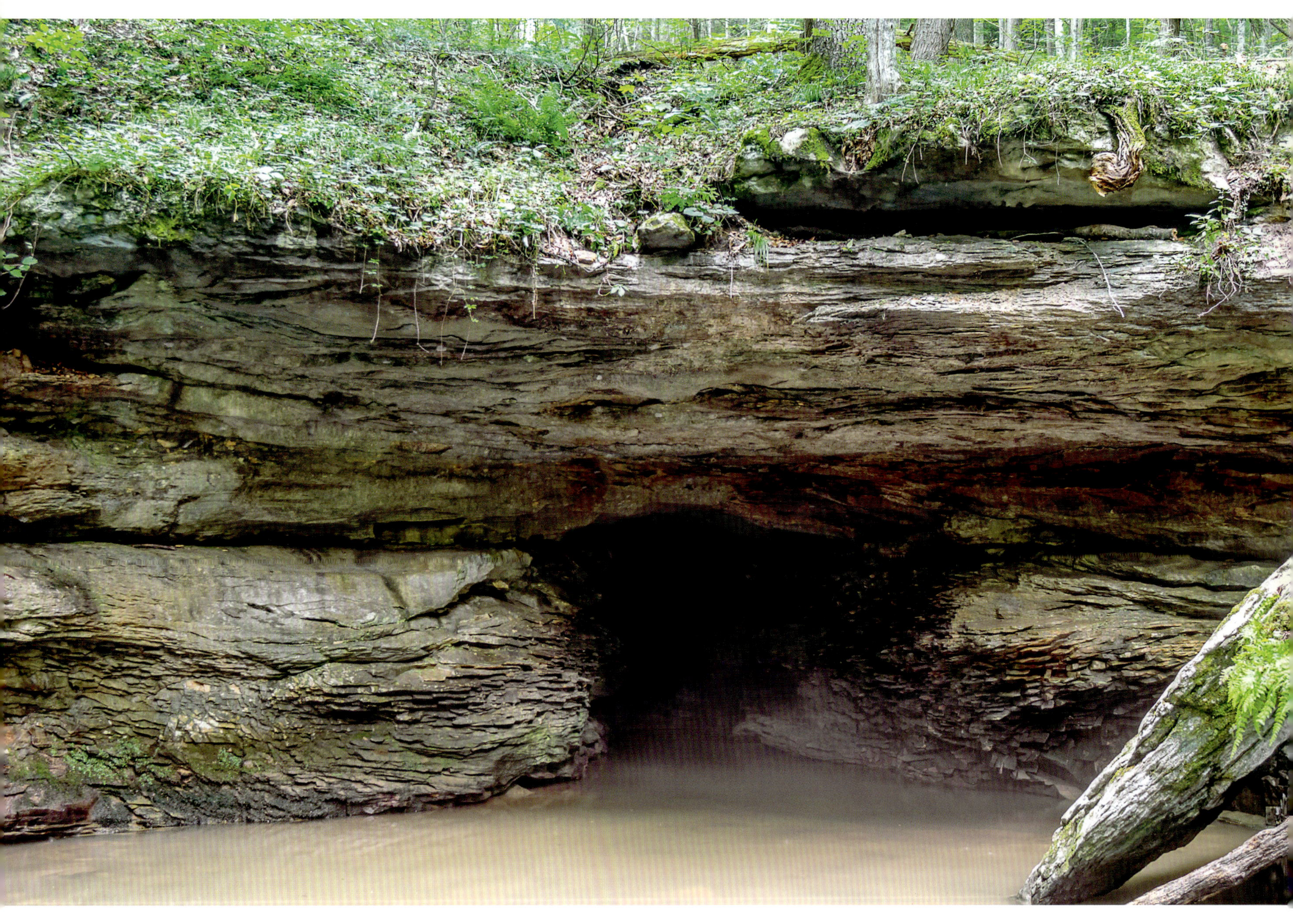

The entrance to Horn Hollow Cave at Carter Caves State Resort Park.

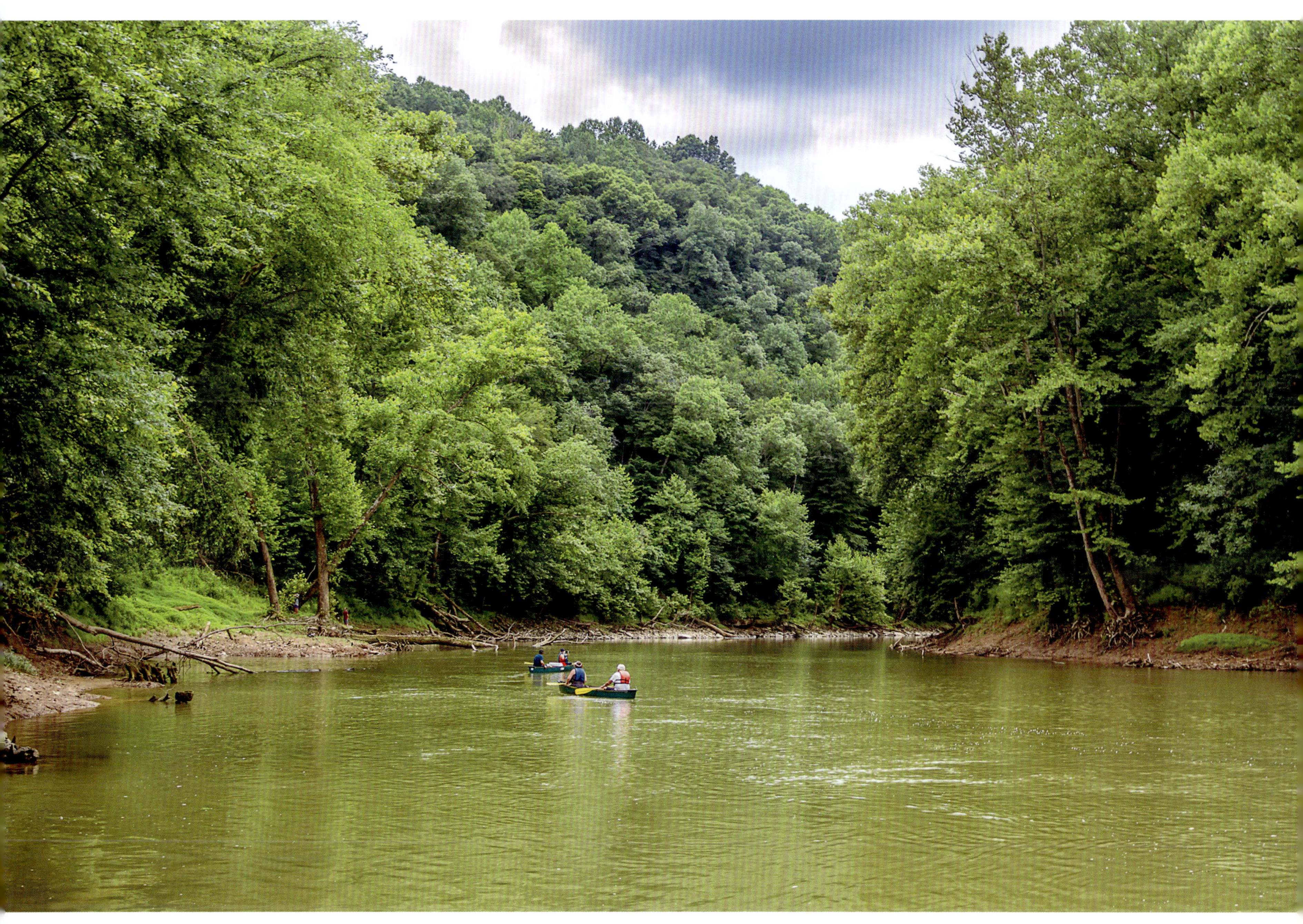

Canoers enjoy a day on the Green River in Mammoth Cave National Park.

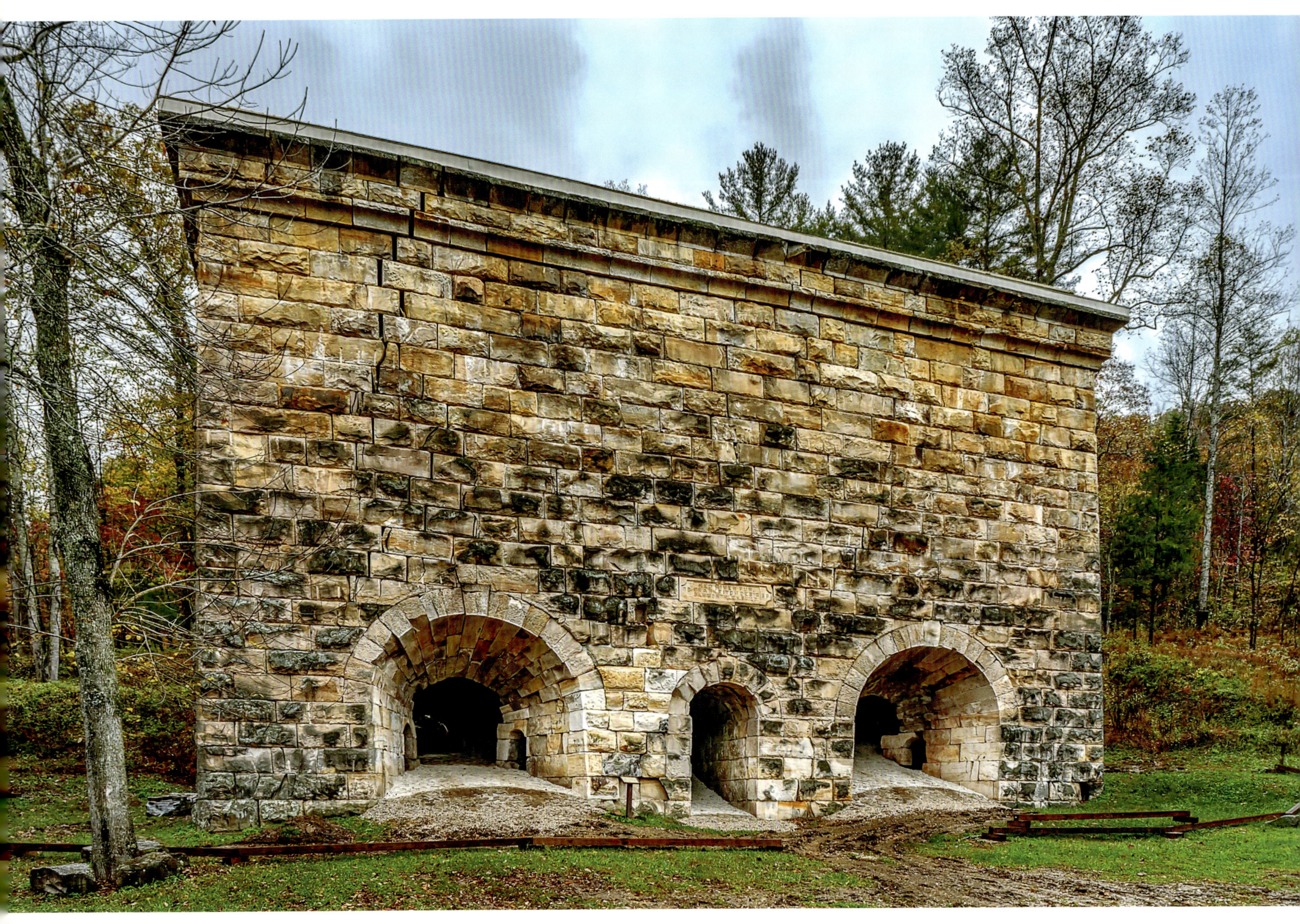

The restored historic Fitchburg Furnace still stands tall in Ravenna, Kentucky.

Mill Creek Lake
on a cool fall day
at Natural Bridge
State Resort Park.

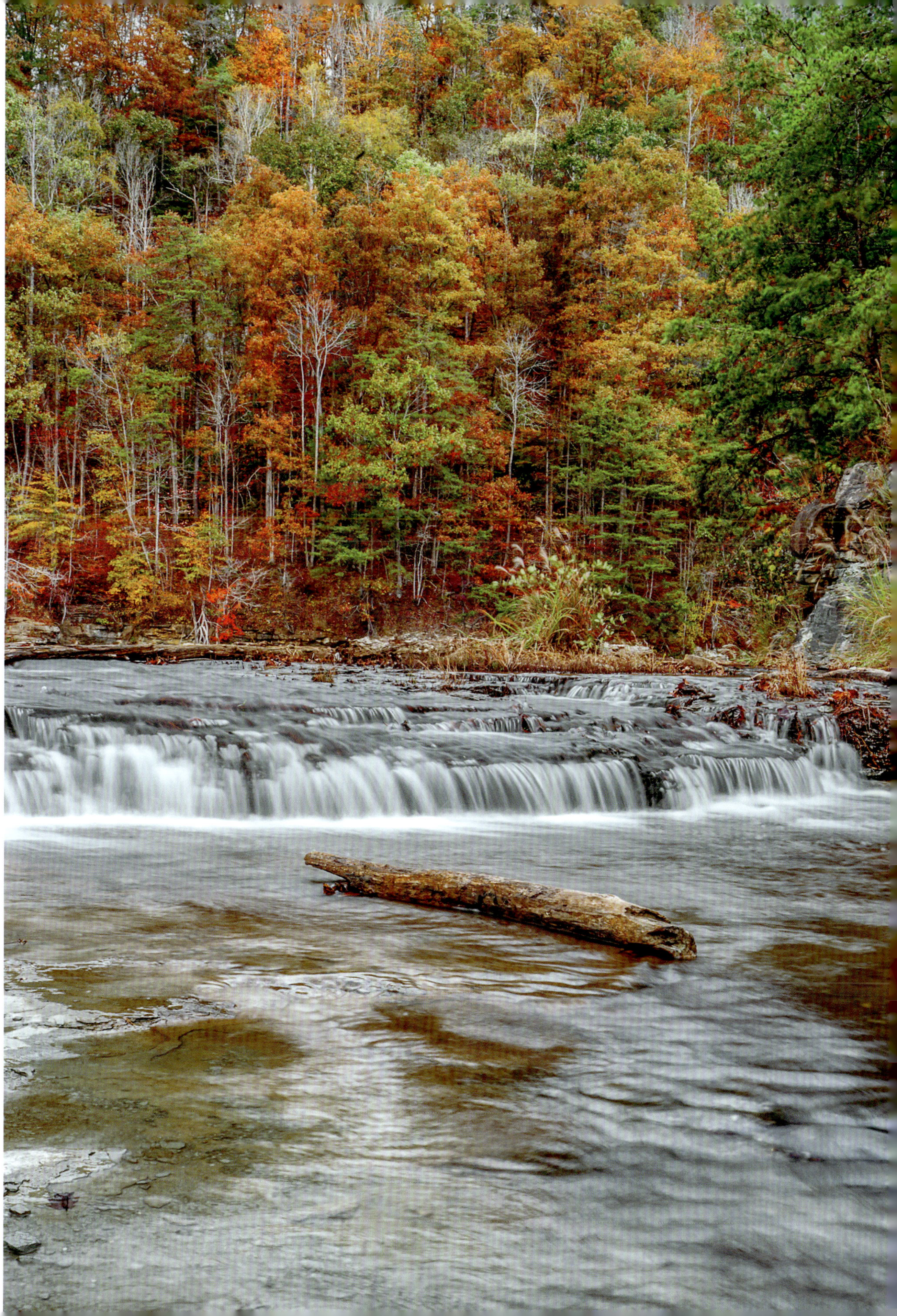

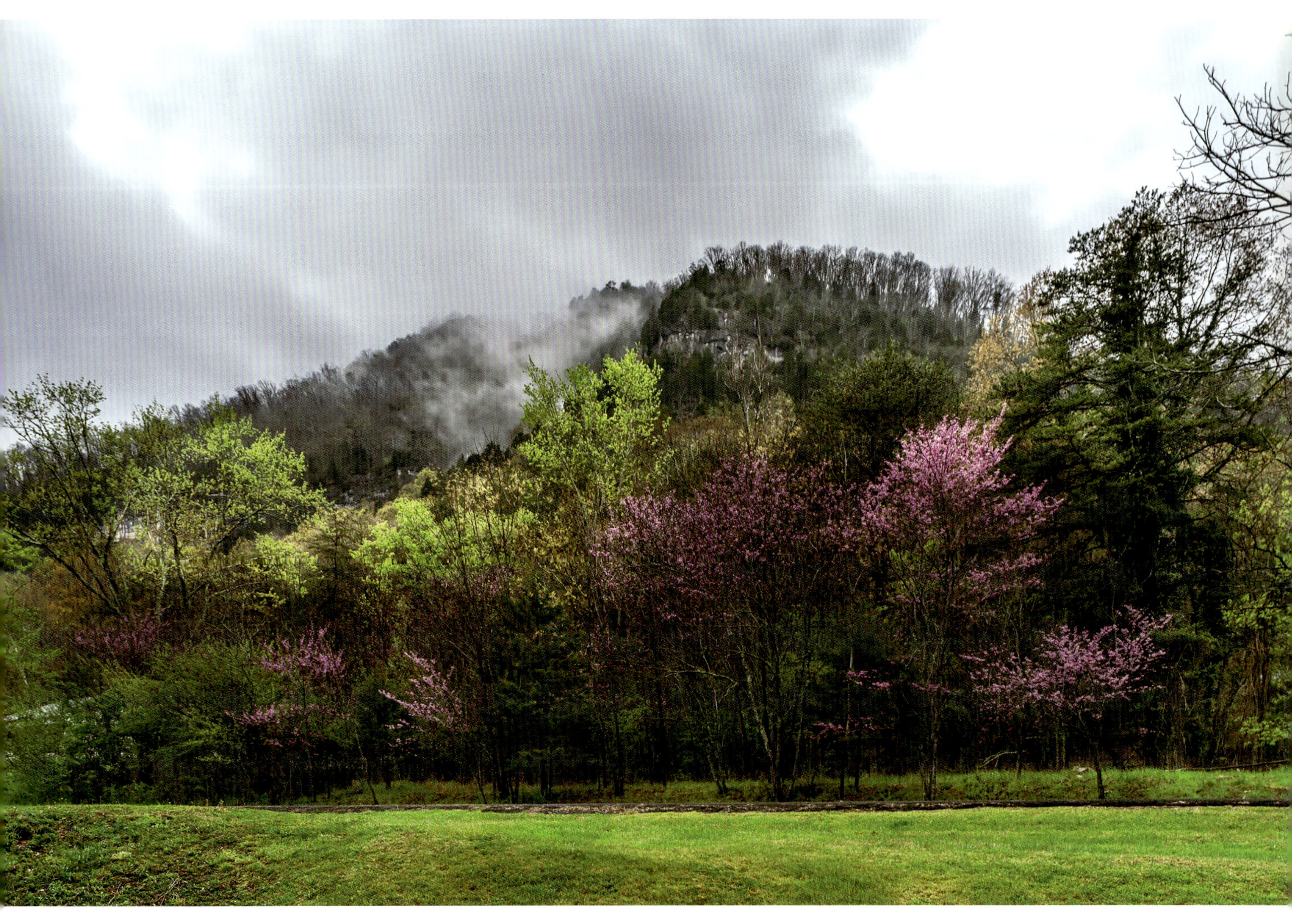

Spring brings a different color palette to the landscape in Cumberland Gap National Historic Park.

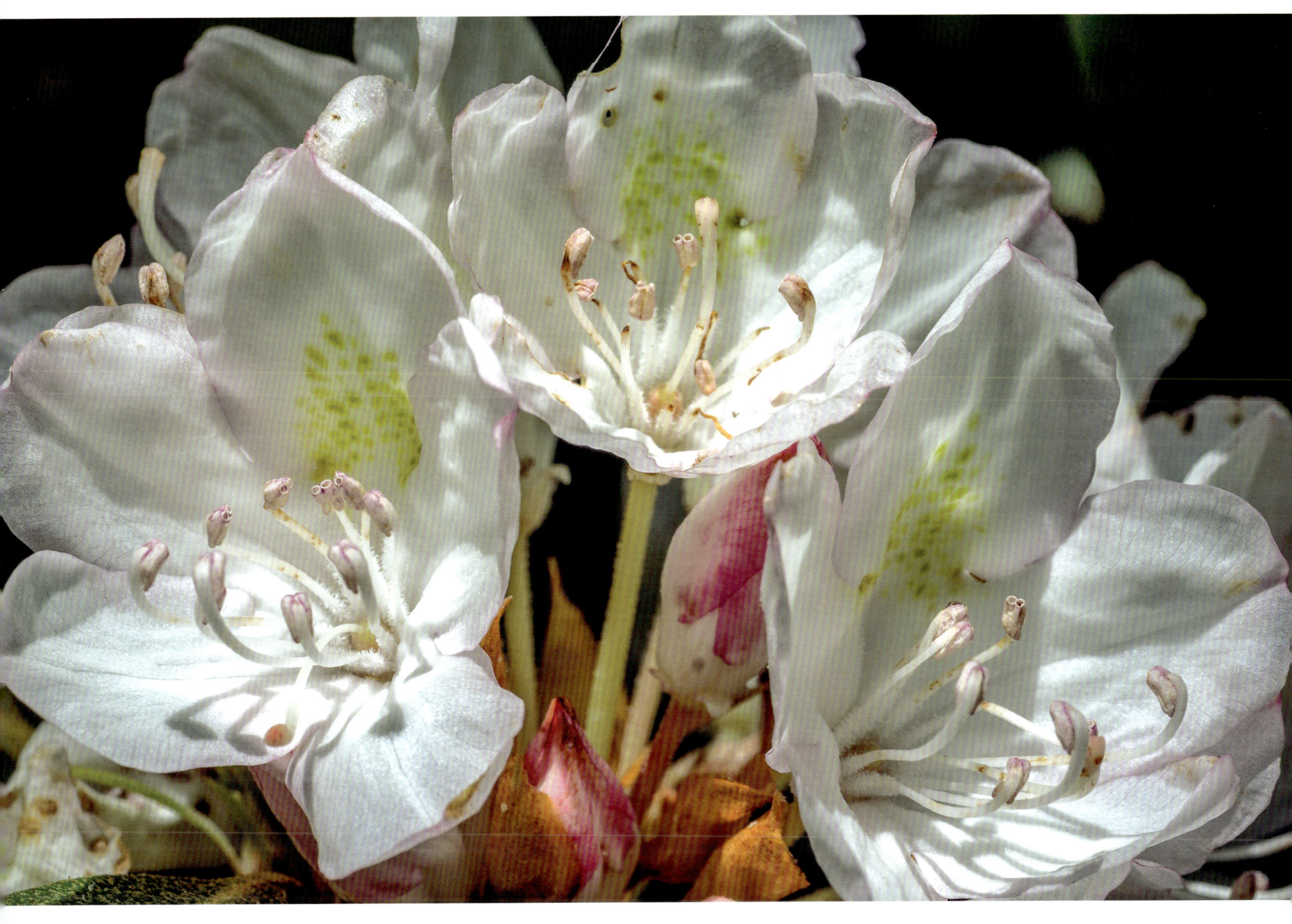

Rhododendrons at Yahoo Falls are a beautiful addition to the surrounding landscape

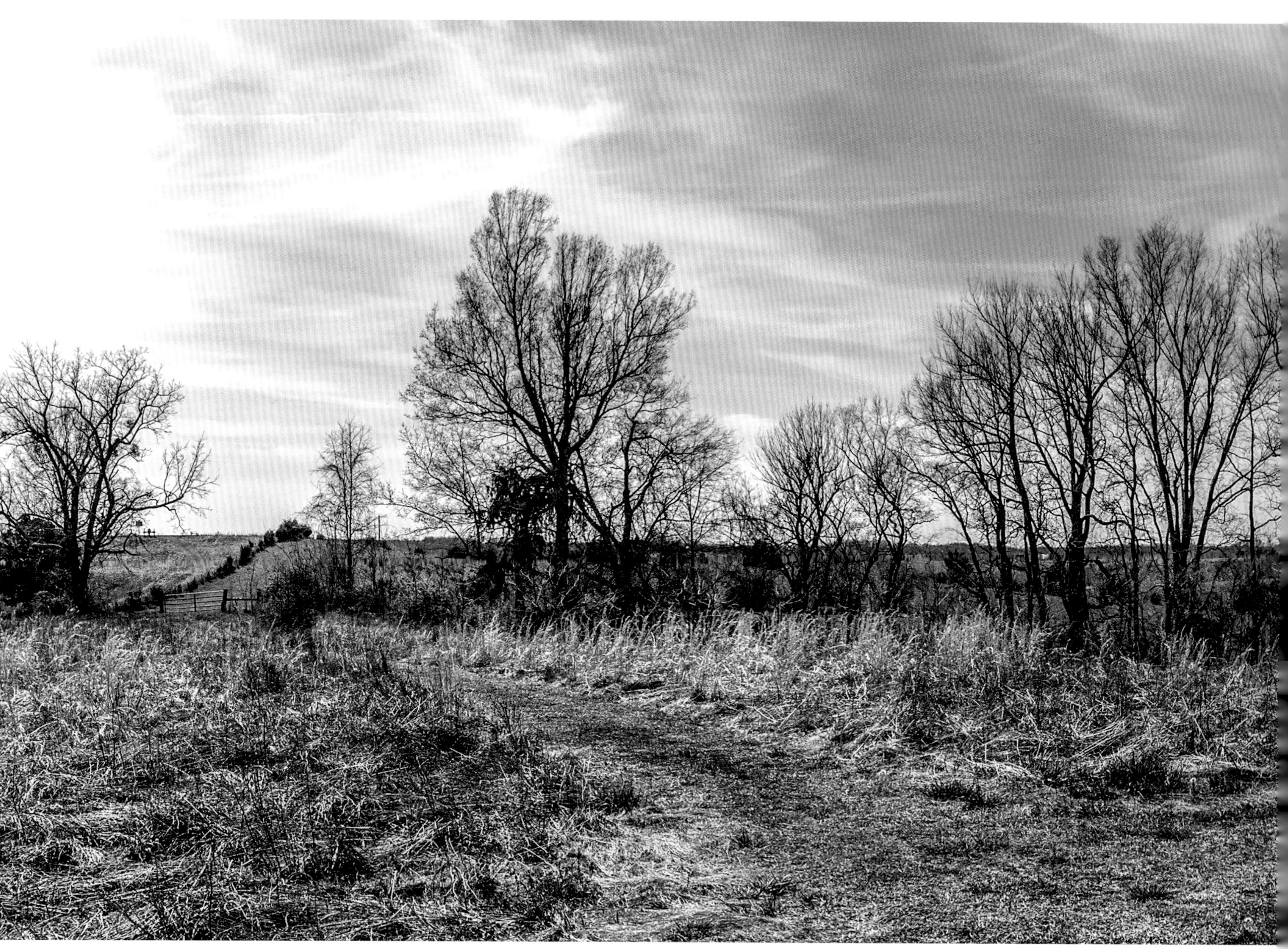

Memories of the Civil War linger at the Perryville Battlefield State Historic Park.

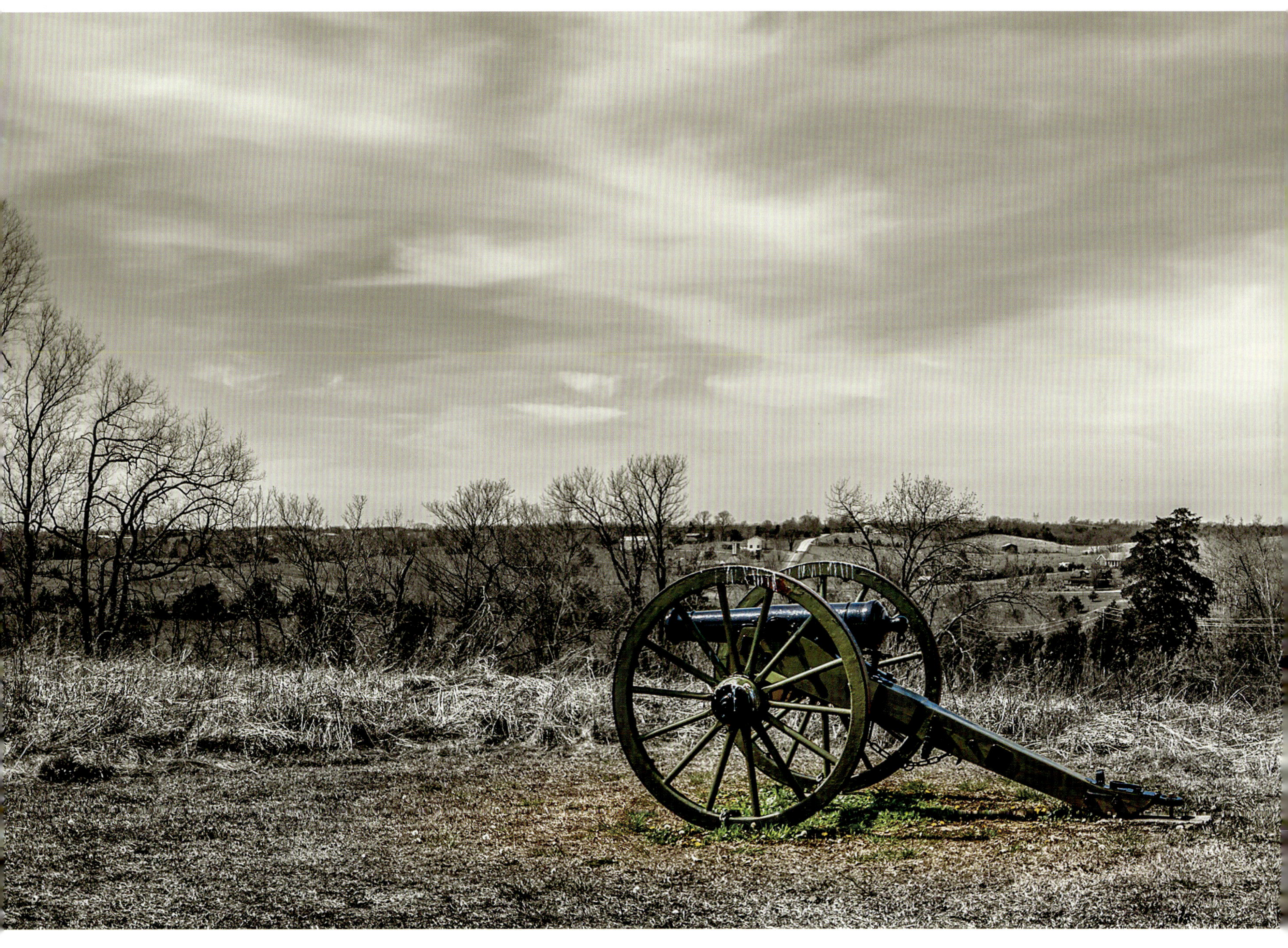

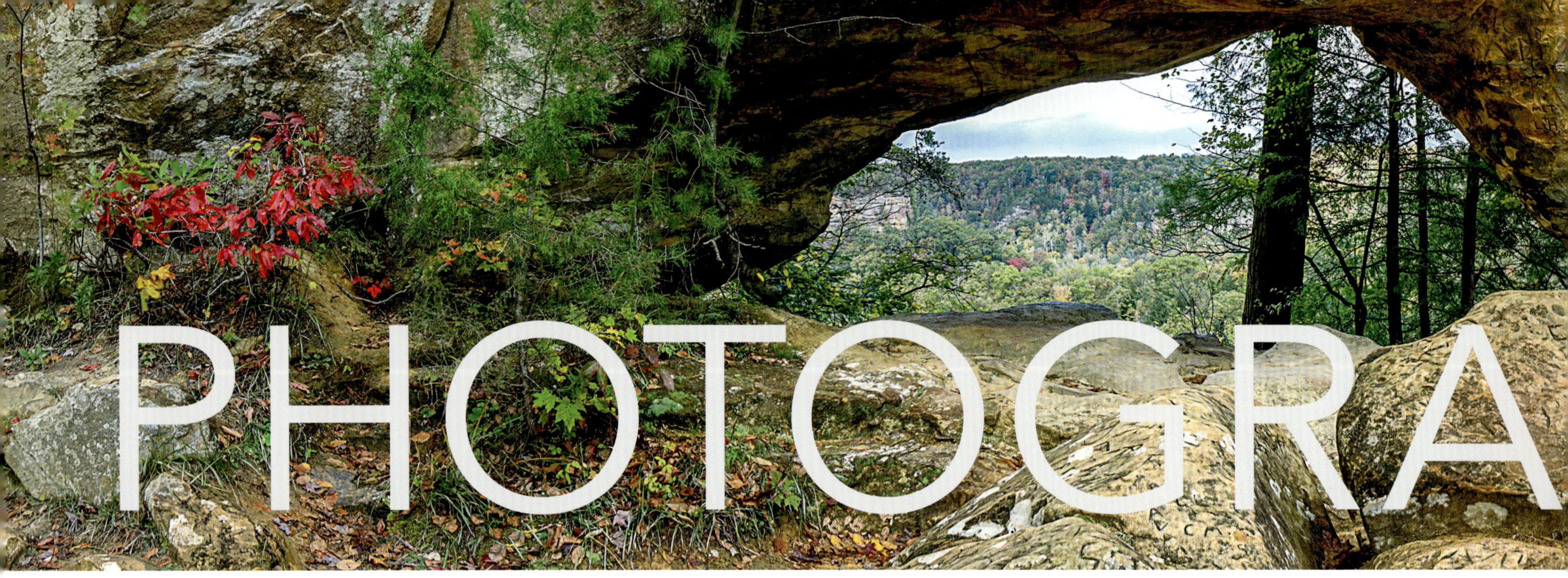

DeeDee and I travel to a lot of places in the central Midwest to photograph the images that are in our series of books, calendars, greeting cards, various print publications, and other media outlets. I do mean a lot. In our travels we tend to bump into quite a few photographers along the way. People who take pictures are anywhere and everywhere. There are casual, serious, and professional shooters alike. They oftentimes occupy the same locations at the same time, and we just join the crowd and blend in when this happens. It's always interesting to talk shop, equipment, or software and discuss ideas and techniques when time allows or the opportunity presents itself. Occasionally someone will ask us to share advice or know-how, and we get to instruct them in a camera function or photo technique. We'll stop what we are doing and give them our best instructions to the best of our abilities. It's always satisfying to assist someone that wants to learn and leave them with some useful information.

Take a quick minute to look at the "about" page on my website, lemansstudios.com, and scroll to the bottom. As you look through the list of equipment that DeeDee and I use for landscape photography, one thing you might notice right away is the lack of new equipment. We don't have an immediate need for it. I find all too often that people I know and meet are swept up in having the newest gear on the market no matter the expense, or they seem to be looking for that magical camera that can take great shots with little more required on their part than pushing a button. This seems to apply to the professionals and the more serious photo crowd more than the casual shooters. As good as cameras and software have become, we still need to know how to use them properly and how to process our images.

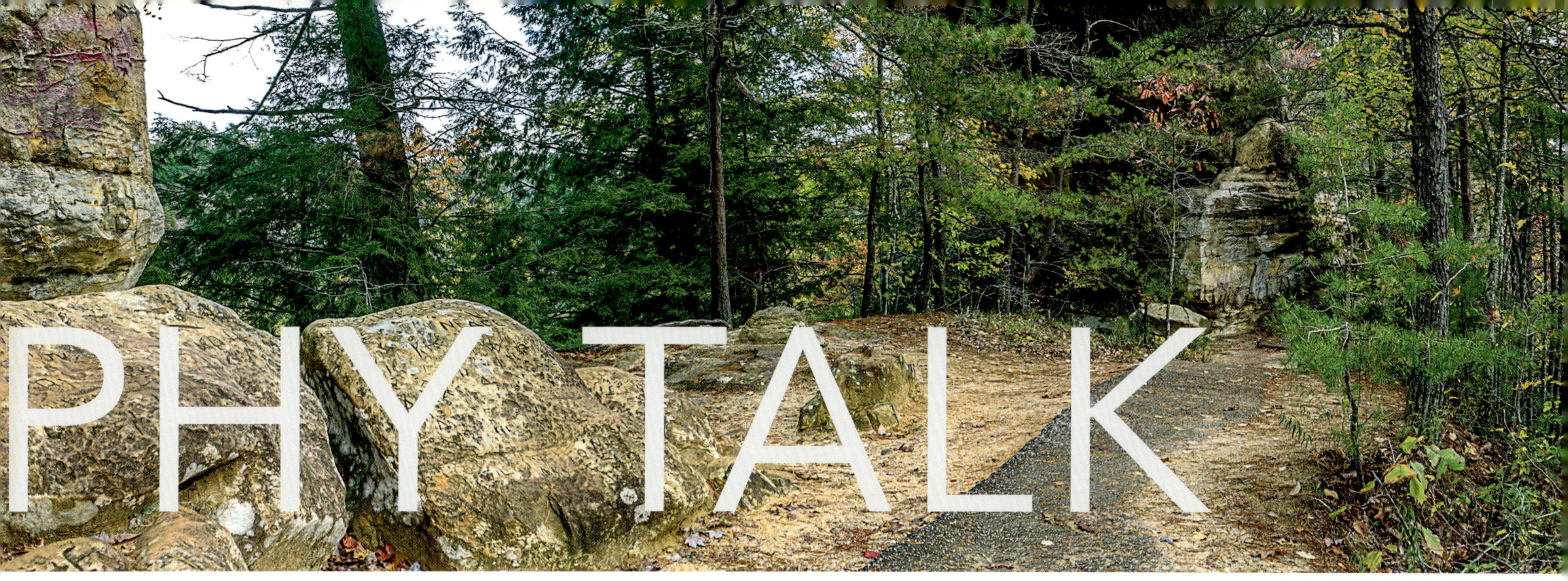

People are also influenced by other photographers and their equipment, especially when those photographers rave about the latest gear they used to get their shots. I have heard people say, "Well, this person on social media said I had to have this camera model and these accessories if I want my shots to look as good as theirs." I ask people to look past new gear on purpose because it's very important to understand that the gear is only a part of making great images. I can't stress this one enough. Gear is only a part of making images. I do agree that people need certain lenses, filters, and accessories. I'm not disputing that. Different types of photography call for specific types of gear. I'm saying you don't have to have new equipment to make amazing images—far from it. You just need to know how to operate the camera you own and know some basic photography fundamentals.

My older gear is of high quality and still fits my needs to this day. It is not at all an obstacle for me to overcome. I have no problem making top-notch images despite not having the newest things on the market. Hanging on to what works is a huge money saver as well, and I always look for used equipment and deals when I do decide I might need to buy something—but that honestly isn't very often. Quality gear is out there that won't break the bank and it doesn't have to be brand new. There are camera shops that carry high-quality used gear and we all know there are online auctions where deals can be had if you are patient and take the time to look for a bargain. Don't fall victim to believing that only a new camera or specific gear is needed to get the images you want to take.

My advice to people that are on the fence about what to do with their time and money is not to invest in new gear, but rather invest in furthering their education by learning about their camera and picking up new photography skills. This is well worth your time, and once you learn a new skill it can never be taken away from you. There are many outlets available today to further learn what interests us. Tutorials are money well spent in my opinion, and there is no shortage of them for any photography technique or craft we want to learn. Research the ones you're interested in and read the reviews to be sure you won't be disappointed with your purchase. Some of them are very pricey, so be sure to do your homework. There are also online subscription services available for photographers to learn their craft that are worth looking into. Obviously, the more you know behind the camera, the better your photos will be. It's a given.

A big area many people tend to avoid learning about is post work and editing. It has gotten to the point where many photographers are now unnecessarily over complicating this task in my opinion. You may find this hard to believe but the images in our book series and showcased on our websites are not overly edited. Yes, they are edited, but we keep what editing we do relatively simple most of the time. I am a firm believer in less is more in my images and I keep the editing grounded in the traditions and techniques I learned in my days as a commercial custom dark room printer. Once in a while I might decide to spend more time on something, but that is purely by choice. I hear some photographers preaching that the only way your images will shine now is to use several software and filter packages. I personally think this tends to scare many people off, not only because of the costs of buying multiple software packages but also because of the investment needed to learn these new programs and filters. In my opinion this is overcomplicating the editing workflow. I can get amazing results with a simplified workflow and minimal software packages.

I use Adobe Bridge for my asset management software. I love the way I can organize, sort, label, mark, and search my images in it. I honestly cannot imagine a better way to keep track of my images. Once they are ready to edit, the raw files are opened into Adobe Camera Raw where I apply a preset with the basic adjustments I want to apply to my images. Once I am happy with what I see here, I bring the image into Adobe Photoshop and do some basic edits there. Occasionally I will have to further reduce noise with Macphun's Luminar Denoise filter if I can't get a satisfactory result from Adobe Camera Raw or inside Photoshop, but aside from that, all of my editing is done between ACR and Photoshop. I can honestly achieve the results I want in one software package and workflow strategy. I spend less time editing but still get the results I want with no loss of quality. In order to be open minded, I have tried looking at other software and filters and have come to the conclusion that I can currently do anything in Photoshop that needs to be done to my images, so I opt to keep things simplified. If your camera work is solid, if you know how to use your equipment properly, and if you apply the correct settings and techniques in a given situation, the editing will be relatively easy and multiple software packages will not be needed.

Photography, like art, is purely subjective. What one person loves in a photo or piece of art, another person will be critical of. I know this is opening a can of worms, but it's important to keep in mind that there is no right way to take a photo and there is no wrong way. There is only the way an individual prefers to take their photos. Sure, we can discuss the fine points all day long—composition, lighting, location, editing or no editing—but in the end, people take photos the way they prefer to take them. I believe it is important to learn to accept and navigate your wants and needs and make images that suit your taste and style and reflect you as an individual. People that do their own thing and are not worried about public acceptance tend to stand out. They bring forth their own visions and not those of someone else. These are the people who are happiest in what they do. In the end, if the way you are taking photos, editing, and sharing them makes you happy, then keep doing it. We should never overlook what makes us happy no matter the public opinion. This is what makes your work unique to you, regardless of whether someone else deems it good or bad.

All of this has basically been to say that I'm a firm believer that the newest gear isn't a necessity, but rather it is learning to use the gear you have and how to process your images correctly that is essential to making quality photos. I'm convinced this is the secret ingredient people are looking for, not some magical new camera or software package.

Lee Mandrell

Kentucky is known for distilleries, horse racing, bourbon, moonshine, coal, tobacco, bluegrass music, and Kentucky Fried Chicken. But I think that list is missing something—photography! This state has a variety of landscapes and treasures that just cannot be ignored. Rolling green hills are nearly everywhere, sprinkled with farms, historical sites, caves, and other photo-worthy scenes.

The northern part of the state, bordered by the Ohio River, creates a perfect setting for the city of Louisville. Louisville is a beautiful, bustling city with much to do, see, and photograph. Sports, art, gardens, cityscapes, and architectural photos will keep a camera busy for days. Louisville is also close to several other interesting features, like Mammoth Cave State Park and O'Bannon Woods State Park among others.

Traveling farther south you come to Red River Gorge Geological Area. Rocky cliffs and arches are a main feature here, along with the Red River itself. There are opportunities for lots of sports and outdoor activities ranging from boating to rock climbing in the Red River Gorge. Along a few of the hiking trails you will see arches and waterfalls too. Going home with a gallery full of images is never a problem!

A little farther to the southwest is Frankfort, Kentucky, the state capitol, with its lush landscaped grounds. Frankfort is a fascinating historic town that definitely takes pride in its history. It is also home to one of Kentucky's earliest bourbon distilleries, Buffalo Trace Distillery. Buffalo Trace is a beautiful place to photograph, on the grounds as well as on the tours. Frankfort is a place you will want to visit.

Not too much farther south is Lexington, Kentucky. Lexington is known for being home to thousands of horses, horse ranches, and of course horse racing. Driving through this area is a treat in every way. The landscape, the ranches, and the horses are just a delight to the eyes and the camera. A day in the Kentucky Horse Park and surrounding area is a fantastic experience and photo excursion.

Hiking shoes are recommended for the southeast end of Kentucky. State and national parks and recreational areas are abundant in this part of the state, including places like Cumberland Gap National Historic Park, Big South Fork National River and Recreation Area, and Cumberland Falls State Resort Park, to name just a few. Kentucky claims only a small part of Cumberland Gap National Historic Park but it is still a site to see. Cumberland Falls State Resort Park offers very photogenic waterfalls, including Eagle Falls and Cumberland Falls. Cumberland Falls is also one of the nation's best places to see a moonbow when conditions are right. Nearby Yahoo Falls, in the Big South Fork National River and Recreation Area, is said to be the state's tallest waterfall at 113 feet. This area is also home to natural arches, an array of wildflowers in season, and enough photographic opportunities to stay for days.

The Daniel Boone National Forest ranges over eastern Kentucky from the Red River Gorge to the Tennessee border. Throughout the forest and surrounding areas there are a variety of geological features, state parks, historical sites, wildflowers, and outdoor activities. There is just no shortage of places and things to photograph.

Traveling from east to west in Kentucky, you can't miss the rolling hills and sweeping landscapes. Taking the back roads will take some time, but places of historical interest are everywhere—as long as you can take your eyes off the scenery long enough to notice them. Quaint little towns speak of times gone by, and some look like they never left the era they were built in. They make wonderful photos that take you back to an earlier, simpler way of life.

On the far west side of Kentucky, Land Between the Lakes National Recreation Area offers 170,000 spectacular acres to photograph. Wildlife, nature, historical sites, and of course lakes always make great photos. Land Between the Lakes has plenty of all of these to offer. There is even an Elk and Bison Prairie in the area that offers a glimpse of past times when these animals roamed free. Driving through a herd of these large animals is an experience to remember. They are amazing animals to photograph and in this park you will be up close and personal.

Photographing Kentucky has been a fun and exciting experience! The hardest part about photographing this state has been deciding which images would make it into the book. No matter what you like to take pictures of, Kentucky has something for you. I hope this book is as enjoyable to look at as it was to make and that it will inspire you to go on your own journey through Kentucky.

DeeDee Niederhouse-Mandrell

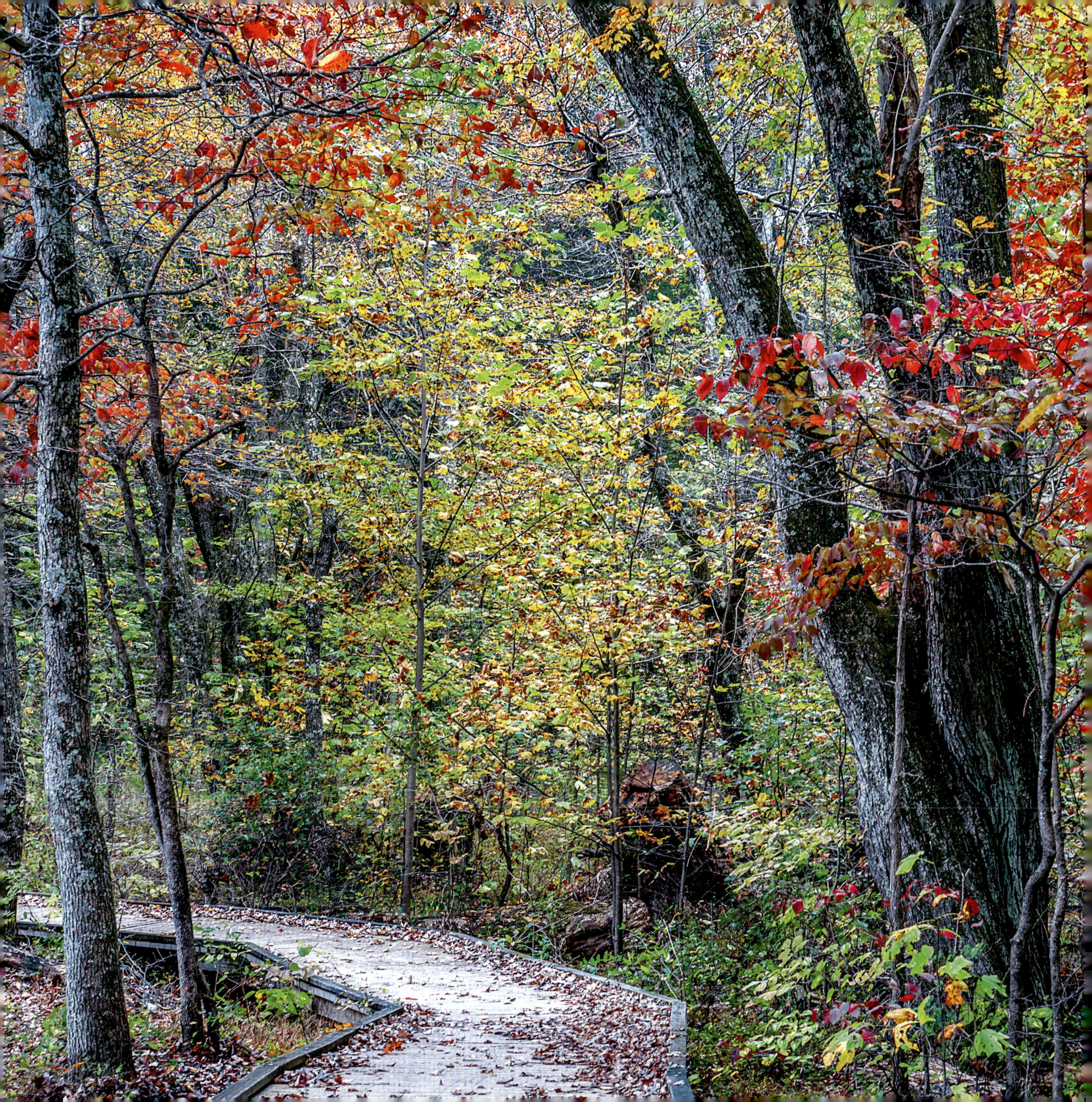

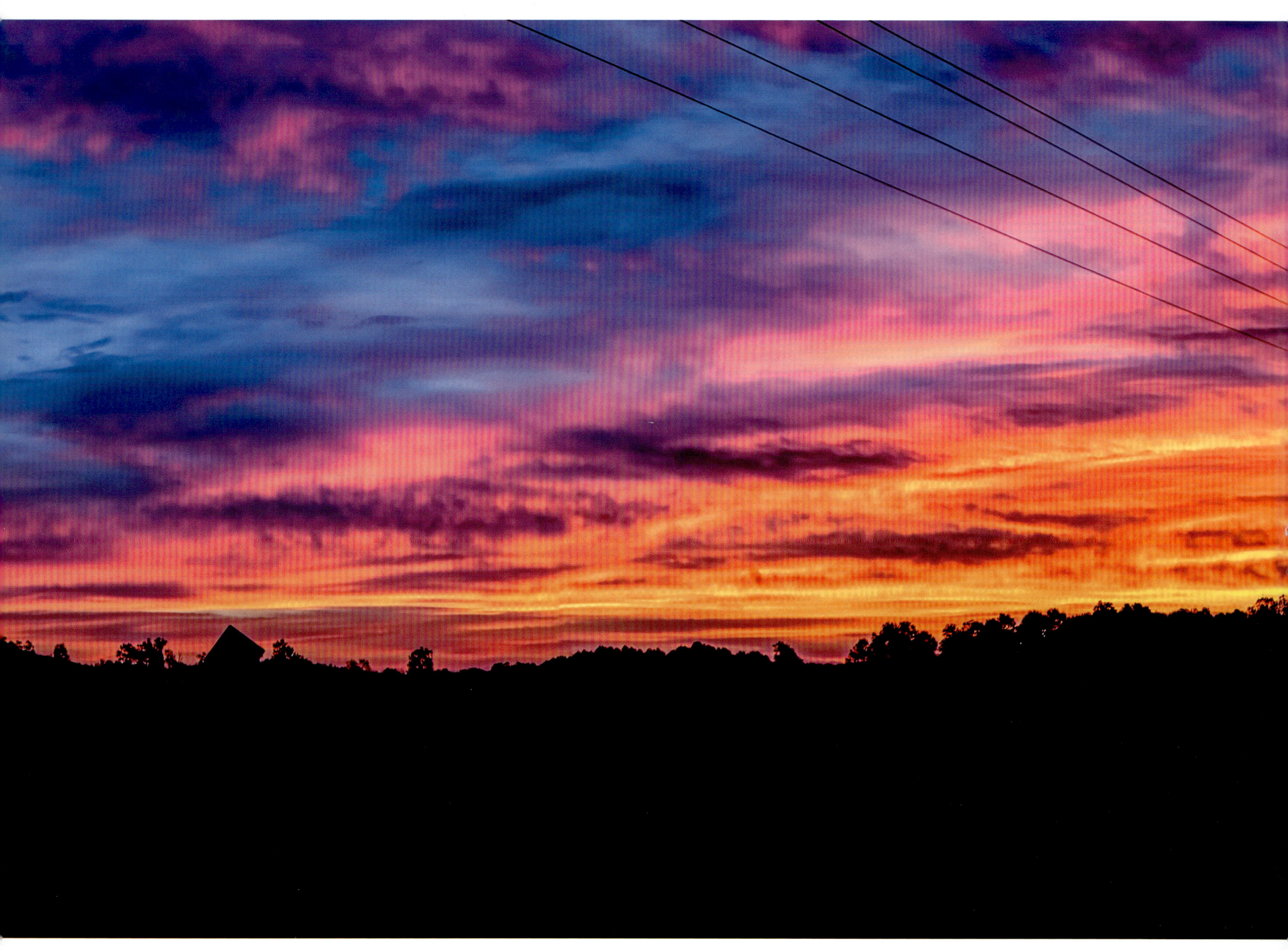

A painterly sunrise near Land Between the Lakes.

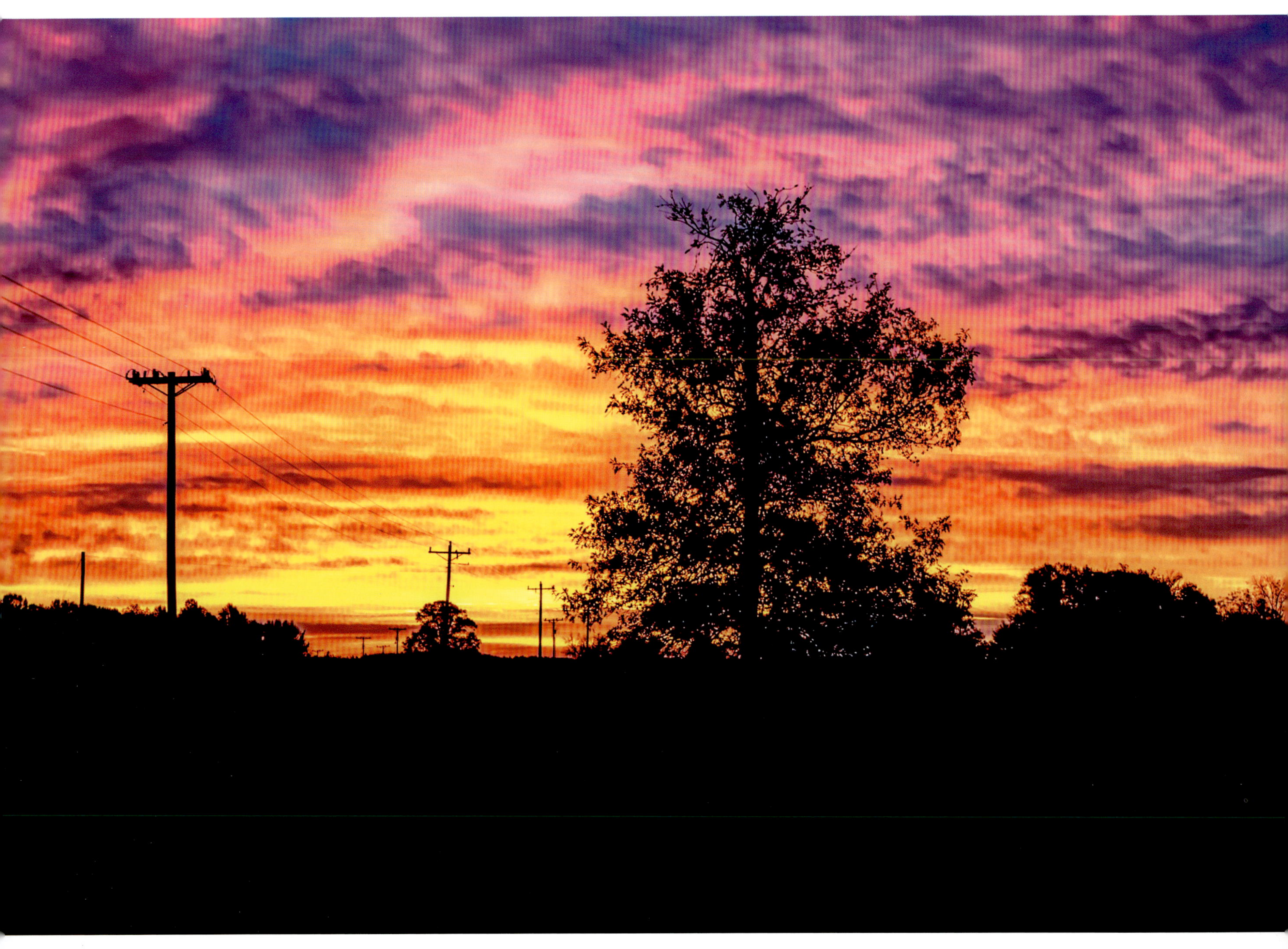

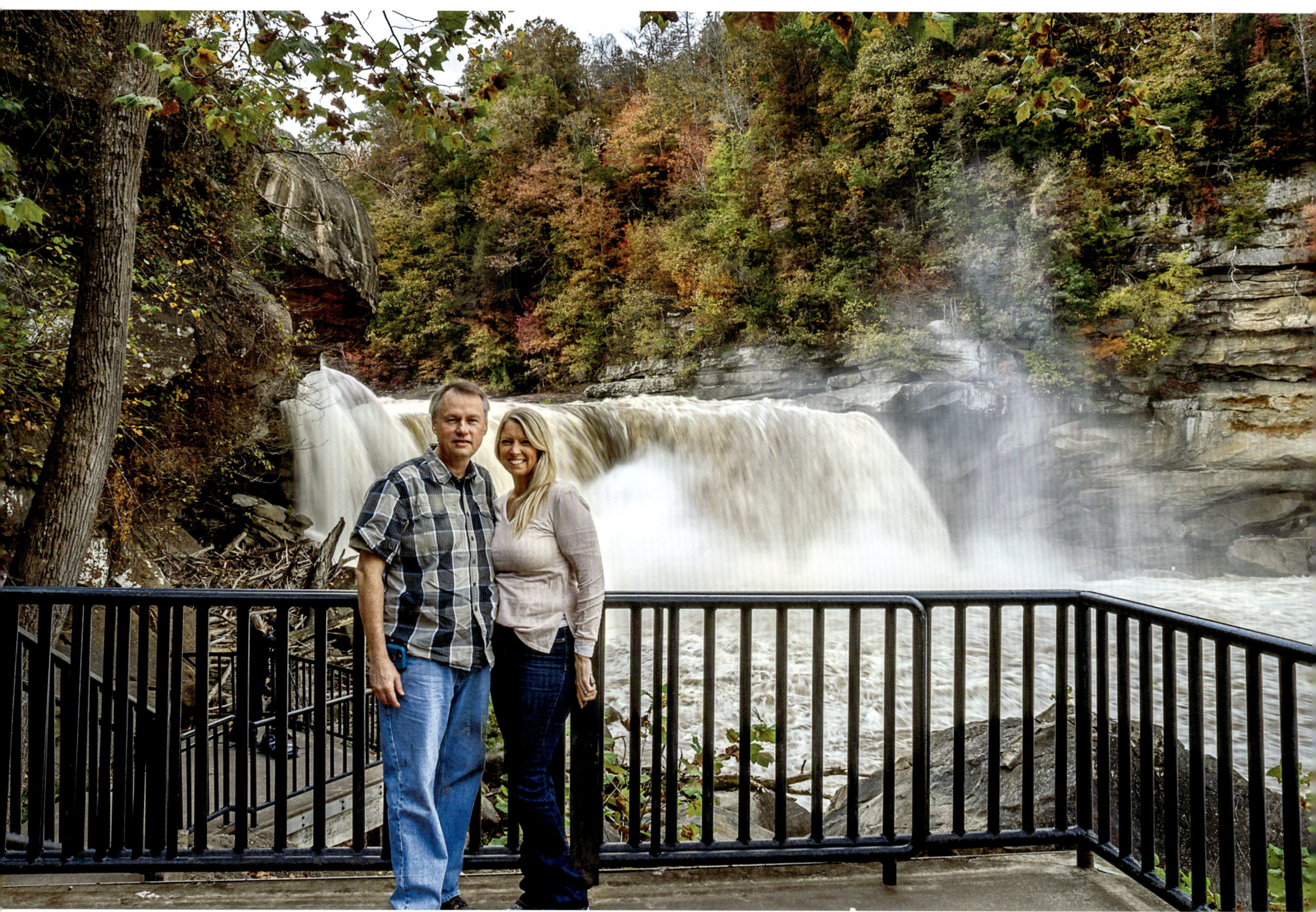

For Lee Mandrell, photography started out as a hobby that quickly ignited into a fiery passion and then a lifelong career. He started out at age fourteen with a secondhand Minolta Hi-Matic E rangefinder. Mandrell worked as a custom darkroom technician in a professional lab for years and was eventually promoted to production manager. An early adopter of both digital technology and Photoshop, he is still actively involved in all current photography techniques and practices. He is author of *Indianapolis: The Circle City* and coauthor of *The Great Smoky Mountains: A Visual Journey, Indiana Across the Land, Illinois Across the Land,* and *Illinois State Parks.*

DeeDee Niederhouse-Mandrell's interest in the art of photography began over twenty-five years ago. What started out as a hobby eventually turned into a paying photography job—she is now the principal photographer for the Ray Skillman Corporation. After several years, Niederhouse-Mandrell became the corporation's creative photography manager for their upper-end magazine advertisements. She is coauthor of *The Great Smoky Mountains: A Visual Journey, Indiana Across the Land, Illinois Across the Land,* and *Illinois State Parks.*

ACQUISITIONS EDITOR	Ashley Runyon
PROJECT MANAGER	Nancy Lightfoot
BOOK AND COVER DESIGNER	Pamela Rude
COMPOSITION COORDINATOR	Tony Brewer